SHAPING IDENTITY IN EASTERN EUROPE AND RUSSIA

Also by Stephen Velychenko

National History as Cultural Process

SHAPING IDENTITY IN EASTERN EUROPE AND RUSSIA

Soviet-Russian and Polish Accounts of Ukrainian History, 1914-1991

Stephen Velychenko

Palgrave Macmillan

© Stephen Velychenko 1993
Softcover reprint of the hardcover 1st edition 1993 978-0-312-08552-0

All rights reserved. For information, write:
Scholarly & Reference Division,
St. Martin's Press, Inc., 175 Fifth Avenue,
New York, NY 10010

First published in the United States of America 1993

ISBN 978-1-349-60653-5   ISBN 978-1-137-05825-6 (eBook)
DOI 10.1007/978-1-137-05825-6

Library of Congress Cataloging-in-Publication Data

Velychenko, Stephen.
 Shaping identity in Eastern Europe and Russia : Soviet-Russian and Polish accounts of Ukrainian history, 1914-1991 / Stephen Velychenko.
   p. cm.
 Includes bibliographical references and index.

 1. Ukraine—Historiography. 2. Historiography—Poland.
 3. Historiography—Soviet Union. 4. Ukraine—History—Errors. inventions, etc. 5. Ukraine—History—20th century. 6. Ukraine-
 -History—20th century—Bibliography. I. Title.

DK508.46.V45 1992
947'.71084—dc20   92-17764
                                                          CIP

CONTENTS

Introduction 1

PART I: BACKGROUND AND CONTEXT

1. Nations, States, and History 11
2. The Institutions and the Ideology 27
3. Delineating the Past 47

PART II: POLISH HISTORIOGRAPHY

4. Neoromanticism and Positivism (1914-1944) 69
5. The Imposed Continuity (1944-1982) 87
6. Monographs and Articles on Ukrainian Subjects 101

PART III: SOVIET-RUSSIAN HISTORIOGRAPHY

7. Degrees of Inclusion, Exclusion, and Affinity 135
8. The History of the Ukrainian SSR (1948-1982) 155
9. Deductivist Discourse and Research 179
   Conclusion 199
   Appendix: Perestroika and Interpretation 213
   Abbreviations to Notes 223
   Notes 224
   Index 259

I saw that Solomon had thought of practically everything, and that there was no escaping his favour. I also saw that I might end, as some writers did, with my head cut off and my body nailed to the city wall, but that, on the other hand, I might wax fat and prosperous if I guarded my tongue and used my stylus wisely. With some luck and the aid of our Lord Yahveh, I might even insert in the King David Report a word here and a line there by which later generations would perceive what really came to pass in these years. . . .

—Ethan ben Hoshaiah
Stefan Heym, *The King David Report*

But it should be understood that for no nation does the obligation and increasingly burdensome dialogue with the outside world mean an expropriation or obliteration of its own history. There may be some intermingling but there is no fusion.

—Fernand Braudel

Introduction

Although in the late 1980s people in the USSR and Poland were shocked when they learned just how far the Party had systematically distorted the past for political and ideological reasons, few today would be surprised to read that "Soviet-type" regimes had sponsored circumscribed and corrupted versions of national history. Accordingly, this book does not review the authorized Polish and Soviet-Russian elite accounts of Ukrainian history merely to illustrate their inadequacy and to condemn the mendacity of the regime that sponsored them. Rather, *Shaping Identity in Eastern Europe and Russia* surveys the origins and evolution of official versions of Ukraine's past to illustrate how historical writing and interpretative change occurred in Soviet-type systems. It traces the peregrinations of ideas from Party resolutions to survey histories and studies how the administrative bureaucracy kept scholars within predefined interpretive guidelines. The book also shows that, despite the nominally monolithic ideological structure, historians in these countries did express different opinions, and that after Stalin's death those who placed facts above theory were able to influence, if not change, official interpretations. Although Marxist-Leninist regimes had disintegrated in Russia, Poland, and Ukraine, by 1991, an examination of the methods of thought control, conditions of scholarship, language, and deductivist logic characteristic of Soviet-type systems has relevance for the 1990s. Not all in the old "Soviet Bloc" have been able to rid themselves of Soviet-Marxist ideas and habits of thought, while hardship and confusion has produced nostalgia among some for the security and certainty of the old system. In Asia, Marxist-Leninist regimes still control almost one-quarter of the earth's population.

A study of historical writing in Soviet-type regimes also focuses attention on differences in historiography and methodology between liberal-pluralist and dictatorial societies. In the USSR after 1934 and in communist Poland, one way historians perpetuated the official image of the past was by omitting details that confuted generalizations derived from *a priori* axioms and principles. But as Herbert Butterfield and Lucien Febvre pointed out, historians in general tend to ignore details that belie broader generalizations. The former observed:

> We cling to a certain organization of historical knowledge which amounts to a whig interpretation of history, and all our deference to research brings us only to admit that this needs qualification in detail. But exceptions in detail do not prevent us from mapping out the large story on the same pattern all the time; these exceptions are lost indeed in that combined process of organization and abridgement by which we reach our general survey of general history.[1]

Febvre later remarked:

> We like to talk about the machines which we create and which enslave us.... Any intellectual category we may forge in the workshops of the mind is able to impose itself with the same force and the same tyranny—and holds even more stubbornly to its existence than the machines made in our factories. History is a strongbox that is too well guarded, too firmly locked and bolted.[2]

If *a priori* categories influence all historians and veer their writing "over into whig history," then what was damnable about historiography in Soviet-type systems? Additionally, it should be remembered that for most of recorded history man has been a subject rather than a citizen and, as such, was content to accept interpretations of the past given by authority. An "historiography of citizens," concerned with accuracy, is the product of participatory democracy, as suggested by Moses Finley, and existed for only a short time—in fifth-century Greece and, in its positivist-critical variety, for a relatively short time in modern Europe and North America. In this context Soviet-type historiography appears less an aberration than a norm, and it may be argued that the removal of Party control over scholarship was a necessary but insufficient condition for the emergence of dispassionate academic study and pluralist "citizen historiography" in what was the Soviet bloc.[3] Without democracy, to follow Finley's line of argument, people will not want nor need to know what really happened in the past. In a society predisposed to accept myth and seeking to express an earlier repressed nationalism, accordingly, critical historiography based on accuracy and open debate could prove a slender reed. New authorities seeking legitimacy and support might be tempted to sponsor historians to replace old pseudo-Marxist myths with new monolithic nationalist myths—and few would oppose.

The communist regimes in the USSR and Poland assigned historians the task of creating narrative continuity out of past diversity. In the USSR, this involved imposing a single pattern of socio-economic development, ideas of popular "solidarity," and "friendship among nations" onto the past of more than a dozen major nationalities. Both regimes required that historians downplay if not eliminate reference to past animosities and plurality in their writings, and use Marxist rhetoric, concepts, and categories. Nonetheless, national categories and concepts persisted, and the continuity of official narratives was tenuous. Postwar and interwar Polish historians, like post-1934 Soviet historians who wrote survey histories, produced, respectively, Polonocentric and Russocentric interpretations incorporating selected events and issues from the pasts of minorities that once had been under Warsaw's or Moscow/St. Petersburg's authority. In postwar Poland, a country stripped of almost all its Ukrainian territories and dominated by Moscow, the official account of the country's past represented a radical break in Polish historiography insofar as it did not treat Ukraine as an integral part of "Polish history." The Stalinist "history of the USSR," by contrast, resembled the pre-1917 tsarist understanding of "Russian history."

Shaping Identity in Eastern Europe and Russia summarizes the official elite Polish and Soviet-Russian images of Ukraine's past as presented in survey histories of Poland, the USSR, and the Ukrainian SSR. The narrative does not classify interpretations according to criteria of truth and validity but does identify monographs and articles written according to the rules of academic method as understood in the West, and tries to distinguish the reprehensible or tendentious from the merely defective.[4] As this book studies how images of a national history emerged and changed, it classifies the examined material chronologically, by country and by form. Only by reviewing and summarizing separately monographs on selected issues, political circumstances, official directives on historiography, and in the case of the USSR, typologies derived from Marxist axioms, can the impact of each be determined and the pattern of interpretative change reconstructed.

The book assumes some knowledge of Polish, Russian, and Ukrainian history on the part of the reader, and begins with a review of the past historiography of the subject and the institutional and ideological context of scholarship. Because the Soviet-Russian and, to a lesser degree, the postwar Polish regimes claimed legitimacy on the basis of Marxism and obliged historians to use an officially defined Marxist method, Part 1 reviews the evolution of dialectical historical materialism. It highlights differences between Polish and Soviet variants of Marxism-Leninism and the limitations this method placed on historical investigation and interpretation. Both countries had Marxist thinkers, but their influence on historiography was negligible in Russia before 1917 and in Poland before 1948. In both countries the sudden subsequent dominance of Marxist-based historiography was not the product of consensus and evolution but of political decisions. Part 1 also examines the organization of historiography and the limits state-controlled institutions and resources placed on thought. This matter was of particular significance in the USSR, where academic research and publishing from the 1930s was a state monopoly. The political control of historical writing in the USSR after 1930, and in Poland between 1948 and 1956, forced historians who wanted to hold jobs and publish to write according to axioms and dictated guidelines derived from a deductivist official version of Marxism. Part 2 reviews 53 of an estimated total of 93 survey histories of Poland, 8 Polish surveys of Ukrainian history, and 82 monographs published between 1944 and 1982—when martial law in Poland and the death of Brezhnev marked the end of the neo-Stalinist order. Part 3 reviews 21 survey histories of Russia and the USSR of an estimated total of 60 published in Moscow, Leningrad (St. Petersburg), and Kiev between 1914 and 1982, 9 of an estimated total of 13 histories of the Ukrainian SSR published between 1948 and 1982, and 26 monographs and articles by Russian historians. Readers not interested in a compendium of Polish and Soviet-Russian writings about Ukraine may skip the second parts of chapters 4, 5, and 6, and the second and third parts of chapter 7. The Appendix deals with the interpretation of Ukrainian history in the USSR between 1985, when Gorbachev came to power, and the dissolution of the Soviet Union in 1991.

Twentieth-century historiography was more impersonal and institutionalized than in preceding centuries, and historians were no longer as prominent socially or politically. During the period under study in Poland and the USSR, there were good historians who were respected by their colleagues, but the realm of historiography in the latter part of the century was no longer populated by great men whose names were synonymous with the national histories of their countries. In the USSR, obscure political functionaries often were more instrumental in formulating interpretations than scholars, while during the 1930s persons would suddenly emerge on the pages of journals with "pioneering" articles written according to the demands of the moment and then disappear just as suddenly in the whirlwind of repression, together with any hope of mention in encyclopedias and directories.[5] For the moment, we only know their names. But as archives are now open, historians will be able to provide information on these men as well as others, more fortunate and less outspoken, who are mentioned in this book if they wrote about one of the examined topics.

The "bureaucratization" of historiography in multinational states did not, in itself, have deleterious consequences for the national histories of minorities. In liberal interwar Poland, historians of all nationalities were free to write as they wished, and during those years there were bodies of knowledge that can be classified as "Polish," "Ukrainian," or "Jewish" historiography. In the USSR between 1917 and 1948, the fortunes of "national history" varied. After 1948, the lines between USSR, Russian, and non-Russian history became so blurred it is possible to argue that "national history" as a distinct body of knowledge ceased to exist in the non-Russian Republics. Strict administrative control imposed after World War II, a state ideology and relatively detailed centrally compiled guidelines, circumscribed the study and presentation of non-Russian pasts in the USSR to such a degree that the survey histories of these Republics published between 1945 and 1990 may be regarded as products of "Russian" historiography about the region rather than native national historiography.

A third major development in historiography during this century was the unprecedented proliferation of "new subjects." In the USSR, these included Ukraine in 1812, the Russian revolutionary movement in Ukraine, "solidarity" between nineteenth-century Russian, Ukrainian, and Polish "revolutionaries," and the history of the proletariat and the Bolsheviks in Ukraine—all marginal to what historians before the 1930s and outside the USSR considered the core of "Ukrainian history." In the wake of the increased attention given these "new subjects," the amount of research devoted to "old subjects" declined. In the USSR after 1934, and in Poland between 1948 and 1956, historians tended to ignore political, legal, and administrative history, and they published little on the events of 1169, 1340, 1386, 1569, and 1596 in Ukraine. Historians in the USSR published few biographies and little on church and intellectual history, the history of national movements, or the non-Bolshevik parties and governments that emerged in Ukraine between 1905 and 1922. Much was published on the economic history of the non-Russian territories, but from the 1930s interpretation of how their forces and relations of production developed depended not on research but on whether or not the area was part of the Tsarist empire.

Because "traditional" subjects figured less prominently in USSR historiography than in prerevolutionary Russian historiography about Ukraine and because the amount of published materials increased dramatically after 1914, the articles reviewed in this book represent a smaller proportion of the total publications related to the representative sample of issues examined than did the selection in my *National History as Cultural Process* (1992). Both volumes review the treatment of the following: Andrei

Bogoliubsky's sack of Kiev in 1169, the Polish occupation of Galicia (Western Ukraine) in the 1340s, the Ukrainian-Rus' lands in the Unions of 1386 and 1569, the Union of Brest and the Orthodox Church in the Polish-Lithuanian Commonwealth (*Rzeczpospolita*), cossack-peasant revolts (1590-1648), the 1654 Treaty of Pereiaslav and the 1659 Hadiach Treaty, Russian-Ukrainian political relations and Cossack-Ukrainian autonomy (1654-1782), socio-economic history (circa 1500 to 1783), and the Haidamak revolts (*Koliivshchyna*). Additionally, this book reviews treatment of the Ukrainian national movement, in particular its institutional expressions, the *Holovna Ruska Rada,* the *Hromady,* and the Cyril-Methodius Brotherhood. Also covered are the events of 1917-1921, with particular attention given to the Central Rada and the West Ukrainian People's Republic.

In quantitative terms, publications about these subjects represent a small proportion of the corpus of post-1914 historical writing, and these topics were not always mentioned or discussed at length in survey histories. Obviously, in itself this reflected a specific bias and sense of priority. But the decision to analyze the treatment of these particular subjects is justified insofar as they were central to pre-1914 historiography and became so again after the disintegration of the Soviet regime. These subjects represent turning points in Polish-Ukrainian and Russian-Ukrainian relations and are nodal points of national images and identities. Under the Soviet regime, events connected with the Bolshevik party and the Revolution fell within the realm of Party history. They were studied by separate research institutes and were covered in survey histories of the Party as well as of the USSR and the republics. This volume does not review the five Ukrainian party histories, nor the 25 histories of the Communist Party of the Soviet Union (CPSU) published between 1923 and 1982 and their many revised editions. Also excluded from the reviewed writing were memoirs, eyewitness accounts, and "regional histories" relating to 1917-1922.

The research for this book was made possible by a Research Fellowship from the Social Sciences and Humanities Research Council of Canada. In 1988, under the auspices of the Canada-Soviet Academic Exchange Program, I was able to work in the libraries of Kiev and Lviv.

For their comments and observations I am grateful to George Enteen, John Keep, Alexander Nekrich, the late Oleksander Ohloblyn, Iaroslav Dzyra, Iaroslav Dashkevych, Iaroslav Isaevych, Serhyi Bilokin, Fedir Shevchenko, Zbigniew Wójcik, Jerzy Maternicki, and Władyslaw Serczyk. I have used my transcripts of formal interviews with some of them as sources and in the footnotes identify by numbers others who also shared with me their knowledge of historians and historiography, but wished to remain anonymous.

In the text, all place names in Ukraine and names of ethnic Ukrainians are given in modern Ukrainian spelling, with the exception of those with established English equivalents; thus "Dnieper" instead of the Ukrainian form "Dnipro." Polish and Russian proper names and place names are given in their respective languages with the exception of those with commonly accepted English forms. The term "Galicia" refers to the Habsburg province that between 1795 and 1918 encompassed Polish and Ukrainian ethnic territory. Before and after those dates the term refers only to Western Ukraine (*Halychyna*), known under Austrian rule as Eastern Galicia.

PART I

BACKGROUND AND CONTEXT

1

Nations, States, and History

UKRAINE AS PERIPHERY AND THE HISTORIOGRAPHY OF THE HISTORIOGRAPHY

In the nineteenth century the lands of the old Polish state were divided between Prussia, Austria, and Russia. Western Ukraine was part of the Habsburg province of Galicia and the site of Polish as well as Ukrainian national movements. Limited attempts by representatives of both nations to compromise were overshadowed by rivalry that grew more intense with the passing decades as each side lobbied for Austrian support and claimed political dominance in Eastern Galicia. In 1918 the Polish state was reconstituted and fought a war against the newly formed Western Ukrainian People's Republic (in Ukrainian: ZUNR). Within a year, Poland defeated the Ukrainians and established its eastern border on the Zbruch (Zbrucz) River.

Political parties differed over the location of Poland's eastern frontiers, but the overwhelming majority of Poles thought in terms of an historic rather than an ethnic Poland, and debate revolved around how far east the country's border should be. Most agreed it should include Western Ukraine, and disapproved of Józef Piłsudski's treaty with the Ukrainian People's Republic and the subsequent war with Soviet Russia. Piłsudski's ambition to form a Polish-dominated Eastern European federation that included an independent Ukraine without Galicia came to nought when a militarily exhausted Poland accepted Lenin's offer of peace in 1920. The Riga Treaty of 1921 and the decision of the Council of Ambassadors in 1923 established the Soviet-Polish border on the Zbruch River and recognized Polish control over some Ukrainian regions. Western Ukraine (renamed Małopolska Wschodnia) was divided into three provinces, while Volyn (Wołyn) was made a fourth.

Roughly one-third of interwar Poland's inhabitants were non-Polish. The 5 to 6 million Ukrainians living in eastern Poland made up 14 to 15 percent of the total population. In Western Ukraine and Volyn Poles made up 40 and 18 percent, respectively. Poland's eastern provinces had the lowest level of urbanization and industrialization. Poles dominated the local administration, police and army, the large landowner class, the professions, and the working class, and they constituted over 50 percent of the two largest cities Lviv (Łwów) and Ternopil (Tarnopol).

Polish leaders had varying opinions about non-Poles. On the right, National Democrats argued for complete assimilation and advocated Polish colonization and bilingual schools in Western Ukraine. They made no claims on Ukrainian territories in the USSR. Spokesmen recognized the existence of non-Poles but claimed their native consciousness was low and should be molded into a Polish national consciousness. Moderate socialists grouped around the Polish Socialist party (PPS) supported cultural autonomy and even discussed the possibility of territorial autonomy for Western Ukraine. They also supported Pilsudski's ambition to create a bloc under Polish hegemony including a Ukrainian state without Western Ukrainian lands. State policy, despite obligations imposed by international treaties, and pressure from the minorities and Polish liberals, was directed at integration and assimilation of all non-Poles except Germans. This included support for efforts to latinize the Uniate Church and opposition to Ukrainization of and broader lay authority within the Orthodox Church. On the other hand, after Pilsudski's 1926 coup, the government recognized the Ukrainian National Republic Government-in-Exile as part of its covert strategy to destabilize Soviet rule.[1]

The Hitler-Stalin pact gave Western Ukraine to Moscow and established the German-USSR border along the San River. In 1945 a new Poland-USSR border was drawn along the Bug River, and by 1950 Poland's population, for the first time in 600 years, was overwhelmingly Polish. The Polish minority in Ukraine and the Ukrainian minority in Poland are today insignificant numerically, socially, and economically.

In interwar Poland perhaps the first to call on Polish historians to keep studying the history of the "lost regions" was K. Sochaniewicz. At the IV Polish Historians Conference, he remarked that Russians published more on central and Western Ukraine than did Poles because they took the regions' archives after the Partitions. He urged Polish historians to counter selective Russian and Ukrainian publications of these documents with their own "objective" selections and to retrieve lost archives.[2] Observations on the interpretation of Ukraine's past were made in 1933 by O. Górka, who pointed out to his countrymen that their attitudes about Ukraine were dictated by feelings, not by historical or political knowledge. He attributed this to Catholic romanticism and the historical novels of Henryk Sienkiewicz, which had "greater influence than hundreds of learned treatises" on Polish mentality. Górka reminded readers that Sienkiewicz wrote to buttress Polish national consciousness during a period of decline and that since Poland had attained independence there was no longer an excuse not to revise the image his works had produced.[3] The year 1933 also saw the publication of a review of interwar literature pertaining to the history of Galicia.[4] Lewicki in 1936-37 published a survey of Polish writing on the cossacks and the Orthodox Church and concluded that work on the former was sparse and weak.[5]

After 1945, study of the interwar Polish interpretation of Ukrainian history was neglected. Maternicki mentioned aspects of it,[6] while Papierzynska-Turek provided a succinct survey of interwar writing on the Ukrainian churches.[7] Reviews of Polish historiography on the USSR Republics,[8] and on Ukraine specifically,[9] revealed only how little Poles wrote about the past of territories once part of the Polish state. S. Zabrovarny provided a particularly thorough annotated bibliographical review of post-war Polish historiography about Ukraine published between 1948 and 1975.[10] He also compiled a review of Polish historical and political-polemical literature about the nineteenth-century Ukrainian national movement in Western Ukraine and noted that the prevailing Polish view was that it had been "invented" by the Austrians to keep the Poles in submission. Postwar studies, on the other hand, argued that the Ukrainian movement had been a variant of a typical European phenomenon.[11] The first scholarly analysis of the Ukrainian movement was published in 1907 by W. Feldmann (*Stronnictwa i programmy polityczne w Galicyi*). The most comprehensive survey of Polish historiography about Western Ukraine is by P. R. Magocsi, who observed that almost all modern Polish historiography about Habsburg Galicia focused on the western Polish part despite the prevailing Polish opinion that the entire province was an integral part of historical Poland.[12] Serczyk wrote an interesting but superficial overview of modern Polish historiography about Ukraine, while Biernacek examined the treatment of Polish eastern affairs in selected histories of twentieth-century Poland published in the 1980s and found that authors downplayed the statist aspects of events in Ukraine during 1917-1920 and indirectly justified Polish claims on Western Ukraine made at the time.[13]

By 1922, the Bolsheviks controlled most of the old Tsarist empire. In the Ukrainian provinces Russians and Jews, some 15 percent of the total population, made up 60 percent of Party members. The Russian Social Democratic

Labour party (Bolshevik), between 1918 and 1925 the Russian Communist party (RKP) and from 1952 the CPSU, spoke in the name of the international proletariat, but did so in Russian. In the elections to the 1917 Constituent Assembly, it received approximately 40 percent of the votes in Russia and 10 percent of the votes in Ukrainian provinces. One of the Bolshevik strongholds was the Donbass industrial region, which accounted for some two-thirds of its membership in Ukraine in 1917. The first seat of Soviet power in Ukraine was the city of Kharkiv.

Unlike the tsars, whose initial interest in Ukrainian lands was dictated by strategic considerations, the Bolsheviks during the Revolution were interested in the economic potential of the non-Russian regions of the old empire. Kievan Bolshevik G. Piatakov said in 1917, "Russia cannot exist without the Ukrainian sugar industry; the same can be said about coal (the Donets Basin), grain (the black earth belt), etc." In 1920, G. Zinoviev explained that Russia could not exist "without the petroleum of Azerbaijan or the cotton of Turkestan. We take these products which are necessary for us, not as the former exploiters, but as older brothers bearing the torch of civilization." The new Russian Soviet Republic did not sign peace and trade treaties with the various non-Bolshevik governments formed after the fall of tsardom. Muravev, commander of the Bolshevik army that captured Kiev in early 1918, declared to his troops on the day they took the city, "We have brought this [Soviet] regime from the far north on the points of our bayonets, and wherever we have established it, it will be maintained at all costs by the force of these bayonets." Leon Trotsky, in 1920 commander of the Red Army, wrote: "Soviet power in Ukraine has held its ground up to now (and it has not held it well) chiefly by the authority of Moscow, by the Great Russian communists, and by the Russian Red Army."[14]

To 1921 the Party was hostile to Ukrainian national demands as well as to the small freehold peasants who constituted the vast majority of Ukrainians until collectivization. The difficulties in establishing Bolshevik authority during the Revolution, however, enabled Lenin to convince his associates to countenance limited cultural autonomy for non-Russians and small-scale farms. After 1932 policy changed again as individual commercial farming was totally abolished, while by the 1960s, in the wake of centrally planned industrial expansion, more than half of Ukrainians had become urban dwellers. This was matched by a huge influx of Russian workers and officials into Ukrainian cities that by the 1960s had more than doubled their turn-of-the-century share of the population.

Cultural autonomy in non-Russian Republics was circumscribed after 1932. Stalin's policy of fostering aspects of Russian culture to buttress his regime led to a reintroduction of ideas previously associated with tsardom into the "socialist" USSR. Official ideology became an amalgam of Marxist phraseology, tsarist statist-Russian nationalism, and elements of non-Russian national-populist ideas, while state sponsorship of Ukrainian national development was limited to Ukrainian "folk culture," Ukrainian scholarship on Ukrainian subjects, and selected aspects of Ukrainian "high culture." Simultaneously, the state promoted Russian as the language of urban life and administration, of scholarship in Ukraine on non-Ukrainian subjects, and of non-Ukrainian "high culture."

With the incorporation of Western and Carpathian Ukraine into the USSR in 1945, almost all Ukrainian territories were united within the borders of one state for the second time in history. In 1954 the Kremlin placed the Crimean peninsula under Kievan administration. Although Russians ruled the Ukrainian SSR, from the 1920s native Ukrainians administered it.[15]

Soviet-Russian surveys of post-1917 historiography about Ukraine stopped distinguishing between Russian and Ukrainian scholarship after 1934. Until then, S. Piontkovsky seems to have been the only Soviet historian who looked at how Russian historians after 1917 interpreted the past of non-Russian nations in the USSR. In 1930 and 1931, he accused older Russian historians writing during the 1920s of chauvinism because they included in "Russian history" non-Russian regions from the moment they became part of the empire. He explained that territories became part of the "Russian historical process" not simply because they had the mark of Russians on them, but because they became an object of exploitation.[16]

Surveys of Ukrainian historiography by scholars outside Poland and the USSR, as a rule, exclude Russian scholars who wrote on Ukrainian subjects and implicitly distinguish between Soviet-Russian and Soviet-Ukrainian writing. But no one has yet studied Soviet-Russian historiography about Ukraine systematically nor attempted to clearly distinguish Soviet "Russian" from "Ukrainian" interpretations of Ukraine's past. B. Krupnytsky and O. Ohloblyn observed that post-1945 historiography in the Ukrainian SSR lacked Ukrainian character or traditions and implied that the prevailing interpretation of the country's past could not be regarded as Ukrainian.[17] Western historians who have written surveys of official USSR historiography about non-Russians have characterized it as politically dictated, Russocentric, statist, and Russian nationalist in tone since the 1930s.[18]

Until 1985 Soviet historians who criticized Western analysis of the official interpretation of non-Russian pasts argued that concentration on relations between Party directives and historians amounted to studying gossip and did not reconstruct the milieu in which writing occurred.[19] Under

Gorbachev, reformist historians were able to assert in print that Stalinism and its ideological atmosphere were conditions of scholarship in the USSR since the 1930s and not merely obstacles to scholarship that were overcome after 1956, the accepted view to 1985. Nevertheless, historians during *glasnost* failed to examine how the interpretation of the pre-1917 past of non-Russian nations was affected by Party guidelines after 1934.[20]

"NATIONAL HISTORY": A PERVASIVE CATEGORY

In the nineteenth century, nations and nation-states displaced kings and dynasties as the focus of historical writing in the major European states. The underlying idea was expressed by Leopold von Ranke, who regarded the nation as a transcendental unity that was simultaneously the object and proper framework of historical study. In general terms, national history involved consideration of national historical individuality and distinctiveness. It assumes national identities as defined in the nineteenth century were primary and that people within specific territories shared unchanging "national" values, features, and institutions through time.

The horrors of World War I led many liberals to see nationalism as a major cause of the slaughter. They began to scrutinize the intellectual adequacy of "national history" and its role in creating and perpetuating national animosities. Arnold Toynbee observed that no single nation or nation-state has a self-contained and self-explanatory past. Others asked whether the category was applicable in studying the past of established states such as France or Germany if for long periods provincial differences between Brittany and Gascony were as great as those between the Île-de-France and Brandenburg. It was pointed out that subjects such as the history of physics were unintelligible within exclusively national frameworks.[21] "National history," whether of the ruled or the ruling nation, failed to recognize that "nation" meant different things to different people at different times. It ignored the role of minorities, diversity, and particularities in the past as well as the impact of alternative local and/or supranational identities.

Theoretical inquiry was matched by international commissions established to encourage and coordinate revision of national images in school texts. Their purpose was to foster international understanding by removing one source of chauvinism. As early as 1890, a private organization, the International Peace Bureau, had passed a resolution to this effect. In 1922, the League of Nations charged its International Committee on Intellectual Cooperation with the task of realizing this resolution. Four years later, the League adopted the Casares resolution and established the first international organization of textbook revision. Participation was voluntary with member states invited to set up committees to examine their foreign history books and report chauvinism and bias to the country concerned. In the 1930s, the first international agreements on compulsory revision of textbooks were signed. Efforts to eliminate national bias from school history texts were continued after 1945 under the auspices of a UNESCO committee and after 1951 by the Brunswick International Schoolbook Institute. These programs function as bilateral exchanges of which one example was the Polish-Soviet Commission on History Textbooks formed in 1968.[22] There were no Ukrainian, Lithuanian, or Belorus sections.

Doubt about the adequacy of national history as an analytical category and organized international efforts to eliminate chauvinism from textbooks were paralleled by historians increasingly using non-national categories of analysis such as class, institutions, or mentality. The supranational tendencies inherent in federalism, economic integration, and the rise of multinational corporations, all of which infringed on national states as the focus of loyalty, also lessened the popularity and utility of "national history." As a result, Western historical culture no longer attaches exclusivist nationalist loyalty to national history. Historians since 1945 have tended to study kings as administrators rather than as nation-builders or conquerors and to attach more significance to minorities, cross-cultural influences, chance, irrationality, particularist ambitions, and local interests than national unity, virtue, destiny, and ideals. The voluntary directed international cooperation and methodological diversification made national history in the West an unlikely agent of extremist nationalism. Critics who claim regulation and new methodologies threaten to eradicate the "national soul" are few. Nevertheless, most historiography and historical culture remain national. Contrary to Enlightenment-based liberal and Marxist expectations, and despite centralization, urbanization, and McDonald's restaurants, a universal homogenized mass culture has not displaced or diminished the need for more intimate forms of collective identity, of which nationalism is one. Nationalism is still with us, as is the national category in historiography.

Reflecting on the persistence of nationality, Gellner and Szporluk have argued that the end of our century has seen the principles of universalism, rationalism, and the rights of the individual, once coterminous with centralist assimilating multinational states, become identified with centrifugal national-state movements.[23] Armstrong, meanwhile, has observed that although national identity and memory are socially constructed "imagined communities," they are nonetheless indispensable for identity maintenance.[24] In countries east of the Elbe these broader trends, which give social importance to national history and which can link it more closely to patriotism and nationalism—but not necessarily chauvinism—than in the West, are reinforced by political and economic circumstances. In short, national-based group solidarity tends to be weaker in wealthier, pluralist, constitutional, consumer societies than in poorer, authoritarian societies. In the former, national identity, if invoked politically, usually appears as a means to attain social or economic goals. In the latter, national identity becomes an end in itself and insofar as historiography preserves collective national memory, it becomes essential to group survival.[25] Given the emotive, even explosive potential of national history, restrictions on expression of national pride in Soviet bloc history books published between 1947 and 1989 were perhaps inevitable. It must be remembered only that these were less the result of spontaneous restraint by authors or the recommendations of international commissions than of state censors whose mandate included excising negative appraisals of Russia and Russians. In reaction, oppositionists accused official historiography of intentionally eradicating national identity.[26] Such criticism had particular public resonance in Poland due to popular dislike of Russians, and the deliberations of the Polish-Soviet Commission in the 1980s sometimes became a matter of national concern.

Western states in the past and nation-states formed this century sponsored and used national history to inculcate citizens with patriotism and to counter the anomie and rootlessness produced by mass urban culture.[27] In Eastern Europe, elites, who regarded World War I not only as a time of unprecedented slaughter and bloodletting but also as a prelude to the resurrection of national life, saw nationalist national history as desirable and politically useful. This attitude was shared by the leaders of nations who failed to establish states after 1918 and found themselves under foreign rule. In such conditions, interpretations of national history could be and were used as weapons in the struggle between ruling and ruled nationalities. Historians belonging to the former stressed what united and integrated, and historians belonging to the latter emphasized distinctions and differences. Although the historiography of the minority was usually derided and often dismissed as "nationalist," it must be pointed out that the scholarship on both sides had its share of good and bad.

The fate of "national history" in the USSR was not influenced by Western programs designed to lessen national bias and must be examined in the light of two considerations. First, as Marxism was a state ideology in the USSR, the evolution of national history as an intellectual category must be viewed in the context of administrative coercion and Marxist theory about nations. Second, the CPSU ruled a multinational state where Russians averaged 50 percent of the total population and where non-Russians were not immigrant minorities but compact groups living on native territories. Accordingly, the Party attached particular political significance to national issues and closely supervised historiography.[28]

Marx and Engels thought the significant cleavages in mankind divided horizontally according to class, not vertically according to nation. To them, nations and nationalism were secondary and derivative "mediations" that contributed to human alienation and impeded self-realization. Sharing classical liberal ideas about nations as groupings that mankind will evolve through, Marx and Engels explained them as products of the rise of capitalism destined to decline if not disappear with the onset of communism. Although Marx thought nationalism was usually a device the bourgeoisie used to present their interests as those of society and to dampen proletarian consciousness, he did grant nationalism a "progressive" role sometimes. Thus, he grudgingly supported the nationalism of big "modern" nations and in *Capital* conceded that individual nation-states could be units of economic development. He did not apply this thought in his assessment of anticolonial "national liberation" movements. If these occurred in an area without a bourgeois economy, "liberation" would be "reactionary" because it could impede centralized capitalist economic development and forestall socialist revolution. Marx believed that a successful and industrially advanced European proletariat had the right to take over non-Europeans in colonies only if it then led them as fast as possible to independence.[29] National minorities in European states, on the other hand, were no more than parts of the states they were tied to economically, and as annexed "historyless" people they were destined by capitalist centralization to assimilate into larger nations. Since "progress" involved the replacement of local attachments by successively wider, more inclusive identities, Marx opposed federalism because it hindered this "inevitable" process. With the exception of the Irish and Poles, he dismissed non-state nations as "ethnic trash," "dying nationalities," and carriers of counterrevolution up to the moment of their denationalization. Engels called hatred of Czechs after 1848 a "revolutionary virtue," and in early writings he referred to Ukrainians as a Polish tribe.[30]

Lenin, unlike the radical leftists of his day, was prepared to exploit nationalism. After coming to power, he did not adopt the Austro-Marxist position that argued that nations were a permanent form of socio-economic organization, but he did advocate cultural autonomy for non-Russians and federalism as a long-term transitional structure for the USSR. Yet Lenin left no theoretical pronouncements on the national question with the exception of comments made in 1903 and 1918 about the proletariat of each nation representing the nation. He confused the national question with the colonial question, argued that "backward" countries were revolutionary, and left his followers with only tactical political prescriptions on how to exploit nationalism when possible and limit it when necessary.[31]

For Stalin, the nation was permanent and autonomous: "a historically evolved stable community of language, territory, economic life, and psychological make up manifested in a common culture." This was never criticized by Lenin but was not consistent with Marx's conception of nations as a historically conditioned and temporary bourgeois phenomenon. Stalin stressed characteristics independent of socio-economic development and assumed that just as nations were permanent so were their differences and conflicts.[32] To defuse the threat he thought nationalism might pose to the USSR, Stalin subordinated the smaller nationalities to the largest, the Russian, and used Marxist rhetoric to justify this arrangement. After 1934, when the leadership adopted policies to foster assimilation of non-Russians into a supranational "Soviet nation" whose cultural makeup was to be Russian, they also called for a "national history" that would minimize, obfuscate, and even omit reference to conflict, differences, oppression, and rebellion in relations between Russians and non-Russians. The resultant historiography initially stressed Russian influence and similarities in non-Russian and Russian development. After 1947 Russians became historical "elder brothers" and bearers of a superior culture.

Marx and Lenin considered economic, not national-cultural, ties to be primary despite occasional references to countries and national social groups as units or agents of development. Lenin passingly noted in a pre-1917 essay that Russian nobles had been "progressive" for a time and implied that the revolutionary movement in Russia had a national as well as a class dimension. But no Marxist historian ever developed a conception of the past as a history of class struggle ignoring state and national borders. Such a schema might have focused on the great revolts of the lower classes, from Spartacus and Wat Tyler to the Paris Commune, and treated nations and states as secondary phenomena.[33] Marxist historians also failed to explain how national cultural phenomena could be delineated in materialist determinist terms.

RUSSIAN OR SOVIET HISTORIOGRAPHY?

Stalin after 1934 imposed upon the history of the nations of the USSR a conceptual model called the "history of the USSR." Ostensibly anational, Marxist, stressing socio-economic issues, and incorporating elements from non-Russian historiography, the new schema of history for the new state seemed to reflect the antinationalist trend of Western historiography. But the "Soviet" schema was in fact statist and Russocentric. It differed little from the prerevolutionary tsarist Russian conception of "Russian history" and reflected the isolation of the USSR from the West. How did this new schema effect the writing of national history in the non-Russian republics?

Marxist thought postulates the ultimate disappearance of national differences. However, Lenin justified federalism as an expedient transitional political form reflecting the temporary importance of national sentiment, and during the 1920s in the USSR "national history" could also be regarded as a tolerated transitional category of analysis. There were plans to abolish the distinction between Russian and European history in Party schools and to teach only the history of the forces and relations of production. The leading Bolshevik historian, Mikhail Pokrovsky, in principle supported this move and rid universities of Russian history departments. But as there were no people qualified to teach according to the proposed model, Russian history had to be retained as a separate subject.[34] Thus, necessity and theory led the regime to recognize the persistence of "national history" as a category of analysis after the Revolution, and Soviet historians could write histories of their respective countries—but only from historical materialist perspectives.

The USSR was not party to international textbook agreements, but up to 1934 its various national survey histories could not be slighted for chauvinism. Narratives focused on changes in modes of production, exchange, class struggle, and technological development. National pasts fit into a "process" that culminated in 1917 with social and national liberation for non-Russians and social liberation for Russians. Pokrovsky cried when he heard Ukraine had been lost at the Brest-Litovsk peace talks, and his history of Russia began with Kievan Rus; yet his interpretation was not nationalist, and he subjected Russia's past to an anational Eurocentric Marxist schema of development. He discussed Russian history in a global context and characterized Russian colonialism as barbaric. Alongside this 1920s Russian Marxist interpretation of Russian history was a Ukrainian Marxist interpretation of Ukrainian history that did not ignore or justify past Russian domination of non-Russians, and treated non-Russian ruling classes as "progressive" during certain historical periods. This shared condemnation of the Russian colonial legacy did not eliminate rivalry or dislike between Russian and Ukrainian Marxists, however. The former thought there were no "real" Marxist historians in Ukraine, whereas the latter took sharp exception to such accusations.[35]

A concerted effort to rid historiography in the USSR of its Russian nationalist legacy was made in 1928 and coincided with the first attempt to coordinate historical research centrally. The Russian Academy was already named the Academy of Sciences of the USSR, while in 1929, the first Russian "bourgeois" historians were arrested and accused, among other things, of Russian nationalism. At the First All-Union Conference of the Society of Marxist Historians (1928), Pokrovsky announced that the term "history of the nations of the USSR" would henceforth be obligatory. This reflected the official desire to decisively break with the nineteenth-century tsarist perspective, which saw Ukraine's past as the rightful preserve of "Russian history."

There seems to have been only one attempt to specify what the new term was supposed to mean. In 1931, the Ukrainian historian M. Redin pointed out that the focus of interest should not be nations as such but how at a certain stage the class struggle took national form and then culminated in proletarian dictatorship in each republic. Redin remarked that the history of the USSR was still thought of as the history of Russia, and he called for work not merely on Russian colonization but on colonialism, which halted development of capitalism in the non-Russian regions and held back evolution in Russia itself. Conversely, the history of ex-tsarist colonies had to specify that nations were historically determined and not ignore class conflicts within.[36]

These observations were not followed by debate, for in 1934 Stalin declared that the history of the nations of the USSR was not the sum of the parts. In May of that year, he called for the writing of a "history of the USSR," the first use of this term, and three months later declared that the history of the USSR cannot separate the past of Russians and non-Russians.[37] Given the Bolshevik dictum that national differences and corresponding federal forms were transitory, and that the nationalities of the USSR would ultimately merge, it was reasonable to demand a history justifying the envisaged fate by deemphasizing past differences, dissimilarities, and conflicts. But as Stalin gave the single centralized USSR state a Russian national face, its official history became Russocentric, statist, and de facto conterminous with the history of Russia. Within the official schema, separate non-Russian national histories as distinct bodies of knowledge were circumscribed and threatened with extinction. A single centrally defined official interpretation that emphasized common links and the desirability of Russian dominance initially included only Russian, Ukrainian, and Georgian history. By 1954 it encompassed the history of all Soviet nations.

Stalin did not intend to make the USSR into a polity ruled by a Russian nation-state. He expanded use of Russian, permitted and encouraged glorification of the Russian "people" and some tsars and generals, and permitted the fostering of Russian patriotism. In the interests of political stability and integration, Stalin also made Russians dominant within the CPSU, ensured that Russians held all major positions of authority, and sponsored Russian historical and national pride by giving the state and its official historiography a distinct Russian character. In short, he enforced Russian hegemony in the USSR.[38] Yet Stalin also diminished the separate institutional identity of the Russian RSFSR, and Russians did suffer in his system like all the other nationalities. Between 1939 and 1991 the Russian Republic had no Academy of Sciences, Party organization, Republican capital or government, or national "History of Russia."

As a result, the USSR was not a Russian-ruled colonial empire with a historiography denying all non-Russian distinctions and particularities, nor was it a national confederation of equals whose official history was the sum of its parts. The Party demanded loyalty to the USSR as a socialist state, yet the USSR's official "national" identity and past were constructed primarily from Russian culture and historiography. The "history of the USSR" differed in terminology and periodization from tsarist histories of Russia; unlike tsarist historiography it recognized non-Russians as historical, if only transitional, national entities, and incorporated selected ideas ransacked from non-Russian historiography. The official interpretation recognized non-Russian Republics and "people" as distinct historical entities, allotted them official survey histories, and denied the Russians a history of the RSFSR. But none of this altered the fundamental statist Russocentrism of the official view.

Stalin, in *Marxism and the National Question* (1913), explained that incorporation of non-Russian regions into the tsarist state and the formation of a multinational state were necessary if Russia were to defend itself from foreign invaders. This simplistic notion, with its overtones of inevitability, became dogma in the 1930s and was used in official accounts to conceptually link Russian relations with non-Russians prior to 1917.[39] Since multinational states and annexation to Russia had been "progressive" and since the future presaged the unification of nationalities, there was no reason for guilt or excessive criticism of Russian in corporation of non-Russian territories. To make his case, in 1934, Stalin explained that Engels's condemnation of tsarist foreign policy as expansionist was wrong.[40] Within this context, Russian nationalism was expressed in patronizing claims about non-Russian love for, emulation of, deference to, and desires to "join" the Russian "people" by becoming part of the tsarist state. Russian state interests were described as altruistic, motivated by friendly concern for neighboring peoples, legitimate defense needs, and "historical tasks." In the histories of the non-Russian Republics, only what could be linked in some manner to Russia and Russians merited favorable assessment and praise.

Guidelines determined in Moscow reduced non-Russian national history to a species of local history and "local historians" to assistants supposed to illustrate *a priori* ideas with facts culled from the past of their respective countries. Initially the guidelines were general, dealt only with two republics, and until the middle 1940s non-Russian interpretations of their pasts could still be regarded as "national history." The need to assuage national feelings during the war slowed down this homogenization of historiography. After 1947, the drive for uniformity was renewed. More detailed guidelines and more stringent central control minimized the expression of plurality, diversity, and national conflicts in official historiography to such a degree that the histories of non-Russian Republics became "Russian historiography" about the particular territory, rather than native "national history." Historians in the Republics after 1947 still studied their countries, but non-Russian "national historiography" was at best a marginal pursuit and verged on antiquarianism. It could not be regarded as a continuation of the various pre-1934 national historiographies. Specialist studies about Republic pasts that offered new perspectives or information that perhaps questioned an official tenet appeared only in tiny editions for specialists. More importantly, the universal proclivity to organize the past in terms of "whig history" was reinforced in the USSR by the controlled, centralized nature of scholarship. The degree to which research not confirming *a priori* Russocentric guidelines found expression at the level of generalization and synthesis depended on political authorities. Thus, mass-edition histories were almost identical and ensured that only the official image of the past was disseminated to the population.

In 1945, the ideological secretary G. Aleksandrov made it known that the pasts of the nations of the USSR were to be amalgamated into a "single organic process." "The history of a separate nation," he wrote, "can be properly studied and understood only in connection with the history of other nationalities and first of all with the history of the Russian nation."[41] In the 1960s, the ideological chief Boris Ponomarev reasserted this idea:

> It would be impossible and incorrect to depict the history of the country as if it were a mosaic, as a summary of the surveys of the history of each separate Republic. Such an approach diminishes the significance of centuries of interrelationships and would not illustrate how the friendship of working peoples of separate nationalities was formed during their struggle against a common enemy.[42]

The "history of the USSR" did not begin in Russia in 1917 or 1922 but in prehistoric Asia. The official histories imposed periodization and categories derived from Russian historiography on non-Russian pasts and highlighted the moment non-Russians became part of the tsarist empire as the most important event in their histories. Comparison of the space devoted to Russian and non-Russian history in any "History of the USSR" illustrates this Russocentrism. Four randomly chosen histories published between 1939 and 1980 devote no more than approximately 30 percent of their texts to non-Russians. If sections devoted to Russian contact with non-Russians and beneficial Russian influences are classified as "Russian history," the percentage of pages on non-Russian history declines. In 1988 the chairman of the State Committee for Public Education admitted publicly that "textbooks on the history of the USSR to a considerable extent remain the history of the Russian people and the Russian state system."[43]

The Russocentric statist bias of Soviet historiography may be illustrated by contrasting the official treatment of Russian relations with the rest of the world before 1917 and the treatment of relations between nationalities in the USSR before 1917. The official view condemned foreign attacks on tsarist Russia and did not refer to "common struggles" of the Russians and Tatar commoners against Mongol oppression, to a "progressive" Polish occupation of 1610-1612, or French invasion of 1812 on the grounds that these countries had been multinational states or on a "higher plane" of development. The presence in Russia of Poles or Frenchmen was not interpreted as an opportunity for Russians to fight alongside them against common class enemies for liberation. In an official Soviet history of Poland, for example, the formation of the multinational Polish state was interpreted as a threat to Russia because the event preceded a war with Russia.[44] The multinational Russian state, conversely, never threatened its neighbors with war. Between 1934 and 1991, in official Soviet historiography there was no "Russian feudal aggression."

Post-1934 official historiography required historians to downplay or omit past differences and conflicts between Russia and non-Russians belonging to the tsarist empire. In Ukraine, the official view, as will be shown, was an amalgam of the nineteenth-century tsarist "pragmatic schema," with the eighteenth-century Ukrainian Cossack "loyalist" and nineteenth-century Galician "Old Ruthenian" and "muscophile" populist interpretations. The latter two, formulated on Ukrainian territory either before the appearance of modern Ukrainian national consciousness or little influenced by it, were written by men for whom an imagined Eastern Slavic unity and loyalty to "Rossiia" was compatible with loyalty to their particular regions of Ukraine and equality under tsarist rule. But once the tsarist government saddled the idea of Slavic unity with autocracy and Russian primacy, Ukrainian allegiance to the center diminished and Ukrainians began thinking less of coexistence and more about Ukraine. By the end of the century a new generation of Ukrainian historians replaced an interpretation of Ukraine's past that stressed Slavic commonality with one that stressed the differences and divergences between Slavs.[45]

Non-Russian nations and Republics were still officially recognized after 1934, and for a time guidelines were broad enough to allow historians to accent in survey histories what was unique in their national pasts. Between 1947 and 1982 control and interpretative limits contracted and widened, and non-Russian "national history" found expression at the level of generalization during periods of liberalization in nuances and shifts of emphasis that were related to the political climate in each Republic. The "reformist" historians were usually the most competent persons in their field, and they sometimes risked their jobs and careers in pursuit of accuracy and truth. But within the context of the Soviet system, their attempts could amount to no more than meanderings and cannot be classified as an indigenous independent interpretation of the history of the Republic. The survey histories of the USSR and the Republics remained defined by a centrally imposed Russocentric statist framework that assumed its objects of analysis, the non-Russian Republic and its native inhabitants, were transitional historical phenomena and continued to portray the Republics as integral parts of the whole.[46] Survey histories still emphasized common links and claimed a "friendship of nations" predated the annexation of the particular non-Russian territories to Russia. Where issues such as Russian domination, diversity, differences, and conflicts among nationalities were not ignored, they were skirted by claims that they stemmed from class-based exploitation. Thus, even during periods of "liberalization," native accounts of Republic history remained merely regional Russian history.[47]

Can distinctions be made at all between "Russian" and "Ukrainian" historiography in the USSR given the similarity between the official view of the Eastern Slavic past and two pre-twentieth-century Ukrainian interpretations? Given these similarities might it be argued that the official Soviet interpretation in fact has "Ukrainian" roots? The answer is no for two reasons. First, the post-1934 official interpretation obfuscated past differences between Ukraine and Russia and thereby failed to meet a basic criterion of "national history"—consideration of the historical distinctiveness of the subject of analysis. Second, the official view postulated Russian political primacy in Eastern Slavdom from as early as the thirteenth century, which brought it closer to the tsarist Russian "pragmatic schema" than the aforementioned Ukrainian interpretations.

2

The Institutions and the Ideology

THE ORGANIZATION OF HISTORIOGRAPHY

Historians in the tsarist empire were grouped within universities, the Academy of Sciences, and private associations. After 1917 the Bolsheviks retained this institutional division of labor, which allotted research to the academy and teaching to the universities. The academy was called the Russian Academy until 1925, when it was renamed the Academy of Sciences of the USSR. Until the mid-1930s, there were independent and semiautonomous institutes associated with universities, such as the Institute of History of Material Culture in Leningrad. Marxists were organized in the Socialist Academy (1918). Renamed the Communist Academy in 1923, this body became part of the Academy of Sciences of the USSR in 1936. Until they were incorporated into the All-Union Academy, Marxist institutes and their historical sections existed alongside the Russian Academy of Sciences, which had its own Historical-Philological Section.

Until 1929 in the USSR, non-Marxist historians were allowed to publish, and the Party demanded neither Marxist method nor interpretations from them. After 1929, it expanded its control to include historical writing and no longer permitted historians who wanted to publish the option of neutrality toward official Marxism-Leninism and dialectical historical materialism. By 1930, a Party member was permanent secretary of the All-Union Academy, Party officials controlled each level of the institution, and all of its activities were linked to state policies. The academy's Institute of History was formed in 1936 from the Institute of History of the Communist Academy and the Historical Archaeographical Institute of the Academy of Sciences. There were sections on the history of the nations of the USSR, but no separate RSFSR section. The Socialist, and then Communist, Academy was subordinated to the Central Executive Committee. Non-Party academics were under the Republican Commissariats of Education (SOVNARKOM) to 1930 and afterward were transferred to the jurisdiction of Republican Central Committees (CC). In 1936, the All-Union Ministry of Education was given supervision of Republican ministries.

The Party's role in scholarship has yet to be fully studied and only in 1989 were documents relating to this question first made available to scholars. These reveal that between 1929 and 1934 Party Bureaus, *biuro tsykl,* were attached to each section in the academy and that they not only judged finished work but determined research plans and who was to work on which topics. The relationship of this subunit to its parallel and superior bodies is unclear.[1] Before 1929, within the academies the Party had only cells within the Section of Scientific Workers, a branch of the Union of Education Workers. These sections were renamed in 1924 the Society of Militant Dialectical Materialists and in 1928 the All-Union Association for Workers in Science and Technology for Cooperation in Scientific Construction (VARNITSO). After 1930, this organization was put under the Secretariat and the Culture and Propaganda Section and included Party-dominated committees of academic "workers," corresponding to factory committees, who advanced Party interests within the institution. These were composed of newly introduced graduate students who were Party members. In 1934, the Party Bureaus were abolished, while the Culture and Propaganda Section was subdivided among ministries. In 1939, the Section was recentralized and renamed the Propaganda and Agitation Department (AGITPROP).[2] During World War II, the authority of Republican AGITPROPs increased, while in 1948 a Culture and Science Department specifically responsible for research was added to the Central Committee. These bodies formulated directives defining historical themes and indicated directions for and supervised research through the mechanism of an Academic Plan under the formal control of the Cultural and Scientific branch of the State Planning Commission (GOSPLAN). Stalin intervened directly in matters he thought were of exceptional importance.[3]

After Stalin's death, the institutional structure of Soviet scholarship remained intact and historians still could not choose their own subjects and methods. But interpretive authority devolved from the CC AGITPROP to Republic Institutes of Marxism-Leninism and the Social Sciences Section of the All-Union Academy. After 1956, these institutions still controlled and allocated resources. They no longer issued detailed guidelines but rather ensured that specialists worked within established parameters.

The All-Union Academy established a council to coordinate research with Republic academies in 1945. In 1963 this authority was expanded when All-Union Academy decisions became mandatory for Republic academies, and semiannual coordinating sessions were instituted, while the Social Sciences Section of the All-Union Academy got the power to supervise all research in the USSR. An additional supervisory body, the Ideological Department, was set up in 1963 within the CC with the specific task of ensuring consistency in phraseology and interpretation.[4]

Historians of the Bolshevik coup and the 1917-1921 revolution were directly under CC control and between 1920 and 1929 were organized into the Commission on the History of the October Revolution and the History of the Communist Party (ISTPART). This organization was divided into central and Republic organizations with the latter studying regional Party history under the supervision of the Republican party. The name was changed to the Institute of the History of the Party and the October Revolution in 1929, and in 1939 the Republic institutions were reconstituted as subunits of an All-Union Institute of Marxism-Leninism (formed in 1931). After 1956, Republic organs regained some of their pre-1939 autonomy, and "Institute of Party History" was added to the Institute of Marxism-Leninism filial title.

This institutional structure was more constrictive than academic hierarchies in Western countries. After 1945, in particular, it was characterized by a high degree of coordination and triple checking, though perfect unanimity and centralization were never attained. Yet despite shortcomings, the system functioned well enough to ensure that after 1956 no general history of the USSR or of a Republic was ever withdrawn after publication. Up to 1956, almost every survey was later condemned for "errors."[5] There was rivalry and tension between authorities and academics, but just as important in accounting for interpretive evolution were factional rivalries between academics. As scholars were dependent on Party bureaucrats for funding, prestige, prizes, paper allocation, travel, and press runs, there was an impetus to appeal to them as arbitrators, which carried in its wake politicization of differences over interpretation between groups of academics or individuals. In the struggle for favor and resources incumbent with the status of "correct" interpreter, rivals only had to express their ideas in the required official Marxist jargon. "Reformists" sought to prove that good scholarship was not incompatible with official views and policy, while "conservatives" warned of "nationalism," lack of "objectivity," or "ideological deviation."

Besides the Party monopoly of jobs and resources, "ideological control" and informal censorship set limits on thought and expression. The former refers to the pressure that could be exerted on historians by ideological workers in security and Party organizations, committees of co-workers, editors, and heads of publishing firms. In the 1930s and 1940s, if anyone dared refer either directly or in Aesopean subtexts to matters of significance to the secret police and Ministry of the Interior, the passages rarely escaped editors' attention. If, after "consultations," the author did not make required changes, his work could be banned by a simple telephone call to the publisher. Given the climate of the time, formal censorship was usually unnecessary. During the 1930s there was even a branch of the secret police (LITKONTROL) assigned the task of determining what authors were planning to write and supervising censors.[6] Postwar censors and editors were lazier, and penalties were less severe. If authors inserted subtexts and "liberal" interpretations into otherwise dull colorless texts containing suitably worded modifiers or introductions, they stood a good chance of getting published. Only in the event of denunciations by rivals or negative reviews were texts rigorously reviewed, and even then the final decision depended on the political climate and whether the author enjoyed the protection of a high-ranking patron.[7] Interpretive meandering was risky but no longer carried the threat of imprisonment.

Simply getting published was another means of control. Procedure dictated that works had to appear on a plan prepared as much as two years in advance. If it did not, authors had great difficulty obtaining paper. Unsolicited works—even if they passed out-of-house reviewers, who were very critical and usually erred on the side of stringency—then had to be accepted by the head of a publishing firm and an institute director. All works were read by a responsible editor, department, or section, and then institutional review committees, an editorial council, and then senior editors. Finally, the State Committee on Publications, which determined paper allocations and in 1963 forbade the publication of monographs longer than 140 pages in Ukraine—280 pages with special permission—determined when and how many copies of a study would appear.[8] Understandably, Soviet historians often complained that they did not recognize their own texts after editing. The pressure to accept changes determined by ideological considerations and by the wish to appear in print was intensified by authors' fears that if they argued about changes too long with editors they would not meet the signed contract deadline. This could bring judicial proceedings, especially if an author had already accepted payment.

A centralized system of institutions and resource allocation, factional rivalry, peer pressure, and editorial supervision all made formal external censorship merely a final, even minor, means of control. The Chief Administration for Literary and Press Affairs under the Commissariat of Education (GLAVLIT) was established in 1922. In 1953 or 1954, the name was changed to Main Board for the Protection of State and Military Secrets in the Press, and in 1966 the term *State* was removed. According to its 1922 statute, publications of the various academies were to be subjected only to checks for military secrets. As of 1936, academy publications were censored like all others, and anything published in more than ten copies without approval led to the arrest of the printer, the responsible editor, and the author. Lists of censored subjects, names, and books were compiled by AGITPROP and published in a frequently updated "Index of Information Not to Be Published in the Open Press."[9] After 1924, there was a centrally directed listing, and "ideologically unacceptable" publications were destroyed except for four or five copies. These were deposited in "special collections" (SPETSFOND) of the major Soviet libraries.[10]

Polish historiography up to 1918 was centered in the universities of Warsaw, Krakow, and Lviv, and in independent privately funded associations, the most important of which were the Akademia Umiejętności (Krakow), the Towarzystwo Naukowe (Lviv), the Towarzystwo Milosnikow Historii (Warsaw), and the Towarzystwo Przyjaciol Nauk (Poznan).[11] With the reestablishment of the Polish state in 1918, some of the private institutions were dissolved while the major ones remained as professional associations publishing journals. The main centers of historical research were the universities of Poznan, Krakow, Warsaw, Vilnius (Wilno), and Lviv. Ukrainian history also fell within the mandate of the Eastern Institute (Instytut Wschodni) and the Institute of Nationality Studies (Instytut Badan Narodowościowych)—the latter established in the early 1920s and after 1926 sponsored by the Ministry of the Interior. Two important Polish historians of Ukraine affiliated to the latter were Oswald Górka and Marceli Handelsman. Scholarship was decentralized and suffered little interference from the state.[12] National minorities had autonomous historical associations.

The establishment of communist rule in 1944 did not bring immediate direct political interference into scholarship. Until 1948, the state supported all scholars, allowed them to reorganize prewar professional associations, and sponsored only a small group called the Association of Marxist Historians (AHM). After the war, the Akademia Umiejętności became the central scholarly institution in Poland, the Soviet-style equivalent of a national academy of sciences, and had "Polish" prefixed to its title.

Sovietization of Poland, begun in mid-1948, was not very successful in the realm of historical scholarship, as the tiny AHM attracted few historians. However, all professional organizations were transformed into Societies of Material Culture and placed under the Ministry of Education together with all the universities. New initiatives were taken in 1951-1952 when a short-lived equivalent of the Russian Communist Academy was established. The

Institute for the Formation of Marxist Leninist Academic Cadres (IKKN) was formed in 1953 and later renamed the Institute of Social Sciences, but it was abolished in 1956. An Institute of History existed within the Polish Academy of Sciences (PAN) formed in 1952.

The drive to unify and centralize on the Soviet model stopped in 1956, but even during those years ideological control, academic planning, and self-censorship were never as restrictive as in the USSR. Unprecedented in the Soviet bloc was the status of the Polish Historical Association (PHT), a major prewar professional association allowed to become a partner of the Institute of History, which, for its part, declared it would operate independently of the secretariat of PAN and elect its own directors.[13] In 1956 a Central Committee Plenum Resolution forbade Party interference in scholarship and replaced the Section on Culture and Learning with a Committee of Education and Science staffed by intellectuals instead of administrators. The Party made these concessions to Polish scholars partly out of fear of a mass exodus of intellectuals from its ranks. Indicative of the resulting "liberalism" was that in one of the few studies on this subject written under the Communist regime the author was able to assert that Party academic policy between 1948 and 1956 had been wrong and that the decision to withdraw from direct interference in scholarship was good.[14] The CPSU never enacted a similar resolution.

Thus, after 1956 there was a restoration of professional ethics and standards in Polish scholarship. Historians enjoyed very broad interpretative limits by Soviet standards, and autonomous associations alongside PAN and the universities provided a counterbalance to the conformist inertia of the latter. But although the Party no longer specified what historians had to write, it retained administrative control over scholars, particularly in the Academy, which was not the informal oligarchical discussion club of prewar days. After 1956 the Academy remained a centralized bureaucracy where officials decided who could publish or travel officially abroad and could even inquire why members may have decided to have their manuscript typed by someone outside the institution.[15]

Poland had no academic institute specifically devoted to Ukrainian affairs. Ukrainian history was studied by individuals at universities, all of which from 1954 had Chairs of the History of USSR. The most active, renamed History of the Nations of the USSR in 1969, was at the Jagiellonian University. Ukrainian affairs were also studied in two subsections of PAN; the Commission for Slavic Studies and the Section of the History of Polish Soviet Relations (*Zaktad Historii Stosunków Polsko-Radzieckich*, 1961-1972). In 1973 its name was changed to the Institute of Socialist Countries

(*Institut Krajów Socjalistycznych*) and thereafter it published fewer monographs devoted to Lithuania and Ukraine than before.¹⁶ Another institution relevant to Polish study of Ukrainian history, insofar as it influenced the writing of survey histories, was the Polish–Soviet Commission for the Improvement of the Contents of History and Geographical Textbooks, formed in 1968-1969.¹⁷

The main organ of censorship in Poland was established in 1945 and was subordinated to the Press Department of the Central Committee: the Main Office for Control of Press Publications and Public Performances (GUKPPiW). In 1981, academic writing was freed from formal censorship and authors needed approval only for publications of more than a thousand copies. Infringement originally incurred a ban and a monetary fine. The 1981 censorship statutes dropped the penalty of one year imprisonment and reduced substantially a 10,000 zloty fine required since 1952. What was to be banned, presumably, was decided by the Propaganda Secretariat, which, like its Soviet counterpart, compiled a thick book of Rules and Recommendations, biweekly Reports on Materials Censored, and occasionally published Informative Notes.¹⁸

VARIANTS OF HISTORICAL MATERIALISM

At the beginning of the twentieth century, neoromanticism, positivism, and Marxist historical materialism were the major methodological and ideological trends. The first two dominated in interwar Poland, while Marxism received state support in the USSR.

Initially, the Party was circumspect in imposing Marxism on non-Party members. According to the leading Bolshevik historian, Mikhail Pokrovsky, Lenin said:

> Give them themes which will objectively force them to take our point of view.... As well, require from each of them a basic knowledge of Marxist literature.... I assure you that even if they still do not become orthodox Marxists, they will nevertheless assimilate things which were completely excluded from the programme of their courses before; and then it will be the business of the students under our political guidance to use that material as it ought to be used.¹⁹

This indirect approach was dropped after 1931 when academics were obliged to espouse and use "Marxism-Leninism"—a series of propositions culled from the writings of Marx, Engels, and Lenin and formulated into an official ideology by Stalin, which as applied to historiography may be termed Marxist-Leninist Dialectical Historical Materialism (DHM). Until the 1980s,

DHM was not simply one method of analysis, but an authoritatively defined and administratively imposed theory binding on all historians who wanted to hold positions and publish in the USSR. After 1956, the Party rescinded almost all ideological control over scientists but still required that historians defer to the Central Committee Secretariats for Agitation and Propaganda, Culture and Learning, and the Ideological Department.

DHM was a product of positivist, unilinear, determinist Marxism, variously identified as "scientific," "orthodox," "vulgar," "neopositivist," "deductivist," or "stalinist." DHM derives from Enlightenment rationalism and its intellectual high point came in the 1860s after the appearance of Darwin's *On the Origin of Species* and Marx's *Contribution to the Critique of Political Economy*. As explained by Marx, the sum total of the relations of production is the economic structure of society, which is the "real" foundation upon which legal and political superstructures arise and to which definite forms of social consciousness correspond. The relations themselves vary in accordance with the different stages in development of productive forces, and every change in the economic foundation leads to radical transformation of the superstructure. This determinist strain of Marxism discounts human agency, gives economic laws primacy over individual will, claims the same laws govern natural as well as human and social changes, and attaches more significance to socio-economic forms than to class conflict. Individuals do not emancipate themselves but are emancipated; will and feeling, in the final analysis, do not influence the "course of history."[20] DHM preserved a margin for human agency but stressed man's dependency on circumstances and claimed consciousness was only a reflection of the "objective" world. The economic "base" in the "last instance" was the most important element in evolution—but when this "last instance" occurs remained undefined.[21]

Marx distinguished six epochs in human evolution: the Asiatic, Primitive Communism, the Ancient, Feudalism, Capitalism, and Socialism. Although Engels and Stalin argued that these forms succeeded each other in chronological mechanical succession, others have noted Marx thought in terms of a nonchronological succession of particular modes, did not assume inevitable unilinear progression, and imagined his stages as analytical rather than chronological categories.[22]

Positivist Marxism was presented as the definitive Marxism by Engels in his *Anti-Dühring* (1878) and G. Plekhanov in his *A Contribution to the Question of the Development of the Monist View of History* (1895). Both men stressed "objective laws" of development in history and argued that "subjectivity" was not important and that internal contradictions caused change.

Reduced to its essentials this theory merely asserts that whatever happened had to happen.

Some have argued that Marx's historical materialism was more hypothesis than theory because it was based on a number of verifiable elements: the claim that the economic had primacy over thought, that the "objective" world was material, and that thought, not reality, was dialectical. Only later, when Engels, Plekhanov, and Lenin added a number of unverifiable propositions did the mentor's ideas freeze into dogma. The most important of these accruements were the claims that the past is a "process" that can be known and that reality, as well as thought, is dialectical. The latter idea, introduced by Engels and presumably accepted by Marx, attributed to the universe a quality that materialist thinkers of the 1860s thought it should have. This idea provided a basis for the claims that development was independent of man and thought and that nothing can be fortuitous.

A key element in DHM is the proposition that an irreversible "historical process" is moving towards a known end that can be known by the discovery of laws. In Marxist parlance the description and analysis of this "process" is termed "objective," while ignoring it is condemned as "subjective," naive, and ill-conceived. Thus, partisanship is desirable because it converges with "progress." From such premises it is easy to argue that since the proletariat is the agent of "historical progress" because its subjective interest corresponds with the "objective flow" of history, and since the Party represents the true interests of the proletariat, what Party spokesmen say is always correct because it is "objective."

Lenin's revolutionary activism and conception of the Party as an all-powerful history-making force led him to a voluntaristic interpretation of DHM, but his revision had little relevance to analysis of events occurring before the formation of his organization.[23] More important for Soviet DHM was Lenin's condemnation of other points of view as wrong. He attributed disagreement to class origins and interests, not to difference of opinion or honest doubt, and he regarded his version of Marx as the only valid way of understanding anything. Lenin stated in the opening pages of his *What the Friends of the People Are* (1894): "Now since the appearance of Capital the materialist conception of history is no longer a hypothesis but a scientifically proven proposition.... Materialism is not 'primarily a scientific conception of history,'... but the only scientific conception of it." The Bolshevik leader saw skeptics as cheats or stupid children to be reprimanded or repudiated through invective in polemics. For Lenin the purpose of debate was not truth but to strike down adversaries by proving there was no authority except Marx and Marxism as defined by himself.[24]

Lenin's method and confusion of fact with assumption had a profound impact on Soviet scholarship: "When Marxist Leninists say, 'There are historical laws,' they do not mean, 'It is our conjecture that there are historical laws and for this reason we search for these laws and encourage others to follow in our footsteps.' The statement there are historical laws means literally there are historical laws for they have been discovered."[25] Moreover, because Marxist-Leninists imagined Marxism was universally valid and facts to be things rather than ideas, and because they assumed there were no non-existent, but only undiscovered, facts,[26] they thought any derived postulate could ultimately be proven. Thus, DHM reduced research to proving theory and permitted historians to make do with evidence others would not find conclusive. If there was no evidence to indicate events followed a predefined model, historians could rest assured that future research would find it. The result of such deductivism was "objective knowledge."

But while Lenin was molding DHM, Croce, Sorel, Weber, Pareto, Labriola, Bergson, and Durkheim were questioning the cult of material progress, the validity of theories of scientific fatalism, and the rigorous distinction between Being and Thought. By 1910, in the "New Knowledge," Heisenberg, Planck, Mach, and Einstein had empirically disproved the Cartesian materialist interpretation of the universe. Quantum theory suggested that the idea of continuous and infinite changes in matter was false and that matter could not be measured as if it flowed in endless streams, while relativity theory demonstrated that there was no absolute space and time as distinct dimensions. In short, absolutes were giving way to relativism and the epistemological premises of realist determinist Marxism were threatened. Philosophical certainty was giving way to uncertainty as neo-Kantians convincingly argued that there was no absolute historical truth and that the past could never be known, as it was a complex not reducible to a single line of development culminating in "liberty" or communism. Dilthey, Rickert, Berr, and Beard explained that historians at best could only provide explanations that were better because they accounted for more evidence.[27]

When leading European thinkers were rejecting the empirical positivist epistemological basis of DHM and argued there could be no facts in history apart from a point of view or theory and that no theory could emerge by itself solely from facts, that is, from the object of study, Lenin still insisted human history was a "process" of the kind found in natural sciences. When this model became outdated in Europe, as scholars realized that assumptions and theories that led to conflicting interpretations could not be tested by observation because there was no common body of evidence recognized by all historians irrespective of their adopted point of view, it obtained state backing in the USSR. When in Europe it was accepted that historical facts were relative to interpretation and could not confirm interpretation in the same way natural facts could test the validity of hypotheses, in the USSR the notion that facts had real existence and had only to be discovered was given an uncontested monopoly on thought by Stalin.

When Pannakoek, Adler, Korsch, and, in Russia, Bogdanov began to modify determinist mechanistic Marxism in accord with the New Knowledge, Lenin condemned them. In his *Materialism and Empirio Criticism* (1907), written after Mach, Planck, and Einstein had published their work, Lenin argued that materialist metaphysics was valid despite evidence to the contrary and that relativity was incompatible with dialectics. The philosophical basis of his argument lay in Engels's rigorous distinction between idealism and materialism, a distinction that, it might be argued, did not reflect Marx, who recognized that thought is governed by practical needs and that the mind's image of the world is regulated not exclusively by the perceived objects, but by the practical task at hand. Marx presumably did not regard matter as something in space capable of being perceived and then defined, but as "social practice."[28] But despite the scholarly sounding title of his work Lenin ignored these details. He was writing a political polemic intended to discredit the New Knowledge because it was incorrect from the standpoint of Party work.[29]

Lenin was a contemporary of Weber, Freud, English logic, and German critical philosophy yet knew nothing of them. He glibly dismissed the New Knowledge as "bourgeois reaction" and remained a determinist Marxist. His book threatened to freeze Bolshevik thought in the 1860s. During his life this did not happen, though he did have Mach, Descartes, and Kant removed from libraries.[30] Bogdanov and a few like-minded thinkers continued to publish and remained in the Party, and until about 1930, thought in the USSR was not totally isolated from the New Physics.

Stalin's Marxism is elaborated in three works published under his name between 1923 and 1938. *Foundations of Leninism* and *Questions of Leninism* introduced the concept of "Leninism," which was defined not as a form of Marxism developed in an agrarian country without traditions of liberalism, but as an internationally valid theory: "Marxism of the era of Imperialism." In 1938 the *History of the CPSU (B)* summarized the key philosophical aspects of Stalinism as follows: the world is material, matter is independent reality existing outside the observer, and nothing is unknowable. Like the young Marx, Stalin explained that history moved through five successive stages in particular order through which all societies would climb at different speeds. The task of scholars was to search for fundamental laws governing each stage and illustrate how the main mover in the "historical process" was the struggle of faceless "exploited masses."

On the subject of individual will, Stalin was unclear. On the one hand, he extended the scope for activism and the idea that man makes himself to the past preceding the formation of the Party. On the other hand, he stressed the determinist nature of economic evolution wherever convenient. As a result, he transformed Marxism into a series of justifications without theoretical foundation:[31] "Marxism under Stalin cannot be defined by any collection of statements, ideas or concepts; it was not a question of propositions as such but of the fact there existed an all powerful authority competent to declare at any given moment what Marxism was and what it was not."[32]

Stalin in his *Marxism and Linguistics* (1950), perhaps unwittingly, provided academics with a theoretical provision to free humanities and social sciences from Party control. If, as Stalin claimed, linguistics belonged neither to base or superstructure, then it was not a product of a class but of society as a whole and, therefore, ideologically neutral. This argument actually did serve to free science in the USSR from political control. Other forms of consciousness, including historiography, however, remained defined as "class products" and therefore, as "weapons in the class struggle," remained under Party control.[33] After 1956 Soviet historians did introduce elements of nondogmatic, multilinear, and evolutionist Marxism into their scholarship, but by the early 1970s the innovators were condemned and official writing sank back into torpor.[34]

The thought of Plekhanov, Lenin, and Stalin constitutes the body of knowledge called Russian Marxism, which after 1931 was imposed throughout the USSR as Marxism-Leninism. In Poland before 1917, Marxism and historical materialism were not popular among Polish radicals; however, Rosa Luxemburg and Ludwig Krzywicki were two notable Polish Marxist thinkers. The latter was critical of determinist, positivist Marxism, and his work influenced the evolution of Polish Marxism. He claimed historical materialism had no universal application, that there was no general pattern of change applicable to all societies, and that although Marxism had limited application in the study of mass social phenomena it was unsuitable for study of primitive communities.[35]

Before 1948 historical materialism had little if any impact on the interpretation of Poland's history. Between 1948 and 1956, the Polish Workers party tried to impose "Marxism-Leninism" on Polish scholars but failed. A student at a Party school in the 1950s, for instance, related that for his oral exams he had to demonstrate knowledge of the important nineteenth-century

Polish historians, not the Soviet historians of Poland then in vogue, and that he was complimented for his knowledge of Ukrainian scholars then unmentionable in the USSR.[36] By the 1960s, DHM had almost disappeared from Polish historiography. The remaining Polish "Marxist-Leninists" understood they were only one school among many, while their method was not the dogmatic historiosophic metaphysics found in the USSR. Polish Marxists as a rule exhibited consistency, showed respect for evidence, considered arguments on merit, and paid due attention to political and cultural history. In 1981, the Party formally recognized that the historical diversity of Polish culture and worldviews had always been beneficial, that tolerance was a valued product of Polish history, and that it would commit itself to continue these traditions.[37]

The work of the major postwar Polish Marxist historians, W. Kula, J. Topolski, and A. Wyczanski was less indebted to Marx or Lenin than to the interwar economic historians centered in Poznan under J. Rutkowski and in Lviv under F. Bujak. Post-1956 Polish historiography was also influenced by the French Annales School, Marc Bloch, Henri Lefebvre, and Henri Berr.[38] Polish historians after 1956 tended to analyze in terms of long-term structures and a descending hierarchy of categories: geography, demography, economy, nature, popular culture, and politics. In their writing, economics was not primary, industry received little attention, and interpretations were built around exchange rather than production relations. They recognized no universal law of stages and rejected periodization based on such stages.

THE PARAMETERS OF INTERPRETATION

Institutional inertia restricts initiative and by determining patterns of personnel selection helps exclude free thinkers from organizations. Policy and personnel, however, can sometimes redefine the objectives of institutions and the limits of imposed parameters. During World War II, for example, A. S. Shcherbakov, head of the Political Directorate of the Red Army, convinced Stalin of the utility of non-Russian nationalism in the struggle against Hitler, overrode the more conservative AGITPROP, and directed the ideological apparatus to encourage rather than circumscribe expression of non-Russian national pride. This was reversed after 1947. Against the backdrop of intense official exploitation of Russian nationalism, stricter central control and the appointment of Mikhail Suslov as Chief of AGITPROP[39] historiography returned to its prewar role as a tool abetting the homogenization and integration of the population around the Russian nation. Between 1965 and 1982, Suslov was in charge of ideology, while the hardliner S. P. Trapeznikov headed the Section of Science and Learning, but intensified centralization failed to produce total uniformity. The Ukrainian First Secretary Petro Shelest used his authority during the 1960s to support writers and academics who tacitly resisted centralist pressure. By following interpretive guidelines loosely rather than rigorously, they cautiously emphasized and celebrated what was unique and particular to Ukraine.[40]

Changes in policy and predispositions of major officials could thus lessen or mollify the restrictive and centralizing tendencies of institutions. The political climate, sometimes more liberal in the peripheries than the capital, and the post-1956 impetus of professionalism among some scholars that led them to dispense with the more absurd of the dictated guidelines also countered the restrictive centralizing inertia of institutions.[41]

But the institutional structure of Soviet scholarship was only one mechanism of control. Another was the official ideology. Inasmuch as hypotheses, presuppositions, conceptual categories, and methods determine what evidence historians deem significant and use, they also determine what aspects of the past are described, ignored, emphasized, or downplayed. Thus, a less dogmatic version of DHM in Poland between 1948 and 1956 restricted the field of historical inquiry to a lesser degree than in the USSR after 1937.

DHM regards the evolution of the forces of production, class structure, and class struggle as the most important aspects of past societies. Because it regards culture, race, nations, and religion as secondary, individuals, their passions, motives, rationality, and irrationality fade or disappear in narratives. Within the DHM worldview persons are replaced by "typical" representatives of a class who act according to predefined interests of either "the oppressed" or "the oppressors," regardless of motives expressed in documents. Standards of living of "the masses" must be low, differentiation within peasant society must be high and permanent. Egalitarianism and aspirations for it are good by definition, as is violence if it is "antifeudal" or "anticapitalist." From the perspective of these purportedly universally valid juxtapositions, international politics, differences of religion, or dynastic interests become secondary or even irrelevant as mere superficial manifestations of "real class interests." The past becomes fixed within a Manichaean schema of "progressive-reactionary" with the former including all those who contribute to intensifying class struggle and the latter all those on the other side or uninvolved. Such categorization forces culture, thought, and politics into one of two molds and effectively dissolves the discipline of intellectual history as differences between thinkers became trivial and truth unimportant.[42] In DHM, differences of opinion cannot be genuine but only derived, while the importance of ideas is not determined by their contribution to the

The Institutions and the Ideology 41

evolution of thought, but by the "being" of the thinker and the class that benefits from them.

DHM assumes causal connection between rationalism and radicalism, and by focusing attention on change it is inadequate as a conceptual tool to study institutions. DHM is useful for study of moments of violence and destruction/reconstruction such as rebellions or revolutions, but it warps understanding of such subjects insofar as the assumption of merciless class struggle excludes consideration of mediation by law, custom, kinship, fortune, self-interest, or Christian morality.

> Both Marx's enlightenment rationalism and his nineteenth-century scientism led him to treat immediate sociality and tradition as essentially arbitrary and thus divorced from fundamental truth. Only such immediate sociality and traditional premises in thought make it possible to conceive of social action, however, rather than some form of socio-structural or culturalogical determinism. It is the weakness of this part of Marx's argument which has led to the analytic separation of "objective" and "subjective" dimensions of class. This has led on the one hand to asking what objective circumstances are required to make (in some simple causal sense) a class into a subjective actor. . . . On the other hand, those emphasizing the subjective dimension have tended to reduce it to a matter simply of what people think, than consideration of all the conditions which may produce collective action.[43]

Direct pronouncements by the founders also left later practitioners with difficulties. Engels, for example, thought the Magdeburg Law inhibited economic growth and that centralized government was historically more important. These tenets, taken as dogma, left little scope for study of nations that lacked indigenous states and for whom any development that did occur was thanks to pockets of autonomy within multinational medieval states defined by institutions such as Magdeburg Law. Similarly, Marx's comments about the "idiocy of rural life" and dismissal of peasantry as a "sack of potatoes" incapable of independent political action was hardly conducive to balanced study and understanding of preindustrial society.

The inherent limitations of DHM do not mean it is a totally useless method. It can produce a coherent, even intricate image of the past, but never an adequate one. The image is not necessarily mendacious, but because the method can lead practitioners to ignore much that cannot be fitted into the model, DHM facilitates tendentious interpretation. At its worst, the method is totally inadequate to examine certain kinds of problems. Its products can be imprecise, and amount to mere truisms or absurdities that explain that what happened had to happen. The worst products of DHM are not bad simply because they are biased and distorted. They are bad because they are biased and distorted in the wrong way. In particular, practitioners of DHM subject to an interpretative authority are prone to neglect fundamental rules of method like accepting conclusions only when there is good evidence, and considering contradictory evidence.

The systematic abuse and manipulation of language by the regime represented another means of controlling scholarship and restricting thought. Scholars conforming to DHM inevitably ended up using phrases and words in structured slogans that related not to reality or documents or internationally accepted definitions, but to *a priori* definitions derived from DHM. "People" (*narod*), for instance, did not mean all human beings at a given time and place. As explained in the *Great Soviet Encyclopaedia,* the word referred only to those who "actively took part in the progressive development of society." Stilted meanings and the failure of DHM as a philosophy to distinguish between fact and value, or what was from what ought to have been, produced convoluted narratives without context and made criticism and thinking clearly difficult. The greater the press run of a book or article, the more frequent did the ritualized official jargon of DHM appear in it. Such texts, as George Orwell noted, consist of phrases tacked together like the sections of a prefabricated henhouse; they are monotonous and difficult to verify since the words bear little relation to what they are supposed to refer. DHM texts may fail to persuade or convince. But insofar as the semantic form of language and syntax rather than reason determines initial perception, and "reality" is more of a verbal grammatical construction than a perceived object, Soviet texts could powerfully influence thinking and understanding, particularly among readers with no access to any other kind of writing. The jargon of formulas and euphemisms also facilitated identification of deviation, as authors who used different word sequences or adjectives would stand out and reveal themselves as free thinkers.

For example, the words "quiet noises run and sleep furiously" formulate an unintelligible abstraction, but because they are in a grammatical order they seem to constitute a sentence that says something. Soviet history writing, with its repetition of passive-mood sentences without subjects, use of verbs in the continuous tense, and phrases like "friendship—or exploitation—intensified" or "the process of bringing socialism to perfection," similarly produces narratives that seem to say something. In fact, they often mean nothing and can paralyze the reason of anyone trying to understand them. At a higher interpretive level, persons schooled in the belief that "material" interests determine motivation and that ideas in themselves have little if any influence on behavior, are predisposed to dismiss the relationship between politics, ideas, and mentality as incidental or even irrelevant.[44] In DHM writings individuals tend to disappear because human beings are designated by collective abstractions such as "vanguard" or "peasants," while the assumption that everything is in constant motion and changing absolves historians of the need to describe in detail. In Soviet texts words do not depict the past as a world of individuals interacting but as a semimythical battlefield where impersonal forces collide as part of an epochal conflict. The result is an image of everything and everybody in a perpetual process of "organic" progress or reaction, liberation or oppression. The juxtaposition of pejorative or positive words to events or concepts prejudges them as required and reinforces the Manichaean image of the universe.[45]

After 1956, academics strove for broader rather than narrower understanding of DHM, and rigor in testing, critical use of evidence, as well as judgment on the basis of results rather than *a priori* principle may be discerned in good Soviet historical writing. But in 1973 the Party reminded historians that their duty was not to reinterpret Marxism-Leninism in the light of new data but to interpret new data in the light of Marxism-Leninism.[46] This injunction echoed a similar warning made in the 1940s:

> Among a certain group of Soviet historians incorrect views have become prevalent which hold that the advancement of historical science consists exclusively of the accumulation of new factual material and that the object of historical works is the fullest exposition of the facts. This is a harmful trend.... The striving for the collection of facts means slipping into bourgeois objectivist positions and a refusal to recognize the objective conformity to the laws of the historical process.[47]

The Party used DHM to justify repression of documents containing discordant or contradictory information. Such justifications may be found in Soviet guides for publishing archival documents.

Establishment of standard rules for publication of archival documents was begun in 1929 and the first draft of proposed guidelines explained that publication could not be narrowed to "technism." The author meant that publication of documents without Marxist-Leninist method, under the guise of "objective documentalism," would lead to falsification and promotion of "bourgeois historical conceptions in documents." He suggested that when choosing documents for publication the archivist had to be sure they reflected facts by using political class analysis as well as textual criticism.[48] In 1935, in a discussion on rules a participant noted it was axiomatic for publishers to work in accord with sociopolitical commands and that all publication "could and should be regarded as weapons in the political struggle."[49] No guidelines and very few documents were published during Stalin's lifetime.

When, in 1955, the first regulations did appear, article 1, part 1, read: "The choice of subject area is determined by its academic value and political relevance, corresponding to the tasks of historical scholarship and the demands [imposed] by the economic and cultural construction of communist society." In choosing a subject, publishers were to be guided by the tenet that history is concerned with the toiling masses as well as with the development of the means of production.[50] The guide of 1969 was more restrictive. Part 3, article 20, specified that documents chosen for publication must be "in agreement with the Marxist-Leninist principle of Partymindedness and historicism, and have a scholarly, political or practical value." Choice of material for specific collections "must be done with the intention of illustrating the law determined [*zakonomernyi*] character of social development and the role of the popular masses in history." Documents originating from the camp of the class enemy were to be chosen "with the purpose of better revealing the plans and activities of the class enemy."[51]

Post-Stalin guidelines included strict requirements on verification and correct rendition of documents, and probably after 1956, outright forgeries or doctored texts were not printed. On the other hand, published documents still were not representative either of actual collections nor of anything except what the interpretative authority wanted illustrated. The preferential selection of published primary materials thus reinforced the ideological and institutional parameters within which historians worked. Documents published under such conditions simply provided another method of ensuring conformity.

Party control of access to libraries and archives and regulations about what could be published or quoted restricted thought and independent research by keeping exploratory and revisionary work within small circles. Such measures successfully reinforced the tendency of historians to speak to each other and encouraged them to say different things to different audiences. A precedent for this kind of cynical manipulation may be found in Lenin's behavior. In a letter to Lunacharsky, the leader expressed dismay about a Mayakovsky book being published in 5,000 copies and wrote that no more than 1,500 copies should have been printed: for libraries and "cranks."[52] In his letter of 1934 on the importance of textbooks Stalin made a similar distinction between specialist and mass publications. He reminded officials that because the proposed history of the USSR would be read by millions he was "not talking about irresponsible journalistic essays where one can twaddle on as one will about everything with no sense of responsibility."[53]

The post-1934 Soviet academic system had its weak points and was never as uniform or monolithic as the Party wanted. Nevertheless, it was an awesome mechanism of control that, until the last years of the regime, ensured those below remained dependent on those above not only administratively, but for interpretive nuances in method and even for sources.[54] Alongside the centralization, the institutional monopoly of the Party, the ritual jargon, the ranking of access to information according to the principle *quod licet jovi non licet bovi,* and formal and informal censorship, the system also included guidelines on how to interpret specific events, persons, and subjects.

3

Delineating the Past

GUIDELINES IN THE USSR

The official interpretation of the "History of the USSR" was formulated between 1927 and 1953. Up to 1932, historians had some scope for debate, although it was increasingly directed and restricted. Afterward, interpretation evolved according to politically determined guidelines. Scholars had little choice but to acquiesce to direction.

The Party began interfering in its own historiography as early as 1925 and initially focused on how historians interpreted its role in the Revolution, but only after Stalin's 1931 letter to *Proletarskaia revoliutsiia* did independent research in this field of study cease. In reference to an issue in Party history, Stalin made statements such as, "The question as to whether Lenin was or was not a real Bolshevik cannot be made the subject of analysis," "Slander must be branded as such and not made the subject of discussion," and "Who save hopeless bureaucrats can rely on paper documents alone, only archive rats judge parties and leaders by words instead of deeds?" His words effectively forbade Party historians from indulging openly in critical analysis. Mobilized on the "historical front," their public task was to confirm axioms and denounce deviations in a fight "for the final victory of socialism."[1] Course outlines in history and other subjects became *"political directives from the organs of the proletarian dictatorship [sic]."*[2]

In 1934, Stalin personally contributed to guidelines on the history of Russia and its empire. In 1937, these were reflected in a survey history by A. Shestakov that provided the basic model for all subsequent histories of the USSR. Stalin also contributed to volume 1 of the *Istoriia grazhdanskoi voiny v SSSR* (1935). According to the memoirs of a student at the Institute of Red Professors between 1933 and 1937, I. I. Mints, the doyen of Soviet historians of the Revolution from the 1960s, actually thought up the book's basic theme: that Stalin, rather than Zinoviev, Kamenev, and Trotsky, played the key role in the Revolution. In 1933 or early 1934, Mints submitted a draft to this effect to the Central Committee. Stalin approved the outline and appointed Mints as his personal secretary in charge of writing the envisaged three-volume history. Thereafter, Mints ensured that Stalin's additions and revisions were incorporated into the final version of the book. The dictator's insistence that the book claim the Revolution occurred in the "USSR," although no such entity existed in 1917, and that "great" and "socialist" be always prefixed to the phrase "October Revolution" seems trivial. But as these phrases effectively defined how historians were supposed to write about the subject, their impact was profound.[3]

By the 1940s Stalin's personal interventions in historiography had given way to a more or less predictable routine. First, a Party plenum decision or comment by Stalin on a given issue was followed by a lead article in a major journal. There followed a "discussion," and then the new ideas were formally introduced into historical articles and textbooks. Finally, monographs "proved" the particular point or adopted specific subjects to the desired interpretation.

Party staging of historical debates between 1927 and 1932 has yet to be studied, but preliminary work on Russian academics between 1928 and 1932 indicates that there was manipulation of differences of opinion and of clashing rivalries and ambitions in academia and that it was directed toward establishing uniformity of thought.[4]

The instrument of manipulation was the Party apparatus headed by Stalin, who from 1922 headed the Secretariat and thus made appointments.[5] The subjects were the young and ambitious eager to win prestige by criticizing established opinions. Some, perhaps most, may have been intimidated, but many submitted willingly and were emotionally prepared to appeal to the Party to establish themselves as intellectual authorities.[6] For those less concerned about issues, the regime could offer material incentives, professional advancement, and status in return for carrying out tasks. The campaign against established opinions and persons was called the struggle for "proletarian hegemony," and the criteria of truth were what Marx, Lenin, and Stalin did or did not say about history. Participants tended to cite Marx and Engels when dealing with theoretical issues such as stages or shifts in relations of production, and Lenin and Stalin on matters relating to national history. In Ukraine, quoting Marxism-Leninism, even by non-Marxists, became the norm after the 1930 trial of the fictional League for the Liberation of Ukraine.[7] Ironically, little from these sometimes interesting discussions found its way into the post-1937 official interpretation, while the origins of what did was not admitted.

Documents released in 1989 indicate that debates in the Ukrainian Academy were guided and exploited by the Secretariat through the *biuro tsykl* and that the most vociferous critics of established views were young men motivated as much by career ambitions and/or naive sincerity as by fear. After being chosen by the Party Bureau to cover a certain subject in a seminar, the person first submitted a draft version of his essay for criticism and approval. The subsequent seminar, duly recorded in protocols, inevitably included discussion of what was or was not the correct "Leninist" understanding of the subject.[8]

Particular points of view became official guidelines because allegedly they represented what Marx, or more often Lenin and/or Stalin, had said or meant. But as these men wrote little about Russian or Ukrainian history, there was considerable latitude for interpretation. In Lenin's writings, for instance, there are numerous comments on events, persons, or issues in Russian history, and a few on Ukrainian history. He even wrote a major historical work, *The Development of Capitalism in Russia,* and formulated a few generalizations relevant to historians. But because he used ideas primarily for resolving current political issues there are many contradictions in his writings. He also confused concepts such as industrialization and capitalism and nationalism and colonialism. On the one hand, those forced to work with Lenin's concepts were intellectually restricted, but on the other hand, his ambiguity did provide maneuvering room.

In 1929, Pokrovsky claimed there was a "Leninist" concept of Russian history, even though Lenin was not a specialist in it.[9] Stalin's subsequent elevation of chosen sets of Lenin's observations to the dignity of theory limited scholarly debate in the "struggle for proletarian hegemony" to the demonstration that points of view on given issues were "true" if they represented the "correct" application of Lenin's thought. In 1932, for the first time, a "Leninist era in historiography" was identified and equated with study of "the masses," the proletariat, and the "world history" of Bolshevism.[10] Karl Radek quipped in 1936 that "Lenin would be a great specialist in Russian history even if he had not written one specialist historical monograph because all his political works were permeated by a profound understanding of all the basic problems of Russian and World History." He added that the same held true for Stalin.[11]

During Stalin's lifetime, and more so after than before World War II, his scattered observations ranked alongside Lenin's as canon. In 1949, the head of the Institute of History in Kiev informed readers that Stalin had drawn attention to the "progressive" role of the Russian nation in Ukrainian history and that "every more or less important problem in the entire history of

Ukraine found [in the 1938 *Short Course* history of the CPSU] its profound and deeply learned characterization."[12] After 1956, Stalin's works were no longer formally part of official ideology, but Lenin's writing on history was declared a "scientific method" and 1890 the beginning of a "Leninist era" of historical scholarship.[13]

In Ukraine, political interference in Party historiography may be dated from 1925, when the Central Committee criticized the existing history as "Trotskyist" and commissioned the historian N. Popov to write another. In the summer of 1926, Politburo member V. Zatonsky criticized the view that the 1917 Ukrainian revolution was distinct from the Russian.[14] A few months later, in 1927, another Politburo member, P. Postyshev, went further and made observations about non-Party historiography in a speech at a jubilee dinner for a senior Ukrainian historian. He praised D. Bahaly for not juxtaposing the Ukrainian and Russian nations in his works and for seeing them as brother nations. Since the Bolsheviks took power in Ukraine under the banner of national liberation and equality such public utterances by a high official were unprecedented and ominous. Postyshev made it clear that the Party respected Bahaly because he was a non-Marxist who had adopted Marxism-Leninism and not because he was a good scholar.[15] Both remarks echoed Stalin's April 1926 criticism of the rapid pace of Ukrainization. Stalin noted that fostering Ukrainian culture was "here and there" assuming the character of a struggle against "Moscow in general, against the Russians in general, against Russian culture and its highest achievement, Leninism."[16]

On the All-Union level, portentous for non-Russians was the rehabilitation in the summer of 1931 of recently purged non-Marxist Russian academics who later became the leading Soviet historians B. Grekov, V. Picheta, S. V. Bakhrushin, and M. V. Bazilov. Ominous as well was a September CC decree condemning "pedagogical extremists" in schools that revealed the leadership supported those who criticized Pokrovsky's syllabus as lacking in Russian patriotism.[17]

Party interference in the interpretation of pre-1917 Ukrainian history may be dated from 1928 with the publication of an article by P. Gorin, a close associate of Pokrovsky and chief administrator of the Society of Marxist Historians. In a debate on the Ukrainian and Russian revolutions Gorin argued that differences between the two were minimal and claimed that he had found nothing in documents to illustrate divergence between the revolutionary "process" in Ukraine and Russia. The proletariat led the Revolution, he continued, and mistakes made in nationality policies could not be blamed on the whole Party in Ukraine but only on isolated groups.[18] At the 1928 Moscow historical conference, Gorin directly criticized the leading

Ukrainian Marxist historian, Matvei Iavorsky, for exaggerating differences between Ukraine and Russia and the role of the Ukrainian bourgeoisie in the February Revolution. A history of Ukraine separated by a "Chinese wall" from Russian history, he said, would be a caricature of the past.

Gorin's intervention was probably arranged. His mentor, Pokrovsky, before the conference had decided to support Stalin, who had just triumphed over Bukharin, replaced O. Shumsky as Ukrainian Commissar of Education, and had the Communist party of Western Ukraine expelled from the Comintern. These circumstances, Gorin's zeal, and reference in correspondence between him and Pokrovsky on the need to "prepare for the Ukrainian conference" suggest the attack on Iavorsky was planned as part of Stalin's move against Ukrainian communists.[19]

Between 1928 and 1935, the Party used unwilling accomplices or sincere but naive zealots, to discredit prevailing interpretations of non-Party-related subjects. Two who figured prominently in attacks on established Ukrainian historians and who expressed ideas later found in official guidelines were Trokhym Skubytsky and Mykhailo Rubach (Rubanovych). Nothing is known about Skubytsky, whereas Rubach from 1923 was the deputy head of ISTPART and then head of the Institute of Party History in Kharkiv between 1929 and 1932.[10] As it is likely that these men did Party bidding, their lists of unacceptable ideas and alternative concepts in detractive if not outright defamatory essays represented official as much as personal opinion. Although the majority of their monographs, as well as those of other "critics," could be considered "guidelines by proxy," this chapter will review only their direct and extended criticisms of the two major historians of the period, Iavorsky and M. Hrushevsky, and their reviews of survey histories of Ukraine.

Soon after Gorin's attacks, and the year before his own promotion, Rubach explained that Iavorsky was not guilty of mere factual errors but of "non-Bolshevik views." These included his treatment of the bourgeoisie as an independent force in the "bourgeois democratic" revolution in Ukraine and his depiction of Ukrainian leftists as precursors of Ukrainian Marxism and independent of the Russian Workers Movement. Rubach claimed that Iavorsky exaggerated the ties between the national movement and the workers movement in Ukraine and their respective links with the West, while ignoring links between the Russian and Ukrainian workers movement. Rich farmers, depicted by Iavorsky as "progressive," were, for Rubach, part of the unreservedly "reactionary" bourgeoisie. Peasants, he continued, could not be subdivided into "feudalist" and "progressive capitalist" leaders of revolutionary struggle.[21] Skubytsky, the most vociferous detractor and vicious defamer of the established historians, took Iavorsky to task in 1929. In a major condemnation of Iavorsky's interpretation of Ukrainian history that echoed Gorin's words, Skubytsky identified the exact target of official policy: "The basic shortcomings of comrade Iavorsky's book lead to Ukrainian history being seen as a distinct process."[22]

These ideas were repeated by the majority of speakers at a conference on Iavorsky's view of Ukrainian history. They condemned him for overemphasizing Western influence and ignoring Russian influence on Ukraine, for claiming the Ukrainian bourgeoisie and the Central Rada government in 1917 were revolutionary, for presenting the history of the USSR as the sum of Republic histories and for not understanding that the 1648 Khmelnytsky uprising had been an "antifeudal" peasant revolt. The comments on nineteenth- and twentieth-century history appeared separately in a formal condemnation by the *Istoryk Marksyst* editorial committee. Particularly important was the comment that the Ukrainian bourgeoisie and its left wing were not revolutionary in the nineteenth and twentieth centuries.[23] Guidelines for Party activists condemned interpretation of Ukraine's past as a struggle for statehood led by petty producers who in 1917 produced a third "national democratic revolutionary" center in Ukraine alongside the Bolsheviks and the Provisional Government.[24]

Thus, as of 1930, in the wake of what was likely a centrally directed offensive, historians risked administrative censure if they claimed Ukraine's historical distinctiveness found expression in a revolutionary bourgeoisie because this idea would deny the pivotal role of the proletariat and its agent, the Bolshevik Party. In 1930, to the list of heresies of distinctiveness were added ideas from the prevailing view of early-modern history. Authors of survey histories were criticized for focusing on interclass as opposed to intraclass conflict thus ignoring the revolutionary role of the peasantry in the seventeenth century and erroneously labeling the Khmelnytsky uprising as a "national bourgeois" revolution against Polish trade capitalism.[25] Particularly harsh was Skubytsky, who now directed his barbs at all the leading Ukrainian historians of the 1920s. Hrushevsky was wrong to have focused on intellectual instead of social history and on the struggle for a nation-state led by intellectuals, thus ignoring the proletariat. Iavorsky's major error was to have claimed that

> the class and national struggle in Ukraine was subordinated to the idea of forming an independent Ukrainian state, and that the major force in the bitter class struggle of the seventeenth and eighteenth centuries was not the conflict of peasants against feudal exploitation, but the struggle by middle and lesser gentry and the cossack elites to form an independent Ukrainian state, and that in the nineteenth and twentieth centuries the central and basic struggle was for national liberation of Ukraine.[26]

Skubytsky condemned "fascist" historians claiming that only the masses "made history" and that Ukrainian elites merely fought among themselves for the right to oppress the rest of the nation. He added to the list of heresies all the major ideas found in the prevailing Soviet interpretation of Ukrainian history: that in 1917 there had been a separate revolution in Ukraine, that Ukraine was more dependent on the West than on Russia, that the Ukrainian economy developed independently of Russia, that the bourgeoisie had never led the revolutionary struggle, and that for most of its history Ukraine's ties with Russia were of little significance.[27] In a 1935 review essay of a Soviet history of Ukraine published three years earlier, he identified as "errors" its giving primacy to exchange over production in analyzing the early-modern economy, its postdating of class differentiation within the cossacks to the second half of the sixteenth century, and its treatment of cossack officers as leaders of a national revolution instead of as counterrevolutionaries—a role that included making Ukraine a colonial part of the Russian market. He specified that in the nineteenth century all bourgeoisie and the "Slavic movement" in 1848 had been reactionary.[28]

With one exception, "proxy criticism" of the prevailing non-Marxist accounts of Ukraine's past contained less conceptual substance than did the attacks on Ukrainian Marxist historians. In 1925, Party officials were already considering banning Hrushevsky's survey, described in a secret police circular as "pseudoscholarly history, hostile and harmful to the Soviet regime,"[29] but the man himself was criticized only three years later.

In the mid-1920s Rubach was analyzing modern Ukrainian historiography as a product of the "federalist school" of Russian historiography "progressive" for its time because it reflected the interests of a rising bourgeoisie and challenged the prevailing Russian nationalist historiography. In his subsequent article, not published until 1930, Rubach explained that before 1917 Hrushevsky had not been hostile to Marxism and that Hrushevsky's conception of Ukraine's past had some merit even though it laid excessive importance on statehood and took conclusions about differences between Ukrainian and Russian history further than the evidence warranted. By the turn of the century, however, the Ukrainian bourgeoisie Hrushevsky represented was no longer "progressive," and therefore overemphasizing Western influences in Ukraine's past, as Hrushevsky did, became "reactionary" because it justified Ukraine's wartime alliance with Imperial Germany.[30]

Iavorsky was actually the first historian to "formally" launch the campaign against Hrushevsky and his interpretation of Ukrainian history. At the 1928 Moscow conference, Iavorsky accused his rival of constructing a "classless Ukrainian historical process" by ignoring class differentiation within the peasantry and focusing on intellectuals.[31] Few commentaries on Hrushevsky's interpretation followed. An extended review of the ninth volume of his multi-volume survey criticized him for approaching facts without a clearly defined approach, for stressing national as opposed to social issues and for claiming that in 1648 the cossacks had wanted to establish a Ukrainian state—thus denigrating the "peasant revolution." Other articles either focused on his politics or vilified him as a "fascist" and leader of the "Hrushevskians."[32]

In 1934, N. Horenshtein explained that the nineteenth-century Ukrainian socialists M. Ziber and M. Podolynsky could not be considered among the founders of the Marxist movement and that Marxism had never been part of the Ukrainian national movement. It was incorrect, he continued, to argue that "economic laws and capitalist development in Ukraine had been different than elsewhere in the empire, and that some landowners had been agents of modernization."[33] That same year, I. Smirnov condemned everything published by the Ukrainian Academy as propaganda aimed at fomenting chauvinism and separating Ukraine from the USSR. Smirnov claimed the Khmelnytsky rising was not a "liberation war of the Ukrainian people" but a "peasant war"; he criticized Ukrainian historians for not contributing to the discussion on socio-economic formations and condemned some for highlighting bourgeois elements in economic development. Smirnov condemned a Soviet history of Ukraine published in 1932 as insufficiently Marxist and too nationalist, because, among other reasons, it claimed Ukraine's history began the moment Slavs appeared on its territory.[34]

The first direct and open interference by high Party authorities in non-Party national historiography occurred in March 1934 when Stalin, Kaganovich, and Molotov criticized a book submitted to a competition for an official history. They rejected it as too abstract, with too little on non-Russians and too few names, places, and dates. More significant in light of subsequent development than a reminder to criticize tsarist expansion was the phrase: "We must have a text book about the history of the USSR where the history of the Great Russians would not be separated from the history of the other nations of the USSR," a stricture that soon took priority over a second, not to separate history of nations of the USSR from European or world history.[35] In Ukraine, 17 historians were instructed to produce a history of Ukraine by the end of 1935. Their writ was vague but did specify no subdivision of "feudalism" and the need to study Lenin and Stalin on Ukraine. They never fulfilled their task.[36]

Although the decree of 1934 concerning history was cited by historians already that year, it was actually published two years later. Alongside it in the main historical journal was an article by a Party functionary, P. Drozdov, that informed historians it would be incorrect to focus attention only on oppression, to see nothing positive in the popular Russian uprisings led by Minin, Pozharsky, and later Pugachev, and that at certain times princes and members of the ruling class had played a "progressive role."[37] The 1934 decree, however, did not glorify or claim primacy for Russia or Russians before 1917. This evolved later, in a process that likely began in February 1936 when a *Pravda* editorial criticized Bukharin for calling Russians passive, lazy Oblomovs, and an editorial in *Izvestiia* pointed out that non-Russians saw Russians as occupiers and wardens in tsarist times. *Pravda* retorted that not all Russians were oppressors and that much more significant than Russian domination of non-Russians in the past was a "common struggle" of all nations against tsarism.[38]

In January 1937, an editorial in a Ukrainian newspaper explained the "great Russian nation" had not been involved in tsarist oppression and had fought a common struggle with the Ukrainian nation for liberation,[39] while in March, Drozdov condemned Pokrovsky for "insulting" the Russian nation and the Russian working class by ignoring their heroic struggles against foreign invaders and by claiming society in 1917 had not been ready for socialism. He remarked that it was incorrect to analyze past mass movements solely from the perspective of struggle between the masses and their leaders and claimed that Pokrovsky had ignored the "Ukrainian national liberation struggle" and had falsified Ukrainian-Russian relations. "It is known," he continued, that both peoples were fraternal and that the treaty of 1654 reflected a desire for union.[40] Also in 1937, Stalin qualified his earlier decree when he sanctioned the idea of "lesser evil" as the basic concept for explaining past relations between Russians and non-Russians. In practice this led historians to ignore the stricture about links with the West as they had to explain that tsarist incorporation of non-Russian territories had not been as bad as incorporation into other neighbors would have been.[41]

The implementation of these general dicta was influenced by changes in the political climate. In 1938, for example, one historian dutifully pointed out that the history of Russia must not be separated from the history of other Republics.[42] But the outbreak of war and incorporation of Western Ukraine made tolerance of Ukrainian national feelings expedient, and in 1940, another historian interpreted the dicta to mean that non-Russians could not be isolated from nor incorporated into the history of Russia, and that events not fully part of USSR history could be accented.[43] A valuable insight into the relationship between guidelines and interpretation in 1943-1944 is provided by A. M. Pankratova's account of discussions about her *Istoriia Kazakhskoi SSR* (1943).

Written in 1942, in accordance with the policy allowing limited expression of non-Russian patriotism, the book portrayed the Kazakh past as a national history in its own right. It condemned Russian colonialism and favorably treated anti-Russian uprisings. In 1944, reviewers condemned the book for precisely this reason. One, in particular, against whom Pankratova leveled the serious charge of "Bernstein revisionism" because he made "unhistorical nations" of all non-Russians in the USSR, argued that colonialism was "progressive" and that leaders of national liberation movements against Russia should not be portrayed as heroes. A. I. Iakovlev complained that textbooks for Russian schools had to be Russian national textbooks and should not be infused with the interests of one hundred other nations. He voiced opposition to the idea of a history of the USSR and wanted to see instead a history of Russia whose main theme was "Russian nationalism." Pankratova rejected her critics and in her report/petition asked for another "objective" discussion.[44] Neither Pankratova nor her more nationalistic-minded critics suffered for their opinions, but an official review published shortly afterward indicated the latter had either echoed or heralded a shift to a more "hard line" policy toward non-Russians.

After the discussion, a reviewer took Pankratova's book to task for ignoring class struggle and for placing too much attention on the Kazakh struggle for independence, which made eighteenth- and nineteenth-century Kazakh history look like a struggle between pro- and anti-Russian groups. Praised in 1943 for not referring to annexation to Russia as a "lesser evil," the book was now criticized for presenting the event as an absolute evil. Historians were supposed to treat annexation as a "lesser evil" that brought capitalism to the regions concerned and to focus attention on a common struggle of Russians and non-Russians against tsarism.[45]

After 1945 five important statements channeled the official interpretation of non-Russian history into the direction mapped out in the 1930s, and more detail in Party articles on historiography constricted the limits of interpretation. The new tone was publicly announced in 1945 when Stalin described the Russians as the "leading nation" of the USSR.[46] The implications of these words for non-Russians were probably worked out by M. Suslov who took control of ideology in early 1947. Presumably under his direction, S. Kovaliov, an AGITPROP official, pointed out that Ukrainian historians during the war had been guilty of stressing the distinctiveness of Ukrainian history and claiming Kievan Rus and the Ukrainian nation were separate from the Russian nation. These "errors" he labeled "nationalist" as well as the practice of presenting all nineteenth-century Ukrainian writers as fighters for Ukrainian independence regardless of their views about society.[47] This was followed by a detailed rebuttal of Hrushevsky's interpretation by a little-known historian who explained that Ukrainian history had to be written from the premise of Ukrainian-Russian unity and class struggle.[48]

Kovaliov's words determined the content of a second statement on historiography in the form of two Ukrainian Central Committee resolutions. One, in 1946, condemned the editors of a literary magazine for printing an article that "idealized" conservative and "bourgeois liberal" members of the Cyril-Methodius Brotherhood. The use of such terms to categorize all the major figures of the brotherhood, except Shevchenko, effectively obliged historians to treat the organization as if it were divided into two distinct political groups of which only one, supposedly "led" by the "revolutionary democrat" Shevchenko, was "progressive."[49] The implications were profound. The brotherhood marked the beginnings of the nineteenth-century Ukrainian national movement, and because this resolution stipulated that Ukrainian activists who were not socialist radicals in their time should be regarded as part of the political right, it meant that almost all of them, their deeds and writings, fell outside the pale of official scholarship. A second resolution issued in 1947 stipulated that Ukraine's past was not to be treated in isolation from the past of other Soviet nations and primarily from Russia's. It also condemned official histories of Ukraine published during the preceding seven years for ignoring the class struggle, the wish of the masses to join Russia, and the influence of Russian centers on the revolutionary movement in Ukraine.[50]

More detailed was a third key statement relating to historiography signed by the Ukrainian ideological secretary K. Lytvyn. He reiterated Kovaliov's ideas and added that Kievan Rus had an ethnic unity. Historians were supposed to examine this affinity between Ukrainians and Russians and depict wherever possible the "unity of the historical processes of the Ukrainian and Russian peoples." Lytvyn called association with Russia "progressive" and a "desire" of Ukrainians to unite with Russia "natural." He added that Ukrainians who sought to separate from the tsarist empire were traitors, that the bourgeoisie was only interested in a national market for itself, and that the workers movement in Russia and Ukraine evolved in tandem. He explained that Poland in the fourteenth century had "seized" Galicia and that the national movement had been a product of the bourgeoisie, which had divided the "fraternal" Ukrainian and Russian nations and thereby weakened their common struggle and, implicitly, helped tsarism.[51]

The increasing Russian nationalist tone of postwar resolutions included an anti-Semitic campaign that possibly prompted the Jewish "old Bolshevik" I. Mints in 1949 to observe that it was wrong to judge events from a perspective of "bourgeois nationalist patriotism" and "bourgeois chauvinism," instead of "Soviet patriotism."[52] Soon after, despite his cautious wording, Mints lost his positions as an editor of *Voprosy Istorii* and head of the section on USSR history at the academy, while AGITPROP sponsored a more forceful assertion of Russian nationalism under the guise of "struggle against cosmopolitanism." A 1949 CC resolution, which may be regarded as a fourth postwar historiographical guideline, informed scholars that the time had come to relegate to the archives "the dangerous underestimation of the leading role of the great Russian nation" in all spheres of life.[53]

By the end of that year, the new tone was echoed in Ukraine by a younger historian who illustrated how the "common historical unity" of Ukraine and Russia had been expressed through time, while the head of the Institute of History of the Ukrainian Academy, O. Kasymenko, stressed the great significance unification of the Russian state and the Russian Social Democrats had for non-Russians. He added that not Galicia but tsarist Ukraine was the historical center of the formation of the Ukrainian nation and, more substantially, called for the inclusion of Western Ukrainian history into survey histories.[54]

The fifth postwar guideline on interpretation of Ukraine's past was the 1953 "Thesis on the Reunification of Ukraine with Russia." Issued on the occasion of the tercentenary of the Treaty of Pereiaslav, the "Thesis" explains that Russians and Ukrainians are descended from a single "root" called the "Old Rus nation" and that the desire to be "reunited" with Russia was the dominant theme of Ukrainian history. Ukrainian lands were "seized" by Polish magnates, and their population was subjected to "inhuman" oppression. The Union of Brest, an initiative of the Vatican and Polish lords, was intended to Polonize and "spiritually enslave" Ukrainians thereby destroying their ties with the Russian people. The culmination of the alleged aspiration to unity was realized in 1654 by the Treaty of Pereiaslav. According to the "Thesis" Khmelnytsky was not a cossack leader with personal and class interests but a providential emissary destined to bring about "reunification" through the "eternal" agreement of Pereiaslav. The "Thesis" associates, wherever possible, Ukrainian achievements with Russian events and claims the great historical achievement of the Russians was to have produced the CPSU. The "Thesis" denies that Ukraine's past was appreciably distinct from Russia's and depicts past events within the context of a teleological progression driven by a striving for an ever more perfect form of union with Russia. Thanks to "reunion," Ukrainians could struggle together with Russians against common class and foreign enemies. Then, in 1917, under the leadership not of the Russian proletariat but the "Russian people," Ukrainians were able to win social and national independence. The "Thesis" contains a reference to 51,000 combines working in Ukrainian fields but mentions Western Ukraine only once: in an expression of thanks to the USSR for realizing in 1939 a "centuries long yearning" of Ukrainians to reunite with each other.

In contrast to Lytvyn's 1947 article, the "Thesis" contains a distinctly un-Marxist stress on the role of ethnic affinity and identity as historical forces and the claim that the 1654 treaty represented a "reunion," not merely "union," of nations—let alone an "annexation" of Ukraine by Russia. The "Thesis" only mentioned in passing the division between exploiting and exploited classes, did not refer to periodization according to socio-economic criteria, and made no references to pan-Slavism, all of which had figured in Lytvyn's article. The "Thesis" let historians know they were not to interpret Ukrainian history from the point of view of class struggle and socio-economic formations but from the point of view of Ukrainian relations with Russia.[55]

These guidelines, like those of 1947, were the result of a political decision made in Moscow. It is unlikely that Ukrainian Party leaders were involved. Ukrainian historians, however, did play a role in creating this interpretation of the Eastern Slavic past, which blurred and minimized the differences between Ukraine and Russia and placed many issues of Ukrainian political and economic history outside the pale of acceptable research subjects.

Andryi Lykholat, between 1949 and 1956 in charge of the Higher Educational Institutions Section of the CPSU CC Culture and Learning Department, was a writer of the "Thesis." In the middle of 1952, he received orders from Suslov, which included three or four general themes, to organize committees of leading historians in Moscow and Kiev to write the first drafts of the "Thesis." Working closely with A. Rumiantsev, CPSU CC secretary in charge of Culture and Learning, Lykholat conscripted the services of the Moscow historians A. M. Pankratova, K. M. Bazilevich, M. N. Tikhomirov, A. L. Sidorov, L. V. Cherepnin, and V. I. Picheta, and the Kiev historians O. Kasymenko, I. Boiko, K. Huslysty, V. Holubutsky, and F. Shevchenko. After about one year, each group submitted outlines to Lykholat, who then compiled a final version in consultation with P. M. Pospelov, director of the Marx-Lenin Institute and deputy editor of *Pravda*; S. Chervonenko, head of the Ukrainian CC Culture and Learning Department; and Rumiantsev. This version was then sent for comments to I. Nazarenko, the Ukrainian Ideological secretary, and to A. Korniechuk, Ukrainian Politburo member and head of the Ukrainian Writers Union. Sometime in mid-1953, Suslov gave final approval to the "Thesis."[56]

After 1954, the Party no longer issued detailed resolutions on how to interpret national pasts. Rather, the ideas expressed in 1947 and in the "Thesis" were reiterated in editorials and/or articles that periodically reprimanded historians for exceeding permissible limits. At issue was the degree of emphasis on the specific and unique in Ukraine's past.[57] After 1953, between periods of "liberalization" in historiography there were two major interventions aimed at restricting the limits of interpretation.

The first post-Stalin criticism of "reformist" accounts, whose authors were accused of "idealizing" Ukraine's past, came in 1957.[58] The following year, perhaps related to policy against China and Yugoslavia, a *Voprosy istorii* editorial directly equated the USSR with Rus and Russia: "And this Rus [referring to the establishment of the Russian Soviet Republic], Socialist Rus, was created by the heroic exertions of the Soviet nation led by the Communist Party."[59] The same year in Ukraine, Kasymenko made it known that a narrow interpretation of the "Thesis," emphasizing similarities in Russian and Ukrainian history, was the only permissible one.[60]

Reformist accounts were taken to task again in the early 1970s. In 1972 the Lviv oblast Ideological secretary, V. Malanchuk (Milman), published a long article condemning Ukrainian populist and statist historians for ignoring class struggle and Ukrainian–Russian fraternity through the ages,[61] while historians at a major All-Union conference were told that their duty was to interpret new data in light of Marxism-Leninism and not vice versa.[62] In 1973 reformist historians were again instructed that only a narrow interpretation of the "Thesis" would be allowed by an extended unsigned review of a book by the Ukrainian First Secretary P. Shelest, *Ukraino nashe Radianske* (1970). The book was condemned for its "liberal" interpretation of Ukrainian history that supposedly devoted too little attention to the post-1917 period, idealized the Ukrainian cossacks as a group without class divisions, illustrated events in Ukrainian history in isolation from the rest of the USSR, presented the 1654 Treaty of Pereiaslav as a simple political fact, and failed to illustrate the great influence of "progressive" Russian culture on the non-Russians. In short, the book "overemphasized the specificities and uniqueness of the history and culture of the Ukrainian nation."[63]

In 1974, a Plenum of the Ukrainian Party again condemned "idealization" of the past, departures from class and Party criteria in historical evaluations, and "incorrect" treatment of aspects of Ukraine's past. These "errors" included "exaggerating" the role of individual bourgeois liberals and "idealizing" the cossacks. For the next ten years, allegedly owing to Suslov's personal instructions, Ukrainian historians were not permitted to publish anything on pre-twentieth-century Ukrainian history.[64]

Although the guidelines of 1947 and 1953 produced an image of the past that glorified Russian achievement, its nationalist tone is not blatantly obvious to outsider laymen observers. Official historiography ostensibly distinguished between Russia and the USSR. However, its methodology and categories of analysis effectively eclipsed the historical diversity and multinational plurality of the tsarist state under the canopy of Russian hegemony. The particularity of non-Russian histories and conflicts between them and Russians were ignored or minimized, while anything Russians and non-Russians may have had in common was stressed and exaggerated. To buttress the image of historical unity and integration texts synchronized events in the Russian and non-Russian pasts. To reinforce the illusion that the parts had always been an integral part of a whole, official historiography imposed periodization and concepts derived from Russian history onto non-Russian history. Terminology was chosen with the same end in mind. In survey histories of the USSR Russians were never called "enemies," the "people" of what was the USSR appear as "friends" from time immemorial, and any hostility that could not be ignored was treated as incidental and fomented by evil ruling classes. In the official post-1954 schema of Eastern Slavic history, a "desire for reunion" was both a driving force in history and a product of an alleged ethnic unity of Ukrainians, Belorussians and Russians, that was supposedly more significant than the political, social, or institutional differences that separated them.[65]

Official guidelines issued between 1934 and 1953 circumscribed the non-Russian past and implicitly identified Russian national history with the history of the USSR. These unilaterally imposed decrees, which can appear as attempts to transcend national history, emerge on closer scrutiny as the basis for the imposition of statist Russocentric categories on non-Russian pasts—including even the centuries before a given territory came under Russian rule. The official guidelines of 1947 and 1953 took the 1934 initiative to its logical conclusion, and notwithstanding shifts in emphasis during "liberal periods," the "History of the USSR" was never a "sum of parts," an account of the past of a multinational polity. It was a presented as a "single organic process."

GUIDELINES IN POLAND

The interwar Polish state was liberal to 1926 and authoritarian to 1939. Although from 1926 Poland recognized the Kievan Ukrainian Government-in-Exile as legitimate, its policies toward Ukrainians under its jurisdiction had little to commend them. Nevertheless, these did not include administrative imposition of an official interpretation of Polish or Ukrainian history and interdiction of all others—with the possible exception of school history syllabi.[66] Similarly, although it is possible to discern a direct relationship between policy toward Ukrainian churches and historiography about this subject, there is nothing to indicate that historians formally received ministerial instructions to write as they did about this subject.

After 1945 the Polish government did instruct historians how to write. Initially the Party (PZPR) demanded a specific interpretation of Ukrainian-Polish relations only in school history textbooks, but by the 1950s an official interpretation figured in all published histories of Poland. In the absence of Soviet-style decrees on historical interpretation, the most important indicators of how the authorities wanted Ukrainian-Polish relations interpreted were school course outlines, the first of which was compiled in 1944 in Moscow.

The *Program historii dla klass III-IV i VI- VII szkol Polskich dla dzieci polskich w ZSRR* was sponsored by the Polish Soviet Committee on Issues related to Polish Children in the USSR (*Komitet do spraw dzieci Polskich w ZSRR*) headed by Deputy Minister of Education of the RSFSR G. Ivanenko. On the Polish side, the most important representatives were E. Kuroczko, an Ukrainian-born PZPR member, and PZPR historian Ż. Kormanowa. The Russian historical advisor to the Committee was V. Picheta.[67] The 1944 program called for very critical assessment of role of the gentry in Polish history. It condemned their "neocolonial" activities in Ukraine and the other non-Polish eastern territories of earlier Polish states and explained that they brought only wars and problems to the Polish people. All the political and religious unions signed by Poland with its eastern neighbors and the activities of eastern magnates were henceforth not to be presented as something Poles should be proud of, and teachers were to stress examples of "friendship and fraternity" between Poles and the nations of the USSR. They were to focus on oppression of non-Poles in historical Poland and not draw attention to how these minorities may have contributed to Polish statehood and culture.[68] A second version of the program, released in 1945, was similar in tone but avoided detailed elaboration of specific events and issues in order not to alienate Polish opinion—as few Poles were predisposed to a critical view of Polish presence east of the Bug River. Accounts of Poland's past were to dwell on social conflict, the centuries of peasant suffering, causes of backwardness, and the errors of gentry foreign policy that surrendered western lands to expand eastward.[69] After 1948, subsequent versions of the program became more explicit.[70]

Until 1956, under the guise of struggle against Polish nationalism, outlines demanded more references to Russian events, more emphatic positive assessments of anti-Polish revolts in Ukraine, and less mention of Polish events on territories east of the Bug. In general, historians were not to treat events in the area as if they were an integral part of Poland's past. Soviet intervention in Polish historiography, as far is known, was not direct but was exercised through intermediaries like Kormanowa and Kuroczko and the Association of Marxist Historians.[71]

The high point of Kremlin intervention in Polish affairs occurred between 1948 and 1956. In historiography, this influence now spread beyond school course outlines to historical research, as USSR historians began commenting at length upon various issues in Polish history. From 1947, there was an increase in the number of pages devoted to Polish and Polish-Ukrainian subject matter in USSR journals where articles sharply criticized past Polish policies in the East, their favorable interpretation in earlier Polish historiography, and failure of Polish authors to reiterate the Soviet view of Ukrainian-related issues. In hindsight, it appears these articles were intended as a prelude to an official call for total revision, which the PZPR made in 1948 at the Seventh Congress of Polish Historians.[72]

As Soviet-Russian involvement played an important role in the evolution of postwar Polish guidelines on the interpretation of Ukraine's past and Polish-Ukrainian relations, it is important to be aware of the utilitarian and neo-Slavophile bias of Western Slavic historiography in the USSR at the time. In the 1920s, the subject, like Byzantine studies and ancient history, received little attention. This changed first in response to international coordination of Slavic studies in Europe that began at the end of the decade and then to Hitler's rise to power and increasingly strident German claims about Slavic backwardness and the beneficial result of past German rule over Slavs. These events made the Kremlin willing to channel funds and cadres into the study of subjects like Gothic settlement and Slavic civilization. A separate Institute of Slavic Studies was established in 1931. The first published reference to the importance of Slavic ethnogenesis as a means of countering "fascist propaganda" appeared in 1938. After 1945, Moscow's political ambitions in Eastern and Central Europe gave added importance to Slavic studies as it became a subject that could provide justification for Moscow's hegemony over Western and Southern Slavs. The Slavic Academic Commission for the Study of the History of the Slavs, established in 1942, became the Institute of Slavic Studies of the Academy four years later. The purpose of both institutions was to disseminate anti-German propaganda and the idea of Slavic unity under Russian leadership. Russian/Soviet Slavic studies, in line with the Russian nationalist tone of humanities scholarship in the USSR, were permeated with the idea that all Slavic rivers flowed into the Russian sea.[73]

The clearest expression of what Polish historians were supposed to write about Ukraine and its relations with Poland are found in 1951 guidelines published by the USSR Institute of Slavic Studies—which at its inception was assigned to write a survey history of Poland. In the introduction, Kormanowa explained that there was nothing to commend Polish presence east of the Bug, while a Russian historian explained that Poles should deal with Ukrainian events only to the degree necessary to understand Polish history.[74] Polish policies in the eastern regions of historical Poland were to be condemned as exploitative and detrimental to Polish interests because they distracted attention from western affairs. The Union of Krevo (1386) was judged a just defensive arrangement, but the Union of Lublin (1569) marked the formation of a multinational state and was condemned as a tool of expansion like the Union of Brest (1596). Both were responsible for embroiling Poland in peasant revolts. Events connected with Cossack uprisings were to be seen from the perspective of "liberation wars." Explanations had to include the idea of "common struggle of Polish and Ukrainian peasants against feudal oppression" and demonstration of mass Ukrainian support for intervening Russian troops. The Hadiach Treaty (1659) was to be condemned. The plans of nationalist-liberal nineteenth-century Polish intellectuals were labeled "great power chauvinism" together with the anti-Ukrainian policies of Poles in 1848. Ukrainian and Polish national movements, dismissed as "bourgeois" and Austrian-inspired instruments of an anti-Russian policy, were juxtaposed to "democratic intellectuals" who fought for "social and national liberation" while the policies of Poland in 1918-1922 were treated as products of Western capitalist imperialist machinations against the Revolution.[75] No published Polish survey of national history ever incorporated all the details in this guide, but a three-volume *Istoriia Polshi* (Moscow, 1956-58) provides a model of the *Istoriia Polskoi SSR* that might have been.[76]

A few interpretative guides also appeared in the Party journal *Nowe Drogi*. In an unsigned reply to a reader inquiring about the uprising of 1648, the editors explained that hitherto Polish historians falsified the event that actually represented a mass national revolution in which Polish peasants participated.[77] Two other articles published in 1954 echo ideas in the 1951 outline. The historian B. Baranowski noted that the Khmelnytsky uprising could not be seen through the eyes of landowners, that the Polish nation looked sympathetically at Ukraine's "reunion" with Russia, and that the policies of the magnates who had oppressed Ukrainians in the past had not been in the interests of Poles. In the same issue, a literary scholar summarized Ukrainian history and Ukrainian-Polish relations similarly, with the observation that Polish bourgeois historians ignored the cultural evolution of Ukrainians and that nationalism could not be allowed to destroy the brotherhood that existed between the two nations.[78]

In 1956, the proceedings of a conference on the tercentenary of the 1654 Pereiaslav Treaty provided more details for historians about Ukrainian-related topics. The theme of the published essays centered on the influence of Poles on Ukraine and "Polish-Ukrainian brotherhood" in a "struggle against oppression." The introduction explained that the task of Polish historical scholarship should be to provide a true history of the Ukrainian nation and its centuries' long struggle for liberty. Historians had to destroy the myths spun by Polish bourgeois historiography that merely "reflected the interests of its class" and the wish of partitioning powers to weaken both nations' "revolutionary energies by setting up mutual resentment and barriers of nationalist enmity between them." The book includes a call for more studies on Ukraine and greater interest by Polish scholars in their "brother nation."[79]

Yet there was no subsequent expansion of Ukrainian historical studies in Poland, for it seems that the fate of this subject depended not only on Soviet tutelage and strictures but also on a belief that the less written in Poland about Ukraine the better. Between 1948 and 1954, officials of this persuasion may have been in a minority. After 1956, their views, presumably, became policy. One can only speculate about the reasons for this. In any case, the 12th Party Plenum in the autumn of 1958 seems to have formally decided to discourage historians to write anything about the "East" and to direct their research towards Polish-German relations and Poland's north and west.[80] Such a tendency was already evident in the two-volume proceedings of the VII Congress of Polish Historians (1948) of which about one-third covered relations with Germany, Russia, Austria, and Czechoslovakia. Ukraine was mentioned in scattered phrases and sentences.[81] Criticism of earlier views of Polish eastern affairs alongside deemphasis of the subject are found in the proceedings of the First Congress of Polish Learning (1950), and the First Methodological Conference of Historians (1951). The multivolume proceedings contain calls for a "principled" approach to Ukraine's past and a revision of established views, but no articles on any Ukrainian-related pre-1917 subject.[82] Ukraine was not mentioned at the 8th Congress of Polish Historians (1958), while the proceedings of the Second Congress of Polish Learning (1973) contain but one remark about the lack of work on eastern regions of the historic Polish state.[83] There is a similar lapsus in the contents of the major journal devoted to eastern affairs during the 1950s, the

Kwartalnik instytutu Polsko-Radzieckiego—as of 1957 *Slavia orientalis*. Although the aim of the journal was to spread information about USSR nationalities, during five years of publication only three articles touched Ukrainian issues—two were on the writer Ivan Franko and the other on Shevchenko. The periodical of Polish history teachers, *Wiadomości* Historyczne, meanwhile, between 1958 and 1982 had not one article on how to teach Ukrainian history, although it did have one on Polish-Swiss relations! Only in 1981, in an article on the formation of Poland's eastern border in 1919-1920 did it mention Ukraine.

After 1956, historians interested in Ukrainian history and Ukrainian-Polish relations faced a small number of strictures on specific events. The fact that official pronouncements about these particular subjects were rare, in itself, amounted to an informal "unwritten rule" discouraging study of the eastern regions of historical Poland. The Polish Party's purpose seems to have been to keep study of Ukrainian history and Polish-Ukrainian relations underdeveloped, and a simplistic utilitarian image of "fraternal relations" between "good" Russian and Polish "people" uncomplicated by the realities of their rivalry over Ukraine. The resulting interpretation of Ukrainian-related subjects in Polish publications was similar but not identical to the official Soviet view.

An insight into the mechanism of control is provided by a comparison of page proofs of articles written in the early 1980s about Ukrainian issues with their later published versions. Removed from a survey of Polish-Ukrainian relations were statements about no political structures being eternal, references to nineteenth-century Polish leaders denying Ukrainians a historical right to nationhood, and the comment that postwar Polish-Ukrainian relations left much to be desired and had to be openly discussed. Also excised was a sentence noting that third parties, in particular the tsars, benefited from Polish-Ukrainian animosities. In another article, sentences referring to the Uniate Church in nineteenth-century Galicia as a part of the national movement, but simultaneously independent and critical of it, were cut. Revealing also was the removal of a passage observing that misguided and erroneous opinions lead people to judge nations and societies, rather than individuals, to be good or bad, victims or perpetrators.[84] Finally, in an article discussing national stereotypes, the censor passed a list of uncomplimentary Polish sayings about Ukrainians, but not one of distinctly unsympathetic Ukrainian sayings about Poles. These and other omissions were justified on the basis of items 1 to 3 of article 2 of the 1981 Censorship Code, which forbade expression of ideas attacking the integrity of the state, advocating the overthrow of or insulting the Polish constitutional system, and "attacking" the principles underlying the foreign policy of Poland and its allies.[85]

PART II

POLISH HISTORIOGRAPHY

4

Neoromanticism and Positivism (1914-1944)

THE MAJOR HISTORIANS

In interwar Poland, historians followed the established rules of critical method and "scientific history." The dominant interpretations of national history were usually either positivist or neoromantic and the treatment of Ukraine's past reflected the assumptions of one of these two approaches.[1] Neoromantics shared a Catholic-messianistic view of Poland's past and argued that "the nation" was the major subject and object of history. They regarded Poland's historical gentry-republican order as ideal, saw its expansion east as the spread of liberty, and placed the onus of responsibility for the Partitions on foreign powers. Positivists regarded Poland's gentry order as anarchical and claimed that since it had been the major cause of the Partitions it had little to commend it. They argued that the state was the major subject and object of history and were critical of Poland's eastern expansion. Whereas neoromantic historians could be found among the supporters or sympathizers of the National Democrats as well as Pilsudski, positivist-inclined historians tended to favour the latter. Those who believed historical narratives should be based on political history and those who advocated "integral history" were in both political groupings and interpretative schools. Interestingly, until Pilsudski's coup the important academic survey histories of Poland tended to reflect the positivist rather than the neoromantic persuasion.

The first major postwar history appeared in 1920-1921 as volume five of the *Encyclopedya Polska*. Edited by Stanisław Zakrzewski (Kazimierz Brzoż, 1873-1936) and published under the auspices of Akademia Umiejętnosci, the book provided a factual, dispassionate account, and, unlike most histories of Poland, incorporated a considerable amount of Ukrainian research.

The text explains that Poland's "task" of "winning over" Rus was accomplished by King Casimir IV (The Great), who inherited the Galician principality from George II in an agreement for which there is no evidence. The people were indifferent to the change in rulers and the region enjoyed autonomy, although its status was unclear.[2] The king recognized Orthodox rights but also introduced the Catholic Church into Western Ukraine to help integrate the region into his domains. Because their church was not persecuted and they realized the benefits of the Polish order, the local population remained passive despite Polish colonization and Polonization.[3] In theory, The Union of Krevo attached Ukrainian lands to Poland but in fact they remained part of Lithuania. There is only passing reference in the text to "Polish spirit" as the force that welded the eastern territories into a polity, situated between east and west, that, based on equality, served as a bulwark of Christian culture. The Union of Lublin is interpreted as a consequence of reforms in Poland and defense needs that ultimately failed because of shortcomings that developed in the following two centuries.[4]

The 1596 Union of Brest was not depicted as an intrigue but as a historical necessity and basic postulate of Polish politics. The reasons for the Union lay in the Reformation and Counter-Reformation, the steady conversion of the Orthodox nobility, corruption in the Orthodox church, and the need to counter pro-Russian tendencies among Ukrainians. Its immediate cause was the refusal of Orthodox bishops to tolerate lay interference in the running of the church. The Uniate Church ultimately failed to attract the nobility because its bishops were not given seats in the Senate, while the leaders of cossack revolts, who used religion as a pretext because they were under the corrupting influence of Russian and Turkish–controlled prelates, only alienated the Rus gentry even more from Orthodoxy. Social rather than national in character, these uprisings stemmed from peasants' natural dislike of the gentry and their plantation politics. The gentry refused to meet cossack needs, which would have been in the interests of the state, and their stubbornness merely enraged the cossacks.[5]

W. Konopczynski (1880-1952) discussed in the same volume the reasons for the fall of Poland and linked the country's problems to the Union of Lublin. He argued that the 1569 Union weakened the nation because it led Poland to expand its production through extensive rather than intensive agriculture, blinded its people with endless horizons of expansion, and burdened them with Ukrainian and Lithuanian issues. This in turn bred laziness, sloppiness, and wars. Konopczynski was critical of the Church

Union but justified this break in a tradition of tolerance with the claim that it had been politically necessary. The Union failed only because it was badly implemented; that is, it did not provide Senate seats for Uniate bishops and forced peasants to follow the faith of their lords.[6]

Khmelnytsky began his uprising in the name of cossack estate rights but soon attracted all social groups to his banners. Whether or not the fire of rebellion would forge a distinct political nation out of the chaos of interests and social, national, and religious ideas in seventeenth-century Ukraine depended on Polish politics as well as the creative forces of Rus society. Initially, Khmelnytsky's attitudes toward his neighbors were unclear but as the cossack commons had only one hated enemy, the Polish gentry, agreement between them was impossible.[7] The Treaty of Pereiaslav represented Khmelnytsky's long-term ambition, and although the alliance with Russia gave him some immediate benefits, it provided very weak guarantees of autonomy. While he lived, the terms of the treaty were a dead letter but they worked against his successors. Faced with the alternative of their country becoming a province of Moscow or a Polish protectorate, Ivan Vyhovsky and Iuryi Nemirych (Niemirycz), the architects of the Hadiach Treaty, chose the latter and were supported by those who understood the idea of political liberty. Among their maximal demands was the inclusion of almost all of Ukraine into a Grand Duchy of Rus, but the mass of Ukrainians rejected the treaty because of its provision for ennobling only a small portion of the cossack army. Subsequently, Ukraine was split by civil war.[8] Although Konopczynski regarded this treaty as a wise and just compromise, which the Poles finally accepted, if reluctantly, he described Mazepa as an ambitious adventurer with no political principles who in 1709 merely "felt within himself a kind of urge to defend Ukrainian independence from the moment Menshikov, the tsar's favorite, threatened his hetmanship."[9]

The last Ukrainian issue mentioned, the Haidamak revolt, was blamed on cynical leaders who used religion for their own ends as well as on Orthodox priests who went too far in their protestations. The Haidamaks, "wild lovers of freedom and theft," took to arms because of a rumor of impending religious persecution. Significantly, this is the only chapter dealing with Ukraine in the book where the author did not use Ukrainian sources and limited himself to Rawita-Gawronski's prewar studies on this subject.[10]

The years 1920 to 1921 also saw the publication of two surveys by Adam Szelągowski (1873-1961), of Lviv University. The first was a popular history divided into 36 chapters intended to correspond with the number of generations passed since the legendary founding of Piast state.[11] The author explains that Casimir took Rus lands to compensate for Polish losses in the west and claimed the Krevo Union was envisaged by Jagiello as the keystone in a plan of eastern expansionism. Whereas the Union of 1569 is presented as an offshoot of the reform movement in Poland at the time and the need to secure the eastern border against Moscow, the author presented the 1596 Union as a Jesuit-inspired plot. The 1648 uprising is presented as basically a social reaction to gentry attempts to impose serfdom in central Ukraine and control cossack raids against Turkey. The historian claimed that by 1649 Khmelnytsky was thinking of a separate duchy for himself and that the 1654 treaty was only one of many political combinations directed toward this end. The author mentions Ukrainian issues again in the section on World War I, where he explains that thanks to Austrian support in 1918 Ukrainians took Lviv, but that the city was saved thanks to the heroic efforts of the Poles who eventually took control over all East Galicia.

More academic was Szelągowski's *Dzieje Polski w zarysie*. The book's tone was the same as the earlier work but devoted more space to Ukrainian issues. Added to the discussion of events in Galicia in the 1340s was the observation that the region had straddled routes useful for Polish trade and that Poland's neighbors were rivals for control over it. Whereas the first edition made no mention of whether the Polish occupation had been a conquest or inheritance, the second noted it had been the latter.[12] A second edition contained no major changes in the treatment of the Union of Brest but, unlike the first, it explained the Union of Lublin in the context of Polish economic expansion. Szelągowski described the cossacks as a threat to this expansion and the power of the magnates, but he made no mention of revolts and referred only to problems in controlling the steppe population, who were better off and had fewer duties than commoners in Poland proper. He also added that the Kiev Academy contributed to a national as well as religious revival in Ukraine.[13]

The author placed the origins of Khmelnytsky's revolt in the context of Wladyslaw IV's failed dynastic and Turkish war plans. Khmelnytsky's successes "befuddled his mind," and upon meeting in Kiev with Orthodox clerics he decided he wanted to be not only a cossack hetman but a lord of a separate Rus stretching from Kiev to Lviv.[14] The Treaty of Pereiaslav was but one of many alliances, and Khmelnytsky soon dropped it because he disliked tsarist centralism. The historian claimed it was Vyhovsky who proposed the alliance with Russia as well as the Hadiach treaty with Poland, which failed because the cossacks divided over it. In this book the author remarked that Mazepa's aim was to throw off Russian rule and that in the 1760s Russia provoked and supported the Haidamak revolts.

The first major survey written from the neoromantic perspective was *Polska jej Dzieje i Kultura,* a huge three-volume work printed on bond paper and with an excellent selection of reproductions and maps. This book contains chapters on numismatics, art, music, and literature as well as political history, but none on social and economic history. Ukrainian events are dealt with in the chapters on political history. The main authors of sections on Ukraine were Roman Grodecki (1889-1964), Oskar Halecki (1891-1973), and Wacław Sobieski (1872-1935).

Polska explained that Casimir took Western Ukraine because of trade interests and implied the occupation was legal because it had been done in agreement with the Hungarians and the Galician king, George II.[15] The account of the Krevo Union includes the first extended exposition of the "Jagiellonian idea" found in a major history of Poland. Supposedly, Jagiello's ambition was to convert Lithuania and Rus and draw them into Western civilization through political union—though the latter was not actually attained until 1569. His immediate political aim was to obtain access to the Baltic and Black seas.

> The attainment of these cultural, structural and political tasks, prepared by Jagiello and Jadwiga and many of which were [later] accomplished by Jagiellonczyks, was possible only thanks to what grateful posterity has called the Jagiellonian idea. Essentially, it involved dealing with internal difficulties guided by the slogans of love and unity as announced in all the acts of Union, as well as using similar peaceful and conciliatory principles whenever possible, despite their frequent interference with foreign policy, [*a ilekroc oni tam zawodziły*] in self-sacrificing cooperation of united nations. Every digression from this idea would bring only competition and failure.[16]

Ukrainian lands, though part of Poland de jure as all its princes swore allegiance to Jagiello, became so de facto only in 1569. The Lublin Union of that year was treated as a reflection of the Jagiellonian idea, which was invoked as the reason for its success and longevity.[17] The major flaw in the Union was that it did not provide for the immediate social and structural assimilation of the newly joined regions, and instead preserved particularities. Thus, because the cossacks could organize into a privileged estate, they became the basic source of chronic problems in the East.[18]

In a section dealing with Ukrainian culture, written from the positivist rather than neoromantic perspective, the literary scholar Alexsander Bruckner explained that until the seventeenth century Ukraine had been culturally stagnant and that assimilation into Polish civilization was to have been expected. For this reason the Ukrainian defense of Orthodoxy until the late sixteenth century had been on the level of ritual and only later did it shift to the higher plane of theology. Bruckner was critical of the gentry's expansionist national desires and wrote that they were checked in the seventeenth century by the hostile reaction to Church Union and the "turbulent anarchy" of Rus blood "made primitive" by its ancestors.[19] There was no section on Ukrainian culture at the end of the second volume.

Polska noted that the Union of Brest coincided with Polish state interests because it counterbalanced a threat posed to Poland by the newly established Russian Patriarchate. But because Uniate Catholicism remained a peasant faith it undercut Polonization of Ukraine by restricting the spread of Roman Catholic churches. As Polish peasant settlers had no choice but to attend Uniate churches they were Ukrainized. Thus, the Union won peasants for Ukraine but repelled the country's native nobility. The authors saw early revolts in Ukraine, caused by local Rus magnates trying to control the cossacks and peasants, as social rather than national or religious in nature and claimed they had been exploited by foreign powers in order to destabilize Poland. Tatar raids forced inhabitants to seek protection from the Polish army, but Tatar looting of gentry estates incited the otherwise peaceful Ukrainian peasant to do likewise and to thereby emulate the violent anarchy of the cossacks.[20]

The book attributes the 1648 uprising primarily to this frontier tatar-cossack temperament but also draws attention to the impact in the 1640s of the expiry of free settlement terms. The cossacks, meanwhile, had begun to see themselves as gentry and defenders of the faith, which widened the gulf between both groups and frustrated the cossacks even more. Khmelnytsky took up arms in the name of estate rights but Turkish agitators had helped him organize in order to deflect Wladyslaw's intended crusade.[21] Once incited, the radical masses forced Khmelnytsky to go further than he had intended and the result was social war. "Stupefied" by Greek incense—a reference to his relations with the Jerusalem patriarch—the hetman began to conduct himself as a monarch, and, when drunk, he imagined a separate Rus kingdom whose borders included the city of Lviv. Under the influence of Greek clerical agitation the lesser Rus gentry also decided to separate from Poland, break the links established at Lublin, and join the cossacks.

In 1654, Khmelnytsky was forced to turn to the tsar because Poland had convinced the Turks to stop supporting him. The book gives no details of the 1654 treaty that granted "protectorate" status to Cossack Ukraine, but notes that it was opposed by the Orthodox clergy, who regarded Moscow as heretical.[22] Near the end of his life, overwhelmed by the tsar's power, and then by the defeat of his Transylvanian ally, Khmelnytsky turned again to

Poland. Relations between the two sides were facilitated by the cossack's Polonophile cultural orientation and their ambition to become gentry in the Polish style. The resultant Hadiach agreement, where the term "Rus nation" appeared in a treaty for the first time, had three main flaws. It contained no mention of the fate of Uniates, provided for return of lost gentry lands, and gave Vyhovsky a separate military force with which he could become completely independent of Poland. These shortcomings, alongside the selective ennoblement clause and the later Polish refusal to permit Orthodox prelates into the Senate, laid the ground for opposition and the ensuing political division of Ukraine.

The author depicted Mazepa's policies in the context of Polish court policy for a Hadiach-type arrangement with Ukraine and opposition to this by a magnate party partial to alliance with Russia as a guarantee against future cossack uprisings. Mazepa rose against autocratic despotism but the cossacks didn't support him from fear of Russian punishment.

In contrast to these relatively detailed accounts, the Haidamak revolts were passed over in a few sentences as products of Russian provocation.[23] Similarly short is the account of 1848 in Galicia. It is explained that Ukrainians and Poles cooperated until the Austrian governor of Galicia, Stadion, told the former to send a statement of loyalty to Vienna. The text concedes the "Rus movement" had to arise, but describes it as an anti-Polish tool in 1848 funded by police agents and used by Vienna alongside the drunken lumpen proletariat of Lviv. Events finished with a compromise: no division of the province into Ukrainian and Polish parts in return for the use of Ukrainian in schools and equal status for Uniate priests with Catholic.[24]

In 1931, W. Sobieski published his own neoromantic survey history of Poland that, unlike other surveys, had a marked focus on Polish-German affairs. He presented Casimir's eastern acquisitions as a compensation for losses in the west. The King claimed dynastic right to Galicia and came in 1340 to protect Catholic traders in Lviv because Rus princes had been using Tatar troops against them. Sobieski does not refer to Polish settlement as a cause of Polonization in Western Ukraine, though he did link German settlement in western Poland with Germanization.[25] Sobieski used the term "Jagiellonian idea" in a subheading and explained it was born of the conflict between the Poles, who historically represented Christian love, and Germans, who represented violence. Sobieski saw post-1386 Polish eastern affairs in terms of this idea and claimed that after the sixteenth-century Poland's parliament (*Sejm*) realized that union with eastern territories had to be based on the Polish nation.[26] The Union of 1569 was not decreed but achieved through the negotiated agreement of the two parties. He gave no details except that the union was finalized once the quarrel over Ukrainian lands had been resolved by linking them to Poland. The success at Lublin led to "imperialism," which Sobieski used in a positive sense.[27] He also praised the Union of Brest as a means of keeping Ukraine apart from Turkey and Russia. He observed that the Union won the Rus gentry but lost the peasants in the east and that Poles began having doubts about the event only when the cossacks took up the Orthodox cause. Khmelntysky's uprising was caused by estate grievances and rapacious leaseholders and was fueled by Greek clergy, Turks, and drunken dreams. He added that since the Orthodox Church had been legalized in 1632 religious conflict in Ukraine was artificial and provoked by Constantinople. He was also critical of the Zboriv treaty (1649) which gave the cossacks de facto autonomy. The cossack leaders had wanted a heaven on earth for themselves, where peasants would be their serfs. What they got were anti-Khmelnytsky revolts.[28] In 1654, Muscovy recognized central Ukraine as "Little Russia."

Reflecting on seventeenth-century Polish eastern politics, Sobieski remarked that it had wavered between the alternatives of peace or unions, and that the latter, based on federalist ideas, provided a better alternative for Cossack Ukraine than did alliance with Moscow because Polish cultural influences had made it more similar to Poland than Russia. An opportunity of realizing the federalist option occurred again when Vyhovsky took power and the Polish queen planned to use cossacks to strengthen royal authority. Sobieski speculated that the Hadiach treaty might have been her initiative. He assessed the treaty favorably and attributed its failure to Catholic opposition to Orthodox prelates in the Senate and Russian agitation among the Ukrainian masses.[29] Sobieski remarked that after 1709 Ukraine ceased being of any importance in European politics and he does not mention it again until his discussion of the events of 1919, when he noted that the commander of Polish troops in the east, saved "Eastern Little Poland for us."

The last major academic history published in interwar Poland was *Wiedza o Polsce* (1932), which consisted of five heavy, well-illustrated volumes, intended to serve as a university course in humanities for interested laymen and teachers. Written from a positivist perspective, it included chapters on economic and social history and a considerable number of drawings and reproductions on Ukrainian themes, including all the hetmans. The sections on Ukraine were by Kazimierz Tymieniecki (1887-1968), Ludwig Kołankowski (1882-1956), and Włodzimierz Dzwonkowski (1880-1954).

The authors described Casimir's eastern politics as offensive rather than defensive, and not the result of a turn away from the West. The Polish king, they explain, inherited Galicia and Tatar attacks prompted him to claim his right against his main rivals, the Lithuanians. He was content with overlordship and did not want to rule the area directly. In discussing the Krevo and Lublin Unions the authors do not mention Ukrainian lands or the "Jagiellonian idea."[30]

The sections on Ukraine have a marked socio-economic emphasis and highlight the link between settlement and economic development and trade. Price rises necessitated higher incomes for the gentry who, in turn, extended serfdom and provoked flight to open lands instead of to towns, as had happened in Western Europe. The emerging society of free settlers and fugitives was armed and unstable. The narrative noted that the first revolts were social in nature and did not mention any related foreign intrigues or plots. Revolts were sometimes incited by adventurers but also broke out when cossacks were not paid after campaigns or prevented from raiding Turkey. Notable in this survey was a reference to the beginning of the Ukrainian national movement in the sixteenth and seventeenth centuries, while the account of the Church Union traced it to Orthodox bishops' dislike of lay interference and made no mention of a Polish or Jesuit role. When "the people" began looking to the cossacks as defenders of the faith the latter began to identify with it, but had the gentry accepted the cossacks' 1632 demand for elector status, they would have neutralized this threatening alliance and tied this formidable fighting force closer to Poland.[31]

The account of the Khmelnytsky uprising attributes it to estate grievances. There is an extended if grudging description of Khmelnytsky's talents, which includes the judgment that his heavy drinking and intense emotions had no effect on his politics. The authors do not mention Khmelnytsky's aims but do note that his decision to submit to the tsar met with opposition from his officers as well as Kievan prelates conscious of how different their church was from the Russian. By the end of his life Khmelnytsky was de facto ruler of Ukraine.[32]

The narrative depicts the Hadiach treaty as a base for the restructuring of the Polish-Lithuanian Commonwealth into a tripartite federation and explains that it was signed by officers influenced by Polish ideals who preferred the Commonwealth to Muscovite despotism. While Polish bishops rejected the maximalist version of this treaty, the Ukrainian masses revolted against their leaders from fear of serfdom. Consequently, Ukraine was split and "greatly weakened."[33] The book ignores Mazepa and explains that the Haidamak revolt was provoked by the heroic but politically foolish anti-Orthodox Bar Confederation. Such rashness gave the Russians an ally in the form of peasant revolt.[34]

In its account of nineteenth-century Galicia, the Ukrainian national movement in 1848 appears as a product of Austrian intrigues. Ukrainians formed their own organizations but these were later used by Austrians to spread Russophile propaganda. The book mentions the Ukrainian-Polish compromise of 1914 and notes it was not implemented because of the war.[35] Events in Ukraine between 1917 and 1921 receive passing mention, with the Kievan Central Rada described as an artificial creation. In Galicia, the authors explain, the Habsburgs initially promised Ukrainians a separate state but after their demise an Austro-Ukrainian coup usurped power in part of the province until Poland "resurrected itself" and was able to reestablish control.[36]

TEXTBOOKS AND POPULAR HISTORIES

The interpretation of Ukrainian history in four of the nine interwar textbook histories of Poland examined in this chapter was neoromantic.[37] The most widely used was Friedberg's revised version of A. Lewicki's prewar *Zarys historii Polski*, which differed only slightly from the 1899 edition of his *Dzieje narodu Polskiego w zarysie*, revised by Lewicki himself. Curiously, unlike Lewicki, who listed the anti-Orthodox policy of the Bar Confederation as a major cause of the Haidamak revolt in his 1899 text, Friedberg followed the 1897 edition and placed the blame on Russian provocations.[38]

More nationalist in tone was a survey by J. Kisiliewska, sponsored by "The Civil Board of The Eastern Lands," and intended as a guide for teachers in Poland's Ukrainian territories. The introduction explained: "The first task of the Polish state was to realize its age old task in the east: to fight against barbarism in defense of its liberties and those of its brother peoples . . . In the wake of the victorious army goes an army of teachers, the quiet builders of tomorrow." Kisiliewska claimed that Poland's greatness was built on love of Lithuania and Rus. In the 1340s Rus boiars, we read, offered no resistance to Casimir's occupation of Galicia in the wake of the death of his relative George II, because they knew the Polish king was wise and munificent.[39]

The other three examined histories provided slightly more balanced accounts of this event. Wanczura noted simply that Casimir had inherited Galicia, while Wysznacka wrote that the region had belonged to Poland from the tenth century and Casimir only decided to return it to Polish rule because he feared that Rus would be unable to hold off the Tatars alone. Friedberg noted that annexation brought economic benefit to both sides. Only Wanczura referred to the "Jagiellonian idea" in her discussion of the 1386 Union, which, she explained, gave Poland the mission of carrying Western civilization east. Friedberg noted that the Union won over two nations to Western civilization and that since Poland was on a higher level it had to predominate. All give a similar account of the Lublin Union. Wysznacka saw it as a culmination of the "Jagiellonian idea," Wanczura noted that it took civilization east, while Kisielewska called it the "most beautiful event in history." Friedberg pointed to the importance of the Russian threat and family and cultural ties as elements convincing the king to push the act through by fiat once he was sure of gentry support. Wysznacka made no mention of the Brest Union while Kisielewska remarked that it divided the Orthodox and Uniates and caused great problems. She identified the Jesuit Piotr Skarga as the main instigator of the Union and attributed Orthodox opposition to Russian intrigue. Friedberg, who provided the most detailed account, explained that Prince Kostiantyn Ostrozhsky opposed Church Union because he faced the prospect of losing his authority within the church, and that because of his opposition Uniate bishops did not get Senate seats. The resulting conflict turned the Orthodox eastward and prompted the church to ally with the cossacks.

No author dealt with the early cossack revolts, while three gave only fleeting accounts of the Khmelnytsky period. Wysznacka did not even mention Khmelnytsky's name or deal with the period separately, but incorporated it into a section entitled "The Battle of Berestechko" that followed the section on the 1621 Khotyn battle. "These were [Poland's] saddest hours, when some Polish citizens called cossacks rose first against Polish magnates in Ukraine and then against the king and the Rzeczpospolita."[40] Kisielewska did provide a political history of this period, while Wanczura wrote that the war dragged on because Khmelnytsky's terms had been unacceptable. "Having betrayed in turn Poland and Turkey he submitted to Moscow which truly promised cossacks freedom and independence, but once it had them under its rule it crushed all cossack attempts to assert their liberty, forced them into obedience with the knout."[41] Only Friedberg provided details. He wrote that Polish colonization brought Western civilization to Ukraine but also that excessive exploitation and Ukrainian reluctance to render rents after the expiration of free settlement terms were causes of hostility. He explained that the conflict was not national because magnates and gentry in Ukraine were Rus'ian (Ukrainian) as well as Polish. He wrote that the cossacks had been provoked by greed and that Muscovite priests convinced them to claim they were fighting for the faith in order to attract the clergy and nobility to their revolution. Khmelnytsky was competent but without scruples, as mere personal injury provoked him to foment the revolt. He became de facto ruler of Ukraine, a vassal of the sultan, and unchecked pride led him to want to establish a dynasty. Failed political plans by 1654 forced him into Russia's hands, and the cossacks became dependent on the despotic tsarist regime that could withdraw their privileges at any time.

All four writers praised the Hadiach treaty and claimed it could have guaranteed Polish-Ukrainian peace had not Moscow fomented divisions among the cossacks. Friedberg added that the Poles blundered when they failed to strongly support the agreement and did not give Senate seats to Orthodox bishops. Kisielewska added that during the war cossacks and peasants developed a sense of national identity and that Khmelnytsky failed to attain his aim of statehood. Mazepa represented those cossacks who disliked being "treated like Russians" by the tsars, and who desired an alliance with Poland. But not all cossacks supported him in 1709 and ultimately cossack Ukraine became a Russian province.

For Wanczura and Friedberg the Haidamak uprisings were a Russian provocation, while Kisiliewska accused Orthodox priests of instigating the destruction of all that Polish ability and spirit had created in Ukraine. Wysznacka does not mention this subject.

Friedberg provided the best and most detailed treatment of nineteenth- and twentieth-century Ukraine. He criticized the Galician Ukrainian national council (*Holovna Ruska Rada*) for opposing Polish demands in 1848 and for demanding a separate Ukrainian province, thus creating a national conflict where none had existed before. Friedberg wrote that the Ukrainian movement originated within a small group of intellectuals and idealists who claimed Rus was not Russia. The Russians persecuted their first ideologist, the poet Shevchenko, but the Austrians used the Ukrainians against Poles in Galicia. Initially, the Poles tolerated the Ukrainian movement. The Polish sense of justice and fair play, in light of the fact that 40 percent of Galicia was Ukrainian, led them to accept Ukrainian language and school demands. Nonetheless, ungrateful Ukrainians began to advocate political separatism because Poles in Galicia were weaker than the Russians in tsarist Ukraine. Relations worsened as radical social demands emerged and linked the Ukrainian national movement with a "strange historical ideology that saw in old cossackdom a moment of Ukrainian patriotism, and portrayed Khmelnytsky, and even Gonta and Zalizniak [Haidamak leaders] as national heroes. This misconstrued patriotism led Ukrainians to regard Poles as their main enemies and [they thought] absolved them of the brutality they used in their struggle."[42] Cooperation became more difficult and the situation was worsened by foreign backing of the Ukrainian movement. According to Friedberg, only thanks to Austria and Prussia did the Ukrainian movement become anti-Polish and their influence created within the culturally young nation dangerous illusions of grandeur—a state from the Caucasus to the Danube and Vistula.[43]

In 1917-1918 these illusions and Viennese backing led to the creation of a small Habsburg state in Western Ukraine through a "brutal act of force" based on the principle of self-determination. Although the West Ukrainian People's Republic (ZUNR) was not a legitimate state, the West did not formally recognize Polish annexation of Western Ukraine until 1922. The author called Pilsudski's alliance with Petliura a fiasco and claimed that Ukrainians were basically politically immature and pro-Bolshevik.[44] Wysznacka mentioned Ukraine in 1917 in a section entitled "Polish Military Organization in the Borderlands" and remarked that the Austrians created the conflict between Poles and Ukrainians. As the Poles could not allow Austria to give Galicia to Ukrainians, a bloody war had to ensue. She concluded that this war and the preceding events should be best forgotten.

The other five texts examined here share the positivist view of Ukraine's past.[45] They presented Casimir's politics in the 1340s in terms of dynastic inheritance and noted that a war was necessary in face of opposition. S. Arnold referred to Poland's "striving to expand" but related this to economic and political interests and depicted Ukrainian-Polish relations in dynastic terms. Arnold was the only author to mention that the 1386 Union linked Rus with Poland. Martynowiczowna and Jarosz wrote little about early Polish-Ukrainian relations but stressed that the Rus people at the time were faithful to their church and language and loyal Poles.

Both authors discussed the socio-economic background of the cossack revolts. Martynowiczowna linked the Ukrainian-Polish conflict to the expiration of free settlement terms and the severity of estate overseers in Ukraine, whose cruelty drove peasants to see the cossacks as their defenders. Jarosz treated the Union as a direct consequence of Skarga's book criticizing the Orthodox Church, which, he claimed, had stimulated the union-inclined Rus bishops to act, while Arnold saw the Union of 1596 as the product of Jesuit-inspired intolerance and the internal decay of the Orthodox Church—particularly manifested in the influence of the laity. The initiative for Union came from Rus reformers, while the king was interested because he feared Russian Orthodox influences in his kingdom. The issue was complicated by Ostrozhsky, who initially supported and then opposed the Union. The cossack problem was explained in the context of Russian and Turkish relations.

These five surveys gave different accounts of Khmelnytsky's revolt. Arnold and Jarosz saw events not in national but in social, political, and religious terms; the former did not use "Ukrainian" or "Rus" in reference to the cossacks. Martynowiczowna warned against confusing peasant revolts with cossack insubordination that culminated in Khmelnytsky wanting his own state in Ukraine. Like Jarosz and other neoromantics, Martynowiczowna discussed the Khmelnytsky period in a section titled "The

Battle of Berestechko," and devoted more space to the battle than to the politics before and after. These two authors also provided more detail than Arnold on Ukrainian-Russian disagreements over rights that preceded the Hadiach treaty. According to Martynowiczowna, this treaty failed because Turkey and Moscow opposed it.

Arnold's rather superficial account of post-eighteenth-century Ukrainian events claimed that the Haidamak revolts were incited by Russian priests and other "agitators." His account of 1918, without mentioning ZUNR, noted that Austria had given authority in Galicia to Ukrainians. Jarosz did not deal with the Haidamaks or 1848 in Lviv. He noted that in 1917 the Ukrainian national movement began forming a state and in the section "Liberation of Borderland Areas" he explained that before leaving the Austrians had given Lviv to the Ukrainians, who were a majority only in the surrounding countryside. After three weeks of fighting, Poles "freed the city from the Ukrainian army" whose aim had been to join the Ukrainian state ruled from Kiev. Jarosz mentioned the Petliura-Pilsudski alliance, that Kiev was to be the Ukrainian capital, and that Ukrainians were too weak to effectively help Poland.[46] In his 1933 edition, Jarosz added that after three weeks of heroic fighting the Poles took Lviv but another half-year elapsed before they "sent the Ukrainians beyond the Zbruch [river]."[47]

Of 14 popular histories of Poland reviewed in this chapter, five provided a positivist treatment of Ukrainian events.[48] Rydel, for instance, merely noted that Lviv was "acquired" in 1340, that the Union of Brest was intended to supplement the Union of 1569, and that the 1648 uprising was a reaction to oppression by agents of magnates. He did not mention the Pereiaslav or Hadiach treaties and, concerning the Haidamaks, noted only that they provoked massacres. Zimowski wrote that in 1648 the cossacks wanted to be a "free nation," not subject to Polish lords living in Ukraine. Only Dobrzanski mentioned Ukrainian issues in 1918 and noted that Austria had caused the Polish-Ukrainian war because it had hoped to weaken Poland by exploiting an old conflict.[49]

Within this group of writings may be included a short survey history by Polish Marxist Feliks Marchlewski. He wrote while in a German prison during World War I, then published a pamphlet in Moscow based on Polish history lectures he had given there in 1923. There is only one passage relating to Ukraine: "After the political Union with the Lithuanian Duchy and the enslavement of the free cossacks of Ukraine, the possibility of colonial activity opened up for the gentry." This was built on oppression and carried the threat of peasant cossack revolt.[50] Marchlewski's prison notes, published in *Ocherki iz istorii Polshi,* introduced by Polish Marxist Stanisław Bobinski as the "basic Marxist work on the history of Poland," also contained only a few lines on Ukrainian issues. Marchlewski wrote that lands in the east were conquered, that peasants were oppressed there, and that in Galicia conflict between Ukrainian peasants and Polish lords had a national aspect. He was critical of Pilsudski's federalist plans and labeled his Galician policy a tool of French imperialism.[51] During his lifetime Marchlewski had no influence on Polish historiography but his scattered remarks and their subsequent condemnation became one source of the official postwar interpretation of Ukrainian history.

The other nine popular histories examined here presented Ukrainian issues in the neoromantic vein.[52] The most influential and controversial was by A. Chołoniewski, republished in Poland four times between 1917 and 1932. The book was the subject of heated polemics—one reviewer commented that it was rare to see a book that combined significant literary talent with such ignorance of Polish and world history.[53]

Chołoniewski gave few facts. Rather, he made sweeping generalizations glorifying Poland's past in the spirit of the prewar conservative-romantic historians. In his introduction to the second edition he rejected all criticism with the assertion that others had written too much about negative aspects of Poland's past and that it was time to write about the glory. He gave an appropriately stirring account, equating early Polish political ideals with nineteenth-century European republicanism and democracy. These ideals attracted Poland's neighbors who received liberty in the wake of voluntary political unions that soon led to their voluntary Polonization. Poland's political unions with her neighbors were internally indestructible, while the country's peasants were no worse off than elsewhere at the time. Poland could not handle only two problems; the peasants in Ukraine and the cossacks. Religion had little political significance at the time because Church Union had been voluntary, successful, and attained within the context of tolerance and liberty. He admitted that the Orthodox were treated badly but laid the blame on Russian anti-Polish machinations, thus implying that the Ukrainians deserved the treatment they got because they were disloyal. Poland could not deal with the Ukrainian cossacks and peasants because they became a problem when Polish political thought and tolerance were in decline. Poland's greatest error was to have rejected the principles that made her great when she needed them most.[54]

A similar tone is found in two books for children and peasants by S. Bukowiecka, also published in 1917. Here we read that King Bolesław I had to go east to "establish order" but he did not conquer Rus, because he already had enough land. He respected the Rus as brothers and only wanted to establish some order among them. Bukowiecka wrote that God told nations to build just kingdoms and the Polish order emerged as the best. Accordingly, others joined voluntarily. Lithuania was offered the "sacrament of eternal Union" and together with Rus was happy under Jagiellonian rule. She compared the four constituent parts of the old Polish state (Ukraine, Lithuania, Prussia, and Poland) to a wagon that moved well as long as there was a good driver. The mass of the nation did not have rights, but this was because of the moral decline of the gentry. Bukowiecka called the entire population of the southeast cossacks, and wrote that since they were not paid they had no alternative but to plunder gentry estates. In revenge, the gentry forced them to work like peasants. But the cossacks then rebelled and shifted their allegiance to Moscow, for which they were later sorry because the tsars rescinded their liberties. Failing to break from Russia, they turned into "savages," and are later described as the direct ancestors of nineteenth-century tsarist cossack troops. Bukowiecka saw the Haidamaks as good people forced to extremes by oppressive lords and led astray by pro-Russian Orthodox priests and Russians who sowed dissension and provoked bloody mass murder. She concluded that it was very sad that dull-witted peasants had allowed themselves to be turned into bandits.[55]

In the second edition of her children's history (1917-1919), she adopted a more hostile tone in her account of the Khmelnytsky revolt—now called a war of brother against brother. She wrote that Khmelnytsky behaved very badly because as a Christian and a Pole he allied with enemies and, blinded by hate, sought out all those with Polish last names simply because of a personal injustice. He was a primitive drunkard who, like most inhabitants of Ukraine, was oblivious to the fact that his activities would only destroy the liberties his people enjoyed.[56]

Smolenski, in a history written before 1914 for Western European audiences but not published until 1919 because of censorship, noted that alongside political considerations the idea of "raising" eastern lands to the "dignity" of Western civilization played a key role in Polish history. Whereas the Lublin Union promoted a beneficial Polonization of non-Poles, the purpose of the 1596 Church Union was to bring about final "union" of the masses with Poland. The nineteenth-century Ukrainian national movement in Galicia he treated as an offshoot of the Habsburg bureaucracy's use of the masses against the Polish gentry.[57] Rydel announced that a survey he published in 1919 was the first history of Poland to be published without a censor, and indeed this text departed markedly from his earlier 1917 history in its treatment of Ukrainian issues. In the "uncensored" text he treated Boleslaw I's campaign against Kiev as a conquest and referred to the need to spread Western civilization and "life forces" as driving Poland east after 1386. Rus and Poland, who shared similar blood and language, had different spirits but Poland had "always strived to attach to Rus the beneficial influences of the Roman church and Western civilization."[58] Rydel criticized King Sigismund III as well as opponents of the Church Union but praised the Union itself. Admitting that a morally dissolute gentry had forced the cossacks to rebel, he wrote that Khmelnytsky was politically exploited by Moscow and Turkey. The second edition of Rydel's history provides an example of how lifting of foreign censorship can release pent-up nationalism and messianism rather than the findings of dispassionate scholarship.

Histories by Śliwinski, Kisielewska, and Czertwan were more muted and factual. These authors presented the events of the 1340s in the context of dynastic inheritance, wise policies, and religious tolerance. Śliwinski remarked simply that in 1340 Galicia had been "joined" to Poland, while none of the authors dealt with the Union of Lublin in detail. Kisielewska described it as one of the finest moments in history, while Śliwinski referred to it as a stage in Poland's peaceful expansion that protected people threatened by Moscow and the Germans. Only nobles Polonized. The peasants did not and therefore could not benefit from Poland's grand deeds. Peasants were worse off in Ukraine than in Poland and, because they maintained their sense of difference, their revolts presented a greater threat to the state than they would have otherwise. Whereas Kisielewska saw the 1596 Union as the work of the Skarga and attributed tensions to the bad will of Orthodox priests and agitators sent from Moscow, Śliwinski assessed the Union negatively as an unsuccessful Jesuit plan supported by a fanatical king that led only to disorder, wars, and civil war among Ukrainians. The Union weakened the country because it replaced religious toleration with fanaticism and led to the moral decline of the gentry and more oppression. Śliwinski's account of the cossacks, described as settlers who became primitive robbers in the steppes, was also more critical than Kisielewska's. They sided with the Orthodox Church, took up the struggle against the Union, provoked Tatar raids on Poland, and raided Ottoman lands. The 1648 uprising was caused by religious oppression and Khmelnytsky's personal injury, but the Hetman carried on the war when it was no longer necessary because pride had inflated his sense of his own greatness. Czertwan grudgingly admitted that the cossacks had been loyal in their own way and that Poland's problems with them had less to do with the moral qualities of the gentry than bad policies and the lack of a politically competent person to handle them. Khmelnytsky took up arms because he was dissatisfied with the outcome of his attempted legal redress against the man who had ruined his properties and his revolt represented a "complete withdrawal of obedience." Czertwan thought Khmelnytsky merely used cossack complaints as a pretext,[59] and explained that in 1654 the cossack leader had to turn to Russia because the Turks had dropped him.

Śliwinski and Czertwan claimed that the Haidamak revolts were incited by Orthodox priests who provoked drunken peasants to murder and destroy the fruits of centuries of Polish enterprise. Only Kisielewska included a section on Ukraine between 1918-1920. She explained that in return for food Germany promised Ukrainians a state cut from Poland's "living flesh" while Austria gave the Ukrainians Lviv. She devoted two pages to describe heroic Polish youth fighting against ZUNR for control of Lviv. Once the city was taken, the struggle continued against the Rada.[60]

5

The Imposed Continuity (1944-1982)

A NEW VERSION OF THE PAST

Although nineteenth- and early-twentieth-century Polish publicists and intellectuals discussed whether the future Poland should be a national or multinational state and have a border defined ethnically or historically, their debates had no impact on historiography. Neither interwar nor postwar historians clearly indicated how and where to draw the line between the history of the Polish state and the nations belonging to it. Survey histories mentioned or ignored Ukraine without providing explicit criteria. Nine histories of Poland published in Poland between 1944 and 1956, reflecting official guidelines, were the first widely circulated histories explicitly dismissive of past Polish control over eastern territories but these also failed to delineate clearly the history of the state from the nation. As will be shown, the new treatment of Ukrainian issues was less a radical break with earlier interpretations than a continuation of minority prewar Polish positivist and communist views.[1]

Party spokesmen formally announced the main ideas of the postwar interpretation at the First Congress of Polish Learning (1950). Historians were told that in the nineteenth century historiography had been used by the ruling class to exploit the patriotism of the masses and poison it with nationalism. Glorification of the various Unions, identified as part of an ideological platform to justify rule in the east and "anti-Ukrainian" interpretations of 1596 and 1768 were strongly condemned, as well as the tradition of "unjust expansionist" wars which in 1917-1920 directly or indirectly had served the interests of Capital. The Party arbitrarily imposed its official interpretation and made no attempt to justify it by identifying its intellectual roots. The prevailing image of the past was simply condemned as part of the burden of Polish nationalism that weighed down especially heavily with respect to Ukrainian affairs.² As Kormanowa bluntly explained in 1947: "With the change in our foreign policy is linked revision of a number of formulations and judgements about our past. Today we see many moments of our past differently. Among them we see the eastern expansionism of the gentry commonwealth differently—we see more clearly that therein lay the roots not only of the partitions but of the many misfortunes that befell us after the partitions."³

One of the sources of the official postwar interpretation lay in late-nineteenth- and early-twentieth-century works by National Democrat and extreme left-wing publicists. F. Marchlewski's history is among these and was the first survey to use the term "colonialism" in a detractive sense to refer to Polish activities in Ukraine. A second source of the postwar interpretation was official criticism of Marchlewski published in 1934.

B. Szmidt, an émigré Polish communist, in the Moscow-based *Z Pola Walki* criticized the hitherto "basic Marxist work" for being non-Marxist, "Luxemburgist," and heavily influenced by bourgeois ideology. He accused Marchlewski of ignoring the peasants and national liberation movements, and for claiming that Poland had only peaceful intentions toward Moscow. Marchlewski, under the influence of the bourgeoisie, had justified its aggressive policy toward Ukraine. He was wrong to have treated Austrian Galicia as a unit, to have failed to identify a Polish imperialist bourgeoisie, to have ignored national conflict, and not to have explained that Polish imperialism was responsible for the 1918 expansion into Western Ukraine.⁴ These ideas were elaborated in a Soviet history of Poland published in 1940,⁵ and in the Polish Party press during and immediately after World War II.

A third source of the postwar interpretation of Ukraine's past were "liberal neopositivist" Polish historians. Sometimes their views clashed with those of the Party, which criticized some of them for not distinguishing between the tsarist and communist regimes when invoking historical parallels to justify cooperation with Russia, and for their critical attitudes toward nineteenth-century Polish uprisings. The views of other neopositivists, critical of Polish policy in Ukraine and Polish-Ukrainian affairs, however, echoed those of some pre-1914 National Democrats and coincided with Party ideas. Thus, Henryk Barycz in 1944 condemned the "Jagiellonian idea." A. Bochenski, on the other hand, in the best known and most influential publicist work of the immediate postwar period, echoed the neoromantic Cracow school interpretation. Bochenski did not condemn the Polish presence in Ukraine and wrote that the country had failed to live up to its "task" because Polish society was in decline when it had to come to grips with Ukrainian problems.⁶

Against this background of prewar positivist and radical socialist thought critical of Polish presence in the east, it emerges that the compilers of the Party interpretation added little original thought. Their efforts were limited to working out details and appending to Polish historiography formulas such as "National Liberation War of the Ukrainian People," "anti-feudal" revolts, and "international class solidarity."

The first postwar official histories of Poland devoted little space to Ukrainian issues and noted only a few dates in what may be classified as transitional interpretations.[7] Hoszowska (1947), alongside a section on the fate of the peasantry and a reference to the formation of the cossack army, which brought glory and liberty to themselves and the peasants, included an explanation of how Rus and Polish gentry after 1340 lived side by side, and defended the country from Russia and Tatars.[8] Dłuska (1947) called the 1648 uprising a peasant war during which fraternal Ukrainian and Polish blood was spilled, and wrote that Khmelnytsky "submitted" to Russia, which then used the pretext of defending him to attack Poland.[9] Before 1949, texts treated Casimir's annexation of Galicia as an inheritance, though they clearly stated that Ukrainians were socially and nationally oppressed and revolted in response. New in Polish historiography was the claim that in 1654 ethnic affinity played an important role in Russian-Ukrainian relations.

After 1949 and the campaign to rid Polish historiography of "chauvinism and nationalism," the last vestiges of neoromanticism disappeared from survey histories. Authors even ignored known facts. They referred now to Casimir's 1340 campaign as a conquest or "taking over" that brought oppression to Ukrainians and nothing good to Poles. They explained that due to the eastward turn in foreign policy Poland lost sight of its proper "tasks" and became entangled with Turkey, Austria, and Russia, and referred to the Union of Lublin as Polish political blackmail; merely the legal form of gentry usurpation of lands in the east. The results were devastating for Poland as they prolonged and extended feudalism, hindered the emergence of a strong national state, gave a legal basis for lords to keep Ukrainian lands in submission, and provided a surplus, which the gentry used to maintain itself and throttle the rest of society.[10] In their accounts of the Union of Brest the new histories ignored the basic findings of nineteenth-century scholarship, such as the Ukrainian initiative in bringing it about. They labeled the event a Jesuit plot that led to denationalization. All published histories now explained that uprisings in Ukraine were justified responses to oppression. This echoed the view of some prewar historians, but unprecedented was reference to the Khmelnytsky uprising as a "War of the Ukrainian nation for liberation and independence." Unable to compromise and too weak to win the war alone, the cossacks allied with their religiously and culturally similar Russian neighbors on conditions of broad autonomy.[11] A history of Poland used in Party schools claimed that feudalism had lasted longer in Poland thanks to surplus extracted from Ukraine after 1569. After 1648, the stubborn class egoism of the gentry ensured the war would continue and bring in Ukraine's "natural ally," Moscow. S. Arnold added that the Pereiaslav treaty was a lesser evil for Ukraine, a country that was historically underdeveloped and had to join Russia because independence was not an option.[12] Arnold was the first postwar historian to mention Polish oppression as the cause of the Haidamak revolts and the cruelty of Polish in suppressing it, without dwelling on the atrocities perpetrated by Ukrainians.

Of these early histories, only Missałowa's mentioned Ukrainian events in the nineteenth and twentieth century. Hers was the first history of Poland to unequivocally assert that in 1848 the *Ruska Rada* reflected the national desires of Ukrainians and that in Galicia Poles had oppressed Ukrainians. Missałowna was also the first survey author to unequivocally condemn Polish policies in Western Ukraine in 1918-1921. She explained that this area was occupied by the "nationalist imperialist" Piłsudski, who represented the Polish bourgeoisie and landowners. In 1918, Polish capitalism allied with the counterrevolution and declared war on Ukraine, and the driving force behind the scenes was French and English imperialism—the "real rulers" of Poland. In the 1952 edition of her book she summed up events in Ukraine after 1917 with the phrase "the Soviet Republic concerned itself with the non-Russians living on what was the territory of the tsarist state."[13]

ELABORATION AND OMISSION

After 1956, the PZPR dispensed with its self-proclaimed right to interfere directly in cultural affairs. Professional ethics and standards reemerged in Polish scholarship, and historians eventually rid themselves of almost all interference in interpretation. By 1978, the Polish Historical Association could place "striving for historical truth" before Marxist method in its statement of goals and purposes, and two years later Stefan Kieniewicz, the senior historian, noted that only Polish-Soviet relations and postwar and Party history remained subject to interpretative control.[1] During the 1960s there were more studies dealing with non-Poles in pre-1945 Poland, and in survey histories the treatment of Ukraine and Ukrainian-Polish relations became less dogmatic. Yet survey histories continued to be titled "History of Poland," thereby implying an account of events in a multinational state, while actually recounting the history of the nation on its national territory that minimized or obscured the diversity of the Old Commonwealth, and oversimplified relations between Poles and non-Poles. Liberalization led to better accounts of Ukrainian issues in histories of Poland, but these did not always incorporate the findings of monographs and some totally ignored all Ukrainian-related subjects.

The major survey sponsored by the communist regime was the multivolume *Historia Polski* (1958-1972). The introduction explained that eastern territorial gains had been temporary and that conflicts with eastern neighbors had weakened Poland in the West, but also drew attention to Poland's positive cultural role in the east. The narrative tried to depict the history of a multinational country but fell short of presenting the history of a state as implied in the title, and was not, as claimed in the introduction, a history of the nation on its native territory.[15]

A balanced exposition of Polish-Ukrainian affairs is found in the discussion of Casimir's campaign in Galicia, which draws attention to the economic interests of the nobility, burghers, and king as the backdrop to occupation in the wake of dynastic inheritance. Ukrainian resistance was called defense of independence, while economic interests were given as a reason the Rus gentry supported and later helped introduce the Polish order. Casimir set up a Catholic hierarchy in his new acquisition, it was claimed, in order to weaken the Orthodox church.[16]

The authors criticized the various Unions as expansionist, but also noted that the Polish order had provided regional defense as well as firm support for Rus gentry class interests. The text presented the Union of Lublin as a purely political issue and mentioned the threat to use force against opposition. The Union provided areas for colonization and latifundia and thereby laid the basis for Rus and Polish magnate dominance in Poland, but its effect on Ukrainian development was not mentioned.[17] A balanced account of the Union of 1596 was followed by characterization of cossack revolts as social and national responses to "feudal oppression" and estate grievances. Ukrainian cultural development at the time was noted but not categorized as a "national revival," while Polish urban and burgher (but not gentry) cultural influences were deemed "progressive": "Those elements that went [east] via relations between feudalists did not have this progressive significance, this included models of administration (gentry liberties during the Time of Troubles) or fashions."[18]

In 1648, a social revolt turned into a "Ukrainian national war of political liberation." An inability to come to terms prolonged the war and Ukraine's bad military situation in 1653, combined with Moscow's willingness to enter the fray, resulted in the Pereiaslav treaty. The authors noted that

Khmelnytsky wanted to "join" Russia, and that the "nation" desired the agreement, which had a great influence on both countries, but they did not reiterate official Soviet formulations. They described the Hadiach Treaty as an agreement signed by a group of magnates who did not want to lose their possessions in Ukraine and listed the treaty's terms without comment. Mazepa appears as a traitor who wanted to unite Left- and Right-Bank Ukraine under Swedish control and who was opposed by "the people."[19] The Haidamak revolts were caused by forced religious conversion and the expiration of free-settlement terms. The revolts were bloody for all concerned and provided Russia with a pretext to intervene in Polish affairs.[20]

The *Historia* provided the first extended treatment in a history of Poland of Ukrainians in nineteenth-century Galicia, called an artificial creation that was half Ukrainian with a backward economy dominated by a Polish minority. Like some prewar histories, this text noted that Austrians played both nations against each other in 1848, but it then added that such tactics had been possible because Poles had ignored Ukrainian demands. The book treated the Ukrainian movement sympathetically and noted Polish democrats' as well as conservative hostility to it. In a period when the Ukrainian national movement in Galicia was not mentioned in Soviet surveys, the official history of Poland provided short descriptions of Ukrainian groups and their objectives of national equality with Poles. Authors claimed that the Ukrainian movement represented the better-off and therefore could not reflect the interests of the Ukrainian poor—but they did not condemn the movement because of this. The Galician Radical Party, which tried to work with Polish leftists in 1890, was treated sympathetically, while the conservative Ukrainian National Democrats were condemned because they tried to channel the Ukrainian national liberation struggle into narrow nationalism.[21]

The account of events in Lviv in 1918 held that the city was initially under control of the armed "Ukrainian nationalist liberation movement" and that by annexing Eastern Galicia the Polish government only created a national problem for itself. There is a sociological characterization of Polish settlement alongside the claim that big landowners were the main force behind incorporation. France's willingness to support Poland turned it into a "tool of imperialism" once its leaders began to fear Bolshevik victory. Incorporation of Ukrainian lands was supported by many Poles but they were divided over how much to include and on what terms. Pilsudski's federalist party was condemned together with the right-wing Polish National Democrats but the former was regarded as more democratic than the latter. The major enemy in the East, hostile to Poland and the Bolshevik revolution, were the two Ukrainian Republics, and as they weakened in the struggle against the

Bolsheviks, the Poles moved east. Oil in Eastern Galicia gave the Entente a special interest in the region and led them to eventually stop supporting Poland, but by then its armies had occupied Western Ukraine. Resigning themselves to the situation because they regarded Poland a stronger anti-Bolshevik force than Ukraine, the Western powers obliged Poland to give national autonomy to Ukrainians. Nevertheless, Ukrainians ended up worse off under Poland than they had been under Austria.[22]

It is stated that Pilsudki's alliance with Petliura and the 1920 Kiev offensive was risky and that there was much opposition to it. The book also provides the text of the agreement and mentions that in the wake of the Bolshevik counteroffensive the Soviet regime in Ukraine, in the form of the Galician Revolutionary Committee, declared an independent Galician Soviet Republic—two facts not mentioned in Soviet historiography at the time. By 1921, Pilsudski was politically isolated and accepted previously rebuffed Russian overtures for peace. In the Riga treaty both sides resigned from their claims.[23] The volume included pictures of Petliura and Polish troops celebrating victory in Kiev and Ternopil!

The multivolume history of Poland highlights moments of particular political importance in Polish-Ukrainian relations and contains few clichés like "common struggles" of peasants of both nations against oppressors. Unlike the first official histories, it included no extremes of self-castigation or guilt. Regardless of shortcomings in its account of Poland's past, its interpretation of Ukrainian issues has much to commend it. The account fell basically within the Polish positivist tradition. It had no underlying theme of failed secular mission in the East and, significantly, contained more factual material on Ukraine than any other history of Poland. The authors did not use Soviet categories or terminology.

Five other major histories of Poland published up to 1982 devoted less space to Ukrainian affairs but had similar interpretations.[24] Eastern issues were noted in historicist socio-political terms without exaggerated criticism, broad schemes, or generalizations implying that Ukraine was an integral part of Polish history. Even guarded comments about cultural influences were absent.

Whereas Topolski (1982) referred to economic interests as a cause of Casimir's 1340 campaign, the others claimed the annexation had been the result of dynastic inheritance. Only Samsonowicz noted that Galicia became an area where national and social conflict merged. For Topolski the Union of Lublin involved Poland in foreign policy problems, while Tazbir remarked that it had been a logical result of the previous 200 years, as it finally regulated political relations between the regions concerned. Perhaps the best summary was written by J. Gierowski, who drew attention to favorable as well as critical assessments of the Union, and mentioned Lithuanian and Ukrainian views on the subject. He explained that Poland created problems for itself by not granting Ukrainian lands separate status, while their direct incorporation provided a region in which magnates could build private empires. These shortcomings might have been counterbalanced by more liberal policies toward the cossacks.[25] Gierowski also provided the best treatment of the 1596 Church Union. He listed the interests in favor of the Union and noted that the Polish gentry and lower clergy were indifferent and that the Union created more problems than it solved. Tazbir, meanwhile, like the others, described the Counter-Reformation background to the Union and reminded readers that it was initiated by Orthodox bishops. From the perspective of Polish interests the Union represented a failed attempt to strengthen state authority as it provoked Ukraine to look abroad for support and provided the cossacks with an ideology for revolts. Others noted that the Union stimulated religious animosity that intensified tensions in the east. All pointed out that the cossack revolts did not initially involve the peasantry and were caused by social, economic, and national oppression brought to a climax by the wavering nature of Polish cossack policies.

The examined surveys called the Khmelnytsky uprising a "national liberation war" whose aim was an independent state, and they described the Pereiaslav treaty as a political agreement joining Ukraine to Russia. Samsonowicz wrote that Ukrainians only changed one lord for another in 1654, while Tazbir observed that those opposed regarded the agreement as representing neither independence nor union. Not all mentioned the Hadiach accords, while those who did provided few details except that Ukrainian peasants opposed it. Topolski noted that Khmelnytsky's agreement with Moscow became meaningless for him by the end of his life because of his agreement with Sweden. While Topolski wrote that Mazepa's aim was independence, Tazbir stated that the hetman's aim had been to "rebuild a great Ukraine."[26] The surveys see social and religious causes for the Haidamak revolts, do not blame them on Russia, and note that both Poles and Ukrainians indulged in mindless bloodletting.

Accounts of nineteenth- and twentieth-century Ukrainian issues were generally sympathetic, very short, and usually limited to noting two tendencies within the national movement: the conservative and national-populist. There was also some divergence between historians. Tazbir, for example, remarked that Austria exploited Polish-Ukrainian antagonism, which was intensified by social differences between Poles and Ukrainians in Galicia. Samsonowicz noted that Poles reacted with hostility to Ukrainian demands, which led to growing antagonism and Ukrainians offering Austria loyalty in return for support against Poles—a tactic first proposed by Austria's Governor Stadion. Only then was the antagonism exploited by Vienna. A survey edited by Topolsky noted that the Ukrainian movement, whose aim was independence, was used but not created by the Austrians after attempts at Polish-Ukrainian agreement failed. Gierowski also pointed to Stadion's initiative in supporting the Ukrainians in 1848 but added that the government was only exploiting an error of the Polish liberals. They had refused to recognize that Ukrainian demands in 1848 signaled the emergence of Ukrainian national consciousness and that this inevitably had to challenge Polish dominance in Eastern Galicia.[27]

The surveys contained very little information about Ukraine between 1917 and 1921. Most mentioned that the allies gave Eastern Galicia to Poland, on condition it receive autonomy, in order to prevent the territory from falling into Bolshevik hands. The volume edited by Topolski added that the Austrians and Germans did not create but only courted the Ukrainian movement in order to counterbalance the Poles and weaken Russia. This laid the basis for the formation of a "bourgeois" Ukrainian state, the Central Rada. The volume explained that Ukrainians, like the Poles, took advantage of the fall of Austria, but it did not credit Vienna with the formation of ZUNR.[28]

There are a number of differences between these academic histories and ten popular and textbook survey histories of Poland.[29] To begin with, the latter, from the 1960s to the 1980s, devoted progressively less space to Ukrainian issues. Centkowski and Syta (1978) mention Ukraine in only three sentences—without actually using the word "Ukraine." They imply Casimir inherited Galicia, note that it was a bad thing for Poland to have turned east as a result of the 1569 Union, and that in 1919 the country lost its western lands because it was engaged in the East. The authors claim that gentry economic interests were the major motive in Polish eastern expansion.[30]

In this group of surveys may be found the only post-1956 history of Poland to refer to a "desire" of Ukrainians to unite with Russia and to initial improvement under Russian rule for the peasants in Cossack Ukraine.[31] This group also contains the only survey to mention Ukrainian dissatisfaction with Russian rule. Michnik, Bogucka, and Samsonowicz were the only authors of survey histories to link the Torchyn Manifesto of 1767 (see p. 116) to the Haidamak revolt, thus implying that it was caused in part by Enlightenment ideas, while Dubas (1958) wrote that Russian intrigues had caused the revolts.[32] The one text that mentioned the national movement noted that the Austrians had stoked it.[33]

Unique was a five-volume survey by Paweł Jasienica (Lech Beynar, 1909-1970) published between 1960 and 1972. The author claimed his work was only a series of essays, but it became the most reprinted postwar history of Poland, appearing in seven Polish printings as of 1983, as well as in an English translation. Jasienica's volumes were published officially and reflected "liberalization" to a degree not found in other histories of Poland, yet the book was not reviewed in any academic journal. His account included the most extensive treatment of Ukrainian affairs found in any postwar history of Poland and is the only one that treated Ukraine as an inseparable part of Poland's past.

Jasienica wanted Poles to remember what official historiography preferred they forget; namely, that Ukraine and Poland were historically related, that a sharp division along political and national lines between Ukrainians and Poles did not exist in the early-modern period, and that Ukraine had a profound influence on Poland between the fourteenth and eighteenth centuries, just as Poland had influenced Ukraine. Jasienica wrote well and had a talent for linking the seemingly unrelated and drawing pertinent and credible observations. In the context of Polish historiography, his interpretation is eclectic. It is similar to the secular romantic Cracow view because he bemoans the weakness of royal power, yet like the positivists, it dismisses messianistic Catholicism and is even critical of Ukraine's failure to politically assert itself in the past.

Like turn of the century historians M. Bobrzynski and A. Jabłonowski, Jasienica thought it significant that the old magnate elite was not all Polish and that they held in contempt the Polish gentry. It was often the case that in Ukraine the lord was Ukrainian while the peasant was a Ukrainized Pole. Jasienica also stressed throughout his book that the *Rzeczpospolita* was not Poland, and to enforce his message he included numerous photos of icons, Ukrainian churches, and cossacks. When it was first published, his book was the only postwar Soviet-bloc publication in which readers could find pictures of Vyhovsky and Mazepa.

His account of the annexation of Galicia drew attention not to trade or economic interest as causes, though he admitted the Polish economy benefited from annexation, but to the close dynastic links between the two ruling families and the threat Lithuanian and Tatar control of the region would have posed to Poland. Jasienica noted that Polish rule was beneficial because although the Rus elite Polonized, the territory never stopped being Ukrainian. To make his point he reminded readers of the fate of the original Prussians at the hands of the Teutonic Knights, and added that Casimir IV issued documents in Latin and Old Ukrainian.[34] Jasienica wrote that there was no such thing as a "Jagiellonian idea" in the fourteenth century, when Poles did not think of controlling areas as far away as Kiev. Echoing interwar findings, he wrote that in 1386 the status of Ukrainian lands was left intentionally vague to leave open future options. He added that one of the architects of the agreement was Jagiello's Ukrainian treasurer, Dmytro of Horai, who thought the Union would benefit his native land. The Union of Lublin is described as brilliant diplomacy that had very bad consequences for Poland and Polish-Ukrainian relations.[35]

In 1569, Jasienica explained, Poland got control of a region that geopolitically should have been a sovereign state. The act did not solve any problems but only pointed the way toward a solution. For Jasienica, Ukraine could have been "free" as a constituent third part of the Polish-Lithuanian Commonwealth. Poland had to win Ukraine through compromise, otherwise the only alternative was to get rid of it. But this alternative never materialized, not because of the attitude of the Polish gentry but because of the politics of the Rus magnate elite that could have done it. He decried their Polonization as "our great tragedy" and condemned their lack of political wisdom, noting that if there had been a party to negotiate the status of Rus with Warsaw in 1569, Warsaw would have negotiated. The only alternative representatives of Ukraine at the time were still in political embryo—the cossacks. By 1657 they had reached political maturity, as witnessed by the Hadiach treaty, but the Poles failed to provide military support while the opposition of the Ukrainian masses buried this promising plan of tripartite union. In historical terms, Poland's possession of Ukraine gave individuals fantastic prospects, but it brought the state to disaster.[36]

Jasienica pointed out that the most important religion in the country was Orthodoxy, which was benign until Catholic fanaticism questioned the political loyalty of non-Catholics. The Union broke with Polish traditions of toleration. It was brought about by Jesuits, a few bishops, and the king, all of whom represented Catholic reaction and political considerations, introduced ideology into politics, made agreement impossible, and destroyed the Orthodox hierarchy instead of creating one as Casimir IV did. In Ukraine, a violent frontier society characterized by war of all against all, the effect of the Union was to add oil to fire. According to the historian, the Ukrainian clergy could have stabilized the area had their energies not been focused on fighting each other. Jasienica's history of Poland was the only one to note that claims about Poland exploiting Ukraine were imprecise, since the state drew no inordinate tax revenues from Ukrainian and Polish peasants living there, and that cossack revolts involved much more than peasant unrest as they were linked to the European diplomatic game. By 1632 the cossacks identified themselves with the Orthodox Church and Rus nation. Jasienica reminded readers that although the mass of this nation, the peasants, undoubtedly were unfortunate, those who provoked them to fight gave little thought to social justice. Had Poland given the cossacks gentry status in 1632, he added, they would have been pacified.[37]

Jasienica's detailed treatment of the cossack wars underscored the differences between the masses and the cossacks. He argued that Khmelnytsky had basically desired that Cossack Ukraine become a third part of the Commonwealth. The war dragged on because there could be no solution to the Polish-Ukrainian dilemma. Dull Polish conservatism on one side and excessive Ukrainian primitivism on the other simply forced Khmelnytksy to keep fighting. Forced to wage war but too weak to attain his political objective alone, he had to turn to foreign powers and in 1653 had no other choice than Russia. Jasienica reminded readers that the tsar's envoys refused to swear to maintain cossack rights, that the tsars never recognized the existence of a Ukrainian nationality, and that Kiev and Moscow were the Rome and Byzantium of the Orthodox world. Khmelnytsky could defend Ukrainian autonomy, yet realizing the threat posed by Russian centralism he not only kept the terms of the Pereiaslav treaty secret but acted independently despite them. Jasienica explained that the treaty did not "join" Ukraine and Russia, but partitioned the country between Poland and Russia. Khmelnytsky sought an independent cossack state including all Ukraine, but ultimately failed.[38] In a fine account of the difficulties surrounding the hetman in his last days, Jasienica remarked that it was no wonder the old leader finally had a stroke.[39]

Jasienica wrote that the Hadiach treaty reflected well on the Ukrainian cossack elite and that since independence was not possible the agreement represented the best alternative. It failed, and by 1670 the Ukrainian question had degenerated into a game for adventurers.

Although known to prewar Ukrainian historians, the fate of Ivan Vyhovsky's brother stopped being mentioned in Soviet-bloc publications. Jasienica used it to remind readers of the darker sides of Russian rule. On the tsar's orders the cossack colonel's flesh was first cut apart with the knout. His eyes were plucked out and the sockets filled with silver, his ears were then bored out with a drill and the holes filled with silver. Finally, his fingers were cut off and his veins pulled out of his legs.[40]

An extended section on Mazepa began with the comment: "Ukraine does not exist to be subjugated to Poland or Russia." Mazepa himself, it continues, if he had belonged to a less unfortunate nation, would have been internationally recognized as an able statesman under whose rule Ukraine created a stable elite. Jasienica's account of Mazepa's alliance with Sweden explained it as an understandable reaction to the excesses of tsarist centralization.[41] Finally, his book depicted the Haidamak revolt as a reaction to the Bar Confederation's declaration of religious war on the Orthodox. He did not know which side was worse in dealing with its enemies, and condemned the Bar confederates for being as stupid as those Ukrainians who had opposed the Hadiach treaty.[42]

6

Monographs and Articles on Ukrainian Subjects

INTERWAR PUBLICATIONS

Pamphlets dealing with Polish-Ukrainian relations through the centuries usually presented the subject within the following context: "From the East came invasions, murder, and conflagration, while law and order and constructive work came here [Western Ukraine] only from Poland, that is, from the West."[1] One of the surveys of Polish-Ukrainian relations in Galicia was by Zakrzewski and Pawlowski, who argued that the region was originally Polish and that the Rus princes, not Poles, were the invaders in the fourteenth century. Casimir IV, as legal heir, had planned to secure Galicia to enable Poland to fight for Gdansk and its western provinces. His campaigns in the east did not stem from a resignation of western ambitions.[2] From the fourteenth through the nineteenth centuries there was no Polish-Rus problem, as proven by the absence of Ukrainian revolts against the Polish state. Poles initially tolerated the nineteenth-century Ukrainian national movement, which the authors characterized as a "special Rus ideology: containing elements of bandit cossack, haidamak mentality, combined with use of terrorist methods in cultural struggle, and backing by Austrians and Russians." A similar view was propounded in a short history of Eastern Galicia written for the Polish army. The pamphlet explained that the region was Polish because of the economic, military, and political effort Poles had put in through the ages. "Red Rus [Galicia] was indebted to Polish settlers for its agricultural development" and exposure to Western culture.[3]

In interwar Poland the nearest equivalent to an academic survey of Ukrainian history was by the liberal Leon Wasilewski. His book, actually a history of the Ukrainian national movement, summarized pre-nineteenth-century Ukrainian history in the first two chapters. Wasilewski implied that Casimir's occupation of Galicia was a conquest rather than an inheritance, and he mentioned Poland's "civilizing mission" only once, in reference to the Polonization of the Rus elite. He characterized the 1648 uprising as a national-religious war sparked by a conflict over estate rights and saw Khmelnytsky's treaty with Russia in 1654 as a last resort intended to extricate Ukraine from a desperate situation. There ensued a struggle over the degree of autonomy, which led to Vyhovsky's attempt to break with tsarist centralism and later, to a last similar attempt by Mazepa. Wasilewski was one of the few Polish historians to mention the abolition of the office of hetman (1762) and cossack autonomy (1782). He also noted that there had been a cultural revival under Polish rule, but once Ukraine had been divided between its two neighbors elites either Polonized or Russified. He claimed that from the beginning of its rule over Ukraine Moscow had administratively imposed Russification as a conscious policy.[4]

Wasilewski's account of modern Ukrainian history was the most detailed available in Polish during the interwar period. He saw the national movement as a product of Western European liberal-romanticism, which awakened autonomist ideas, stimulated populism, and provided a basis for the emergence of a new national consciousness. The movement reached a high point in 1846 with the formation of the Cyril and Methodius Brotherhood and the work of Shevchenko, who was first to clearly formulate the wishes of reborn Ukraine. Wasilewski regarded the Galician Uniate clergy and intellectuals as an "artificial" Austrian creation and dated the national movement there not from the late eighteenth-century Josephine reforms but from the 1830s. The most important person was Markian Sashkevych, he continued, who had advocated the right of Ukrainians to develop as other Slavs did. Under the influence of Eastern Ukrainians and Polish revolutionaries, Galician-Ukrainians devoted special attention to education to raise peasant national consciousness. The Austrians in 1848, he wrote, did not "create" a Ukrainian nation but only exploited what existed, while the *Holovna Ruska Rada* proclaimed that Western Ukrainians were part of the Ukrainian nation.

In the Tsarist empire, the Ukrainian movement was small and primarily a cultural phenomenon. Persecuted by the regime, which treated it as if it were politically separatist and socialist, activists shifted their activity to Eastern Galicia. Initially there were problems as the more opportunist, clerical, conservative westerners reacted against attempts of the easterners to impose liberal and radical notions into political programs. Wasilewski provided a short account of the parties and platforms in Galicia and tsarist Ukraine, and pointed out that the movement remained a cultural-literary current until the beginning of the twentieth century.[5] The author was critical of Ukrainian populists for not supporting the Polish revolt of 1863, but did not elaborate. He explained that because land was available and cheaper in Eastern Galicia than in Poland proper, Polish settlers settled en masse and contributed to national conflict. Tension was heightened because the province was a center for the Polish as well as Ukrainian national movement.

In 1917, the Ukrainian movement in the Russian Empire became a mass phenomenon. But whereas the Central Rada stood for autonomy and moderation, the peasants demanded political separation, a national army, and radical land reform. Centralist Russian liberals opposed the Rada while the Bolsheviks supported Ukrainian demands in Petersburg but opposed them in Kiev. Wasilewski dismissed the Kharkiv Soviet government as a puppet regime and noted that only the Russians and Jews in Ukrainian cities supported the Red Army. The Rada, which signed an alliance with Germany because of Bolshevik invasion, was dissolved when it protested the excesses of German requisitions. Wasilewski described the program of the Directory, which took power from Hetman Skoropadsky in 1918, as Bolshevist and different from Lenin's regime only insofar as it sought to realize its objectives in a less bloody manner. The Directory failed because it had no control over the countryside where Bolsheviks successfully exploited a radicalized peasantry.[6] In Galicia, Ukrainians took power with Austrian help in 1918 and ignored the rights of Poles. Pilsudski fought the "usurpers" but the Polish right to rule Eastern Galicia was not recognized by the Entente until they were faced with the threat of Bolshevik victory over Poland. War did not bring liberation to Ukraine since the Soviet Ukrainian Republic was a fiction—a concession necessary to maintain Russian power in Ukraine.

As in the nineteenth century, the major Ukrainian subjects of interest for interwar Polish historians were cossack and religious history. The first published monographs on cossack subjects dealt with the Hadiach treaty, and their appearance in the early 1920s coincided with a period when Ukrainian-Polish relations were a major concern of Polish foreign policy. Articles dealing with the Ukrainian churches appeared against the background of a long intensive debate over what their status should be in the interwar state.

Two posthumously published studies by Ludwig Kubala provided detailed factual accounts with clear expositions of reasons for Ukrainian differences with Russia in 1656. Especially valuable in his study was the comparison of the original Hadiach treaty text with the version recorded in *Sejm* protocols. The former stipulated that no Uniate or Catholic senators were to be allowed in the three Cossack-Ukrainian provinces and that the cossacks would be under no obligation to fight Russia. The other version allowed Uniates to remain, permitted alternate Catholic senators in two of the three provinces, and made no reference to the obligation of fighting Russia.[7] Kubala attributed the idea of a tripartite Commonwealth to King Jan Casimir, but opposition on both sides was too strong for the treaty to hold. Rank and file cossacks were more concerned with social equality than the fact that the accords secured for their country a strong position in the Commonwealth from which they could have pursued their interests further. Except for the Court, the Poles disliked giving away gentry status en masse, opposed recognizing the equality of faiths, and disliked the fact that the treaty permitted the hetman to command an army independent of the *Sejm*. Kubala claimed it was difficult to determine whether at the time Poland was too weak to hold on to Ukraine.[8] A. Prochaska (1920), using Vyhovsky's will, drew attention to his important role in formulating Khmelnytsky's politics and observed that although Vyhovsky was shot by the Poles for treason, the charge was unfounded and unjust.[9]

A 1923 survey history of the cossacks by F. Rawita-Gawronski explained that they had been merely nomads and bandits whose anarchic rebellions couldn't be compared to other popular revolts because they had no justifiable reasons or constructive aims. Not representing a national interest, and concerned primarily with whiskey, cossack leaders only used religion to attract peasant support. Their evolution into a Frankenstein's monster was abetted by misguided Polish policy that sought to compromise rather than to destroy them. Gawronski wrote that Khmelnytsky, possibly a Jew, was able but became unbalanced after his successes. Khmelnytsky was motivated by revenge and the cossacks were provoked to fight by the most primitive among them whose only objective had been more booty. The masses joined the adventure because they were by nature anarchic. The Polish-Ukrainian conflict was one of barbarism versus civilization, and although Gawronski did note that Khmelnytsky had a dim idea of cossack autonomy by 1649, he insisted that the hetman continued the war primarily because of his pride and love of fighting. He gave no reasons for the 1654 treaty and argued that Khmelnytsky by then had wanted statehood but ended up with provincial autonomy based on army, not territorial rights. The treaty, he explained, represented a sell-out of Ukraine to the tsar by the officers in return for personal land grants.[10] Faced with tsarist centralism, the hetman changed his mind and attempted to renew Polish ties. Gawronski admits that by the end of his life Khmelnytsky, who initially thought only in terms of estate politics, was thinking in national terms. This evolution was continued by Vyhovsky and was reflected in the Hadiach treaty, which was the first legal document and treaty to use the term "Rus nation." The agreement was based on the principles of 1569, but failed to attract mass support as too few Ukrainians were able to comprehend its importance.[11]

The Hadiach agreement failed not only due to anarchy, ambition, and intrigue in the Ukrainian camp, but also because the Poles did not understand its significance. Gawronski sympathetically described Mazepa as an intelligent man who planned to administratively reorganize the cossacks and to create a Rus state. Mazepa understood the meaning of liberty because he was raised in Poland, but his people understood the concept only in terms of economic independence and regarded all laws as oppressive and tantamount to slavery. Ukrainians wanted to live like birds and such people could not support or be influenced by political ideas. The cossack officers were worse than the anarchic Polish gentry as they had all the bad traits of the latter without any of their redeeming virtues. After Mazepa's failed bid for freedom in 1709, tsarist administrative centralization eventually turned Cossack Ukraine into a province. Because cossack leaders put class above national interests, they failed to create a state in a rich land. Gawronski's account of the Haidamak revolts was as dismissive as his prewar monograph about them. He claimed that those who participated were provoked and deceived by their leaders with the connivance of Catherine II, who hated Catholicism, as befitted a Protestant. If Orthodox priests consented to and took part in the bloodshed, he continued, then their behavior had only reflected their low level of education, spirituality, and morality. Gawronski argued that the Bar Confederation had nothing to do with the revolt and that allegations about its anti-Orthodox policies were merely rumors spread by the Russians.[12]

Z. Stronski, writing on early cossack revolts, explained that Poland could have dealt with the cossacks in only one of two ways: it either had to profoundly change its policies or destroy them. The latter alternative was not viable because the cossacks were not mere brigands but enjoyed mass support, while the first had been possible because the state did realize that cossack revolts were directed against gentry oppression, not the crown. Agreement was theoretically possible. Cossack revolts were not national as Ukrainians had no national consciousness yet, because the masses had no conception of "social revolution," and because religion was not an issue for them.[13] E. Chrząszcz drew attention to Khmelnytsky's extensive ties in 1649 with Turkey and Transylvania and noted that he had planned the destruction of Poland during the winter of 1648.[14] In a second article describing Ukrainian-Turkish relations in 1648-1649, he claimed Khmelnytsky was a Turkish vassal and had signed a trade treaty with the Sultan.[15]

A leading modern Polish historian of Ukraine was Władyslaw Tomkiewicz. In an article on the cossack revolt of 1630, he argued that it had been the first in which religion played the key role. It polarized opinion and ensured that an earlier attempt by clerics from both sides to resolve the religious division would not be successful. Tomkiewicz observed that although the Poles won battles against the cossacks, they never imposed hard conditions.[16] In a second major article he studied the Hadiach treaty and argued that Polish policy faced the alternative of recognizing the cossacks as peasants or as gentry. During the first half of the seventeenth century the gentry had tried to force them into the peasantry, while the treaty of 1659 recognized a selected number as gentry. The treaty failed because it came too late for Ukraine, where civil war had broken out over the issue of equality versus gentry liberties for a few, and too early for the Poles, who were still fighting Sweden. Both sides regarded the agreement as a temporary expedient and necessary evil. Tomkiewicz noted that although Poland accepted the final version of the treaty, the mass of Ukrainians did not because they had no understanding of the idea of statehood. Ukrainian leaders were ultimately more responsible than the Poles for its failure because they thought chaos was normal in politics and that they could balance indefinitely between two powers. Tomkiewicz also drew attention to the destructive consequences in Ukraine of Russian anti-Polish agitation, the small number of Vyhovsky's supporters, and his destructive jealousy of potential rivals. Tomkiewicz, unlike Kubala, believed the Poles had no military forces with which to assist Vyhovsky.[17]

In 1939, Tomkiewicz published a popular history of the cossacks. His theme was that cossacks, an anomaly in the Polish social order, could neither be forced into the peasantry nor all made gentry, and that therefore their revolts had been unavoidable. Nevertheless, cossacks fought as often for as against Poland. The cossack question originated with their raids on the Turkish Black Sea coast, which threatened Poland with Ottoman attack, and later took on a social dimension as magnates establishing estates began threatening to dispossess cossacks already settled on the land. Religion emerged as an issue after 1620, when the cossacks became protectors of Orthodoxy and thus acquired prestige among their own people. What began as an estate revolt in 1648 quickly turned into a religious and national war for statehood. The Treaty of Pereiaslav was only a military alliance, while the Hadiach accords reflected Vyhovsky's desire to establish a state. The latter treaty failed but had great moral significance. Because the politics of Khmelnytsky and Vyhovsky were "doublefaced" and inconsistent, both men contributed to the demoralization of the cossacks, who finally divided into two groups and then split the country. Born in warfare against nomads, the cossacks adopted their psychology and were incapable of creative work in a peaceful social order.[18] Tomkiewicz saw Mazepa's politics as an attempt to break away from the Russian centralization that threatened Ukraine. The historian was critical of the Haidamaks, whom he depicted as robbers used by Russia against Poland. Cossackdom, he concluded, was not a major factor in Poland's decline, only the first nail in the coffin.

Kazimierz Tyszkowski wrote one of the few articles that appeared in interwar Poland on Polish-cossack cooperation—stressed in many survey histories of Poland. Tyszkowski elaborated on an idea of prewar historiography when he outlined the political dilemma the cossacks presented to Poland. The Court could avoid internal problems with them by directing their energies abroad, either in support of its dynastic ambitions or as soldiers in crusades. But such projects provoked the gentry, who feared royal power and opposed foreign wars. Conversely, the cossacks could not be militarily destroyed because they were a major component of the Polish army and needed as a defense force. In 1612-1614, for example, after fulfilling a major role in the Muscovite campaign, the cossacks could not be paid and consequently caused as much havoc plundering on the Polish as on the Russian side of the border. Each campaign they fought in, moreover, increased the cossacks' sense of their own power. Tyszkowski also drew attention to cossack cooperation with Catholics and pointed out that the religious divide had not always been as great as later historians often made it out to be.[19]

Polish historiography of the Ukrainian churches was written against a backdrop of a renewed Vatican initiative to extend the Church Union, and a celebrated 1927 government libel case against the editor of a Ukrainian magazine who had published a letter by Ukrainian members of the parliament condemning Poles for oppressing Ukrainians in the past. Kazimierz Lewicki (1929) was critical and argued that the Union initiative came from the nuncio in Poland rather than the Jesuits, whose main concern had been the conversion of individuals. Success seemed likely because, initially, the de facto political representative of the Orthodox Church in the Commonwealth at the time, Prince Kostiantyn Ostrozhsky, was willing to negotiate.[20] In 1933, Lewicki examined the role of the Union in state politics and suggested that it had been a political rather than a religious affair from the beginning. The Vatican forced the issue, which was at odds with Polish state interests, and thereby created problems for Poland. The Union was established only in Western Ukraine and had successes under Sigismund III, thanks to his Catholic convictions, and again under King Jan Sobieski, thanks to political circumstances. The Polish clergy, for their part, disliked the Union because it denied them the possibility of getting Orthodox land, while the Catholic gentry were indifferent. Ukrainian pro-Union prelates under Jesuit influence hoped the Union would help them reform their church.[21]

In a study of Ostrozhsky's role in the Union, Lewicki argued the matter was a purely social and political affair. He provided a useful summary of literature, simplistically divided into Catholic and Orthodox points of view, and took the side of the latter. He argued that the Jesuits had little to do with the Union and added that he personally thought it had been a good plan that failed because it was badly implemented. The major error lay in trying to impose the Union conspiratorially before publicly convincing the Orthodox of its benefits. Defending Ostrozhsky from those who accused him of opposing the Union for selfish personal reasons, Lewicki claimed he was motivated by conservatism, concern for religious freedom, and fear of absolutism.[22] Lewicki was one of the few Polish historians to describe the Ukrainian cultural revival and the activities of the Ukrainian urban confraternities (*Bratstva*). He pointed out that their cultural achievement would have been greater had they not been distracted by the religious conflict.

Other Polish historians of the Ukrainian churches sought to demonstrate that the Union of Brest had been in Polish interests and did not lead to systematic state-sponsored persecution. Tomkiewicz argued that the Orthodox Church in the Commonwealth had been basically loyal and had split over the question of relying on the cossacks after its last major patron, Ostrozhsky, had died. The resistance to the Union was well organized and Tomkiewicz stressed it was subversive inasmuch as it had foreign backing, but he also identified the internal social interests behind it. He claimed that the lower clergy disliked the prospect of Uniate reforms centralizing the church, while the Patriarch feared losing a source of revenue. The cossacks, he explained, only used religion as a tactic, while the opposition of most of the Catholic gentry meant the Union could survive only thanks to royal support. The Polish Crown faced the dilemma of being unable to nullify the Union yet simultaneously trying to meet Orthodox demands in order to keep that church apart from the cossacks.

In 1648, religion was not an issue during the uprising because the Orthodox Church had been legalized 16 years earlier. Although the provincial clergy supported Khmelnytsky, the prelates were initially indifferent, while Khmelnytsky used religion only for tactical reasons. Influenced by the Patriarch of Jerusalem—described as a Russian agent—he began thinking of an anti-Catholic league and adopted the role of defender of the faith. Tomkiewicz reminded readers that because Russian and Ukrainian orthodoxy were different, the Kievan clergy opposed the Pereiaslav agreement.

During the Haidamak revolt, however, the clergy was used by the Russians as an instrument of anti-Polish intrigues.[23]

Two histories of the Ukrainian churches were published in the interwar period. Kazimierz Chodynicki completed one volume of a planned history to 1919, and the published version of his manuscript covered the years 1370 to 1632. The manuscript of two subsequent volumes was lost in 1944. The main subject of his definitive study was the relationship between the state and the Orthodox hierarchy. Chodynicki argued that, despite conflicts, the Church remained basically loyal and was not repressed by the state. The crown fulfilled its formal obligation to defend and benefit the church insofar as the king and the laws guaranteed its possessions and authority, and supported confraternities. Polish policy, in accord with Orthodox teaching, recognized the principle of separate Orthodox churches for separate states and the decline of Orthodoxy in the Commonwealth during the sixteenth century, he stressed, was not the fault of the state but flowed from the lack of appropriate candidates for higher office. Because Orthodox prelates were not eligible for the Senate, the great Rus families were not interested in pursuing careers in that church.[24] Chodynicki pointed out that Ostrozhsky opposed the Union of Brest because he had not been consulted, as was his right, while the king did not declare himself in favor until the bishops had done so. Yet the king continued to recognize Orthodox rights, as shown by his acceptance of Orthodox petitions.[25] Chodynicki showed that the king opposed the use of force in 1596, and he provided the first extended discussion in Polish of the *Sejm* debates on the Union. This issue, he revealed, was of little public concern until four or five years after the event, and even then protest came primarily from Protestant provinces and areas controlled by Ostrozhsky. Most of the Catholic gentry were indifferent and Moscow played no role until at least 1620, while promising attempts at compromise were sabotaged by the cossacks.

Chodynicki's detailed discussion of the relationship between the religious struggle and foreign politics demonstrated that cossack contacts with Sweden, Transylvania, and Holland had been more important than those with Moscow. These relations posed a serious threat to Poland, but were partly neutralized by internal differences. The cossacks were divided into registered and non-registered, and pro- and anti-Polish factions, while not all Orthodox bishops were prepared to engage in anti-Polish activity. Cossack revolts were initially estate and social rather than confessional in nature, but once the cossacks became involved in religious affairs they hindered attempts at agreement.[26]

A second history of the Ukrainian churches, by Janusz Wolinsky, senior administrator in the Department of Orthodox Affairs (1931-1939), was less detailed but covered events up to 1796. Wolinsky wrote his book to acquaint himself with the institution under his supervision. Like Chodynicki, he noted that Casimir IV introduced restrictions on the Orthodox to protect the Catholic minority, and that proof of Polish tolerance lay in the absence of Rus gentry complaints of persecution. What religious based restrictions existed were dropped in 1572 for all gentry, and the restrictions that remained in towns did not stem from state policy but the Magdeburg Law, which gave full rights only to Catholics. In general, social circumstances, the fact that most Orthodox were peasants, and the decentralized structure of Poland allowed the Orthodox Church considerable autonomy and thus made it different from its counterpart under tsarist rule. Wolinsky devoted considerable space to church organization and noted that the denial of Senate seats for Orthodox bishops had been a factor in its decline. Whereas the confraternities played an important role in reviving the church, their considerable influence within the church was also responsible for the internal conflict that set the stage for the Union. Papal primacy was the major stumbling block to agreement between Uniates and Orthodox after 1596, and Wolinsky reminded readers that in 1628 the Patriarch decreed that all but two confraternities were to submit to church control. After Poland legalized the Orthodox Church in 1632, division of property between it and the Uniates emerged as the major problem. Although the first uprising in the name of religion was in 1630, the Orthodox Church remained neutral in 1648, while under Muscovite rule Ukrainian and Russian prelates were at odds as they each had different rituals and notions of church-state order. Wolinski also briefly described the incorporation of the Ukrainian church into the Russian. He noted that the 1596 royal decree was never used to justify oppression, pointed out that the state did not restrict Orthodox rights in Poland until after the cossack wars, and that the first such act, in 1676, only forbade contact with the Patriarch. He traced the first appearance in Polish documents of the derogatory term "disuniate" to 1668.[27] As Russians attempted to turn the Ukrainian Orthodox Church into their tool, the Poles reacted by increasing restrictions in an attempt to limit Russian interference. Wolinsky claimed that during the Haidamak revolts the Orthodox Church exploited minor issues, made exaggerated claims of persecution, and then used these incidents as a pretext to call for full equality with the Catholics. The Russians supported such tactics in order to weaken Polish reformers and strengthen the conservatives. But Polish conservatives refused even those minimal concessions required by Petersburg, and Ukrainian fear of possible persecution sparked the bloodshed of 1768.

In a major change from the pattern of earlier historiography, interwar Polish historians devoted as much attention to Ukrainian lands in the Unions of Lublin and Krevo as they did to cossacks and religion. Oskar Halecki, Henryk Łowmianski, and Henryk Paszkiewicz wrote major studies about the Krevo Union.

Halecki (1916) concluded that "Rus" in 1386 was not a national but a political term, since some Rus lands (northern Belarus) belonged to the Grand Duchy, while others were separate principalities. He claimed that the provisions of the Krevo Union applied only to Rus lands administratively part of the Duchy and not all Ukraine.[28] In a second article Halecki tackled the question of why Rus did not become a third part of the kingdom. Noting that the word "applicare" in the act was imprecise, in contrast to other key terms, he postulated that those who had compiled the terms themselves were unclear about the nature of future relations. While Lithuania was a distinct political and administrative unit, "Rus" referred to a number of provinces united in the person of the Grand Duke, and when he became Polish king, "Rus" simply became part of Poland. Jagiello kept the region divided into provinces in order to provide himself with benefices for relations, which he distributed to diffuse opposition. Thus, Jagiello controlled "Rus" after 1386 even though its provinces no longer formally belonged to his dynasty. Also, since the Hungarian king at that time included "Rex Russiae" in his title, it would have been dangerous for Poles to treat it as a unit. In 1392, the threat of a Lithuanian alliance with the Teutonic Knights led Jagiello to recognize Lithuanian-Rus (without Volyn) as a separate administrative unit. Jagiello now sought to rid Rus of local potentates and place it under stronger royal control.[29]

Łowmianski (1937) reached similar conclusions and claimed that Lithuania and its Rus lands were incorporated directly into Poland after 1386. After an exhaustive comparison of the Krevo articles with similar agreements made in the rest of Europe, Łowmianski concluded that the Lithuanian Rus lands, like Lithuania itself, after 1386, devolved into separate provinces owing allegiance to the Polish king. Provincial princes who refused to swear fealty to Jagiello as Polish king lost their thrones. Although Poland did not actually control the region after 1392, the Settlement of 1386, which imposed incorporation, was never annulled.[30] Paszkiewicz (1938) devoted more attention to the Ukrainian dimension of the Union and argued that fear of the Teutonic Knights induced Lithuania to seek union with Poland against them and, in return, to give up its Rus lands. Lithuanians used the vague term "applicare" in the text intentionally to keep their own options open. He added that it was impossible to determine the details of relations because many of the original documents were missing.[31]

Halecki (1915) wrote what is perhaps the definitive study of the place of Ukrainian lands in the Union of Lublin. Using sources other than the long-known 1569 *Sejm* diaries, of which the most important were correspondence, and *Sejm* diaries written during the preceding 20 years, he pointed out that Polish claims on Volyn and Podlassia provinces originated in border conflicts. Polish claims received convenient historical legitimation in the second half of the sixteenth century because these disputes coincided with the dissemination of Kromer's chronicle, published in 1555 and 1558, which claimed that lands annexed in 1386 were historically Polish. There were opponents of incorporation on the Polish side as well as supporters on the Lithuanian-Rus side. Indeed, the latter were a majority, and this discouraged the Lithuanians opposed to the Polish Union plan. In a departure from earlier views, Halecki accepted as true the excuses given by the Rus lords Sangushko and Ostrozhsky for their reluctance to swear allegiance. Halecki claimed they had resigned themselves to the situation and only played for time to see how the affair would develop. Their reluctance stemmed from concern about their personal status and the Orthodox religion.[32] Halecki recounts the interesting case of the Polish Catholic Bishop of Lutsk, J. Wierzbicki, who opposed the Union and sent letters to the king written in Old Ukrainian explaining that he would not attend the *Sejm*.

The idea of including Kiev province into Poland came late. It probably originated at court and was realized thanks to the personal efforts of the king. Unexpected support came also from the Volyn gentry, who argued that separation of their province from other Rus lands would break up families as it would lead to some members having Polish gentry liberties and others not. Most of the Lithuanian nobility was little concerned about losing central Ukraine to Poland because the transfer would shift from their shoulders and purses the burden of defense.[33] The annexation of Volyn and Podillia provinces was justified as a tactic to force Lithuania to agree to Union, Halecki claimed, but Kiev province was unnecessary and brought Poland the burden of defending a border against Tatars, Muscovy, and later, cossacks. This region also provided the future base of magnate power. But in 1569, the gentry did not concern itself with these complications as they were attracted by the vast tracts of land that would become open to settlement after incorporation.

A pamphlet on the Lublin Union by Halecki (1916) contains generalizations not found in his detailed studies. Here he noted the weakness of the Union was that it included three nations but only two states, which between them divided Rus lands. He added that this did not come about through force but because a Rus state had ceased to exist long before 1569. The Commonwealth had no third partner because Rus national consciousness was underdeveloped. Rus had not made any demands to this effect but had wanted to join.[34]

In 1919, Halecki studied the history of Polish-Lithuanian relations from Krevo to Lublin with particular attention to the Ukrainian question. In this study, unlike his others, he used messianistic terminology and referred to the Union in terms of "Polish destiny." He claimed that after Rus fell only a Polish-Catholic Union could have ensured the region's future political development. Halecki now labeled the Union of Krevo a "program" of a country on a higher level of political development than its neighbors that provided an example and cultural model to others. Assimilation was necessary if one state was to emerge, and although politically evolving in this direction, progress was uneven. For Halecki, unity was the ideal and separate institutions were undesirable. Accordingly, he claimed that the Rus lands annexed after 1386 were worse off than Galicia, because unlike it, they retained their princes and old order. He called the Union of Lublin the final result of 184 years of synthesis begun by the Jagiellonian union. The Rus gentry saw and demanded Polish gentry rights and no one among them demanded their country be a third part of the *Rzeczpospolita*.[35]

The last major prewar article on the Union drawing attention to the position of Rus lands was by Łowmianski (1934), who, like Halecki, covered Polish-Lithuanian relations from 1386 to 1569 but focused on the socio-economic interests in Lithuania behind Union. He argued that the Lithuanians were too weak to simultaneously control Rus lands and deal with the Teutonic threat and therefore were prepared to ally with Poland even at the cost of surrendering sovereignty.[36] In the years preceding 1569, the Lithuanian gentry were changing from a military servitor group into a settled agrarian gentry more interested in rights vis-à-vis their prince and getting money to pay for a standing army, than serving in levies, which, in any case, could no longer keep enemies at bay. This made them more willing to agree to Polish demands, which included claims on Rus.[37]

Finally, S. Kot (1938) demonstrated that Rus nobles were not as indifferent to the terms of Union as Halecki suggested. On the basis of the letters of the secretary to the Chancellor of the Grand Duchy of Lithuania M. Radziwill, Kot revealed that threatened with dispossession they took the oath of loyalty to the king "with tears in their eyes."[38]

Casimir's occupation of medieval Galicia, the Ukrainian national movement, and the Haidamak revolts received little attention from interwar Polish historians.

In the mid-1930s, Podleski and Głuzinski depicted the national movement as an Austrian creation that Vienna used as convenient and without any long-term strategy. Thus, in 1848, Vienna supported the Uniate Church despite its Russophile orientation because Austrian policy was pro-Russian, while after 1854 it backed the national movement because Austria was then anti-Russian and its aim was to weaken Muscophile influence within its borders.³⁹ Wasilewski, by contrast, using published Ukrainian documents, showed that the Austrians agreed to a long-standing Ukrainian demand to divide Galicia only in 1915, but then withdrew because Ukrainians revealed these plans, which were supposed to have remained secret.⁴⁰

Gołąbek published a fundamental study of the Ukrainian movement in tsarist Russia.⁴¹ He focused on the Cyril-Methodius Brotherhood, whose formation marked the beginning of modern Ukrainian political development, and whose members provided Ukraine with a historical basis for independence claims. The author traced its roots to French, Polish, and German romanticism and memories of cossack autonomy, the Romantic literary awakening, political liberalism, and the Masonic movement. He provided a short biography of the major members, noting that all were concerned with social issues and classified their ideology as liberal Christian-humanist. In one of the first extensive discussions of relations between nineteenth-century Polish and Ukrainian intellectuals, he compared one of the founders, N. Kostomarov, with Adam Mickiewicz and pointed out that both nations were "enslaved" by Russia. Because Ukraine was closer to Poland culturally and socially, he claimed, Poles could play a key role in the Ukrainian awakening. The movement had little social impact, however, because it had no organization.

M. Handelsman (1937) studied the Ukrainian policies of nineteenth-century Polish émigré leader Adam Czartoryski, whose ambition had been to federate a united Right-Bank and central Ukraine with an independent Poland on the basis of the Hadiach treaty. Much of the monograph deals with the early Ukrainian movement, presented as the easternmost expression of the "Young Europe" movement. Using French archives and prewar Ukrainian monographs, Handelsman argued that Polish romantic ideas and revolutionary activity greatly influenced the founders of the Ukrainian movement in tsarist as well as Habsburg Ukraine. Handelsman pointed out that in Galicia the movement had existed before 1848, and that the Austrians had merely decided to exploit it that year to counter Russian influences. He criticized both sides for having failed to come to terms; the Poles for not understanding in 1848 that all Galicia was not Polish, and the Ukrainians for being blinded by anti-Polish sentiment.⁴²

In 1939 J. Skrzypek wrote the only scholarly treatment of the national movement in the early twentieth century in an attempt to fill a major gap in Polish scholarship—as he noted at the beginning of the essay.⁴³ Skrzypek listed political groups and platforms and provided a relatively detailed discussion of their relations with each other, as well as with the Russians and Austrians. He pointed out that the Austrian military and court were especially interested in the Ukrainians and had developed a long-range plan to divide the Empire into national units. They supported these nationalities as useful allies against Russia but offered them nothing specific. Any promises Vienna made were related to the alignment of forces within the government. The Germans were specifically interested in a separate Ukrainian state.[44] The author claimed that Ukrainians were more anti-Polish than Poles were anti-Ukrainian, because except for the right-wing, Polish groups sought agreement. Relations between west and east Ukrainians were weak and there were differences between them. Eastern Ukrainians were less interested in independence, and their national consciousness was weaker, while Galicians feared their countrymen's social radicalism.[45] Although Poles in Kiev supported Ukrainian independence in 1917, their backing quickly faded because of the Central Rada's radical land policy. Skrzypek did not discuss Polish-Ukrainian relations in Galicia and only noted that immediately before the Ukrainian coup in Lviv the Germans had moved Ukrainian military units to the city. The topic of Poles in central Ukraine was taken up the same year by Henryk Jabłonski, who argued that the Rada had attempted to put into practice the nationality theory developed by the Austrian Marxists, Renner and Bauer. He characterized the Rada as socialist and revolutionary and provided readers with a short history of the Ukrainian movement similar to Handelsman and Gołąbek's.[46]

Two works dealing with the Central Rada were published in 1919 and 1921. The first, by Ursyn-Zamarajew, an editor of a Polish newspaper under the Central Rada, gave readers a very favorable account of the Rada that explained Poland would find it easier to exist if Ukraine were independent.[47] The second, by E. Paszkowski, a former editor of *Dziennik Kijowski,* had little sympathy for Ukraine and argued that it had been Poland's obligation to put Ukraine's affairs in order. In the first part of his booklet, Paszkowski provided a detailed and dispassionate account of events in central Ukraine between 1917 and 1919. This was followed by an account that attributed events there to German intrigues, "cossack-haidamak instincts," and semi-intellectuals forced to resort to social radicalism when their nationalist appeals to peasants fell on deaf ears. Paszkowski explained that the Rada, unable to control anarchy in the countryside, tolerated it as a means of ridding Ukraine of Poles and Russians. Giving way to Bolshevik influences, Ukrainian leaders tried to be more radical, with the result that the war between Moscow and Kiev became a struggle between two kinds of Bolshevism.

Germany fomented the chaos in Ukraine by supporting the Directory in the hope of thereby denying the country to the Western powers.[48] In Galicia, Paszkowski wrote, "it's not Ukraine that is fighting in the name of the Fatherland against Poland, but the Ukrainian mob that is trying to break away from a legally run state in the name of centuries old slogans of anarchy and plunder."[49]

Few historians dealt with Casimir's campaigns in fourteenth-century Galicia, but, on the basis of earlier studies on Piast genealogy and scrutiny of available sources, some of those who did suggested that legitimacy of Polish claims to the territory did not have to be based on a written agreement. Stanisław Zakrzewski argued that the king's policy did not represent a sudden turn eastward at the price of a western orientation, but was a continuation of previous policy to maintain peaceful ties with the purpose of securing eastern frontiers. He pointed out that George II of Galicia had closer kin than Casimir to succeed him, and must have made arrangements to regulate succession with Casimir, although there is no extant text of such an agreement.[50] In a later article he noted that historians did not yet have a critical edition of the relevant documents. He doubted whether one often cited on the question of Galicia's legal status actually referred to George II.[51]

In a major and exhaustive study of this subject, Paszkiewicz (1925) concluded that Casimir took Western Ukraine by dynastic right in a move necessitated by Tatar raids, Lithuanian threats, and weak Rus princes. National issues were less important than estate interests, and Galician nobles did not recognize Lithuanian claims because Lithuania had dynastic rights only to Volyn, not Galicia.[52] Paszkiewicz explained that there had been no Polish-Hungarian agreement concerning Rus before Casimir's attack. He argued that the king's claim stemmed from the Piast family system of precedence, which gave him legal right to the principality without need of a formal document. An agreement was reached after the annexation and the king's purpose was total incorporation of the region into Poland.[53] Despite his promises to the pope, Casimir made no concerted effort to spread Catholicism in his new possession before 1370. He limited his initiatives to founding Catholic cathedrals wherever there was an Orthodox one. The king sought to mollify church conflicts where they arose but also was prepared to use conflicts in his own interests.[54] What missionary activity did occur was the work of religious orders and Catholic settlers, who entered the region and began spreading Catholicism and civilization east.

Only one study mentioned the Haidamaks, and it did so tangentially. Gilewicz (1931) argued that the revolts had not been spontaneous but erupted from agitation on the basis ideas found in the "Torchyn Manifesto," a document supposedly issued in Volyn, based on Enlightenment ideals, and calling for limits on serf obligations and political rights for commoners, as existed in Sweden. It was not clear whether this document was circulated by the monarchist reform party in Poland or whether Russians used it merely to undermine Poland.[55]

POSTWAR PUBLICATIONS

Three Polish survey histories of Ukraine were published between 1944 and 1982. One of these was the first scholarly Polish synthesis of Ukrainian history to cover all periods and appeared as part of a one-volume encyclopedia of Ukraine published by historians at Krakow's Jagiellonian University (1970).

The authors saw Casimir's annexation of Galicia as dynastic compensation for lands lost elsewhere that brought benefit to burghers and nobles. The status of the new territory was vague until 1434, when it was incorporated into Poland. Religious issues were not mentioned, and Rus lands in 1386 and 1569 received fleeting attention. During the Lublin Union, Ukrainian provinces were incorporated with the intention of using them to pressure Lithuania to agree to Polish terms. As a result, Poland became entangled in eastern affairs that played a major role in its later decline. The Union of 1596 was the work of the Curia, the Polish court, and a few Ukrainian bishops motivated by personal interests. Sigismund III's policies are labeled as decidedly anti-Orthodox. Although the revolts in Ukraine are called "antifeudal," the narrative makes it clear that they involved primarily cossack estate interests and stemmed from their annoyance with Polish attempts to control their raids on Turkish territory and vassals. The revolts slowly took on a national, social, and religious hue, and what began as an estate rebellion in 1648 became a struggle for an independent Ukraine by the end of that year. Khmelnytsky opened relations with Russia in 1649 because he sought a more reliable ally than the Tatars,[56] and in 1654 the tsar decided it was in his interest to join Ukraine to his domains. There followed a short summary of the Pereiaslav accords, mention of the abolition of cossack autonomy, but no characterization of Russian-Ukrainian relations except for the comment that the Pereiaslav treaty extended cossack liberties and secured religious freedom for the Orthodox.

The Hadiach treaty bore witness to the "profound changes that occurred during preceding years in the political consciousness of those responsible for the border politics of the Commonwealth." Ukrainian leaders, opposed by their own nation, were forced to flee. Similarly, Mazepa, who planned to separate from Russia and give Left-Bank Ukraine to Poland, was "not supported by the masses." The authors noted post-1709 tsarist restrictions on Ukrainian autonomy, but provided no explanation for Mazepa's policies. They did not mention that mid-century tsarist concessions on Ukrainian autonomy were related to Russia's Turkish wars.[57] The "anti-feudal" Haidamak revolts were attributed to the religious policy of the Bar Confederation. During those years, they added, the Orthodox received "much assistance" from Russia.

This survey was the first to provide Polish readers with a discussion of social and economic development in nineteenth-century tsarist Ukraine. It explained that the area initially provided markets for finished goods and a source of raw materials, and observed that political division hindered the evolution of Ukrainian national consciousness, which emerged in Kharkiv, was loyalist, and was rooted in cossack history. The text noted that the Decembrists and Polish intellectuals had little impact on Ukrainians, but claimed that Polish ideas did influence the founders of the Cyril-Methodius Brotherhood. The formation of this group marked a maturity of consciousness among the nation's representatives and the transformation of the Ukrainian movement from a cultural into a political phenomenon. Repressed, the movement revived in 1861. Because its leaders focused their attention on cultural issues, they failed to appreciate the importance of social reform and isolated themselves from the mass of the nation, who supposedly were more attracted by Russian radicals. Liberals, grouped around the politically moderate cultural organizations called *hromady,* very few of which cooperated with more radical populist organizations, were nonetheless repressed for allegedly advocating separatism. The authors claim that in cities Russification mollified the Russian-Ukrainian conflict and led to the solidarity of the working class against the Russian and Ukrainian bourgeoisie.[58]

The national movement developed "normally" only in Eastern Galicia. Vienna tried to win it over in 1848 by offering cultural and religious concessions, and the policy had the effect of making Poles anti-Ukrainian. The origins and evolution of each Ukrainian group is summarized with the comment that by 1876 Galicia, economically backward but part of a state with a limited constitutional order, had become the center of the Ukrainian national movement. The text included short descriptions of the various Ukrainian political parties and their programs.

In 1917, Bolshevik weakness and the political disorientation of the masses allowed the Central Rada to exploit the nationalist atmosphere and lead the national movement. Its initial aim of autonomy led to conflict with the Provisional Government, but common class interests eventually brought the two regimes together and separated the Rada from the Bolsheviks, who initially had supported its autonomist demands. The Rada ruled but could not administer most of Ukraine. With the formation of the Kharkiv Soviet government, promised aid by Moscow, and the Rada's refusal to give up power, there ensued a "bloody fraternal war" during which the Rada had to call on foreign powers. The Brest-Litovsk treaty forced the Bolsheviks to recognize Ukrainian independence, but the Rada was soon disbanded by the Germans. Meanwhile, in Eastern Galicia, Ukrainians, with the consent of Vienna, had taken power and demanded a state including all Ukrainian territory—which met with Polish and Romanian hostility. The allies finally allowed Poland to take over Eastern Galicia from fear of Bolshevist expansion, but they did not give Polish occupation de jure recognition.[59] The authors added that without Russian help the socialist revolution in Ukraine would not have triumphed. The Ukrainian Bolsheviks understood this and wanted closer ties with Russia.

Two surveys by Podhorodecki (1976) and Serczyk (1979) contained more detail than the Krakow text. They were the first Polish survey histories of Ukraine since 1854 to offer relatively detailed accounts of the Hetmanate and its abolition. They differed, however, in emphasis and omissions. Podhorodecki provided more statistics on social structure and economy, more attention to Ukrainian-Polish relations in Galicia, and was the only Polish historian to use the official Soviet concept of "Old Rus nation." Serczyk gave more space to the activities of Russian political groups in nineteenth-century tsarist Ukraine, and his treatment of the decades preceding 1917 closely resembled the official Soviet interpretation.

All three surveys attached little significance to Bogoliubsky's sack of Kiev in 1169. Serczyk did not mention it, while Podhorodecki simply noted it and remarked that the city of Vladimir was politically dominant in Rus for some years after the Mongol invasion. Podhorodecki, unlike Serczyk, noted Polish economic interest and Ukrainian political weakness as causes of Casimir IV's campaigns, but both explained that his aim had been incorporation. Neither historian gave details of Ukrainian lands in 1386 and noted only that they remained under Lithuania afterwards. Both remarked that the Union of Lublin initially stimulated Ukrainian economic development and provided a region for magnate estates. Serczyk stressed that the Union brought Poland into conflict with Moscow. Both accounts of the Union of Brest, cossack-peasant revolts, and economic development resembled the prewar positivist view. Serczyk characterized the revolts as peasant and "anti-feudal," although it emerges from his text that they were motivated initially by cossack estate interests and only later included the peasants. Both surveys had sections on the cultural revival and detailed Ukrainian social structure and economic development. Like Tomkiewicz, Serczyk thought that cossack ennoblement or autonomy had represented the only way Poland could have resolved its cossack problem. He also claimed that the 1625 revolt was particularly significant because for the first time, the cossack issue took the form of a conflict between Poland and a "semi-organized" cossack state. Serczyk did not give similar importance to the 1590 revolts, when Austrians played a role in provoking the cossacks.[60] Neither of the surveys mention the role of cossacks in Swedish and Transylvanian diplomatic combinations. Both authors saw the Union of Brest as the work of Rome and treated the religious question tangentially—as a reflection of deeper social and economic issues.

In Podhorodecki's opinion, Khmelnytsky's aim in 1648 was "feudal statehood," but cossack leaders soon realized liberation would not be possible without Russian assistance. He explained that despite historical, economic, and religious proximity some officers feared Russia would not respect their rights, and that in fact it did not respect them. Khmelnytsky subsequently signed an alliance with Sweden but refused to break the Pereiaslav treaty. Serczyk did not mention a statist aim in 1648 and used the phrases "desires to join" and "natural ally" in his discussion of Ukrainian-Russian relations. Like Podhorodecki, he pointed to the refusal of tsarist envoys to swear in the tsar's name to respect cossack rights, but added that the alliance had been a matter of vital urgency. Both noted that cossack reservations about the Russian alliance stemmed from an incompatibility between autocratic tsarism and the expectations of men accustomed to the gentry Polish order.

Serczyk saw the Hadiach treaty as a reaction to tsarist centralism, and like Podhorodecki, remarked that the agreement was a compromise fated to a short life. Podhorodecki added that opposition on both sides had been too strong for the agreement to succeed, while Serczyk observed that the tragedy of the hetmans, their rivalries and shifting alliances, became the tragedy of the country and its people.[61] Both historians described the cossack state and the slow erosion of its autonomy but neither treated this diminution as a cause of Mazepa's decision to join Charles XII. Both wrote that Mazepa wanted to rule a united Ukraine. Serczyk explained that the hetman betrayed the tsar because he switched sides only when he concluded that Peter would lose the war, but he made no reference to Mazepa betraying Ukraine or its people as did Soviet historians. Serczyk isolated, as the immediate cause of the abolition of the Hetmanate, Hetman Rozumovsky's attempt to make his office hereditary, and like the official Soviet view, claimed that political centralization favored the economic unity and development of Russia as well as its Ukrainian lands. Podhorodecki pointed out that in the eighteenth century, alongside economic development, the tie with Russia also destroyed Ukrainian independence and led to increased exploitation.[62] Neither historian thought Russian policy was a cause of the Haidamak revolt, and for both Catherine II intervened only because Haidamak raids into Ottoman territories had raised the spectre of a war with Turkey. Serczyk added that the Haidamak aim had been autonomy under tsarist rule and that political events responsible for weakening the Polish state at the time were as significant as socio-economic exploitation in causing the revolts.

Podhorodecki saw the origins of the Ukrainian national movement in the turn-of-the-century revival of historical memory, and identified the formation of the Cyril-Methodius Brotherhood as the moment a cultural movement became a political one. In Eastern Galicia the movement became political in 1848, against the backdrop of the national concessions that Vienna gave Ukrainians in return for support against the Polish nobility. Because Poles reacted to this nationalistically, Austria could easily stoke mutual antagonisms and keep both nations subjugated. Serczyk identified the influence of French ideas on the Brotherhood, whose emergence he characterized as marking the first phase in the formation of modern Ukrainian national consciousness. He gave more detail on events in Lviv in 1848, but unlike Podhorodecki did not indict both sides for inflaming national enmity, or mention that Austria played off both nationalities against each other and gave cultural concessions to Ukrainians in return for loyalty. Serczyk, like postwar Soviet historians, implied that the revolution of 1848 was causally related to peasant unrest, while Podhorodecki put events within the context of a politicizing national movement. Serczyk explained that because Polish politicians ignored Ukrainian national demands, Ukrainian liberals and conservatives made initiatives on their own to Vienna, expecting political liberties in return for a role as future "moderators" of Polish demands.[63]

Both authors dealt with the emergence of a Ukrainian "national bourgeoisie" in the wake of industrialization and noted the struggle against Russification. Podhorodecki explained that the liberal bourgeoisie ignored the social question and that because the working class was Russian in Ukraine, Ukrainian parties had little influence on it. Their membership was made up primarily of middle-level and rich peasants, intellectuals, capitalists, and petty bourgeoisie. Without elaborating, he wrote that capitalism "was conducive to the development of national life." Serczyk noted that capitalism led to assimilation and quoted Lenin on the desirability of both.

Whereas Serczyk claimed that the Bolsheviks devoted great attention to the national question, Podhorodecki wrote that they had failed to attract more supporters because they ignored it.[64] Conversely, both men paid more attention to Polish revolts in Ukraine than did the Krakow survey and noted that in Galicia the semi-constitutional order was conducive to national movements and political development.

Serczyk and Podhorodecki, like the authors of the Krakow survey, did not present the events of 1917 in Ukraine as an attainment of statehood by the national movement—neither the Rada nor the Kharkiv government was seen in these terms.[65] Both claimed that there were no differences between Lenin and the Kiev Bolsheviks concerning the Ukrainian question. In the Podhorodecki text there is a section on Poles in Ukraine where he noted that they participated on all sides during the Revolution, although the majority were either pro-Bolshevik or neutral, while Serczyk focused attention on Bolshevik activities in Ukraine and Petersburg. In relating the history of the Ukrainian Bolsheviks Serczyk did mention one instance of differences with Moscow, but in general his account is much closer to the Soviet version of events than Podhorodecki's. For example, the former wrote that by proclaiming political autonomy in its Third Universal, the Rada usurped the right to speak in the name of Ukrainian people at a time when the rural and urban proletariat thought their main task was to support the Bolshevik revolution and social reform, not to separate from Russia—especially once the socialist revolution had triumphed there. Union with Russia, he continued, threatened the Rada with revolution. Serczyk had only one reservation about the course of events in Ukraine: because workers were not Ukrainian, problems in statebuilding were not always resolved in the interests of Ukraine.[66] He did not mention the conflict of interests between the Rada and the Germans, nor the Bolshevik terror against nationalists. Serczyk described Bolshevik activities in Ukraine as if they occurred independently of the Russian Bolsheviks, who merely consented to requested aid. He explained that in Western Ukraine Polish interests were less important in explaining Polish policy than the Western project of an anti-communist bloc. The origins of ZUNR, he claimed, lay in the Habsburg refusal to agree to a separate Eastern Galician province. Neither mentioned, as did the Krakow survey, that the Austrian army supported Western Ukrainian demands. None of the three surveys actually explained why one side lost and the other won.

In postwar monograph studies devoted to Ukrainian subjects the cossack theme was the most popular. Baranowski (1948) discussed Tatar-cossack relations and noted that they cooperated as frequently as they fought. In 1648, the Crimean khan was willing and able to join the cossacks thanks to a treaty recently signed with his enemies, the Kalmucks.⁶⁷ Tomkiewicz (1948) looked at the social and national composition of the cossacks and demonstrated that by national origin the majority always had been Ukrainian. Others had already noted how their social composition had shifted from gentry to peasantry, but Tomkiewicz pinpointed this shift to the 1590s, when the higher nobility stopped joining because they had come to regard cossacks as a threat to their colonization. In the 1630s, the lesser Rus gentry stopped joining and the cossack rank and file quickly became primarily peasant, while the gentry predominated among the officers. From the 1630s, documents begin to refer to the cossacks exclusively as bandits.⁶⁸

The first articles on early-modern Ukrainian and cossack history written in accord with official guidelines were presented at a conference marking the tercentenary of the Pereiaslav agreement. Writing on the attitude of the gentry to the revolt S. Arnold repeated the Soviet view of the treaty as a "natural result" of the previous history of two "brother nations," and the basic underlying cause of the revolt. Arnold has the dubious distinction of being the only Polish historian ever to write that Ukrainian national liberation was attained thanks to "reunification" with the Russian nation.⁶⁹ He provided a political history of the Khmelnytsky period and claimed that the major concern of Poland had been to prevent this "union" from occurring. Presenting what would become a major theme in official historiography, Arnold wrote that Polish peasants and burghers supported the cossacks. Because they were faced with the threat of a serious revolt in Poland itself, the gentry could not deal as effectively with Khmelnytsky as they had wanted. During Khmelnytsky's uprising, "for the first time in history," bonds were forged between the Ukrainian and Polish nations on the basis of common struggle for social liberation. Z. Libiszowska claimed that Polish peasants were not interested in exploiting Ukraine and "opposed the meaningless anti-national class politics of the feudal camp."⁷⁰ Libiszowska described peasant revolts in Poland and identified instances of support which she linked to news of Khmelnytsky's victories and the work of cossack emissaries. O. Górka, writing on Khmelnytsky the man, provided a useful summary of Polish historiography about him and showed he had been a competent political leader and administrator who waged war against magnates, not the king or Polish peasants. The hetman's aim had been the establishment of a separate nation–state tied to Russia.⁷¹ Górka's detailed but slanted discussion of political history from 1648 to 1654 examined why it took six years to attain the "union" to which the hetman allegedly remained loyal until his death. Górka followed official guidelines but did not use Soviet terminology. Wawrykowa explained cossack revolts as popular national revolutions against Polish colonial oppression. More significantly, she devoted considerable attention to the early-seventeenth-century Ukrainian cultural revival. "Struggle for national survival led to the revival of intellectual life and development of culture," she wrote. She included lists of the contemporary publications and organizations in the first extended survey of this subject in Polish since Jabłonowski's 1912 monograph on the Kiev Mohyla Academy.[72]

In the early 1960s, J. Seredyka published a detailed study on Ukrainian-Russian relations between 1648 and 1649. Examining the question in realpolitik terms, he reminded readers that in 1648 the Polish-Russian anti-Ottoman treaty was still in force and that Khmelnytsky in his first letter to the tsar had offered him the Polish throne because he had feared the Russians would attack his rear. This did not occur because the tsar had his own revolts to contend with and feared Khmelnytsky's threat of retaliation. The tsar remained friendly with both sides and interested in obtaining the Polish throne peacefully.[73] In a second article he explained that in 1649 Khmelnytsky made no offer of submission to the tsar, who remained neutral because he mistrusted the Ukrainian leader once he had heard that Jan Casimir had been elected primarily thanks to the hetman's support. With no possibility of election the tsar lost interest in intervention.[74]

J. Perdenia published two studies in the 1960s on the fate of cossacks under Polish rule after 1654 and the dilemma they presented the state. Although the crown needed them for defense, the cossacks presented it with grave difficulties, given their ambition to unite both parts of Ukraine, and their conflict over lands with the gentry, who wanted to get rid of them altogether. The cossacks ignored the 1679 decree to disband since they thought the magnates had passed it against the royal will. Formally reestablished in 1684, the king used them until 1699, when they were again disbanded. There followed a period of revolts, and peace with Turkey after 1712 made the cossacks militarily unnecessary.[75] In a second article, Perdenia discussed the role of the cossacks in Polish-Russian relations between 1689 and 1712. While Poland's objective was to keep Right-Bank Ukraine, the cossacks wanted to unite with Russia, which, although friendly, refused to accept them as they were more useful as part of Poland, where they counterbalanced the gentry. The Russians offered to help Poland control unruly cossacks, but only in return for influence. Once Charles XII had been defeated and the cossacks no longer served a strategic purpose, Peter attempted to take the territory in question. Defeated in 1712, he returned it to Poland. The Right-Bank cossack officers, meanwhile, as the tsar's recent appointees, were loyal to Peter rather than to Mazepa.[76]

The early 1960s also saw the publication of two editions of a survey history of the cossacks to 1659 by Z. Wójcik, a student of Tomkiewicz. Though rich in detail, the book contained no new information on issues examined here. But its theme, that the cossacks presented Poland with an international rather than an internal problem, and that from its origins the cossack-Polish conflict had been a national issue, was novel in Polish historiography. Wójcik argued that the cossack problem could have been resolved within the Commonwealth but for gentry pride and a misguided policy toward the Orthodox Church. Colonization and the Brest Union were the key events that fanned hatreds and turned the Ukrainians and their church eastward.[77] Like Kubala, Wójcik noted that Poles committed their share of atrocities against Ukrainians, and like Jasienica he reminded readers how many magnate families were by origin Rus'ian. Wójcik saw Khmelnytsky's uprising as a struggle for national independence and titled the relevant chapter "Ukraine an Independent Land."

Wójcik explained that Russia in 1648 was not interested in what it regarded as another revolt. He compared Khmelnytsky to Mazarin and Cromwell and claimed the hetman realized his country could not be independent without allies. A faithful Crimean ally would have allowed the hetman to secure independence from Poland, but Tatar policy was to ensure a balance of power, which required a strong Poland. Wójcik viewed Khmelnytsky's alliance with Russia as a last alternative and, like Jasienica, described their initial contact as a meeting of two worlds with different conceptions of politics. Khmelnytsky thought in terms of independence, while the tsar saw Ukraine as an autonomous province.[78] Displeased at the end of life with the Pereiaslav agreement, the hetman moved closer to Sweden and Poland, and Vyhovsky continued this policy. But the majority of Poles and Ukrainians opposed agreement and the latter were backed by Moscow. Wójcik gave less space to details of the Pereiaslav treaty than to the Hadiach accords, which failed, in his opinion, because it was concluded 20 years too late.

In a thoughtful study related to the Hadiach treaty, R. Majewski (1967) traced most of its supporters to the ranks of the older, more established Right-Bank regiments and found very few came from the newer Left-Bank regiments, which feared that the treaty would exclude their closest kin from the ranks of the proposed cossack gentry.[79] Finally, Serczyk demonstrated that early-seventeenth-century Polish policy toward the cossacks in the short term had been dictated by foreign policy and the gentry's fear of the example cossacks set for peasants.[80]

In a major departure from the prewar pattern, when church history figured alongside cossackdom as the main Ukrainian subject for historians, the second major subject of interest for postwar historians was events in Eastern Galicia and Ukraine between 1917 and 1921. H. Jabłonski (1948), studying relations between Poland and Western Ukraine, compared Poles living there to Germans in western Poland. He explained that the West had urged Poland to recognize the ZUNR and that Polish rule over the territory had been illegal.[81] Jabłonski also published a monograph on Polish national autonomy in Ukraine under the Central Rada that reviewed Ukrainian policy toward the Polish minority in the context of Austro-Marxist national theory. The book provided a wealth of information on Ukrainian events, parties, and platforms. It referred to the Rada as a "typical revolutionary organization" that, even if only because of the demands of competition with Bolshevism, had to have a clear socialist hue. Because the Poles were socially petty-bourgeois and politically right-wing, the attempted cooperation, despite good intentions on both sides, was doomed to failure since big Polish landowners could not have come to terms with a radical Rada advocating a policy of estate parcellization. The Rada did not carry out its intentions and tried to win Polish cooperation but thereby alienated its own people. On the basis of the Ukrainian case, Jabłonski argued that Otto Bauer's theory of cultural national autonomy was wrong and implied that Stalin's was correct. In breach of Soviet orthodoxy, he added that the Ukrainian Social Democrats (SDs) and Socialist Revolutionaries (SRs) had truly supported proletarian revolution but that mistakes in their programs led them to try and compromise with those they had declared enemies at the beginning of the revolution.[82]

Stalinization of Polish scholarship obliged historians to follow guidelines and the first "new" essays were read at the First Methodological Conference in 1951. Those on Polish-Ukrainian relations in 1917-1921 examined the issue from the perspective of "Polish imperialism." Poland was characterized as a semi-colony belonging to the bourgeois camp of capitalism and "counter-revolution," and conquest of Ukrainian territory was in the interests of Polish capital.[83]

These ideas were elaborated upon in the proceedings of the tercentenary conference mentioned previously. One author covered events in Kiev in 1917 in an untitled subsection within an article on "Polish-Ukrainian brotherhood" from 1905 to the 1950s. Using Soviet categories, he divided the "nationalist bourgeoisie" into three groups—the clerical landowners, national liberals, and petty bourgeois nationalists—and explained that because rich peasants were stronger in Ukraine than in Russia during the Revolution, they could attract the middle peasants and make them "counter-revolutionary" with their nationalist rhetoric. The middle peasant also opposed the workers in part because of erroneous Bolshevik collectivization policy. In Western Ukraine, "Polish nationalism," supported by American and French capitalism, throttled the "bourgeois West Ukrainian Republic."[84] Jabłonski, in a short history of Soviet Ukraine, explained that the right to national self-determination had been a good thing because it was proclaimed by Lenin, and that the Ukraine's greatest good fortune was to have been in direct proximity to the world avant-garde proletarian Bolshevik party that had created the best possible perspectives for its development.[85] In a significant departure from his 1948 work, Jabonski now linked the Ukrainian SDs and SRs to the bourgeoisie, claimed that they had only used socialist phrases, that their policies were at odds with the interests of the Ukrainian masses, and that they had been incapable of liberating the country. He now depicted the Central Rada as "anti-national" from its beginnings and its socialism as a facade. The masses struggled for liberation through unity with Russia, led by Bolsheviks and with the assistance of the Russian proletariat. The fate of the ZUNR was dictated by Western powers, who waited to see if it could resist Bolshevism and thus, initially, did not allow Poland to occupy Western Ukraine.[86]

Articles on the events of 1917 in Ukraine published between 1967 and 1980 contained significant departures from this schema. Serczyk (1967) observed that the front had divided Ukraine and that leaders on each side understood the national question differently. In the east, people saw no difference between the Rada and the Bolsheviks and supported the former while the latter could only control a small part of the territory. Socially, the Rada was "reactionary," but its national program was "progressive" and initially supported by Lenin.[87] J. Kozik (1972) specified that the Ukrainian political tradition was autonomist, that the Bolsheviks were not interested in the national question or federalism before 1917, and that they recognized Ukraine's right to self-determination but not the right of the Rada to represent the nation—though initially they did support it. Kozik's study was the only Polish article to deal with the formation of the Ukrainian branch of the Party, the Ukrainian SSR, and the question of differences over the degree of centralization.[88] J. Radziejowski (1973) provided another balanced account of events in Ukraine during the Revolution. He noted that Ukraine was economically developed but nonetheless a colony, while its proletariat was Russified and indifferent to the national question. He provided a short description of all Ukrainian parties and groups, and wrote that the Bolsheviks had no position on Ukraine until 1917, and even then their activists in Kiev ignored it. Once the Bolsheviks realized how weak they were in Ukraine, they decided to form a Ukrainian branch. The main weakness of the Rada lay in its failure to implement its pronouncements on land reform, which alienated its peasant supporters. Radziejowski was the only Polish historian to note that the first Bolshevik occupation of Ukraine, in 1918, failed because of Russian nationalist excesses. The Rada fell in the end because of the land issue and its refusal to become a German puppet.[89] Lewandowski (1980) stressed that the Bolsheviks were surprised by the strength of the national movement, which in a few months had evolved from mild demands for autonomy to demands for full independence on its national territory. Ukrainian leaders, he continued, because they were young and naive, allowed themselves to be used by Germans in anti-communist and anti-Polish combinations. Although the Rada had a radical land program, it did not implement it. Peasants then began to take the land regardless, and this was the main reason for the demise of the Rada. That the Rada did attain independence and some diplomatic victories abroad was impressive but ephemeral, as it had no real internal support.[90]

Jabłonski wrote the first postwar scholarly monograph on Western Ukraine in 1917-1921, and like almost all interwar historians who wrote on this subject, he focused on military history. He concluded that conflict over northwestern Ukrainian lands stopped when Petliura, who preferred a partitioned Ukraine under Polish domination to a Soviet Ukraine, surrendered the region to Pilsudski. Poland in 1920 needed the Ukrainian alliance for economic reasons.[91] Kukułka (1963) claimed the French were interested in Galicia because of invested capital and oil interests, and had been willing to support any regime there able to oppose the Bolsheviks. After Brest-Litovsk, France backed Poland since it had lost faith in the Ukrainians, who by then were fighting among themselves.[92]

Sophia Zaks wrote the first study in Polish historiography to examine the international aspects of Polish-Ukrainian relations during the revolution, and in particular, revealed the role of Ukrainian oil in diplomatic bargaining. Contrary to the prevailing Polish view, whose roots lay in the interwar period and claimed that the occupation of Eastern Galicia had been a heroic feat of arms unrelated to international issues, she argued that the Polish occupation was illegal, that the Entente did not recognize the annexation until 1923, and that the Entente was ultimately responsible for the annexation because it had allowed Polish armies to march east in 1919.[93] Zaks saw the Polish-Ukrainian war as a Western-Ukrainian struggle for self-determination that had little chance of victory once the allies decided to back Poland and pointed to the irony of two Ukrainian governments in 1920 negotiating with each other's enemies. She claimed the 1920 Ukrainian-Polish alliance was Petliura's idea.[94] Looking at Soviet policy toward ZUNR, she noted that the region was a backward area that Bolshevik leaders decided to sacrifice in order to concentrate their forces against General Wrangel, whom they regarded as a greater threat than Poland. She claimed that the Bolsheviks realized Western Ukraine was culturally closer to Poland than Russia. At one point they informed the Galicians it was not in Moscow's interest to join the region to Soviet Ukraine and that Russia was willing to recognize ZUNR as a separate state.[95] Soviet historiography at the time did not mention this and merely praised Bolshevik policy as a failed attempt to unify the Ukrainian nation.

A. Deruga (1970) also analyzed the Petliura-Pilsudski treaty. Unlike the official Soviet and Polish Stalinist view, his implicit theme was that Poland had not been a Western tool against the Bolsheviks because the Entente had ignored its interest, which was to rule Eastern Galicia. Deruga reminded readers that Poles were split over the question, that the bourgeoisie were more important than landowners in determining policy, and that political, not economic issues were primary and more important. Petliura took the initiative because he was militarily weaker and made his first overture to Pilsudski when still holding Kiev. Details of first discussions, Deruga noted, are unknown, but Petliura had been prepared to resign from office when he lost Kiev to the Bolsheviks.[96]

Official guidelines did not explicitly mention the Ukrainian national movement. But because they focused research on topics such as "the revolutionary cooperation of Ukrainian and Poles aimed at the destruction of tsarism," or how nineteenth-century "revolutionaries" on both sides tried to reach agreements, they directed historians away from the subject. Issues like Ukrainian autonomy or independence were simply irrelevant from such perspectives. From the official point of view, Ukrainian, unlike Polish nineteenth-century radicals, did not struggle for statehood but for "voluntary union with the Russian nation." "Ukrainian revolutionaries," it was claimed, realized that destruction of tsarism was the task of all three nations. Only "bourgeois liberals" called for Ukrainian separation from Russia.[97]

Serious Polish studies on the national movement did begin to appear in the 1970s. E. Hornowa (1972) described its fate under Alexander II, when new ministers branded Ukrainian cultural and educational endeavors a political threat. They associated cultural revival with radicalism to discredit it and justify administrative repression, though it was led by declared apolitical liberals. The ensuing repression, however, strengthened contacts between tsarist and Western Ukraine.[98]

Kozik (1973) studied the Ukrainian movement in Galicia during the first half of the nineteenth century and argued against the prevailing interwar Polish view of the Ukrainian movement as a treacherous Austrian-inspired plot. Kozik, like other postwar historians, described the region's economic backwardness, but unlike them he explained the movement as a product of Western Romanticism and Polish thought, and compared it with counterparts in the rest of Europe. Before 1830, there were no differences between Poles and Ukrainians because neither side yet had a national movement, he explained, and only after 1848 did conflicts emerge over future borders and social structure—an issue where Ukrainians were more radical.[99] Ukrainians had good reason to be pro-Austrian before 1848 due to the regimes favorable peasant and church policy. Because Ukrainian leaders were anti-Russian while Polish leaders were anti-peasant, Ukrainians really had no choice but to ally with Austria. Poles were hostile to Ukrainians not only because of conservative social views and commitment to historic rather than ethnic frontiers, but because they regarded Ukrainians as economic rivals. What cooperation did occur, Kozik stressed, was limited to individuals and had no long-term significance. Austria, initially hostile to all national movements, later supported Ukrainians to keep them away from Russia and the Poles. The year 1848 marked the evolution of the Ukrainian movement in Galicia from a cultural to a political phenomenon. Polish influence was significant and played a role in the emergence of the idea of Ukrainian statehood.[100] In a second book, Kozik traced the conflict between the nationalist and Polonophile Ukrainian Radas in 1848. The former was conservative and Austrophile, but it represented the only realistic alternative for Ukrainians. Because of their social conservatism in 1848, he continued, Uniate clerics lost their authority among the population.[101]

Radzik (1981) also saw the Ukrainian movement in a European context and noted its transformation in 1848 from a cultural to a political phenomenon. Polish antipathy nurtured it, and Ukrainians became more anti-Polish in 1863 than in 1830, while the Austrians used them as convenient. The institutions formed in 1848 did not mobilize the whole nation, but they were crucial in raising its general level as well as intensifying the Ukrainian intellectuals' sense of their difference from Polish intellectuals.[102]

Among subjects of lesser interest to postwar Polish historians was Ukrainian socio-economic history. Guldon (1966) pointed to the need for more study on early-modern central Ukraine, observing that it was not linked by river to the Baltic trading system and that it had no magnate latifundia prior to 1600.[103] A number of studies on seventeenth-century Western Ukrainian socio-economic history were written by Maurycy Horn, who was the first to quantify, locate, and list the effects of Tatar raids.[104] His articles provide valuable statistical breakdowns of the Galician society and economy and include a study of where fugitives came from and how many there were.

Horn concluded that almost half fled to local towns rather than to the eastern steppes and explained that because people thought in terms of "just rent," protests against perceived injustice involved violence only as a last resort. Horn also demonstrated that economic rather than national issues dominated local conflicts in Western Ukraine, since violence was directed just as often against Orthodox as Catholic owners.[105] Janeczek's (1978) analysis of Polish colonization in Lviv region specifies when it began, where the majority settled, and concluded that by the sixteenth century half the gentry in the province were Polish.[106]

Serczyk published two detailed monographs on the Haidamaks, the first to appear in Polish since the turn of the century. Serczyk reviewed the historiography and identified two major causes of the revolts. The first was an increase in monetary duties that impatient lords had imposed before free settlement terms had run out. The second was the violent reaction of Uniates to missionary activity by the Orthodox, who had expected improvement in their status with the election of a new king. Persecution led them to turn to the cossacks for protection. The spark was provided by the anti-Orthodox declaration of the Bar Confederacy, made during a year of bad crops and high grain prices. Serczyk stressed that the Russians had nothing to do with the revolts,[107] and that they intervened to forestall the possibility of war with Turkey brought on by the Haidamaks' raid on the border town of Balta. Serczyk reviewed the aims of participants by social group and argued that the leaders had no control over their followers' excesses. He pointed out that a decree purportedly issued by Catherine II calling on people to rise in support of the Orthodox Church was a forgery, that the Haidamaks did not expect the Russians to react as they did, and that the movement was unrelated to the Torchyn Manifesto. He expanded his monograph into a book in 1972, which was less analytical, more descriptive, and included a longer historical background. Serczyk, like Lelewel, regarded the Haidamaks as a positive phenomenon in Ukrainian history.

Casimir IV's policies towards Galicia were reviewed by Sieradzski (1958), who summed up some of the major Polish views on the subject. He agreed with O. Balzer, who in 1919 concluded that the legal nature of the tie between Poland and Galicia during Casimir's lifetime was still unknown, and with M. Małowist, who argued that Casimir's eastern policy had been well thought out and not merely the product of eastern Polish noble and merchant expansionist interests. The king's foreign policy was not exclusively orientated eastward but swung back and forth between Germany and Rus throughout his reign. Casimir's use of the title "Rex Russiae" suggests Galicia had been regarded as a kingdom equal in status to Poland at least during his lifetime.[108] Rus lands in 1386 were mentioned, in passing, in only one article devoted to an examination of the "Jagiellonian idea." The author argued that no such idea existed, and that the annexation had been ad hoc. The "idea" represented at most a dynastic and not a national plan, one that was intended to retain Lithuania as well as Rus lands for the Jagiellonian dynasty and to check aggression in the east in order to allow an offensive in the west. The Union led to one dynasty ruling three countries and not to Poland ruling over its two neighbors. Like the major interwar historians, the author noted that Rus lands after 1392 remained part of the Lithuanian Duchy despite the Union. Polish leaders developed ideas of expanding east only in the late sixteenth century, when the death of Ivan IV opened the prospect of placing a Polish king on the Russian throne. Reprinted in 1965, the article elaborated on the point that there was no Jagiellonian aggression eastward in the fifteenth century. It also added that Western Ukrainian lands became Polish domains through inheritance under the Piast dynasty.[109]

There were no studies devoted exclusively to Rus lands during the Union of Lublin. A major study of the Union by J. Bardach, however, mentioned that concessions to Orthodoxy and religious tolerance were important preconditions for the Union and won Rus gentry support for it. Bardach reminded readers that the Crown had opposed incorporating Kiev province, that it officially recognized the Rus language, and that up to the 1580s the return of Rus lands to Lithuania was a major political issue.[109] The Union led to wars with Russia and Turkey and provided a base for magnates and internal conflicts, thus weakening the state. The acquired lands also drained resources and energy that would have been more fruitfully expended in Poland proper. There were beneficial cultural influences in both directions. He observed that insofar as the Union of Brest fomented religious intolerance, it was qualitatively different from the Union of Lublin.

Polish postwar historiography almost totally ignored Ukrainian church history. Perhaps the most important article on this subject appeared as a section in a history of the Polish church (1969). This valuable overview focused on the organizational and social aspects of the Ukrainian churches, the incomes of their benefices, the number of parishes, and the tendency toward centralization that intensified after 1596 in the Uniate as well as Orthodox Church. The author notes there were no explicit anti-Orthodox laws in Poland until the 1670s, and that despite close Papal control over the Uniates, not until the 1720 Synod were Tridentine Council decrees applied to them. He also recorded that the Brest agreement did not guarantee the autonomous structure of the Uniate Church. This was granted by a separate papal decree to the Kiev Metropolitinate, and as such, could be withdrawn at papal discretion.[111]

PART III

SOVIET-RUSSIAN HISTORIOGRAPHY

7

Degrees of Inclusion, Exclusion, and Affinity

THE NATIONS OF THE USSR (1914-1937)

After 1914 at least seven prewar non-Marxist histories of Russia were republished. These included Kliuchevsky's *Kratkii kurs*, Priselkov's *Russkaia istoriia* (1915), and K. Sivkov's *Russkaia istoriia* (1917-1918?).[1]

During the 1920s, three original survey histories of Russia appeared. V. A. Algasov's *Konspekt lektsii po istorii Rossii* (Kharkiv, 1924) was unavailable to me. Another, by Nikolai Rozhkov, actually his second multivolume history of Russia, was published in three editions between 1919 and 1930. Rozhkov focused on political events that could be related to socio-economic conditions and began his narrative with Kievan times. He attached no significance to the 1169 sack of Kiev and gave little attention to Ukrainian events. His account of the cossack period summarized the views of the Ukrainian historians M. Hrushevsky and O. Iefymenko and his original contribution to this subject was to have labeled these years the period of "gentry revolution" in Ukraine, and to see in Left-Bank development an instance of trade capitalism. Moscow, he explained, was driven by economic interests to the Black Sea.[2]

Mikhail Pokrovsky's prewar *Russkaia istoriia* was reprinted seven times to 1934 and once more in 1966. He also wrote the third original survey that appeared during the 1920s; a short popular history reprinted nine times in Russian between 1920 and 1933, and once more 1966. Including all translations, this book saw 90 printings. Pokrovsky devoted about one quarter of the text to the period before the eighteenth century, and made only fleeting mention of Ukraine, in sections on Russian foreign policy. He noted that the Khmelnytsky uprising differed from Russian popular revolts because there were intellectuals in the Ukrainian leadership and that Russia subsequently turned events to its advantage. Non-Russians disappear from his text until the 1905 revolution.[3]

A "History of the Nations of the USSR" was written by N. M. Vanag, Latvian Deputy Head of the Historical Section of the Institute of Red Professors. His book focused on nineteenth- and twentieth-century affairs and had only 70 pages on earlier centuries. A second volume supposed to cover the years up to 1922 was never published. Vanag focused on socio-economic development and his book was basically a socio-economic history of Russia. He admitted in his introduction that he had not devoted sufficient attention to non-Russians, but explained he had decided to publish nonetheless because of the need for a one-volume survey covering all the peoples of the USSR.

Vanag presented Russian relations with non-Russians in terms of "military feudal" colonization by serf-landowners whose class interests led to the formation of the empire through violent conquest.[4] Vanag skirted political events, and like Pokrovsky, explained that oppression led Ukrainian petty-producers to take up arms together with the cossacks, whose aim was to become a ruling class. The Treaty of 1654, which Russia signed only after Ukraine had been exhausted, ended the "peasant war" and transferred Ukrainian peasants from the hands of oppressive Polish lords to a "kabal of Russian serf landowners" allied with cossack officers fearful of social revolution. Left-Bank Ukraine subsequently became one of Russia's most important colonies. Vanag argued that national revolts in the empire were "anti-feudal" but not "bourgeois democratic" or "national liberation" in character despite distinct national tendencies, because capitalist relations in the peasant economy had been weak and were kept so by colonial exploitation. The cossack elite had not been "revolutionary," while the peasants, thanks to a patriarchal social structure, could not organize politically, attain the status of free petty-producers and thereby give direction to their movement. Yet their uprisings were not "reactionary" because at the time they were the only moving force of the "historical process."[5]

The first political organization representing the Ukrainian national bourgeoisie was the Cyril-Methodius Brotherhood, formed in a region of the empire where "feudal remnants" were weak. As one of the non-Russian territories in an empire where capitalism by the end of the nineteenth century had developed into "imperialism," Ukraine served as a source of raw materials and markets for Russian capital. Vanag wrote that tsarist colonial exploitation in the peripheries reinforced and perpetuated backwardness in Russia itself. Ukraine, a region of "agrarian capitalist colonization," experienced faster agrarian capitalist development than other parts of the empire, while Russian leaders built industrial capitalism in its eastern parts. This allowed them to retain feudal relations in the Urals industrial region, which slowed down the tempo of development in Russia proper and thus maintained the economic basis of their "feudal" dictatorship. Ukraine played a key role in holding back Russian development and supporting the tsarist imperial serf-landowner system because it attracted capital away from centrally located industry. Tsarist politics did tie non-Russian peripheries to the world market and destroyed the pre-existing system there, but this "progressive" aspect of Russian rule was counterbalanced by colonial "military-feudal" oppression.[6] Similar in tone was an outline guide for students in higher education published in 1933.[7]

Stalin's call in 1934 for a "History of the USSR" was actually made in a critique of a draft textbook Vanag had edited in accordance with a 1932 CC decision. Following Stalin's thoughts, V. Bystriansky, a specialist in "uncovering anti-soviet activities," now condemned Vanag for focusing on Russia, and for ignoring the anti-tsarist national liberation movements and the progressive role of "gathering the Russian lands"—called "military feudal expansionism" in the reviewed book. Bystriansky also took Vanag to task for not saying anything positive about post-1861 capitalism and for ignoring Russian backwardness.[8]

That same year appeared examination copies of the first histories of Russia written according to Stalin's directive and with the title "History of the USSR." One was by S. M. Dubrovsky (65 copies), and the second was edited by I. Mints, M. Nechkina, and E. Genkina (70 copies). Neither was adopted as the official history and are rarely noted in studies on Soviet historiography. But these draft surveys merit attention as they provide insight into the kinds of interpretations that were being considered for official status in the early 1930s.

Dubrovsky's Russocentric text contained nothing on central Asia despite its subtitle "history of Russia and the USSR." It explained that in 1169 Prince Bogoliubsky destroyed Kiev, and it reiterated the tsarist idea that during his life the center of Rus "shifted from Kiev to Vladimir on the Kliazma."[9] Ukraine in 1569 was called a "feudal" colony under "Polish conquerors," while the 1648 cossack "uprising" was given a religious direction by wealthy cossacks. Khmelnytsky turned to Russia in 1654 because he was unable to deal with peasant revolts against his rule. In a short account subtitled "The division of Ukraine between Poland and Tsarist Russia," Dubrovsky described the Pereiaslav treaty as an agreement struck between the tsar and the cossack leaders at the expense of the peasantry. We are told that the tsar rewarded handsomely "the betrayers of Ukrainian independence." There is a fleeting reference to Peter increasing the subordination of Ukraine and the oppression of conquered nations in the eighteenth century, but nothing on the national movement in 1848 or the 1917 revolution in Ukraine.

The collective work had a different tone. The authors pointed out that all the nations of "our country"—meaning the USSR—had their histories, but that the Russian past was of great significance to all others because Russians had helped them to struggle for liberation and led their fight against landowners. This is the first USSR survey to contain the phrase "All the nations of our country are equal and the Russian nation is the first among equals."[10] The authors did not mention the 1169 sack of Kiev or a transfer of capitals, but did reiterate the tsarist idea of a "gathering of Rus." The authors ignored the Unions of Lublin and Brest and called the 1648 uprising a war of peasants, cossacks, and townspeople against gentry Poland. Cossack-peasant conflicts were not mentioned, while the Pereiaslav treaty was presented as a "transfer" (*perekhod*) of Ukraine to Moscow's rule. The country thereafter became a colony and oppression increased, but Mazepa, who wanted to separate Ukraine from Russia, was identified as someone who "betrayed" Peter.[11] The book did not mention the abolition of the Hetmanate and a section on Ukrainian culture only dealt with folk songs. There was nothing on the national movement and little on 1917 in Ukraine. The authors mention that the Central Rada that year only made cultural demands on the provisional government because it feared a quarrel with Russian capitalism. The workers and peasants, meanwhile, rose to liberate Ukraine from the Rada, which was finally "chased out" by the Red Army.

HISTORIES OF THE USSR (1937-1956)

The work that was finally chosen by the leadership to be the official text was edited by A. Shestakov. Titled the "History of the USSR," it was published in 1937 and subsequently reprinted in millions of copies until 1956 without significant changes. Just after its appearance Shestakov explained that, guided by Stalin's ideas, he had striven to avoid Pokrovsky's "errors." Shestakov located non-Russian pasts within the rubric of "the development of Russia into a multinational state" and applied the concept of "wars of national liberation" only to struggles against "foreigners"—which did not include Russians. Annexation to Russia, he continued, was a "lesser evil," all peasant revolts were "spontaneous" and could not be revolutionary or bourgeois in nature, while in 1917 there was no peasant revolution parallel to the worker's revolution as the "liberation struggle" could only have been led by the proletariat. Shestakov remarked that before 1917, Russia was backward but that the "October revolution" was socialist nevertheless.[12]

Shestakov's book was intended to be a school textbook and had no criticisms of earlier views, as did the two earlier draft surveys. Half of the text covered post-1860 events. The book focused on the development of the Russian state and on Russian leaders and gave little attention to non-Russians. The authors used DHM socio-economic categories but provided little that could be regarded as socio-economic history, while criticism of Russian expansionism appeared only in the sections dealing with Russian foreign policy toward the West. The narrative began with Kievan Rus but subsequently dealt with Ukraine fleetingly. It explained that the Pereiaslav treaty "joined" two people of the same faith and that although the tsar freed Ukrainians from Polish oppression he did not free them from their native ruling class. The book implied that Peter I was "progressive" inasmuch as he "brought order" and that revolts against his rule were "reactionary." Shestakov's was the first survey history published in the USSR to label Mazepa a "traitor." It did not mention the Ukrainian national movement, and, with respect to the events of 1917 in Ukraine, only mentioned that "some" who did not want to submit to Soviet rule formed a bourgeois republic.[13]

A more sophisticated account, intended to be a university text, appeared in 1939-1940. Most of the sections dealing with Ukraine were written by V. Picheta and Nikolai Rubinshtein, a Jewish student of M. Slabchenko and author of some studies on Ukrainian history written in Ukrainian before he moved to Moscow. In the second edition (1948-1949), the Ukrainian historian M. Petrovsky wrote the chapters on Ukraine in the eighteenth century. A particularly striking change in the second edition was its heightened Russian nationalist tone. The introduction of the second volume, for example, omitted a discussion of Marx and historiography and claimed that the Russian nation "from ancient times held an honoured place in human history and has now liberated nations from fascist oppression."

The first edition did not link Bogoliubsky's sack of Kiev to a shift of power or the issue of primacy. It noted that Ukrainian history cannot begin with Kievan Rus, that the Kiev region was not Ukraine, and that in any case nations did not exist at the time. In the second edition, Suzdal was described as the center of the "Rus Union" and an earlier reference to the area having been under the Kievan church and paying tribute to Kiev was removed.[14] Both editions implied that King Casimir conquered Galicia in 1340, but the second omitted a reference to the local population calling itself "Ukrainian" in the sixteenth century. Neither edition mentioned Ukrainian lands in 1386, while the second replaced the chapter title "The Formation of the Russian

State under Ivan III" with "The Russian National State," and "Muscovite Duchy" with "Russian lands."

Ukraine was dealt with at length only in a subsection on seventeenth-century Russian foreign policy, where the first edition referred to a task of "reconquering" Ukrainian lands and the second referred to Russia's "task" to fight with Poland for Ukraine. In the 1948 edition Ukraine replaced Germany as the first source of Western influences on Russia, and the reference to Russian cultural backwardness was removed.[15]

In the section devoted to sixteenth-century Ukraine and Belarus, both editions dealt with the Lublin Union but did not mention who on the Ukrainian side supported it. Only Polish magnates, it continued, benefited from the Union, and they declared an "open campaign on Ukrainian national culture" that was thwarted only by Poland's difficult international situation. The Union of Brest, intended to Polonize the Orthodox church, complemented the Union of 1569, and was signed by ecclesiastical magnates desirous to secure material privileges. The narrative placed the first cossack revolts in a continuum of perpetual struggle that progressed from cultural and ideological forms to armed violence. Cossacks and peasants were not rigorously distinguished and both revolted in supposedly mass reactions to a Polish "state offensive" on Ukrainian lands. Culture during the period in question "developed" despite Polish oppression and reflected an ever-increasing Ukrainian awareness of their national affinity with the Russian "people."

Accounts of the period 1648-1657 in Ukraine differ in both editions. In the first, "the joining of Ukraine was an aspect in the development of the multinational Russian state. Into this union, of course, it is incorrect to project the idealist Great Power concept of the reunion of one Russian nation, which denies the right of Ukrainians to their independent history." The Russian state was the "objective" source of support in the opinion of the more "progressive" Russophile Ukrainians at the time, and historical development solidified the alliance of Ukrainian and Russian nations. The same author in the second edition stressed that only the Russian orientation really corresponded to Ukrainian interests: "The Union with Ukraine was a necessary moment in the creation of the multi-national Russian state. And simultaneously Russian government policy met the wishes of the Ukrainian nation which turned for aid to the fraternal Russian people."[16]

Both editions recapitulated the main events of the uprising and point out that Khmelnytsky raised the issue of submission to tsarist rule in Kiev in 1649. It was still admitted that Khmelnytsky's land policies split the movement and that his wish to secure guarantees for feudal gentry liberties explained his turn to Moscow. Both sides had different political objectives but only Moscow's appeared in the treaty. At the time, Moscow supported the "progressive" cossacks and burghers. Because Ukraine developed late politically it could not form its own state, and although tsarism imposed political colonialism, the Pereiaslav treaty, nonetheless, represented the only alternative and was "the foundation of the union of two brother nations." The account in the second edition was the same except for the omission of the statement that political subordination to Moscow in the "earlier period" did not deny Ukrainians the possibility of cultural and national development. There followed a subsection entitled "Ukraine in the Second Half of the Seventeenth Century." Originally entitled "Ukraine under the Control of the Russian State," it included a quote from Stalin about incorporation involving political and then economic subordination, followed by "real union."[17]

A discussion of Vyhovsky and his politics mentioned Russian conflicts with Ukraine and Ukrainian opposition to tsarist centralism, but this was not given as a reason for Vyhovsky's alliance with Poland—labeled betrayal. The "Grand Duchy of Rus" was noted but not the terms of the Hadiach treaty. The second edition no longer dealt with Ukrainian-Russian relations as if Moscow had only been one political alternative for Ukrainians. The authors sought to give the impression that except a handful of "traitors" Ukrainians were unanimous in desiring "union" with Russia.

The first edition dealt with eighteenth-century Cossack Ukraine in a subsection entitled "Peter I's Colonial Policies." In the second edition this was changed to read: "Peter's Politics in ... Ukraine...." There was a short list of tsarist measures intended to curtail Hetmanate autonomy, but no statement that these policies actually had such a result. Mazepa was significant only because he betrayed Peter, and the author pointed out that his "treason" provided the pretext for infringing on Ukrainian rights. Significant was the omission in the second edition of a paragraph blaming tsarist policies for Ukrainian cultural decline. Neither edition treated mid-eighteenth-century Cossack Ukraine in the subsection "Nations of the Russian Empire and Tsarist Colonial Policy." Whereas the first edition clearly stipulated that Peter formed the Russian Empire and extended its borders to the Baltic and Pacific, the second did not use the word "empire" or claim that Peter did anything personally. The narrative in the second edition "explains" events as follows: "his epoch fulfilled the task which the past and historical life had placed before Russia."[18] The Haidamak revolts, dubbed anti-Polish, anti-Catholic, and anti-Jewish, were attributed to growing oppression without further elaboration. In 1782 the Hetmanate was not "subordinated" (*podchinit*), as written in Shestakov, but "destroyed" (*unichtozheno*).

The postwar effort to integrate Ukrainian with Russian history is particularly evident in the sections devoted to nineteenth-century events. For instance, the first edition placed the national movement in the context of economic difficulties of the 1830s that produced a bourgeoisie with the political aim of independence, whereas the second edition no longer referred to this opposition group as "progressive," nor as the product of tsarist colonial policies in Ukraine. In its place there is a "rising peasant movement" described as the base of a "democratic ideology." Thus in the first edition the Cyril and Methodius Brotherhood appeared as the liberal expression of the "progressive bourgeois" evolution of a national movement from a cultural to a political phase. But the second edition categorized the Brotherhood as "bourgeois" with nationalist tendencies and divided it into two groups, of which only the minority who advocated a revolutionary abolition of serfdom merited the distinction of being "progressive radicals." The issue of Ukrainian separatism and independence was gone.[19]

Unlike the prewar edition, the second explained that in the Ukrainian provinces, industry developed at the same rate as in the rest of the country, and that a national bourgeoisie appeared with manufacturing. The second edition then characterized "bourgeois nationalism" as a product of this industrialization, whereas the first depicted it as a reaction to tsarist colonialism. The first edition noted Lenin's comment about southern Ukraine undergoing especially fast capitalist development and being a colony held back by tsarism, but the second included observations by Stalin about Ukrainian levels of industrialization being the same as in Russia. Finally, the second edition was written when Western Ukraine was part of the USSR, and unlike the first included a section on Eastern Galicia, which it described as an Austrian "internal colony."[20]

A survey by Tikhomirov and Dmitriev (1948) was slightly less polemical tone and provided slightly more detail for some subjects. In this text, Casimir IV did not "grab" or "usurp" Galicia, but "joined" it to Poland thereby "tearing" it away from "the rest of Rus." In the earlier text the local population became the object of "Polish-Catholic aggression," in this one Galicia was described as a base for the "conquest" of the rest of Ukraine. Tikhomirov and Dmitriev noted that the Krevo Union was vague concerning the status of Ukrainian lands, that in 1569 the Rus gentry supported union with Poland, and specified that the gentry, clergy, and burghers led the cultural revival in the early seventeenth century.[21] They did not divide the Cyril-Methodius Brotherhood into two distinct tendencies.[22] The earlier text specified that Rus in 1386 became part of Poland, made no mention of the Rus gentry in 1569, and presented early-modern Ukrainian culture as the product of the Ukrainian nation.

Degrees of Inclusion, Exclusion, and Affinity 143

Along with Shestakov's survey, the most widely read and reprinted history of the USSR was by A. M. Pankratova. The first edition of her textbook for grades eight to ten (which she began to write in 1933) appeared in 1940, and the last edition appeared in 1964.[23] A comparison of the editions indicates that major changes were made in 1948, 1955, and 1958 to reflect the prevailing political climate.

The first important change appears in the section on Kievan Rus, where the 1948 edition dropped the earlier reference to Marx calling Rus an empire in chapter IV of his *Secret Diplomatic History*. Also gone was his comment that Kievan Rus preceded the formation of Poland, Lithuania, the Baltic states, Turkey, and Muscovy as Charlemagne's empire had preceded the emergence of Germany, France, and Italy. Very little space was devoted to Ukrainian lands in subsequent centuries. In 1340, Galicia was "taken over," and in 1569 central lands "became" part of Poland. In the section on Ukrainian lands under Lithuanian rule, however, we find for the first time the idea that Ukrainian masses desired "union" with the Russians because there existed a Russian state. The 1940 edition referred only to "intensifying ties" among brother nations and Russian support for the Ukrainian struggle.[24] A number of changed subtitles in the 1950 edition reflected the presence of a "friendly" Communist Poland on Ukraine's western border. Thus, "Ukraine and Belarus in the Seventeenth Century" became "The Struggle of the Ukrainian and Belarus peoples against the Oppression of Gentry Poland," while "Struggle of the Ukrainian Nation against Poland" became "The Liberation War of the Ukrainian People." Pankratova depicted the Union of Brest as primarily a Jesuit plot, and whereas in the 1940 edition she wrote that "Poles" oppressed Ukrainians, in the 1948 edition she specified Polish gentry did the oppressing.

The 1948 edition related that peasants openly grumbled about Khmelnytsky's policies by 1649, that Ukraine could not become independent, that Russians and Ukrainians were ethnically close, and that transfer to tsarist rule represented a lesser evil. The 1950 text referred to the "Liberation War of the Ukrainian Nation led by the leading statesman and military leader, the son of the Ukrainian nation, Bohdan Khmelnytsky." In this edition there was nothing about cossack-peasant conflict and only vague mention of class struggle occurring simultaneously with the "liberation war." We learn that the first contact with Russians came not in 1652 but in 1648, and that Khmelnytsky turned to Russia because Ukraine was too weak to stand alone against Poland. The 1950 edition also added that "joining" Russia contributed to Ukraine's economic evolution and that transfer to Russian rule was a "reunion" of nations.[25] The 1945 edition no longer referred to the 1654 treaty as a "lesser evil," while the 1955 edition added the formulas of the tricentenary "Thesis."[26]

All editions of the Pankratova survey interpreted the Hadiach treaty as a result of Poles exploiting strife among the cossack officers by offering noble status to the pro-Polish Vyhovsky faction, and they did not detail what the treaty involved. The 1950 edition dropped a reference to Russian culture being under Eastern influence and Ukraine as a second source of seventeenth-century Western influences.[27] All editions described Mazepa as treacherous and explained that the "tsarist administration" sought to make Cossack Ukraine similar to the rest of the empire because the officers were too independent and influential. All editions mentioned the abolition of the Hetmanate.[28]

There were considerable differences in the treatment of the Ukrainian national movement. In the 1940 edition, the Cyril-Methodius Brotherhood was simply "left-wing." This edition also referred to enslaved nations in the empire and to "bourgeois democratic" intellectuals as carriers of national culture during a period of developing capitalism. Mention was made of the Ukrainian movement in Eastern Galicia. The 1950 edition claimed the Cyril-Methodius brotherhood had been split into two radically opposed wings, and omitted the reference to bourgeois democratic intellectuals as carriers of national culture. It classified intellectuals as "democrats" or "bourgeois nationalists," and praised the former because they were in close contact with Russian "progressive" thinkers, while condemning the latter because they sought to separate from Russia and sell their country to Germany. Similarly, whereas the 1955 edition referred to the *hromadas* as organizations of the bourgeoisie, the 1950 edition described them more negatively as bourgeois political organizations.[29]

Accounts of early-twentieth-century Ukraine changed little between 1940 and 1955. "Bourgeois liberalism" continued to be noted as emerging alongside the mass peasant and proletarian movements. In 1917, "bourgeois" leaders of the national movement tried to use the February Revolution to create "their" autonomous states. The Central Rada, however, based on rich peasants, feared separatism because it was unable to face revolution alone. The Rada was explicitly called "counter-revolutionary" after October 1917 when "workers and peasants of Ukraine," hearing of the Bolshevik takeover, took up arms. Kiev fell to the Red Army, "helped by workers." Pankratova called the revolutionary movement of oppressed nationalities the "reserve of the proletarian revolution," according to Stalin's formula, but she did not mention how other Ukrainian governments arose. The slogans of Ukrainian parties had no impact on Ukrainian workers or peasants, she claimed, as they had wanted to overthrow tsarism in "brotherly union" with Russian workers. Pankratova mentions The Directory only as a government that sold out Ukraine's economy to France, and in the section "Civil War in the National Republics" she explained how Russians gave disinterested military aid to all non-Russians and that especially tight ties existed between the three fraternal East Slavic nations.[30] She ignored the ZUNR and noted that in 1920 the Bolsheviks beat off the Polish attack and then accepted Warsaw's peace offer.

The eight-volume *History of the USSR* (1953-1958) traced events to 1800 and tended to treat non-Russian issues in separate chapters. The book's stated purpose was to illustrate how the nations of the USSR fought foreign aggressors under Russian leadership. It attached no particular significance to Bogoliubsky's raid and noted that in 1340 Casimir IV "seized" Galicia because it was weak. The authors call Poles conquerors and offer no discussion of the details of the Krevo Union. In accordance with the "Thesis" the authors wrote: "The three brother nations in the course of their further history did not lose consciousness of their unity based on common origins, culture and language and continually struggled for reunion within one Russian state."[31]

The volume covering the fifteenth through seventeenth centuries sought to "show the history of the Great Russian nation that took upon itself the role of unifier of nationalities," and contains the first mention in a survey USSR history of the idea that the main task of Russian foreign policy vis-à-vis Poland and Ukraine had been "reunification." Notable in this volume was the discussion of the Ukrainian economy because it mentioned the rise of towns, commercial money relations, and manufacturing. Although an improvement over other Stalinist texts that focused exclusively on "oppression," this volume refrained from making generalizations about a "transition to capitalism." The impact on Ukraine of "Polish seignorial culture," allegedly forced on Ukrainians by Jesuits, was downplayed and there was no mention of a Ukrainian cultural rebirth at the turn of the sixteenth century. Class struggles, it was vaguely asserted, "grew over" into struggle for "reunion" thanks to the influence of the centralized Russian state.[32]

The Union of Lublin, a "reactionary alliance" and tool of aggression used to enslave Ukraine, was eagerly supported by Ukrainian "feudalists" who hoped it would help them in their struggle against the peasants. "Feudalists" also signed the Union of Brest, necessary to enforce their "ideological apparatus" in face of mass uprisings against "feudal oppression." The plan, in keeping with Vatican ambition, was to "liquidate" the Orthodox Church, and those higher Ukrainian clergy who collaborated did so out of material interests and the wish to free themselves from the supervision of confraternities.³³ The uprising of 1648 was presented in terms of the "Thesis" and the authors made no reference to any Ukrainian aims other than "reunion," nor to differences between the hetman and the tsar over foreign policy. Vyhovsky appears only as someone who gave Ukraine to the Poles. Although there is reference to the positive influence of the Russian ruling elite on economic development, there was no parallel claim concerning the impact of the cossack elite on the Left-Bank Ukrainian economy. There is no mention of tsarist restrictions on autonomy.³⁴

This was the first "History of the USSR" to use "our fatherland" as a synonym for "Russian Empire" and the first to contain an extended section on Mazepa. He is portrayed as a traitor and man of bad character who hated "the Russian and Ukrainian people." This survey was also the first to claim that the cossack officer struggle for autonomy represented nothing more than their wish to exploit Ukrainians by themselves. The volume described the structure of the Hetmanate in some detail and mentioned that the conflict between cossack officers and Russian "feudalists," who both wanted to exploit the Ukrainian masses, resulted in the victory of the latter and liquidation of the local administration of Ukrainian "feudalists." But the authors saw nothing "progressive" in cossack autonomy, did not mention Ukrainian cultural influence on Russia, and claimed that Ukrainian cultural development occurred thanks to Russian influence. A short section on the Haidamak revolts attributed them to "feudal exploitation," while Russian intervention was presented as a move intended to save the local serf owners.³⁵

HISTORIES OF THE USSR (1956-1982)

In post-Stalin histories of the USSR, the impact of "liberalization" on treatment of non-Russian pasts was limited. Some of the new surveys contained more information about socio-economic development and fewer blatant expressions of Russian greatness, paternal concern, and assistance for non-Russians, but the underlying DHM and Russocentric structure remained in all. The introduction to the second revised edition (1964) of a 1956 survey still specified that the past of the Russian nation had to be closely tied to the past of the "other nations of our fatherland." Russia, it was explained, was significant to all non-Russians, even when they had not been part of the Russian state, because it had a positive influence on their struggles against foreigners—which excluded Russians. The 1964 survey devoted more space to non-Russians than did the earlier one, but did not treat non-Russian economic, social, and political history in separate sections.

Only sections on non-Russian cultures were not subsumed into the broader Russocentric thematic-chronological divisions.

The 1956 survey states that Prince Bogoliubsky in 1169 "appropriated the title of All Rus to himself" and that his ensuing conflict with Galicia for Kiev weakened Rus and made it easier prey for foreigners. Polish "feudalists" in 1340 "entrenched" themselves in Galicia, and the Union of Lublin was a "tool" of Polish-Lithuanian feudal expansion that provided new means for oppressing Ukrainians. The authors noted that, in the face of opposition, Poles had to grant concessions—in the second edition this reference was shifted further in the text and implied concessions were made only after a revolt. The 1596 Union was cited as an example of increasing national oppression, while the first revolts were "already" growing into the struggle for "reunion."[36] The phrase "bourgeois relations" in a subtitle of the section on sixteenth- and seventeenth-century economy, as well as reference to broad perspectives for Ukrainian economic development under Polish rule, were dropped in the 1964 edition.[37] In the account of the 1648 uprising, a new section explained that different groups joined for different reasons but were united around the aim of national liberation and the "desire to reunite." Whereas the first edition only linked this "desire" to the earlier existence of the "Old Rus nation," the second observed that the awareness of historical commonality had never faded. The second edition omitted a reference to the Russians as the strongest East Slavic nation because they were first to throw off Mongol rule, and added that "reunion" had an economic basis inasmuch as during the first half of the century there had been trade between the two countries! Eliminated from the second edition were references to the Russian nation "strongly" supporting "reunion," to Khmelnytsky showing great military talent, and to his allegedly not compromising with the Poles.

The 1956 edition made a reference to eighteenth-century tsarist restrictions on Ukrainian autonomy after 1654 as a cause of dissatisfaction among some officers and their wish to reestablish links with Poland—an ambition resisted by the "masses." But the Hadiach treaty was ignored.[38] Eighteenth-century Ukrainian economic history and culture were not dealt with in separate chapters but lumped together with Russian and Belarussian developments. Peter I was still praised for increasing the authority of the Russian state, but without the previously obligatory Stalin quote to this effect. The authors identified Russian colonialism in central Asia but not in Ukraine, which they dubbed an area of "anti-feudal" peasant revolts.

The authors did not mention a Ukrainian national bourgeoisie, and dealt with the nineteenth-century national awakening in the section on culture as an exclusively literary phenomenon. Mid-century intellectuals were still categorized as either "revolutionary democrats" or "bourgeois," with Shevchenko identified as the Ukrainian founder of the former group.[39] The authors did not mention Ukraine in the chapter on borderlands, but stressed that Ukraine was more developed than other regions of the empire and therefore was not a Russian economic colony. Significantly, they no longer condemned the *hromady*,[40] nor did they relate the nationalist movement to economic development. Instead, it was described as the reaction of "bourgeois intellectuals" to tsarist national oppression. The basis of the national movement lay in that group's wish to control its own national market.

An important change in the 1964 edition was the claim that the national movement was not merely a product of "bourgeois intellectuals" but of the whole oppressed nation. This allowed the national movement to be categorized as "progressive" and the bourgeoisie to be relegated to the status of a group within the broader phenomenon. As a result, the limits of permissible subjects were expanded, as now individuals who otherwise might have been dismissed as "reactionary" could be integrated into the narrative. From the revised perspective, the cultural achievements of Ukrainian moderates could be recognized, and these were not labeled as the product of "bourgeois democrat compromises" with tsarism. Whereas the 1956 edition noted that tsarist chauvinism reinforced "bourgeois nationalism," the second edition noted that national oppression only reinforced nationalist tendencies within the bourgeoisie of oppressed nations, thereby legitimizing non-Russian national opposition. Where the first edition referred negatively to growing local nationalism, the second noted only "bourgeois exploitation of nationalism." But the claim that ultimately the Russian proletariat led the revolutionary movement remained. There was also a slight shift in the treatment of the Central Rada. The 1956 edition noted the Rada was hostile to the Soviet regime and desired autonomy. The 1964 edition still categorized the Rada as "bourgeois nationalist" but dropped the other two remarks.[41]

The most "liberal" history of the USSR was the multivolume survey (1966-1980) edited by CC member Boris Ponomarev. The introduction claimed that "problems during the thirties" affected only the treatment of the Soviet period and that the history of the USSR was not a history of the sum of its parts. Yet the text contains significant interpretive shifts that reflect "reformist" understanding of the 1947 and 1953 guidelines. But although the introduction also called the ignoring of non-Russians by Russian historiography a "sin," the text did not reflect full repentance.

The new survey attached no broader political significance to Bogoliubsky's sack of Kiev and the treatment of Casimir's campaign and the Unions of 1386, 1569, and 1596 was superficial. The latter was still seen as a Catholic-Polish plot intended to better enslave Ukrainians and separate them from their "brother" Russians when the "desire for reunion was growing." The development of Ukrainian social and political thought was identified as part of the religious struggle after 1596, although cultural evolution in general was not linked to the reaction to the Union. Polish concessions to Ukrainians were judged a cunning means of enforcing their rule, while the Kiev confraternity was depicted as the "political centre of the liberation movement in Ukraine"—a kind of proto-party headquarters in the class struggle. The origins of confraternities were linked to a particular bourgeois "wish for a cheaper church."[42]

The authors presented seventeenth- and eighteenth-century non-Russian affairs from the perspective of tsarist alliances with local elites directed against "popular masses," and included details omitted from earlier surveys. They noted that the ruling class of Russia was interested in Ukrainian economic resources, and discussed the international impact of events in Ukraine. The new survey distinguished between the "reunion" of nations and a union of countries in 1654, and did not always use the term "reunion" when dealing with issues in Ukrainian-Russian relations during Khmelnytsky's lifetime. Nonetheless, the authors still did not treat the Pereiaslav treaty as a purely political event and provided little information about Vyhovsky's politics other than to say it was pro-Polish and opposed by "the people." The conditions of the Hadiach accords were not mentioned but it was noted that the treaty that pro-Russian cossacks signed with Moscow in 1659 was more restrictive than the 1654 articles. The survey condemned Mazepa without dealing with his motives and explained that his treason and the separatist ambitions of some officers resulted in appropriate countermeasures from the tsar, which included diminution of rights. There was reference to political centralization ignoring national particularities and traditions and to a tsarist objective of making Ukrainians forget their autonomy by attempting to erase from their historical memory the names of the hetmans. But economic centralization was not criticized and the sections on the economy treated all non-Russian incorporated regions as part of an imperial whole. The Haidamak revolts, like all others, were not explained as the result of specific causes but as episodes in an eternal struggle. In response to Polish social and national oppression, the Ukrainian population of the Right Bank rose to a liberation struggle. The Russian ruling class feared it would spread and helped suppress it.[43]

Interpretive shifts were more evident in sections dealing with the non-Russian areas in the nineteenth century. As before, it was claimed that capitalism brought more oppression of non-Russians, stimulated national consciousness, and that thanks to the imperial economy regions were tied to the world market. But "the forms and methods of this process did not correspond to its objective progressive content because it was weighed down by the military feudal character of the regime ruling the country and the exploitative nature of its society."[44]

Early-modern Russian expansionism was described as the politics of the Russian "military feudal state." It was explained that feudal landowners, faced with class conflicts in Russia, sought to defuse it by expansion south and east. This was supported with a quote from Lenin about "colonial politics" and imperialism existing before capitalism and all wars being imperialist if expansionism was their purpose. But because Ukraine underwent capitalist manufacturing and commercialization of agriculture thanks to incorporation, it never became a colony. Left-Bank and Right-Bank Ukraine were not colonies because they suffered only national, not economic, oppression. Neither region became a market for industrial goods, and both had a level of culture the same as the center's. The authors labeled southern Ukraine, a region of agrarian export and industrial imports, an economic colony, but they did not regard it as a nationally exploited region because the national composition of its population was mixed to a greater degree than elsewhere in Ukraine.[45]

Although the Ponomarev survey did not include Ukraine among Russia's economic colonies, the fact it was the first Soviet history since the 1920s to identify tsarist national colonial policies as a cause of economic backwardness in general is noteworthy.

> By aiding the primary accumulation of capital, the colonial exploitation of the nations of the Russian empire objectively helped the emergence of capitalist elements to a degree. But the great possibilities to oppress and rob the non-Russian population of the regions allowed tsarism to conserve feudal relations within the country and retard the breakup of the serf order. Insofar as this system was the center of all reactionary elements of Russian social life, its persistence was clearly at odds with the fundamental interests of the Russian nation, not to speak of those of the other nations of Russia [Rossia].[46]

Within such a context, liberation movements could receive more attention than before, though not all of these were treated as national in form because, according to Marxism, this required capitalism and a bourgeoisie struggling for a national market. The authors explained that because the peasant liberation struggle was not only "anti-feudal" but anti-colonial, it was often joined by local "feudalists" interested in regaining pre-incorporation rights.

The combination produced a national movement weakened by the predisposition of the "feudalists" to compromise with tsarism out of fear of social revolution. The Ukrainian Left-Bank gentry were mentioned specifically as a group interested in autonomy but fundamentally loyalist because they feared the masses.[47]

In a change from earlier surveys, the Ponomarev history implied that all the members of the Cyril-Methodius Brotherhood were "progressive" because during the 1840s a "national bourgeoisie" was emerging. "Liberal reformists" were identified with its right-wing as supporters of serfdom, but they were not condemned as "reactionary." The differences between members, it was explained, represented only the beginning of a split in the Ukrainian national movement that actually occurred only in the 1860s.

The authors identified "progressive" elements within the national movement when they pointed out that part of the "national bourgeoisie" were not reformists and that some in the then "progressive" liberal movement did not advance national demands. This national bourgeoisie, however, was classified as agrarian rather than industrial. This limited their political significance as their main interest was to maintain "feudal remnants." The authors noted that the Russian Empire was unique because its peripheries were not separated from the center by seas and that consequently, there was no barrier to a common front of oppressed and "progressive" intellectuals critical of colonial policy.[48] The authors admitted there was economic colonialism in Central Asia.

In the early twentieth century, "feudal remnants in the economy" were still significant, and the forms of economic exploitation were particularly primitive under tsarism because it was a military "feudal-imperialist" power. The survey explained that although the "national bourgeoisie" was "anti-imperialist in Asia," in the Russian Empire a revolution led by this class could not have blazed the path of future development because they were too intertwined with a strong finance capital. The survey did categorize reformist democratic bourgeoisie demands for autonomy as "revolutionary" because they were anti-tsarist, but the reformist democratic bourgeoisie itself was still dismissed as "reactionary" because they split the "revolutionary movement" and threatened to limit it to "national liberation." The struggle of Russian workers and peasants in non-Russian areas was described as having been in essence anti-colonial as well, even in the absence of specific national demands! Moreover, the Russian proletariat was still treated as the only force able to unify the national struggle and merge it with the "all-Russian revolutionary movement." In February 1917, the "People of Russia, as one, recognized the leading role of the Russian working class in the struggle against autocracy."[49]

In Ukraine, in 1917, the survey admitted middle peasants had wavered and that the bourgeoisie had mass support initially. Unlike earlier surveys, this multivolume work admitted that the Central Rada had a positive role, that in February the "Ukrainian national liberation movement strengthened," and that the Ukrainian liberal bourgeoisie were the most influential at the time. There was also discussion of Bolshevik mistakes on the national question in Ukraine, among which were the failure to establish a single Party center, forced collectivization, and the formation of a separate Donetsk Republic in eastern Ukraine. Significant was the admission, for the first time in a general history, that different regions in the empire had different levels of development and a different "revolutionary process."[50] The authors explained that, thanks to the chauvinist policies of the Provisional Government, the Rada had support and that only after the Bolsheviks took power did it become "anti–soviet." Attaching increased importance to nationality in general, the text referred not only to an anational "working population of Ukraine," but to Ukrainian workers and peasants as pro-Bolshevik. The survey did not discuss why the Rada signed a treaty with Germany, why the Germans later dissolved the Rada, or events in Western Ukraine between 1848 and 1920.[51]

Three of the ten remaining histories published between 1956 and 1982 examined here, like the Ponomarev survey, were in places less Russocentric and nationalist in tone.[52] Smirnov, for example, mentioned that Galicia was a rival with Vladimir for primacy in Rus—very rare in one-volume surveys— and specified that the Pereiaslav treaty had "reunited" only Left-Bank Ukraine with Russia. Sakharov and Kovalchenko made no references to medieval "desires for reunion," nor did they write that the Rada was "counter-revolutionary" from its beginnings. Diadychenko wrote that Ukrainian statehood appeared in the middle of the seventeenth century, that Hetmanate autonomy had benefited the whole nation, and that Khmelnytsky had desired to "free" all Ukrainian lands. He stressed that Peter's centralization had seriously infringed upon the autonomy of non-Russians.

The remaining seven surveys adhered more closely to the 1947 and 1953 guidelines.[53] Least influenced by post-Stalinist changes were Kondufor and Artemov, who claimed, for instance, that Bogoliubsky had first used the title "Grand Prince of All Rus" and had transferred its capital to Suzdal. They also reiterated a theory, disproven 100 years earlier and not characteristic of official Soviet historiography, that there had been a mass settlement to northeast Rus from the Kiev region after the Mongol invasion. Whereas more "liberal" Soviet surveys stressed that Shevchenko had been under the influence of the Russian "revolutionary democrat" V. Belinsky, these two claimed he had been his disciple. They labeled the Rada a group of German agents and wrote that in 1917-1919 the "Russian nation," rather than the proletariat, provided decisive assistance to its Ukrainian brothers in the struggle against the Rada.[54]

The idea that Bogoliubsky was Grand Duke of Kiev was also in the 1958 edition of Pankratova's textbook. Furthermore, this edition, replaced an earlier section on "Bourgeois Liberal Opposition and the Tsarist Struggle Against the National Liberation Movement" with "The Bolshevik Struggle Against Nationalism," and stressed the leading role of the Russian proletariat in non-Russian liberation struggles, whereas earlier editions had referred to Bolshevik efforts to unite non-Russians around the Russian proletariat. The 1958 edition contained nothing on the revolutionary potential of nationalities in 1917, and unlike earlier editions, it explicitly classified the Rada as "counter revolutionary" from its beginnings, and ignored Lenin's comment about its demands for autonomy being just and restrained. References abounded to the crucial and important role during the revolution of the Russian nation, instead of its working class.[55]

Two other histories, by Datsiuk and Artemov, and Kabanov and Mavrodin, almost totally ignored Ukraine. Almost nothing on non-Russians was in a popular picture history of the USSR by Pashuto. The pictures dealt overwhelmingly with Russia, and Russian-Ukrainian relations were characterized as follows:

> The nations of Ukraine and Belarus aspired to shake off the despised Polish gentry yoke . . . Mass destruction of the population by the gentry and Crimean tatars threatened the very existence of the Ukrainian nation. But the aspiration to liberation from Polish oppression and to reunification with fraternal Russia was irresistible and in the end expressed itself in the liberation war.[56]

In a similar spirit, Malkov explained that "the Union of Poland with Lithuania led to increased feudal oppression in the grabbed Rus lands" and that after the Ukrainian nation had appeared in the fifteenth century, its political, economic, and cultural life "gravitated towards" east Rus. In a sentence implying that non-Russians had no "national culture" before their association with Russia, we read that in the nineteenth century the "nations of Russia in the struggle against tsarism created the basis of their national cultures."[57] References to non-Russians in 1917 are limited to the observation that the Revolution had freed all of them and that the Rada had been counterrevolutionary.

8

The History of the Ukrainian SSR (1948-1982)

THE FIRST ATTEMPTS

Between 1921 and 1946, histories of Ukraine were written by Ukrainian scholars living, working, and usually educated in the country and formally supervised by the Ukrainian branch of the Party. Drafts were probably read by friends and there is no record of formal institutional reviews, structured discussions, or stenographed protocols that authors were obliged to consider while revising. There is no evidence of guidelines from Moscow more explicit than Stalin's two decrees and Drozdov's exegesis. After 1945, conformity was imposed more efficiently thanks to the recentralization and expansion of the ideological apparatus and more detailed and explicit instructions. In 1947, the authorities not only demanded that historians link the Ukrainian and Russian pasts (see chapter 3), but obliged those Ukrainians chosen to write an acceptable survey to spend two months in Moscow at the All-Union Institute of History.[1] Authors of chapters dealing with the early twentieth century were summoned in person to an interview with a commission that included Ukrainian CC member L. Kaganovich,[2] while all concerned were provided with copies of reviews and protocols of the discussions. The result was an outline *History of Ukraine* (1948, 350 copies), subsequently reviewed by 86 historians, of whom no more than ten were Ukrainian. Although formally written by Ukrainian historians, due to such measures the resulting text must be considered a Russian rather than a Ukrainian interpretation of Ukraine's past. But before dealing with this prototype "History of the Ukrainian SSR" it is necessary to note an earlier Russian history of Ukraine published in *Bolshaia sovetskaia entsiklopediia*.

The bulk of the survey, up to 1800, was written by V. Picheta, most likely in 1946—after the liberal course toward non-Russians had been dropped and the appearance of Kovaliov's article condemning recent surveys of Ukrainian history for stressing Ukraine's distinctiveness, but before new guidelines were announced.

The story of subscribers to the Soviet encyclopedia receiving a page with an entry "Bering Sea," which they were supposed to paste over the entry "Beria" is well known. Perhaps the same might have been done with this entry on Ukrainian history had it not been almost 100 pages long. With 45,000 copies in print, this survey could not be withdrawn from circulation despite its "shortcomings," and it remained on open shelves to provide anyone interested with a relatively non-Russocentric interpretation of a non-Russian past closer to the wartime surveys of Ukrainian history than to the 1930s guidelines.[3]

The first of the reviewed subjects Picheta dealt with in greater detail was the Union of Brest. He depicted it as a Polish magnate and Jesuit plot intended to denationalize Ukrainians, but noted the Uniates retained the Orthodox rite. Picheta did not mention statehood as a cossack objective in the seventeenth century or popular revolts against Khmelnytsky, nor did he condemn Russian colonialism and dwell on cossack autonomy. But neither did he mention the benefits that "joining" Russia brought Ukrainians, or treat ideas of Russian-Ukrainian fraternity and "desire for union" as historical forces. Similarly, the anonymous authors of the section covering 1800 to 1917 did not condemn the Ukrainian national movement for threatening the "unity of the revolutionary movement," made few references to Russian influences on Ukrainian socialists, and considered the *Holovna Ruska Rada* "progressive." They wrote that the 1917 Central Rada took the leadership of the national movement and that initially it had expressed the will of the masses despite itself. The Rada became "counter-revolutionary" only after the Bolsheviks took power, and the assistance of Russian workers in its fall was specified. In November 1918, the Ukrainian Soviet state "was formed," while the following year the Poles destroyed the "national liberation" movement in Western Ukraine and occupied it.

The 1948 *Istoriia Ukrainy: Kratkii kurs* gave a different account, and reviewers' comments provide an insight into the optimism wartime liberalization had awakened among some historians. Most of the reviews focused on details and errors of fact and were preceded by comments that the authors had fulfilled their task. Some complained that the specificity of Ukraine's past had been lost, that more information had to be included about the country, especially Western Ukraine, that there was not enough on Russian colonialism, and that the struggle of Ukrainians for liberation was portrayed as if it had only been a struggle for union with Russia. The Galician Russophile and Party member B. Dudykevych observed that the text had ignored Western Ukraine and failed to rationally incorporate its past into the narrative.[4] But such observations were out of keeping with the political climate after the 1949 CC condemnation of Mints for "belittling" Russians, and the authors could hardly have been expected to take their cues from them—with the exception of the last mentioned. Comments that required closer adherence to, and narrower interpretation of, the 1947 guidelines reflected the times (see p. 57).

Mints's comments on the draft text, for instance, did not echo the concern expressed in his 1949 article about excessive Russian nationalism. He observed that the account of Ukraine's struggle against Poland should not imply that nationality was its root cause, called for emphasis on the high degree of popular opposition to Mazepa, and unequivocal demonstration of the "profound influence" on the "revolutionary movement" in nineteenth-century Ukraine of the Russian "democratic movement." Other historians pointed out the importance of showing there could not have been differences between the Ukrainian and Russian "people" in the eighteenth century, and that there were no statistics to show tsarism held back Ukrainian economic development. B. Grekov, known for his Russian-nationalist opinions, said the text had to stress what united the two peoples, while S. Bakhrushin, though critical of the use of the term "Old Rus nation," which he regarded as tendentious, argued that there was no need to dwell on details of Ukrainian autonomy after 1654, as this could lead to "incorrect conclusions" of the sort found in the "Hrushevsky school."[5]

Three more drafts subsequently appeared, and only the fourth (1953) was released as the official history of the Ukrainian SSR to February 1917. Although originally entitled "history of Ukraine," one reviewer in 1949 noted that the title should be "history of the Ukrainian SSR" to illustrate that the culmination of Ukraine's "historical process" was the formation of the Soviet Republic. This change was made between June and December 1950 and the third draft edition was so titled.[6] After Stalin's death a revised edition appeared in 1955, and in 1958 a second volume covering 1917 to 1954 was released. This two-volume work was superseded as the official history of the Ukrainian SSR by another in 1967. With a few exceptions, basically the same authors wrote all of these surveys.

The 1953 edition, written in the spirit of the 1949 resolution, was the most Russocentric. It reflected most faithfully the ideas expressed by Gorin, Rubach, and Skubytsky in 1929-1930, and followed the 1947 and 1953 guidelines most closely. Its Russian bias was reflected even in the choice of pictures, which excluded Ukrainian subjects like Khmelnytsky's 1648 entry into Kiev, found in the first draft, and included pictures, later omitted from the 1955 edition, with purely Russian themes like scenes of the Kremlin, of the Kulikovo battle, or scenes of imaginary Russian-Ukrainian fraternity, such as Gorky dressed in a Ukrainian embroidered shirt reading Shevchenko to peasants. In chapter VIII of the 1948 draft there is reference to Russia controlling the biggest part of Eastern Europe, while in 1953 this passage called Russia the biggest state in the world. In the 1953 edition the Haidamak revolt was "caused" by the appearance of the Russian army in Right-Bank Ukraine, while in the 1955 edition this was changed to read that with the appearance of the Russian army in Right-Bank Ukraine rumors spread that it had come to help. In the chapters devoted to 1917-1921, Stalin, Lenin, and events in Petrograd received more space than events in central Ukraine, while Western Ukraine was ignored. The 1953 text was simplistic and its account of socio-economic history consisted of accounts of ever-increasing oppression rather than descriptions of the evolution of production, national markets, and classes. The amount of space it devoted to Russian as opposed to Ukrainian events was unmatched by any Soviet history of Ukraine published before or after.[7]

As a result of the "Thesis," the 1953 text included the notion of "Old Rus nation" (*drevnyi russkyi narod*), and frequent mention of a metaphysical Ukrainian "striving" to "reunite" with Russians, caused by the ethnic affinity derived from this alleged medieval proto-Russian nation. The "Thesis" obliged historians to treat this "desire" as a major historical force in Eastern Slavic history up to the twentieth century, and to muddle distinctions between the Ukrainian and Russian pasts. Thus, "Old Rus state" replaced "Kievan Rus," and whereas the 1948 edition noted that in the ninth and tenth centuries Eastern Slavic tribes were intermingling and therefore had a "unity," the 1953 edition claimed a single "Rus nation" already existed. Against this background, authors presented Bogoliubsky's sack of Kiev in 1169 as a feudal war between princes of the same nationality instead of a conflict between two proto-nationalities. It was claimed that his aim was to subjugate Kiev and establish his city as the new capital. The 1948 text explained the Treaty of Pereiaslav represented a lesser evil for Ukrainians who "joined" the Russian state, but the 1953 edition referred to the results of the treaty as the best of all possible political alternatives.[8]

After Stalin's death, the authorities retracted the 1949 resolution and authors dropped the more extreme expressions of Russophilism from the 1955 edition and included more information about Ukrainian events. All three subsequent editions devoted no more than a few lines to the Unions of 1386 and 1569 and told readers that Poland "seized" Ukrainian lands. In general, political events remained epiphenomenal in the text, and even revolts were not depicted as the result of specific causes but as part of an eschatological schema of perpetual violent class struggle in the face of perpetually worsening national and social oppression. In post-1953 surveys, revolts become stages on the road to "reunion."[9]

Sections on economic history listed the numbers of craftsmen, noble landholding, and productive enterprises that progressively increased each century, "despite oppression," alongside social differentiation and polarization. A tedious narrative repeated the same phrases chapter after chapter without linking changes in technology and the relations of production to new social groups, politics, or culture.

In the 1953 and 1955 editions, generalizations about the formation of bourgeois relations and national markets in the first half of the seventeenth century were introduced, together with sections on Ukrainian-Russian economic ties, which received more space than economic ties with Western Europe or Poland, and were intended to prove that there had been a "base" for the "objective" and historically determined "reunion."[10] Generalizations about the Ukrainian economy as a distinct entity developing in a specific national territory were absent. Whereas the economy of Ukrainian lands under Russian rule in the eighteenth century provided a "base" for a "bourgeois nation" that was developed favorably thanks to its integration with the Russian economy, the integration of lands under Polish and later Austrian rule did not similarly foster the Western Ukrainian economy, which was treated as a colonial sub-unit. Ukrainian integration into Russia was the result of all that happened before and was "objectively progressive" despite admitted tsarist interference with the economic development of its oppressed nations. But unlike the earlier texts, the 1955 edition did devote some attention to the concept of transition to capitalism in Ukraine.[11]

In dealing with the nineteenth-century Ukrainian economy, the 1948 edition, like the later two, stated that Ukraine was not a Russian colonial dependency because its industrial development was the same as Russia's. The 1953 edition added that there was a "Ukrainian bourgeoisie," while the 1955 edition referred only to a "manufacturing bourgeoisie in Ukraine." Neither implied that this bourgeoisie could have been "progressive." The 1948 edition ignored the matter altogether, while the 1953 and 1955 editions explained that this group's only interest had been to control its own market, which merely led it into insignificant conflicts with other national bourgeoisies. The 1953 and 1955 editions noted that Ukraine's economic integration with Russia was "progressive" even though it was done by force and despite Ukraine's subsequent semicolonial status. This "contradiction" was ended by revolution.[12] Such reasoning was not applied to Western Ukraine, where "oppression," poverty, and the level of development were worse and integration into the larger whole was not "progressive," but a manifestation of economic colonialism.

The 1953 and 1955 accounts of Ukrainian seventeenth- and eighteenth-century political history differed significantly from the 1948 text. They admitted the lesser gentry into the "progressive classes" and explained that they joined Khmelnytsky's revolt not merely to save their lives and interests, but because they had the shared interest with peasants and cossacks of escaping oppression. Reference to Khmelnytsky, "the feudalist" who did not share the social ambitions of the masses, was removed, along with the claim that the Hetmanate was a tool of feudal cossack officers. This state was now "recognized by the whole nation." The 1955 edition added that the nation supported the state.[13] Although all three editions listed some tsarist restrictions on cossack autonomy, none invoked these as a reason for Vyhovsky's and later Mazepa's anti-Russian politics, nor did any give details of their treaties with Poland. Mazepa was given slightly more space in the 1950s editions, which explained that he was perfidious and "hated the Russian and Ukrainian people." These two editions told readers the majority of officers were pro-tsarist because tsarism helped them oppress the masses. Only a minority wanted to rule the masses by themselves, and they betrayed the "national interests of the Ukrainian people" and gave it away into slavery by signing accords with foreign states. The oppressed "national masses" always opposed such agreements because they wanted to maintain and strengthen their tie with the Russian "people." An argument made in the 1953 and 1955 editions but absent in the earlier text was that rule by the tsar and the Russian ruling class, although "bad," was "progressive."[14]

Such logic derived not from socio-economic categories, and were it applied consistently, then Soviet historiography would also have claimed that Mongol or French or Polish rule over Russia was "progressive" because it would have allowed Russian and French or Polish or Tatar commoners to struggle together against a common ruling class. But the Stalinist image of the past did not link Russian independence to the class rule of Russian "feudalists" and their supposed desire for a "monopoly of oppression." Russian statehood was historically "progressive" and "good," as were tendencies toward integration, concentration, centralization and uniformity in the empire, while anything directed against such forces became "bad" and "reactionary." Thus, Soviet historiography could dismiss Ukrainian cossack ttempts to establish statehood, while judging events such as Peter's Treaty f Nystadt (1721) to have been more important for Russia than the defeat of he cossack rebel Bulavin.

Accounts of the nineteenth- and early-twentieth-century national movements also reflect this reasoning. From a Marxist perspective, it was possible o argue that a bourgeoisie was "progressive" for as long as it expanded roduction. Insofar as official postwar historiography denied the bourgeoisie his "progressive" role in the non-Russian economy, it constricted the limits within which national movements, something that did not exist in Russia proper, could be discussed. None of the three editions even used the category when dealing with tsarist Ukraine until the discussion of the 1905 revolution, where they admitted that the "struggle of the Ukrainian nation for national equality had progressive significance." To further minimize the significance of national issues before 1917, they were treated within a framework of conflict between two groups that represented different paths of development. At the beginning of the century there were only "leading sections of Russian society" that in response to an early nineteenth-century "crisis of feudalism" formed a "liberation revolutionary movement." In the 1840s, this "movement" split into two wings. Liberals, supposedly over-concerned with national issues, reflected the desires of the bourgeoisie to control its own market and claimed their interests were those of the whole nation, while "revolutionary democrats" were the representatives of "the people" because they advocated liberty through revolution, which included national freedom.

All three editions dated the separation of bourgeois liberals from revolutionary democrats to the 1840s, but the 1953 and 1955 editions condemned the former as "enemies of the people" whose used nationalism to divide the working class and impede revolution. Thus, the Ukrainian national movement became "reactionary" until the twentieth century. Even the qualification that some of the Ukrainian bourgeois *hromady* were closer to "revolutionary democracy" was removed in the 1953 and 1955 editions, along with the term "bourgeois liberal" from all subtitles.

All three editions referred to a national movement in mid-nineteenth-century Western Ukraine, but the 1953 and 1955 editions condemned its organization, the *Holovna Ruska Rada,* as the "counterrevolutionary" arm of the bourgeoisie, interested only in national demands. Concessions given by Austria in 1848-1849 were attributed to the revolutionary activity of the peasants. By condemning the Austrian parliament as reactionary, all three editions avoided having to explain how Ukrainians in Galicia could have been worse off than their counterparts in Russia if the latter lacked even a bourgeois parliament.[15] Whereas the 1948 edition wrote that the major

Ukrainian political thinker of the late nineteenth century, Mykhailo Drahomanov, had a positive side, the two subsequent editions condemned him because he was critical of centralism. Also, unlike the 1948 text, the 1953 and 1955 texts included mention and condemnation of the "bourgeois" idea that Galicia had been a Ukrainian national "Piedmont." Since the national movement there did make phenomenal gains and this had to be explained, the official histories wrote that because the Galician economy was backward, the bourgeoisie was exceptionally strong and attracted some "revolutionary democratic" radicals. Western Ukrainian cultural achievements were then presented as if they had been the product of this "left wing" that had obliged the authorities to grant concessions to Ukrainians.[16] Nineteenth-century Ukrainian culture was dealt with in a separate subsection that simply listed names and works, while comments on the leading role of "progressive" Russian culture in Ukraine and long excerpts on Russian men of letters to whom Ukrainians were understudies, highlighted Russian superiority.

To present the Bolshevik coup of 1917 as a true Marxist revolution occurring at the "right" time, the authors of the 1953 and 1955 editions depicted the "bourgeois enemy" in as non-revolutionary and loyalist terms as possible. Thus, unlike the 1948 edition, which was not explicit in this matter, the later surveys omitted reference to the Ukrainian bourgeoisie becoming stronger at the turn of the century, competing for markets with its Russian and Jewish counterparts, and using the national liberation struggle in its interest. Authors claimed this social group was interested in the All-Russian market, made compromises with the tsar and the Russian bourgeoisie, and turned to imperialist Germany when it began to doubt the viability of tsarism. Also omitted was reference to Ukrainian "progressives" who participated in the Ukrainian national liberation movement but who failed to understand that Ukrainian nationalism was the enemy of the Ukrainian people.[17]

Accounts of the Revolution in Ukraine differed. The 1958 edition contained greater emphasis on events in Ukraine and the activities of Ukrainians, as opposed to events in Petrograd and the activities of the Bolsheviks, especially Lenin and Stalin, in Ukraine. The 1958 edition also admitted that errors in Bolshevik policy made the struggle for the allegiance of the non-proletarian masses difficult. It clearly stated that "the national liberation movement had a progressive character" and did not label the Rada "counterrevolutionary" until after the Bolsheviks took power. Whereas the 1948 edition attributed the formation of the Ukrainian Soviet state to directions given to the "workers and peasants of Ukraine" by Lenin and Stalin, who were then helped by "Russian workers and peasants," the 1958 edition attributed the idea to "the consciousness of the Ukrainian working class," who decided to call the first congress of Ukrainian Soviets to clarify the question of Soviet power. The 1958 edition did not refer to the Ukrainian Central Rada as "German agents," or part of a single "all Russian counterrevolutionary camp." Also gone was reference to the Ukrainian Soviet state as the first sovereign Ukrainian state.[18]

The 1958 edition dealt with Western Ukraine between 1917 and 1921 but did not treat ZUNR as one of the products of the "bourgeois democratic" revolutions that broke up the Austrian Empire. ZUNR emerged because of the low level of consciousness of the working population and the lack of a Party to lead it. ZUNR tried to divert the "masses" from the "revolutionary struggle" and supported the allies even though they were pro-Polish, while any of its policies that were deemed worthwhile were attributed to the pressure exerted by "revolutionary masses" who realized true social and national liberation lay in reunion with Soviet Ukraine. Because ZUNR was afraid of the masses, it made no serious effort to defend Western Ukraine from Polish invasion, and, allied with the "counterrevolutionary" government in Kiev, was more concerned with repressing workers.[19]

The interpretation of Ukrainian history in these three official histories followed the guidelines of 1947 and 1953. It minimized distinctions between the Russian and Ukrainian "historical process" and sought to show that the pasts of both nations were "indissolubly linked." Narratives highlighted and exaggerated similarities while downplaying or ignoring particularities and differences, a practice that often led to grotesque absurdities and/or omissions. Thus, 500 years of Polish cultural influence on Ukraine were ignored, while more space was devoted to Russian-Ukrainian trade than to Ukrainian trade with the West. Without comparative statistics, it was claimed that this trade was an economic base for "reunion." Most guilty of such practices was the 1953 edition, where it is possible to find an assertion that Jesuit schools trained fanatics and "Vatican slaves." The 1955 edition, by contrast, only noted that there were many Jesuit schools in Ukraine in the seventeenth century.[20] The treatment of events in Ukraine between 1917 and 1921 in the 1958 edition reflected the more "liberal" climate in the USSR. The narrative was not centered on how Lenin and Stalin extended the revolution in Ukraine but presented the Revolution as the result of efforts of the "working population in Ukraine" as well as of the "Ukrainian people." The assertion that the national liberation movement was progressive represented an important interpretive shift.

SUBSEQUENT REVISIONS

Between 1958 and 1982, the Academy of Sciences in Kiev released two major histories of the Ukrainian SSR, one in two volumes (1967), and one in eight volumes (1977-1979). Both contained considerable revisions and most of the authors of the 1977 text did not participate in writing the 1967 history. Since the similarities between these and earlier editions were greater than the dissimilarities, they cannot be regarded as different surveys but merely as revised editions of the 1948 text.

Reformist Ukrainian historians exploited the post-Stalin "thaw" to write a less Russocentric history of the Ukr. SSR. In a number of monographs and articles published during the writing, and after the publication, of the two-volume 1967 survey, reformists also questioned some established views and examined previously ignored subjects.[21] The overall tone of this reformist tendency was expressed before the bulk of these publications appeared, however, in reviews of the draft version of the 1967 text, which challenged statements of fact and addressed conceptual issues. At a meeting of the academic council discussing the draft, an optimistic participant remarked: "The conditions that existed under the cult of personality no longer exist. Solving such problems [the Pereiaslav treaty] could bring on much danger. Now this is all behind us." From the audience someone shouted: "There were not only threats but arrests."[22]

Although there were calls in the reviewer's protocols to identify parallels in Ukrainian and Russian history, the majority of the comments directed the authors to pay less attention to Russian affairs and more to what was particular in Ukraine's past. The underlying theme of the "reformist's" remarks was that loyalty to the USSR was not incompatible with Ukrainian national consciousness or an awareness of the differences between Russia and Ukraine. One participant urged her colleagues to consider the conditions under which the "Thesis" was formulated and not to transform what was a formula into a dogma. Historians called for better treatment of cossack statehood after 1654, more details about the nineteenth-century national movement, mention of the positive role played by individuals such as Drahomanov, and for full discussion of whether or not Ukraine was a Russian colony economically. This was an important issue since if it was not, there would be little sense in even raising the issue of a national liberation movement.[23] Noteworthy were observations made by the rector of the Higher Party School in Kiev in 1965, A. Chekaniuk. He wanted historians to show why the existence of a Ukrainian feudal state was not in the interests of tsarism and to "reveal" not only how Ukrainian bourgeois nationalists but also Russian and Polish nationalists "falsified " Ukrainian history. He wanted to see more material about twentieth-century Ukraine, stress placed on how the national liberation movement was an intrinsic element of socialist revolution, and fewer quotes from Lenin![24] Although these criticisms appear limited when compared with what is found in Polish historiography after 1956, they were outspoken at the time in the USSR.

The 1967 text did not amount to a Ukrainian interpretation of Ukraine's past, but it did reflect the "liberal" tone of the above comments and was the least Russocentric of the postwar surveys. Its authors did not accent the "reunion" theme, Russian primacy, or Russian influence; and highlighted political and economic issues particular to Ukraine. The difference in emphasis was evident in the introduction. The 1967 text referred once to common Russian and Ukrainian historical development and explained that the subject of the book was the history of the Ukrainian nation. The main introduction to the 1977 edition, by contrast, repeated the Ukrainian-Russian idea five times and explained that the subject of the narrative was the history of the "working population of Ukraine." The introductions to the following volumes dealing with tsarist Ukraine emphasized ethnic commonality, Russian primacy, and the benefits Ukraine won from economic integration into the Russian state.

The 1967 edition and the first volume of the 1977 edition contain less Russian subject matter than the earlier editions, and the 1967 text has fewer anti-"bourgeois nationalist" diatribes. Noteworthy was the stress that edition placed on cossack autonomy and the nineteenth-century national liberation movement, which it identified as "progressive" instead of as a hostile current separate from the "revolutionary movement" from the 1840s. The 1977 edition contained more factual information than the earlier surveys, but like the 1948 and 1953 editions it downplayed and minimized differences between Ukraine and Russia. Even "Ukraine" in the adjectival form appeared less often in the 1977 edition than the earlier ones, while "Ukrainian nation" and "liberation movement of the Ukrainian nation" did not figure as the historical subject of the narrative. In the 1977-1979 text, the image of Ukraine as merely a geographical region of a larger all-Russian territory was reinforced by the use of forms like "the popular movement in Ukraine," "the worker peasant masses," or simply "population."

Both editions treated political events as epiphenomena. With respect to the 1169 sack of Kiev, the 1977 account does not mention Bogoliubsky's wish to subjugate the city and make Vladimir in Suzdal capital of Rus, claiming that the incident was blown out of proportion by historians since southern as well as northern princes took part in the attack. The 1977 edition, unlike the earlier two, remarked that the Lithuanian Grand Duke became rightful ruler of Galicia after George II, and that Casimir IV simply ignored its autonomy. More satisfactory was the treatment of the Union of Lublin, which noted the role of foreign policy and Polish blackmail in causing the higher Rus nobles to agree to it. The authors did not condemn the lesser nobles for joining because of the promise of more rights. Unlike earlier editions, it did not portray their move as treachery done to obtain Polish help in oppressing "the masses." Unlike the Moscow histories of the USSR, the Ukrainian surveys stated Orthodox bishops motivated by secular interests were as responsible as Rome, Jesuits, and Polish political leaders for the Church Union. Also, the 1953 and 1967 editions remarked that the Uniate bishops demanded Rome recognize their rite and liturgy because they feared the enraged Orthodox masses. The 1977 text called this condition merely a ruse intended to befuddle the people and added that efforts by the Orthodox Church to reform itself had little success.[25] Like the other surveys, these gave no political dimension to revolts and muddled the differences between cossacks and peasants. The 1967 edition noted that revolts were not only "anti-feudal" but part of the "national liberation struggle." A claim in the 1967 edition about the search of "the population of Right-Bank Ukraine" for "support from the fraternal Russian people" and their desire to reunite with the rest of Ukraine, was replaced in the 1977 text with a reference to the "working population" seeking protection from the Russian state while "being desirous of realizing their old dream of uniting with the Russian people."[26] There was no mention of massacres of Poles during the Haidamak revolts, but the 1967 and 1977 editions cite the Torchyn Manifesto as a cause.

The sections on sixteenth- and seventeenth-century economic history in the 1967 edition and volume one of the 1977 edition placed more stress on the development of forces of production, and on the rise of bourgeois commercial and money relations than did previous surveys. Authors discussed the formation of a Ukrainian national market, urban development, and the extension of hired labor; and they mentioned that the class struggle during this period centered on the emergence of a class of free petty producers. But although these elements were identified, the economy was not actually labeled "early capitalist" until the late seventeenth century, that is, after part of Ukraine was annexed to Russia, thus linking capitalist progress to association with Russia. However, this was a change from the 1955 edition, which dated the transition in the late eighteenth century. Whereas the 1967 edition noted pre-1654 Ukrainian economic ties with Russia in passing, the 1977 text dealt with this subject in separate subsections before discussing trade with the West, and claimed they had been economic preconditions to "reunion."[27] Noteworthy was the absence of the Russian Empire from a list of "foreign states" with "regressive political forms of social structure" who controlled Ukrainian lands, although Russian historians did list Russia among such states in other publications. This omission made logical the claim that tsarist Ukraine developed better or quicker than those parts of it ruled by other powers.[28]

In dealing with the eighteenth-century economy, the 1967 edition made no explicit criticism of Russian interference with development, but unlike the 1955 edition, it did not refer to economic development as one of the blessings of "reunion." It also mentioned, for the first time, tsarist restrictions on Ukrainian exports and the exploitation of Ukrainian natural resources for Russian manufacturing. The 1953, 1955, 1967, and 1977 editions do not refer to the abolition of the Ukrainian-Russian tariff border in 1756 but to the abolition of internal tariffs in the empire that helped expand trade between Left-Bank Ukraine and Russia and the evolution of the "All-Russian" market. Ukrainian economic history, in short, was presented in terms of regional specialization. It was assumed that because concentration of productive forces and integration was good for the empire, it was good for its non-Russian provinces.[29]

The texts differ in their descriptions of the nineteenth-century bourgeoisie. A reference to an appreciable rise of the "Ukrainian bourgeoisie" in the 1967 edition was replaced in 1977 with an observation on their quantitative increase and a comment that the Ukrainian and Russian bourgeoisie was never revolutionary. Both texts claimed Ukraine was economically on the same level as central Russia and therefore was not a colony, but the 1967 text implied the liberal bourgeoisie played a "progressive role." Also, it claimed that because of a weaker position in the world market, the Russian bourgeoisie was more nationalist in Ukraine than in Russian proper, and that Russian feudal military imperialism was more oppressive in the borderlands than in Russia proper. This implied rivalry between the non-Russian and Russian national bourgeoisies was omitted in the later edition, which flatly stated that all the tsarist bourgeoisie were the same. In Ukraine, this group was merely part of an imperial class in one particular economic region.[30] All editions described Eastern Galicia as an exploited, backward colony that did not benefit from the economic specialization imposed on it by virtue of belonging to the larger Habsburg whole.

The official histories diverged in their treatment of issues related to Ukrainian statehood, autonomy, and the national movement. Whereas in the 1955 text the Zaporozhian Sich was only "progressive," the 1967 text called it the "basis of Ukrainian national statehood" and a national political center, and cited Marx's reference to it as a "Christian Cossack republic." These claims disappeared in the later edition, as did the categorization of cossack-peasant revolts as a "national liberation" struggle. Whereas the 1967 edition depicted cossacks as protectors of the Orthodox Church from the 1620s, the later edition explained that the church allied itself with rich cossacks to secure its socio-economic position in Ukraine against "the masses." On the question of statehood during Khmelnytsky's lifetime, the 1977 edition omitted references to mass recognition and support for the cossack state and the comment, found in the 1967 edition, that the tsar's aim was unlimited control and it had not been in Russia's interest for the Hetmanate to exist. Also gone was the observation that near the end of his life Khmelnytsky was displeased with Russian foreign policy and centralism.[31]

Both editions explained the politics of Vyhovsky and Mazepa as a reflection of narrow class interest, though the 1967 text did not brand Vyhovsky and his supporters "reactionary," and, unlike the later edition, mentioned the "Duchy of Rus" and that some officers were supposed to get gentry privileges according to the Hadiach treaty. The 1967 edition contained a relatively outspoken treatment of restrictions on the "autonomy of Ukraine" resulting from the "colonial onslaught of tsarism" that not only circumscribed the rights and privileges of the ruling officers, but worsened the status of "the masses," who also protested against the restrictions placed on the last vestiges of autonomy. The abolition of the Hetmanate, the authors added, deprived the Ukrainian nation of the elements of statehood formed in the preceding century—an important and "inseparable part of its national development." The diminution and restriction of autonomy allowed Russian tsarism to better exploit "the masses," fill offices in Ukraine with Russians, and begin forced Russification and national oppression. This edition did not attack "bourgeois historians" for stressing this issue, nor did it mention any "progressive" effects on Ukraine of Peter I's reforms. By contrast, the 1977 survey, which contained more information about the political history and structure of the Hetmanate, downplayed the issue of statehood and its significance. The 1967 edition mentioned that the 1659 and 1668 Ukrainian-Russian accords were more restrictive than the Pereiaslav treaty, and stated that they served to limit the autonomy of the Hetmanate. The 1977 edition pointed to the 1659 treaty as proof of the common class interests of the Ukrainian and Russian ruling class, and claimed that the 1668 accords instituted "fundamental changes" conducive "to merging the class interests of the cossack officers and Russian nobility." The later survey attached little importance to the diminution of cossack rights. It noted simply that the Russian administrative system functioned alongside the Ukrainian political system and that both were the instruments of the ruling class. Both histories observed that cossack officers needed autonomy only to secure better conditions for exploitation, but the 1967 account also included remarks on some of the unfortunate consequences of diminution of autonomy.

In all official Soviet accounts, the Russian state, "despite oppression," attained "historically necessary" tasks, such as annexing Baltic ports. Ukrainian political structures, on the other hand, were not identified with any function, role, or task except repression. Moreover, no edition directly linked the diminution of the Hetmanate's autonomy with anti-Russian uprisings or politics, and all dealt with Peter's internal reforms before dealing with Mazepa's fate at Poltava in 1709, thereby not explicitly identifying the latter as a cause of the restrictions on Ukrainian autonomy. Perhaps this was to avoid an issue that appeared in two pre- 1917 Ukrainian biographies of Mazepa: why a presumably loyal majority was punished for the activities of one man supposedly representing a minority.[32]

The gist of the interpretation of the nineteenth-century national movement may be gauged from subsection titles. For example, in the 1955 edition we read: "The Birth of Revolutionary Democracy and the Bourgeois Liberal Movement." In the 1967 text the same subject matter is given in a section called "The Birth of Revolutionary Democracy," but there are added sections entitled "The Liberation Movement" and "The National Movement." The later edition contains only subsections called "The Birth of Revolutionary Democracy in the Russian Liberation Movement" and "The National Liberation Movement" in Western Ukraine in the 1840s. In tsarist Ukraine there was only a "Liberal Opposition Movement," while the term "national movement" did not appear at all until the late nineteenth century. These headings reflected the shifting dates during which a "progressive" national movement with two wings was supposed to have emerged. In the 1955 edition, it was the twentieth century; in the 1967 account it was the mid-nineteenth century, and in the later edition it was the late nineteenth century. The dating was significant because it determined for how long social development and political history in Ukraine could be treated as part of a single "All-Russian" social revolutionary movement with two wings, within which non-Russian national issues could be placed on the political right, labeled "reactionary," and therefore irrelevant and unworthy of attention. The dating of the emergence of a "progressive national movement" determined how much of the non-Russian political heritage could be incorporated into the official interpretation and how far back it could be traced. Since there was no "national question" in Russia proper, extending its chronological limits effectively expanded the

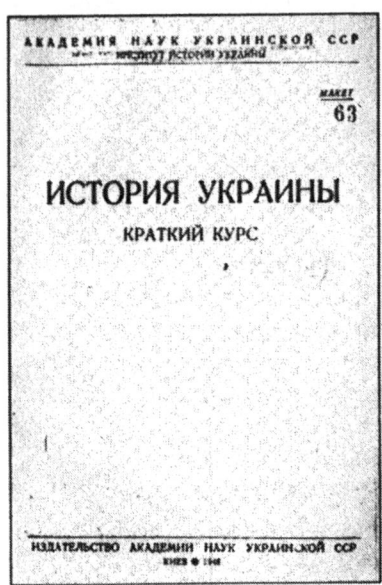

1. Title page of the 1948 draft version of "Istoriia Ukrainy."

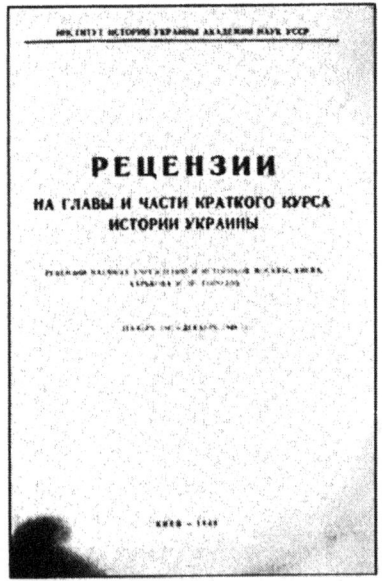

2. Title page of the stenographed protocols and reviews of the 1948 draft survey history.

ЗВЕДЕНИЙ ПОКАЖЧИК
ЗАСТАРІЛИХ ВИДАНЬ, ЩО НЕ ПІДЛЯГАЮТЬ ВИКОРИСТАННЮ В БІБЛІОТЕКАХ ГРОМАДСЬКОГО КОРИСТУВАННЯ ТА КНИГОТОРГОВЕЛЬНІЙ СІТЦІ

Видавництво Книжкової палати УРСР
Харків—1954

3. Title page from a 1954 edition of the list of works not permitted on open shelves in libraries.

framework for discussion of something unique to the non-Russian nations. For example, the later a national movement uniting all classes was identified as "democratic" in a particular country's history, the shorter would be the period of "proletarian hegemony," a euphemism for Bolshevik control. This then allowed historians to claim indigenous historical development for their countries for a longer period of time before 1917. It also gave them the greater leeway for interpreting the Revolution as a product of specific circumstances in each non-Russian region, instead of as a phenomenon basically the same throughout the empire.

These shifts in the treatment of persons and ideas associated with nineteenth-century national issues seem minor, almost trivial. But they represented the best efforts of honest scholars to construct as accurate an account as they could within the deductivist DHM interpretation of the past with which they were forced to work. By dating the national movement from the mid-nineteenth century, for example, the 1967 edition provided a better account of the first organizational expressions of political nationalism in Ukraine, the Cyril and Methodius Brotherhood in Kiev, and the *Holovna Ruska Rada* in Lviv. The latter was not mentioned at all in the 1955 text, which labeled the former a "reactionary" organization except for Shevchenko, the "revolutionary democrat." The 1967 edition, on the other hand, noted that Shevchenko fought "liberals" inside a Brotherhood with "progressive" aims that were not exclusively the result of his or of "revolutionary democratic" influences. Such a formulation served to widen the scope of the permissible in discussing nineteenth-century Ukrainian history. By contrast, the 1977-1979 edition narrowed these limits. It explained that Shevchenko entered the organization to propagate "revolutionary democracy" but that its program, despite "progressive" elements, was dominated by "bourgeois nationalist shortcomings." Differences between members were presented as if there had been a sharp ideological debate between two wings in a "sociopolitical movement" who shared the wish for "national independence." The 1967 edition identified a liberal wing in the national movement whose members all desired "Ukrainian national liberation" but differed over various "liberal and bourgeois views." Dealing with the Ukrainian movement in Galicia, the 1967 edition approved the cultural work of "progressive intellectuals," who, unlike the local bourgeoisie and priests, did not limit their activity to national cultural demands in the name of their class interests but also made social demands. It did not condemn the *Lviv Rada,* as did the earlier edition, but described it as an organization with a "progressive" wing. Polish influences on Ukrainians were noted, and there was no condemnation of the Austrian parliament.

Where the 1955 edition condemned the *hromady* as "counterrevolutionary," the 1967 edition ascribed to them a positive role in the national liberation movement even though they were not politically radical. The later edition equivocated. The authors noted, without judging, their cultural work and, as in the 1948 edition, divided their members into a minority left and majority right wings. They also observed that *hromadas* were repressed although they only were involved with cultural work.[33]

The 1977-1979 survey provided a theoretical description of the national movement. It explained that nations appeared as capitalist oppression developed and that national movements were a reaction in which all social groups took part. In Ukraine, the movement was weaker than elsewhere in Europe and never demanded separatism because the national bourgeoisie was more inclined to compromise, and because "the masses" were tied by blood to the "Russian people."[34] The authors depicted almost all nineteenth-century Ukrainian activists as "liberal-bourgeois" because they were not radicals, and unlike the 1967 text, did not state that their cultural achievements played a "positive" role in the national-liberation movement. The 1977 survey devoted more space than the earlier ones to Western Ukrainians designated as "liberals," but made no note of their cultural achievements as it did when dealing with their tsarist counterparts. Whereas it criticized Kievan "liberals" for compromising with tsarism, their Galician counterparts were described as agents of the Austrian government.[35] The 1967 and 1977 editions provided short descriptions of Ukrainian parties, but the latter edition, like the 1955, was more critical of their behavior after 1912 and condemned them as anti-popular, chauvinist, pro-Austrian separatists. The 1967 survey only divided the parties into three groups and made no reference to "agents." Hrushevsky in the 1955 text was an "agent," in 1967 an "ideologist of the national liberals," and in 1977 a "bourgeois nationalist ideologist."[36]

The 1967 and 1977 editions give little attention to Polish-Ukrainian conflicts in Galicia and their political context. Their theme was that the "revolutionary pressure of the masses" forced Vienna to give national concessions and that the "bourgeoisie" exploited these according to its class interests. The 1967 account claimed the "bourgeoisie" aimed to secure their privileges and keep down the revolutionary movement. Their aim was to place all Ukraine under Austrian rule, while "the working masses" and "progressives" wanted "reunion." In the 1977 edition, Galician Ukrainian cultural organizations were "tools of nationalist propaganda." They were not the achievement of "progressives," as asserted in the 1967 edition, but organizations in which "progressives" only took part. The political events in turn-of-the -century Galicia were dismissed as nothing but interpolations on minor matters in parliament, and there was no mention of the aim of autonomy. Gone as well was the observation in the 1967 edition that Lenin paid much sympathetic attention to the Ukrainian problem in Galicia.[37]

Shifts in the official interpretation of Ukraine's past stemmed from changes in political climate that determined whether those who minimized, muddled, or erased historical differences and distinctions, or those who identified and stressed them, had greater influence on the printed page. During the 1960s Ukrainian "reformists" were unable to ignore the guidelines of 1947 and 1953, but with Party support they interpreted them broadly. Their efforts led to changes in the account of events in Ukraine between 1917 and 1921. Thus the 1967 edition, unlike the earlier one, did not isolate a national movement led by the bourgeoisie from a workers movement. Rather, it redrew the line and referred to a single revolutionary movement of which the national movement had been a "progressive democratic" part and within which two wings fought for leadership. This established a better framework for discussing the national revolution in Ukraine. The 1967 edition drew attention to differences between the Russian and Ukrainian bourgeoisie, whose struggle to exploit the workers was based ultimately on the national question. The authors did not label the Rada "counterrevolutionary" until after the Bolshevik coup and noted that its demands for autonomy from the Provisional Government were "democratic." The 1967 edition did not condemn the shortlived Bolshevik participation in the Rada but interpreted the affair as a well thought-out tactic, thus implying the Rada could not have been very "reactionary." Unprecedented and significant was mention in the 1967 edition that the majority in the Rada were left-bourgeois democrats whose influence increased due to the anti-Ukrainian policies of the Provisional Government. The Rada and the national movement of which it was a part played a positive role in the revolution, according to the 1967 edition, because they weakened the Provisional Government. Similarly, this edition implicitly approved of the Rada's First Universal, which declared Ukrainian autonomy. It explained that the proclamation was made only under the pressure of the "popular masses," and reminded readers that Lenin approved of it.[38]

In contrast, the 1977 edition argued that the Revolution followed a similar pattern throughout the empire and depicted Kiev in 1917 as merely one of many centers. The narrative began with the activities of Bolsheviks in those areas where they were strong (mainly Russified cities), reviewed incidents in army and village soviets, and only then introduced the national question, implying that it was an issue that only concerned the Rada and the Kiev region. The theme of one national liberation movement and two groups struggling for leadership within it was retained, but the Rada was dismissed as "counterrevolutionary from its origins, an enemy of the national liberation movement whose success was founded on popular political naivete. There was no mention of its differences with the Provisional Government over the national question, although there was more detail about Ukrainian parties and politicians than in earlier editions. Bolsheviks who participated in the Rada were "duped" and in error. The author's admitted that the First Universal was issued under popular pressure, but not that Lenin had approved or that the Rada feared losing popularity.[39]

Since Ukrainians in 1917 were an overwhelmingly peasant population, it is noteworthy that the 1967 edition dropped the phrase "under the influence of the revolutionary workers movement" whenever mentioning the peasant movement. Implied tutelage was thereby replaced with implied independence of action. Whereas the 1977 account presented Bolshevik victory as if it were an irresistible wave encountering a few unfortunate complications in Ukraine caused by some bourgeois parties, the 1967 account gave the reader a sense of conflict and drew his attention to Bolshevik difficulties in Ukraine. The 1967 edition did not depict the Revolution in Ukraine as a reflection of events in Petrograd and Moscow following a predetermined pattern, but as a "process" wherein "Bolsheviks in Ukraine" led the struggle of "Ukrainian workers and poor peasants" to establish the Soviet regime. The account stressed that Lenin recognized the independence of the nation in 1917 and described the first Ukrainian congress of Soviets as the result of an idea formed in "the consciousness of the Ukrainian working class." The 1977 edition explained how the Bolsheviks, carrying out the will of the revolutionary masses, took charge of creating Ukrainian Soviet statehood in the course of systematically implementing Lenin's program on the national question. This edition, it may be added, noted mistakes in policy toward the peasants but none toward non-Russians.

Accounts of events in Western Ukraine between 1918 and 1921 differed in the 1967 and 1977 editions, especially with respect to the local communist movement. The former referred to "bourgeois democratic" revolutions in Austria-Hungary but did not classify ZUNR among them. It depicted ZUNR as "counterrevolutionary" and able to take power only thanks to the low level of political consciousness and absence of a revolutionary party in the region. The "mass revolutionary movement" in Western Ukraine aimed to reunite with Soviet Ukraine. The Western Ukrainian Communist Party (KPZU), meanwhile, was formed by Ukrainian Bolsheviks as part of their "internationalist duty" but it does not appear as the leader of the struggle. The 1977 history omitted the reference to "bourgeois democratic" revolutions and claimed ZUNR took power thanks to its military formations. Like the 1958 edition, it dealt with the KPZU as an organization formed in Western Ukraine that began leading the struggle, but omitted reference to the role played in its formation by returning POWs from Russia and added that it got help from the Bolshevik Party. This edition, for the first time in an official survey, mentioned the Galician Soviet Republic, thus indirectly admitting that at the time there were no Soviet plans to unite Ukraine. Whereas the 1967 edition explained that in 1921 Moscow gave up Western Ukraine to hasten peace talks, prevent bloodshed, and deal with White Russian troops under Wrangel, the later edition curtly noted that the Bolsheviks withdrew and backed Ukrainian rights at the negotiations with Poland.[40]

In addition to the major surveys, after 1956 a number of one-volume "popular histories," summary outlines, and text books for colleges and secondary schools also were written.[41] Of six published up to 1982 reviewed here, three had interpretations similar to the 1955 and 1977 editions of the multivolume surveys,[42] and two, like the 1967 edition, highlighted particularities in Ukraine's past. The interpretation in the sixth varied. Published eight times between 1962 and 1975, it stressed or minimized the uniqueness of Ukraine's "historical process" according to the political climate.[43] The remainder of this chapter will only mention illustrative examples from each book.

The texts by O. Kasymenko (1960), like those by Rybalka (1978) and Kondufor (ed., 1981) adhered more stringently to the 1947 and 1953 guidelines than two surveys by Dubyna (1967 and 1965). Kasymenko stressed that Ukrainian-Russian ethnic affinity played a key role in determining events and did not even mention major events such as the Union of 1569. For Kasymenko the "characteristic singularity" of Ukrainian national identity as formed in the nineteenth century was its "shared traits" (*sporidnist*) with the Russian and Belarus people.[44] Whereas the Dubyna texts refer to the "Ukrainian nation's" struggle against oppression, Kasymenko wrote of the "liberation struggle in Ukraine." Kasymenko associated cossack autonomy with the desire of the Ukrainian ruling class to better exploit their masses, but both Dubyna surveys highlighted tsarist restrictions on autonomy and noted that this "colonial policy" forced cossack leaders to seek alliances with other powers.[45] Similarly, Kasymenko dealt with the Cyril and Methodius Brotherhood as a "bourgeois liberal" organization with a radical wing led by Shevchenko, but Dubyna toned down the differences between members. Dubyna (1967) also used the phrase "liberation movement of the Ukrainian nation" where the other authors mentioned only a mid-nineteenth-century "revolutionary movement" or an anti-feudal agrarian movement.[46]

For both Kasymenko and Dubyna (1967) the Central Rada from its origins was "counterrevolutionary," but the latter noted that the Rada had mass support and specifically stated that the Revolution in Ukraine differed from the one in Russia due to the national liberation movement.[47] The gist of the interpretation in each of the surveys was captured in the sentences concluding the sections on the first period of the 1917 Revolution. Kasymenko wrote: "And so thanks to brotherly amity with the Great Russian nation the Ukrainian nation, guided by the Communist party, headed by Lenin, began to victoriously build socialism in its state, the Ukrainian Soviet Socialist Republic, created thanks to the triumph of the Great October Revolution." Dubyna (1965) wrote: "Thus from the first days of Soviet power in Ukraine . . . the Ukrainian nation began the task of statebuilding and socialist transformation of the economy." In Dubyna (1967) we read: "The triumph of the Socialist revolution and the establishment of Soviet power in Ukraine—this is the great historical triumph of the Ukrainian nation, the result of its centuries long struggle for a better fate."[48]

The secondary school text book by V. Diadychenko, F. Los, and V. Spytsky, republished in many editions between 1962 and 1975, provides a vivid example of how interpretation accented or erased historical differences. Major changes are found in the 1964, 1968, and 1974 editions. For example, in the earlier text we read that the tsarist government wanted to totally subjugate, oppress, and exploit Cossack Ukraine. In the 1974 edition the tsarist government, "carrying out the policies of the nobility," wanted only to fully control Ukraine.[49] Interpretative shifts are also revealed by subtitle changes. In the 1973 edition (an unrevised reprint of the 1968 edition) there are headings such as "The Ukrainian Cossacks," "Ukrainian Culture in the Eighteenth Century," and "The Struggle of Ukraine against Foreign Invaders." These were changed in the 1974 edition to "The Origins of the Cossacks," "The Culture of Ukraine in the Eighteenth Century," and "The Participation of the Ukrainian Nation in the Struggle Against French Invaders." A phrase in the 1973 edition about the Zaporozhian Sich as the military base of the Ukrainian nation whose glory was known throughout Europe, was changed in the 1974 edition to read that the Sich played a great role in the struggle of the Ukrainian nation against foreigners.[50] The subheadings "The National Liberation Movement," "Struggle of the Bolsheviks against Bourgeois Nationalism," "The February Bourgeois Democratic Revolution in Ukraine," and "The Anti-Popular Policies of the Rada" were changed in the 1974 edition to "The Struggle of Lenin and the Bolsheviks for the International Solidarity of the Working People," "Events of the February Bourgeois Democratic Revolution in Ukraine," and "The Counterrevolutionary Policies of the Rada." "The Heroic Struggle of the Ukrainian Nation for its Freedom and Independence and for Soviet Power," found in the 1968 edition, in 1973 became "The Heroic Struggle of the Workers of Ukraine."

The 1968 text explained that in 1917 the bourgeoisie desired autonomy within a bourgeois constitutional order, feared revolution, and wanted to solve the national question peacefully but were exposed by the Bolsheviks. The 1974 text noted that the bourgeoisie merely exploited the existence of national oppression in an attempt to prove it represented the interests of the nation, and that the bourgeoisie, fearing revolution, fawned before the Provisional Government and was prepared to implement only cultural reforms. While the 1968 text referred to Rada policy simply as "anti-popular," the 1973 text depicted the Rada as an instrument of foreign powers and "counterrevolutionary."[51]

Some passages changed or removed in 1974 were introduced in 1964 and then emphasized in 1968. For example, a claim in the 1964 edition that Russia was the only power that could defend Ukraine was changed in 1968 to read that the formation of the Great Russian state had a great progressive role in Ukrainian history, but Ukraine had to defend itself. Whereas the 1964 version condemned the "feudal" Ukrainian ruling class for betraying the nation, the 1968 text condemned only part of this class. The two following passages from the 1964 edition were deleted from the 1968 text: "So the Ukrainian nation under the leadership of the great Lenin and shoulder to shoulder with the Great Russian people went towards the Great Socialist Revolution" and "The general development of revolutionary democracy and the emerging proletarian culture lifted the spiritual level of the Ukrainian nation and helped raise its revolutionary consciousness." Finally, the 1968 edition, unlike the 1964 edition, contained a subsection entitled "National Liberation Movement" and specified that the Ukrainian struggle for national equality was progressive. Where the 1964 text accused the Rada of maintaining the landowner order and the apparatus of the Provisional Government, the 1968 edition asserted, without comment, that the Rada proclaimed a republic.[52]

9

Deductivist Discourse and Research

INTERPRETATION AND TYPOLOGIES

Academic discourse in the USSR was deductivist, and research in Marxist-Leninist Dialectical Historical Materialism (DHM) involved looking for evidence to illustrate, not question or disprove propositions. Since DHM postulated that future research would reveal appropriate evidence because there were no non-existent facts, only undiscovered ones, it allowed historians to make do with evidence that otherwise would not be considered conclusive. A lack of evidence to show that events conformed to a predefined scenario was not problematical, since it was assumed that proof that would emerge someday. Therefore, a DHM account was "objective," not because it conformed to evidence, but because it confirmed the predetermined evolution of the subject as interpreted by authority. For historians, the acceptability of interpretation to authority depended not only on logical consistency with *a priori* principles. Acceptability was also related to considerations of patronage, political circumstances, personal rivalries, and even of space and time. Sometimes the intellectual climate was more "liberal" in Moscow than in the Republics, while at other times Republican Party factions supported controlled expression of regional nationalism. Ideological and political considerations, as well as supervision, also became less burdensome for scholars the more remote in time and less politically sensitive a subject was.

After 1953, the epistemological nature of official humanities scholarship in the USSR remained holistic and deductivist. Unlike science, which was declared an ideologically neutral product of "society as a whole," historiography remained part of the "superstructure," therefore "class determined" and necessarily subject to Party control. Restrictions eased, however, and differences of opinion did emerge in print. Historians who believed that theories and interpretations should correspond to evidence and not vice versa, could compete for Party favor against their "conservative" rivals.

Throughout the post-Stalin period, the Party controlled resources and jobs. Deductivist DHM still defined categories of thought as well as language, and revisionist research could not directly influence the evolution of interpretation. However, during the 1960s in particular, interpretation was not determined exclusively by guidelines, and monographs on specific subjects could influence generalizations indirectly, via DHM paradigms.

Between 1929 and 1932, and again during the 1950s and 1960s, scholars debated the "correct" interpretation of what Marx, Engels, Lenin, and Stalin wrote on specific subjects and created models or paradigms of "anti-feudal struggle," "the transition from feudalism to capitalism," "absolutism," "the national question," and tsarist "imperialism." These models were intended to explain subjects such as peasant revolts, economic development, Russian territorial expansion, and state-building in DHM terms, but without unduly ignoring reality. In constructing these paradigms, historians stretched and diluted first principles and guidelines in order to make them compatible with evidence. Alternatively, during these years, it could be argued that existing interpretation was an incorrect derivation from the first principles. The result was what John Keep called a "competition between typologies," which usually ended when the interpretative authority, a senior "conservative" historian or Party official, judged the existing interpretation "correct" and the "reformist" questioning and dissonant information "wrong." But sometimes authority agreed that the interpretation was "incorrect," and permitted revision. At this stage, new information could be incorporated and "reformist" historians could either mollify or eliminate some of the more blatant inconsistencies between fact and interpretation without formally refuting or challenging the "truth" of first principles or guidelines.[1]

After Stalin's death, "reformers" who thought information should not be ignored when it contradicted established interpretation expressed their views among their colleagues. For example, in 1956, E. Burdzhalov stated that great power chauvinism had to be condemned, that tsarist colonial policy could not be ignored, and that national groups and liberals in the empire at the beginning of the century could not all automatically be regarded as "counterrevolutionary."[2] But to appear in print and serve as a basis for interpretative revision of the official image of the past, such ideas could not be presented directly as explicit critical attacks or alternatives. They had to be phrased and structured as "corrections."

To make their case, "reformers" exploited the ambiguity of official axioms. For example, Marxism postulates that a well-developed capitalism must precede socialist revolution, and Lenin in *Development of Capitalism in Russia* (1890) "proved" that the nineteenth-century empire had capitalist agriculture and a highly differentiated peasantry ready to ally with the proletariat. Lenin's analysis ignored inconvenient information, was superficial and tendentious,[3] but not for these reasons did he reach opposite conclusions, that better explained reality, in his *Revision of the Agrarian Program of the Workers Party* (1903) and *The Agrarian Program of Social Democracy* (1907). There he argued that because "feudal remnants" dominated, the peasantry was relatively homogeneous, and small property holding was progressive, the Party should support them. These two works expressed different points of view because they were written for different political purposes, and Lenin ignored the consequences of the differences and ambiguities in his two interpretations. But for later historians faced with the task of legitimizing the post-revolutionary order and obliged to study nineteenth-century economic history in terms of Lenin's ideas, the differences had profound importance. For example, if "feudal remnants" dominated the pre-1917 economy, the legitimacy and timing of the Revolution is opened to doubt, the peasantry takes on a role as a non-capitalist agent acting on its own as a "progressive" force, and the taking of power by representatives of the proletariat becomes merely a coup, not an historically inevitable and legitimate result of evolution. By extension, it could be argued that "remnants" were at different levels in different parts of the empire, which in turn meant that there was not one but many revolutions. This undermined the legitimacy of Bolshevik rule and understandably most historians in the 1920s categorized the pre-1917 tsarist economy as capitalist.

During the Stalin years, the "capitalism now" view was obligatory. After 1953, Lenin's ambiguity permitted historians more concerned with accurate depiction of the past than doctrine to challenge the prevailing interpretation of nineteenth-century economic history by using the "feudal remnants dominated" argument.[4] As of 1982, authority had not passed judgement and the debate went on. Since most post-Stalin survey histories equivocated on the "capitalism dominates but remnants remain" formula to such a degree that it is impossible to determine where the authors stood, the debates seem to have had some influence.

A major venue of the "competition between typologies" during the early 1930s and 1960s were scholarly conferences whose proceedings usually reflected better than articles the kind of change interpretative authority was willing to consider. Some of the ideas propounded at the various conferences and in published literature were remarkable from the point of view of Western observers at the time, and were undesirable from the perspective of the Party. It must, however, be remembered that all the debates were officially organized. In 1959, the Party mobilized intellectuals to "struggle against revisionism" and "bourgeois ideology" and issued guidelines and topics, and during the next ten years the historians fulfilled their duties.[5] Some went further than the authorities had expected, but this does not alter the fact that interpretive changes were as much products of official as personal initiative. Moreover, during discussions about DHM paradigms and models, there is no record of anyone questioning whether they were worth debating at all, thus the Party never faced the threat of scholars rejecting DHM completely. Indeed, reformists, regardless of how they interpreted a particular issue, effectively legitimated and reinforced DHM by virtue of the fact they used and proceeded from premises defined by DHM. Naturally, the published proceedings of post-1934 conferences were censored, but they retained the gist of the disputes, and searching for and identifying these ideas in survey texts provides useful criteria with which to measure interpretative change in Soviet historical writing.

The debates were Russocentric because most participants were Russians and/or students of Russia, because almost all cited examples from Russian history to support or refute theoretical propositions, and because participants assessed events from a Russian perspective. The only Ukrainian who made a major theoretical contribution at the All-Union level was V. O. Holobutsky.[6] In hundreds of pages of published proceedings, direct comment by "reformist" historians on non-Russian subject matter not classified as part of "the national question," though at times very critical and sincere, was limited and without theoretical elaboration. But the debates and resolutions of the conferences did influence the later presentation of non-Russian history. By criticizing a prevailing paradigm and offering a "correct" interpretation of first principles, "reformist" historians at the center redefined analytical categories. Historians in the non-Russian periphery then had the opportunity of utilizing categories more appropriate for the study of their respective countries' pasts.

A major discussion in the early 1930s focused on "socio-economic formations" and covered problems connected with the emergence of capitalism in the Russian Empire and the "transition from feudalism to capitalism." Although not officially admitted, the "History of the USSR" produced under Stalin's auspices contained ideas found in these debates—some of whose advocates were later shot. The most important were that "feudalism" existed from the ninth century to 1861, that production, not exchange, played the determining role in defining socio-economic formations, that there was no stage of "commercial capitalism," that class conflict was more significant than intra-class conflict even in the pre-modern period, and that "internal contradictions," as opposed to "external" influences such as trade, were the decisive forces of history.[7]

From 1934 to 1949, all survey histories noted that the first signs of capitalism appeared in the Russian Empire in the eighteenth century. In 1949, in connection with the "anti-cosmopolitan" campaign, the leadership decided it would be useful to assert the opposite; namely, that Russia did have an early capitalism. There followed publication of Stalin's 1929 article citing one of Lenin's letters (1879) containing a reference to a "new period" in Russian history in the seventeenth century, which saw the formation of the Russian nation thanks to the existence of a national market and a bourgeoisie. This information provided ideological support for an "early capitalism" theory, which had already surfaced in a prior discussion on absolutism. For the next few years, historians wrote articles demonstrating the early roots of capitalism in Russia. In 1965, a conference devoted to the subject rejected "early capitalism" and reasserted the earlier idea that capitalism in Russia began to appear in the late eighteenth century. On the question of absolutism, meanwhile, the academics could not come to a decision.[8] As a result, "early capitalism" and references to what could be construed as elements of it disappeared from, or were interpreted differently in, survey histories of the USSR, although monographs on the issue were still published.[9]

This discussion was relevant for Ukrainian historians insofar as "early capitalism" could provide a better framework for explaining their country's socio-economic history before it was engulfed by the Russian Empire in the mid-eighteenth century. As long as central Ukraine was linked to the European market it experienced European political and economic influences. Because an active class of burghers, significant urban growth and commercialization, the Renaissance, the Reformation, yeoman farmers, and petty producers struggling for places in the export market are phenomena with no counterpart in Russia at the time, study of them could only highlight the particularity of Ukraine's past vis-à-vis Russia's.

While the "early capitalist" theory was in favor it was faintly reflected in chapters on Ukraine in histories of the USSR. It was more evident in the Ukrainian surveys; less so in the 1953 and 1977 editions and more so in the 1955 and 1967 editions, although neither of the latter linked Ukrainian development directly with the rise of commerce and international trade, or used the term "early capitalism." Opponents of the "early-capitalist" theory dismissed it as an ill-founded attempt to "backdate" capitalism aimed at raising the historical level of development of non-Russians "to that of the country's central regions." One detractor said that Ukrainians were especially guilty of such backdating.[10]

Important to the "early capitalism" theory was the issue of how to interpret early-modern peasant uprisings. Lenin was of little assistance here. Except for mention of a "new period" beginning in Russian history in the seventeenth century, he made only one other relevant statement, in chapter 4 of *Agrarian Program* (1907): "Every peasant revolution directed against medievalism, when the whole of the social economy is of a capitalist nature, is a bourgeois revolution. . . . the general Marxist concept of 'bourgeois revolution' contains certain propositions that are definitely applicable to any peasant revolution that takes place in a country of rising capitalism." Engels, in *The Peasant War in Germany* (1850), saw the war as part of the "transition to capitalism," an "early bourgeois" revolution. Although he never used this term in reference to the war, Engels did claim it had a "bourgeois character" and he assumed a "bourgeois revolution" without a bourgeoisie was possible. Because peasant demands challenged feudal authority, corresponded to the interests of the urban burghers, and reflected the interests of "progressive" free small producers, the war was "objectively" part of the "process of transition" to capitalism.

Lenin's scattered comments, Engel's vague discussion of the Peasant War as the first revolutionary attempt to overthrow feudalism, and Marx's view of free market relations as corrosive of pre-capitalist structures as presented in *The German Ideology* and *Capital,* can be combined and used to demonstrate that peasant "anti-feudal" uprisings were not merely revolts but "revolutions" and harbingers of bourgeois development. Some Soviet historians argued this in the 1920s.[11] They saw peasant revolts, alongside a growing bourgeoisie, developing commercialization, and centralizing markets and political authority, as forces making the post-feudal bourgeois socio-economic order implicitly more significant historically than the state against which they were directed. In the early 1930s S. G. Tomsinsky attempted to formulate a paradigm of peasant uprisings that did not equate them directly with capitalist development, and characterized them as precursors of capitalist development. By 1934, in accord with the statist shift in interpretation demanded by the regime, a committee condemned Tomsinsky and the view of peasant revolts as organized proto-bourgeois revolutions. These uprisings, it was explained, were not revolutions but "progressive" localist "wars" with little long-term impact. They did not lead to changes in the means of production.[12] Implicitly, revolts of the "oppressed peasant masses" against the Russian state, were not as "progressive" or significant as their revolts against non-Russian states.

After World War II, Russian historians again raised the issue. Invoking Engels and Lenin on the "new period," they argued that peasants were not merely an object of exploitation and that peasant wars had a revolutionary character because they hastened bourgeois capitalist progress. In 1965, this point of view was again condemned.[13] V. V. Mavrodin gave the last word in 1975 when he explained that whereas Russian peasant revolts did have a revolutionary bourgeois character, the Khmelnytsky uprising, and presumably other Ukrainian uprisings as well, did not.[14]

Interpretation of peasant uprisings as proto-bourgeois revolutions, in conjunction with "early capitalist" theory, had implications for the interpretation of Ukraine's past. If non-Russian "anti-feudal" uprisings were "early bourgeois revolutions," and if they occurred under conditions of a gradual growth of capitalism, then they must involve the formation of "progressive bourgeois capitalist society." If this happened in a region before it was incorporated by "feudal" Russia, then to claim annexation was "progressive" becomes nonsense, since the annexing country is at a lower stage of development than the annexed. Similarly, the uprisings must be "progressive" even if directed against the Russian state. Either the theory or the interpretation had to be changed. In any case, there was no echo of this particular debate in sections on Ukraine in postwar histories of the USSR, or in histories of the Ukrainian SSR.

Party guidelines defined the image of the past, but the interpretation of first principles and related categories of analysis determined what historians could or could not stress within the official image. Within this context, "reformists" clashed with hard-liners over what subjects in non-Russian national pasts could be included or omitted or glossed over, and what could be highlighted. Examples of this process are provided by an examination of the treatment of the national question and tsarist Russian imperialism in discussions that occurred in the 1960s.

The published proceedings of a 1962 conference on historiography in the USSR contain general statements critical of all aspects of official historiography, and for the first time since the 1920s, depicted in print a confrontation between "conservatives" and "reformists." Of the scattered remarks on non-Russian history, the most explicit stated that it was incorrect to glorify all tsarist conquests and ignore conflict within and among the bourgeoisie during the 1917 Revolution. No one questioned the supposed primacy of socio-economic over national interests, an assumption that allowed historians to discount the significance of conflicts between the Provisional Government and various non-Russian governments that emerged in 1917, on the grounds that these were less significant than the supposed underlying class solidarity. But speakers did claim that "national liberation" should be regarded as a component part of the "socialist revolution," and that only "nationalist" leaders, not the movement itself, could be condemned. One speaker noted that Lenin's phrase about the empire as a "prison of peoples" had disappeared from literature. Rubach observed that all classes took part in national liberation movements that were "progressive" insofar as they were not directed against the "revolutionary struggle."[15] At a 1963 session on "History and Sociology," two historians noted that the post-1917 "friendship of peoples" theme should not be read into the past. Others pointed out that they did not know what the "History of the USSR" was or when it was supposed to have begun, that a single periodization could not be applied to the history of all the Republics, and that Republic history was not merely a reflection of Russian history. The same year, during a conference on imperialism, one speaker noted the need to examine the regressive impact of tsarist policies on non-Russian economic development.[16]

The Kazakh historian P. G. Galuzo made important observations on the beginnings of Russian "military feudal imperialism" at a 1964 conference on the national question. He noted that tsarist colonialism was the most primitive sort, and that Russian expansionism had slowed down the transition of primitive "octobrist" capital into more "progressive industrial" capital, as well as the economic development of non-Russian regions. But while making a case for Russian economic exploitation of non-Russian regions, which was novel, Galuzo still retained the idea that the economic interests of Russia and her colonies demanded an "international union" of the "whole peasantry" under proletarian leadership in the struggle for industrial capitalism. Dividing up the tsarist economy, he said, would have served the interests of the bourgeoisie. Rubach also claimed that economic unity had been "progressive" but added that the absence of Ukrainian statehood slowed down the country's development and that in Ukraine industry was overwhelmingly extractive—thus implying economic colonialism. He argued that the bourgeoisie led the national movement in its earlier phase in the late nineteenth as well as early twentieth centuries and that the movement was "progressive" except when directed against the "revolutionary struggle." Other historians raised the issue of reassessing the *hromady* and ZUNR, condemned as "reactionary" in the 1930s. I. Mints observed that Stalin's interpretation of national movements as bourgeois led to all movements not "led by the proletariat" to be wrongly labeled "reactionary."[17]

But the possible interpretive ramifications of these important remarks were circumscribed by the introductory statement of Politburo member Boris Ponomarev at the 1962 conference, where he specified that the Russocentric approach was not a mistake of the "cult of personality," but a principle of "internationalism":

The utmost support should be given to the efforts of the historians of the Soviet Republics who have strived to reveal the objectively positive significance of the merging of the history of their peoples with the Russians and of their annexation to Russia. . . .

In connection with this it is of the utmost importance for the history of the individual republics to be presented as part of the history of the entire country and closely tied with the history of the other nations of our fatherland, as this is what actually happened.[18]

It was Lenin's merit to have distinguished between imperialism, which was not policy but a stage in economic development when the expansion of the capitalist system of production and exchange becomes necessary; and colonialism, which refers to state-led territorial expansion. He also realized that the latter did occur without the former. Nevertheless, his analysis of imperialism was simply wrong, like his work on rural capitalism.[19] More important for our purposes, however, is that the argument in *Imperialism: The Highest Stage of Capitalism* (1916) contradicts a claim made in *The Development of Capitalism in Russia*. In the former, Lenin argued that the imposition of capitalism outside a given core perpetuated backwardness and exploitation and that separation from the metropolis through "national liberation war" led by a colonial national bourgeoisie was part of the socialist revolution. In the latter book, Lenin wrote that the export of capitalism outside a given country was not only exploitative but also led to economic progress for the various annexed regions. With respect to the national question, both arguments point in different directions. The former implies that colonialism is undesirable and that national struggles led by a bourgeoisie and a peasantry are "progressive" because they are "anti-colonial," even though economic conditions in the given country may not be "ripe." The latter argument measures development in the periphery in terms of the center and implies that separatism destroys the political unity necessary for further development of productive forces. There is no room in this paradigm for a "progressive" anti-capitalist bourgeoisie or national liberation war, and from such a perspective socialist revolution demands appropriate conditions and central proletarian, that is, Party, leadership.

Lenin wrote different things at different times according to political need. The resulting ambivalence was frustrating yet useful for those who had to use his tactical ruminations as axioms or categories of analysis. Both the hardliners and "reformist" historians could exploit the mentor's gaps, inconsistencies, and contradictions to claim their respective images of the past were "objectively correct."

In the 1920s and 1930s the interpretive authority tolerated survey histories that implicitly portrayed Russian presence in non-Russian areas of their empire in terms of Lenin's *Imperialism*. Historians could also debate the nature of tsarist colonialism, and up to 1936 they differed as to whether or not Russia itself was a Western colony. Russian political and economic presence in the non-Russian areas, however, was condemned by all as colonialism and regressive for the area concerned.[20] After 1936, according to Stalin's dicta, the Russian Empire became a "semi-colony" of the West, and Russian oppression of non-Russians was defined as political, not economic in nature. Now, the official view was made according to the logic of Lenin's *Development*: that economic development continued in non-Russian provinces, only more slowly than theoretically possible because of political oppression. Interestingly, this reasoning was not reflected in the official Soviet position between 1928 and 1956 on the underdeveloped countries. There, the extension of capitalism, it was argued, still brought destitution, but the colonial "national bourgeoisie" were no longer "progressive" as they had been before 1928.[21]

The most serious flaw of the "semi-colony" thesis lay in its implication that Russia was backward, which meant that the 1917 Revolution was more national than socialist in character. Stalin and Lenin were not perturbed by this dilemma, but after 1958 historians rid themselves of it by dropping the "semi-colony" designation for the nineteenth-century Russian state and its corollary that tsarist politics were dictated by the West. They noted that Lenin had said that financial monopoly capitalism was a precondition of socialism, then proved this had existed in Russia and proclaimed the 1917 Revolution as unambiguously socialist.[22] But from such a perspective, Russia became the prime political oppressor in the empire, not merely an agent of other imperialists, and implicitly blame for oppression of non-Russians could no longer be passed on to the West. The year 1959 saw removal of the unequivocal condemnation of the colonial national bourgeoisie and a return to the position held between 1920 and 1928. This implied that a bourgeois "anti-capitalist national liberation war" was part of a socialist revolution. But the corollary of the notion that Russian capitalism stimulated the economic development of the non-Russian regions of the tsarist empire, that foreign capitalism could develop the forces of production in Western colonies, was not admitted in Soviet literature on underdeveloped countries.

Thinking on colonialism and imperialism in the Russian Empire was taken further in 1961 with the reintroduction of the term "military feudal imperialism" and the subdivision of capitalism into "democratic" and "octobrist" once made by Lenin. This provided the theoretical context historians needed to examine the oppressive and regressive side of Russian–non-Russian relations from their beginnings. The next step would have been reexamination of the Stalinist formula that, although politics in the tsarist empire were damnable, the direction of economic development was not. But only one historian, Galuzo, took this step and published a monograph discussing the deleterious effects of Russian colonialism and imperialism on the economy of Kazakhstan. In his introduction, Galuzo went well beyond his previously noted remarks and provided the finest critique of Stalin's version of the Marxist theory of imperialism ever published in the USSR.[23]

The effect of the post-Stalin ferment on questions related to Russian imperialism and colonialism was not clearcut. In the mid-1960s the notion of Russia as a "semi-colony" with its overtones of political dependency was criticized but not actually abandoned. The concepts of "military feudal imperialism" and "democratic capitalism" were reintroduced but not extended or applied systematically to study of all non-Russian economic development. Finally, although the logic of Lenin's *Development* still determined interpretation of economic effects of Russian rule in most of the tsarist empire, official approval of the ideas that national liberation was "progressive" and that the national bourgeoisie could play a revolutionary role did result in changes in survey histories.

The multivolume 1966-1980 survey history of the USSR admitted and illustrated Russian economic colonialism in the Asian republics. Other surveys also contained minor shifts that gave slightly more emphasis to non-Russian particularities. In the 1967, and to a lesser degree in the 1977, edition of the Ukrainian SSR history, authors gave more attention to the "progressive" role of the Ukrainian national movement. The 1967 edition and two one-volume surveys also dealt more openly with tsarist restrictions on cossack autonomy and their deleterious effect on Ukrainian development. But there was no mention of "democratic capitalism" or study of whether Russian rule turned Ukraine into an economic colony.

These shifts in emphasis were small when compared to the perspectives tantalizingly opened during the debates on the national question and tsarist imperialism. But consideration of where changes in premises threatened to lead explains why. According to the post-1934 official interpretation, Ukraine benefited economically from being part of Russia and its forces of production could only have been unfettered by a proletarian-led socialist revolution occurring at the same time throughout the territory of the empire. Ukraine in this scenario took the same place as did India in Marx's discussion of the relation between it and England, but without an explicitly "progressive" bourgeoisie. Within the limits of this schema, if an historian wanted to demonstrate why the 1917 Revolution in Ukraine was different than in Russia, he could do little but claim that the region had been as developed as the center and that its national proletariat had been able to adequately express its interest. But this would have meant ignoring the Russified character of the proletariat and Bolshevik Party in Ukraine, their relative indifference to national issues, and in the end, not producing a better interpretation. Conversely, if Ukraine was seen as Russia's Ireland, that is, in the terms of Lenin's *Imperialism,* as an economically backward, exploited region, then a national peasantry and bourgeoisie could play a "revolutionary" and "progressive" role as agents of "democratic capitalism," freeing the country's productive forces. This threatened to resurrect the official interpretation of the 1920s and lead to an account of Ukrainian history as different as the history of any periphery can be from the history of an imperial center.

After 1956, the regime was prepared to recognize some "errors" existed in official historiography during Stalin's rule, and the authorities allowed significant changes in the interpretation of the history of the Asian republics. This might have been related to the regime's wish to curry favor in Asia at the time. Perhaps because events in Ukraine no longer had the impact on foreign affairs that they had in the 1920s, the regime did not think it necessary to allow as much leeway in interpretation of Ukrainian history.

MONOGRAPHS AND ARTICLES

The organization and the epistemological nature of USSR scholarship limited the impact monograph research could have on interpretation, and kept even "reformist" views within the DHM mold. But practical considerations also limited the impact research could have on the official Soviet interpretations of Ukraine's past. First, the few surveys of Russian or USSR history appearing before 1939 were short and superficial and could not have been expected to incorporate the considerable findings on the pre-1917 past published during the 1920s. Second, after 1934 when the deductive nature of DHM intellectual inquiry in humanities scholarship was made more rigid by political guidelines, most pre-1934 literature was either destroyed or placed in restricted library collections.[24] Even authors with access to them were allowed to cite only works not explicitly contradicting first principles. Thus, the bibliography in *Istoriia SSSR* (1939-1940) contains more references to pre-1917 than Soviet publications on Russian history and none to Soviet works on pre-nineteenth-century Ukrainian history.

Between 1956 and 1973, reformists exploited the relaxed political climate to question or broaden established interpretations. The scholarly level of historiography improved somewhat, many monographs were published that were good by the standards of critical Western scholarship, and some of these appeared in post-1956 survey bibliographies. Yet the incorporation of research findings into surveys was still related to the acceptability of the broader typology from which the findings were derived, rather than to the requirement that synthesis reflect a critical confrontation of evidence with generalization. Moreover, throughout the 1960s and 1970s, most pre-1947 Soviet works remained in closed collections. Most had no access, and those who did could not freely cite them. In eight pages of bibliography on pre-1922 Ukraine in the two-volume *Istoriia Ukrainskoi RSR* (1967), there are only 12 pre-1947 articles and monographs, and of these the three from the 1920s deal only with the Revolution.

Bibliographies in survey histories of the Ukrainian SSR, and bibliographies of USSR historiography in general, also reveal that except for the Kievan and pre-Kievan periods, Soviet-Russian historiography about Ukraine was almost non-existent. Of the articles on the subjects reviewed for this book no more than 60 can be regarded as "Russian" historiography. The tiny number of Russian studies on Ukrainian history, that is, work by native Russians who lived and worked in the RSFSR and who never made careers in or lived for an extended period in Ukraine, might in part be attributed to a division of intellectual labor imposed by the regime after 1934 or 1947. Presumably from the leadership's perspective it was rational to allot central institutions where the majority were Russians the study of Russia, the rest of the world, and analytical categories and paradigms. This left local Russians and non-Russians in Republic institutions the study of Republic national pasts—to the almost total exclusion of any other national history. A similar division of labor existed in the Eastern Bloc, where the majority of historians were directed into study of their own respective countries. The resulting isolationism in the non-Russian Soviet Republics, and to a lesser degree in Eastern Europe, produced ignorance of the surrounding world and reinforced the intellectual provincialism generated by DHM.[25]

A small number of works by Russian historians on Ukrainian history appeared between 1914 and 1918. Vladimir Picheta published three important articles on the diminution of Ukrainian cossack autonomy. He pointed out that Khmelnytsky's original intention was only to obtain military assistance. Picheta argued that after the hetman's death, Russian encroachments on cossack autonomy contravened the 1654 articles. He then traced the reduction of autonomy by comparing each subsequent agreement signed between tsar and hetman, and concluded that by the 1730s the "articles of Bohdan Khmelnytsky" were mere legal forms with little political substance.[26] I. Rozenfeld (1916) discussed the legal nature of the 1654 treaty and concluded that it represented incorporation with specified conditions agreed upon by two equal partners.[27] V. I. Semevsky's definitive 1911 study of the Cyril-Methodius Brotherhood was not published in full until 1918 due to censorship. The first historian to use the police dossiers compiled during the interrogations of the arrested members, Semevsky detailed the program of the Brotherhood and drew attention to the importance of folk-romanticism and cossack history in forming the world-view of its members. Semevsky explained that the group was influenced by, and did not simply copy, the ideas of the Polish Romantic movement, in particular as expressed in Mickiewicz's *Books of the Polish Nation and its Pilgrimage*.[28]

The war years also saw the publication of about a dozen propagandist, popular, and academic studies devoted to Western Ukraine. One of these was a short, rather balanced survey history by A. Iarynovich (A. Nikolsky), who noted that Russia made no claims upon the region prior to the nineteenth century. He explained that King Casimir had conquered the region in 1340 and respected its rights. The local populace initially opposed Polish rule but then "turned inward" and sought other paths to national rebirth. The author recognized the role of the Uniate Church as well as the Austrian government in the nineteenth-century national movement and explained that in the course of their struggle Ukrainians attained cultural independence as well as a European level of cultural life.[29]

Soviet Russian historiography did not produce one article specifically on Casimir's occupation of Galicia, Ukrainian lands in the Unions of 1386 and 1569, or 1848 and the national movement in Galicia.[30] Some of these subjects were reviewed, however, by V. Picheta in a schematic survey of Belarus and Western Ukrainian history published after their annexation to the USSR in 1939. Picheta explained that although the Lithuanian Grand Duke was the "official ruler" of Galicia at the time, Casimir IV in 1340 "seized" the region, and its people suffered national and social oppression thereafter. In the nineteenth century, Austrian policy had intended to turn the region into an economic backwater and denationalize the population. He mentioned a "bourgeois nationalist" movement and some of its cultural achievements, but not the events of 1848 or 1917-1921.[31] In an article purporting to deal with Ukrainian issues at the time of the Union, Picheta actually focused on Polish-Lithuanian relations.[32]

Little was published on the other subjects reviewed in this survey. One rather polemical review dealt with early-modern Ukrainian socio-economic history. Roughly ten publications, a figure that excludes propagandist tracts, dealt with cossack-peasant revolts, the Khmelnytsky uprising, and the treaties of Pereiaslav and Hadiach. There are no more than a dozen devoted to the Union of Brest and related issues. Five dealt with cossack autonomy, Mazepa, and the Haidamak revolts, while four may be found on the Cyril and Methodius Brotherhood and more generally on the national movement.[33] There is a larger body of Soviet-Russian historiography on the Ukrainian Revolution of 1917-1921; however, most of it is either memoirs of Russian activists or focuses on Bolshevik activities in provincial cities. There is nothing specifically on ZUNR, but at least 15 articles deal with the Kiev Central Rada and the general course of the Ukrainian revolution.[34]

Between 1934 and 1947, historiography on early-modern Ukraine reflected the changing political climate. N. Rubinshtein (1936), who explained that Pokrovsky's account of Khemlnytsky's uprising had ignored intracossack conflict as well as its national aspect, wrote that in Ukraine the lesser gentry, townspeople and peasants stood for "national independence" despite class differences. The cossack officers represented an emerging ruling class with an economic and national program of independence who struggled against the masses as well as the Poles. As a result, between 1648 and 1657, civil as well as national war raged in Ukraine. Rebellions against his authority forced the hetman to turn to Moscow, but the tsar had his own aims and by exploiting class differences in the newly annexed territory he eventually subordinated Ukraine to "eternal servitude."[35] Two years later, V. Mavrodin provided a different view in a popular article about Ukraine's struggle against Poland and the 1654 "union" with Russia. He made no reference to the Pereiaslav treaty as a first step in Moscow's subjugation of Ukraine. Instead, he wrote that Khmelnytsky wanted to "unite with the native, consanguinal Russian nation" but was troubled by the possibility of losing his authority as a result. The alliance, therefore, represented a last alternative.[36]

In 1939, the regime decided to propagate an image of Khmelnytsky as hero and "unifier" of Ukraine and Russia. The first work written from this perspective was a detailed study published one month after the outbreak of the war by K. Osipov (O. Kuperman). This book explained that the hetman had been not only a feudal landowner serving the interests of his class, but an able statesman and hero whose plans included Ukrainian statehood as well as "union" with Russia.[37] This image was simplified in 1944 by V. Picheta, who stressed that cossacks and higher Ukrainian clergy had a "desire" to unite with Russia, while not mentioning the doubts Khmelnytsky had about the Russian option or his differences with the tsar. The cossack officers had desired only improved status within Poland, whereas independence had been the aim of a "national front" made up of peasants, burghers, registered cossacks, urban plebeians, lower clergy, and "better sections" of officers. He did not mention anti-Khmelnytsky rebellions or the consequences of 1654 treaty for Ukraine.[38]

A revised version of Osipov's book appeared in 1948. In the sections dealing with the period before 1654, there were few changes. For example, this edition replaced the claim that Kievan-Rus had been inhabited by Slavic tribes with the claim that it had been peopled by one nation.[39] More substantial revisions appeared in the chapters covering the years 1654-1657. Whereas the earlier edition had implied that the Russian alliance had been a best alternative and claimed that Khmelnytsky understood it was a political necessity, the second described it as a lesser evil and "vital" necessity.[40] Both editions drew attention to popular revolts against the hetman, who ultimately had not been able to reflect the interests of the "whole popular mass," to his differences with the tsar over matters of internal and foreign policy, and tsarist disregard for Ukrainian autonomy. The second edition, however, omitted a section discussing the legal nature of the Ukrainian-Russian agreement and the views of Ukrainians opposed to it, and did not mention that political differences between the two countries arose from different social structures and political traditions. Whereas the first edition only noted that the Pereaislav treaty had been "progressive" for the common people despite Russian policy, the second edition added that it represented "progress" for Ukraine as a whole.[41]

In 1949 Kalashnikova explained that national conflict in mid-seventeenth-century Ukraine was less significant than social struggle and pointed out that the lower clergy were the originators of Ukraine's "desire" to unite with Russia. She noted that, although the higher clergy were "anti-national," they did make positive contributions to cultural development.[42]

With the publication of the "Thesis" in 1953, the margin for interpretation narrowed. Better monographs, however, often included information not strictly in accord with the first principles. G. Lyzlov studied Ukraine in Polish-Russian relations for the years 1648-1649. Less prepared to view Russian policy toward Khmelnytsky in terms of realpolitik than Seredyka, and not mentioning Russian fear of a possible Ukrainian attack (see p. 124), Lyzlov did state that among the reasons the tsar had not intervened in 1648 against Poland was his wish to be elected king of Poland.[43]

In 1940 an article on the Hetmanate by G. Georgievsky provided an informative review of newly found correspondence between Mazepa and Peter I's close collaborator Menshikov. He noted that both men treated each other as brothers and that Mazepa sought to ingratiate himself with the tsar's favorite in order to secure his position in Ukraine. Georgievsky referred to Mazepa's reasons for joining the Swedes, and did not vilify him as a traitor.[44] In a second, similarly informative and dispassionate article, V. Putilov discussed the activities of one of Vyhovsky's associates and a creator of the Hadiach accords, Pavlo Teteria, whose main motivation was given as greed. Putilov argued that the Hadiach accords gave fewer rights, territory, and privileges to the cossacks than did the Pereiaslav agreement. He added that the concept of a Grand Duchy of Rus was not in the first version of the treaty. Introduced primarily thanks to his associate Iuryi Nemirych, Vyhovsky was supposedly opposed to what in any case was a sham. Putilov reasoned that the pro-Polish cossack officers betrayed the nation by opposing Russian overlordship because in spite of political centralization, Russian rule did not interfere with Ukraine's social structure or national and cultural development. These men, he continued, raised in a Polish cultural milieu, didn't really understand what they were doing![45] A third article, by M. Volkov (1961), considered how abolition of the tariff border in 1754 originated in Russian merchants' wishes to dominate the Ukrainian market. Beginning in 1724, they repeatedly petitioned Petersburg to exclude foreign merchants from the Hetmanate. They also sought to weaken their competition by abolishing the tariff border between Russia and the Hetmanate. The government, bending to cossack officer pressure, refused on the grounds such an act would contravene Ukrainian autonomy. But it changed its position in 1754, when a shift in court factions weakened the influence of the Ukrainians Rozumovsky and Bezborodko, and brought to prominence P. I. Shuvalov, a decided centralizer.[46]

The 1930s saw three Russian studies devoted to the Haidamak revolt. In two booklets, A. Dmitrev (1934) claimed that the revolt was neither a national movement or national war, but a purely spontaneous eruption of peasant hatred of serfdom. He tortuously argued that Haidamak leaders unwillingly took up religious slogans because these only interfered with their struggle against serfdom. He claimed that cossack officers supported the Haidamaks because they realized that the uprising would ruin their grain-producing Polish rivals, that the Orthodox clergy backed the Haidamaks to protect their lands from them as much as from the Catholic church, and that Russian officers actively fostered illusions among Ukrainians about tsarist support.[47] I. Golovchiner (1939) gave some attention to the religious issue and characterized the revolt as spontaneous, "anti-feudal," and without long-term objectives.[48]

The second Russian scholar to study the Ukrainian national movement was P. Zaionchkovsky, who in 1947 published a summary of his 1940 dissertation on the Cyril-Methodius Brotherhood. Although appearing during an ideological campaign against "nationalism" in Ukrainian historiography, the article contained no Russophilism, nor did it claim that the Brotherhood was sharply divided into reformist liberals and revolutionaries. Well researched and unpolemical, the article pointed out that the organization reflected the interests of a colonial and implicitly "progressive" bourgeoisie struggling for social and national liberation. Although he noted differences between members, Zaionchkovsky argued that they were not divided into two groups and were all equally committed to the ideal of a nationally and socially liberated Ukraine. Shevchenko, because of his uncompromising radical stand on serfdom, was isolated.[49] In his book on the same subject (1959), Zaionchkovsky provided more detail for his argument. He statistically demonstrated Russian domination of the Ukrainian economy and added that liberals were undeniably progressive in the 1840s because they did not split with the revolutionaries until the 1850s. Among minor additions was a reference to Ukraine as a "semi-colony."[50]

Among the historians in the Ukrainian Party history organization (ISTPART) during the 1920s, it is sometimes difficult to determine who should be categorized within Russian and who within Ukrainian historiography. Classification by language of publication would be misleading, as in the case of Latvian R. Eidemanis (Eideman), who played an important role in Ukraine during the Revolution and later took up an academic post in Leningrad, but sometimes published in Ukrainian. D. Erde (Rakhstein), like the Belarussian Jew M. Maiorov (Biberman), published in Ukrainian, but unlike Eideman they both lived and held important posts in Ukraine for some time as well. For this reason they are included within Ukrainian historiography. This chapter includes historians of the Revolution in Ukraine into Russian historiography if they were born outside Ukraine, and were associated with it or lived there for only part of their careers.

Articles published during the 1920s argued the Bolshevik point of view as a matter of course. But they lacked the polemical and even vicious tone that characterized writings during the 1930s, contained more information than the latter on non-Bolshevik governments, and discussed Bolshevik errors alongside the strengths of the opposition. Eideman and Kakurin's short history (1928; Ukrainian translation, 1931) noted that Ukraine's historical peculiarities were the source of the specific dynamism of events in the country, and referred to the great role of the Rada in the Revolution and the counterrevolution—albeit without details concerning the former. The book had no references to a "crucial role" during the Revolution of the "Russian people" nor to Lenin. The authors explained that at the beginning of the Revolution in Ukraine, only the "radical peasants" were alienated by the

Rada's land policies and that the Ukrainian proletariat could not expect support from their brother class in the RSFSR. Since the bourgeoisie had allied with Ukrainian bourgeois governments, the Soviet regime was too weak to establish itself in the country. The Bolsheviks finally intervened because the Rada was destabilizing the front by its policy of "Ukrainizing" the army and was denying Russia raw materials and resources. The authors were more concerned with military than political affairs, but in the last chapter they concluded that the history of the Revolution was basically the story of peasants switching from one government to another until, on the basis of experience, they decided that the proletariat and its party were the only acceptable alternatives. In the list of reasons for Bolshevik victory among the most important were the class consciousness of the Red Army and the support of the working class. The leadership of Lenin was placed well down on the list.[51]

P. Gorin wrote the first articles on the Revolution in Ukraine that followed Stalin's prescriptions (see p. 50). He argued that differences between Russia and Ukraine did not nullify or negate the "basic similarity of the class process occurring in Ukraine and Russia." He explained that the leading role was played by the poor peasants, led by the working class, not middle farmers, and that if the approach he used was not adopted by historians, they would portray the national question as a supra-class phenomenon.[52]

This line of thought was taken further by I. Gorodetsky, who condemned the Rada and the Provisional Government as counterrevolutionary. The former's declaration of autonomy and later independence, as well as its land policies, he claimed, were mere cynical maneuvers forced upon it by circumstances. In his articles, Gorodetsky explained that the Rada, hostile to the proletariat, was not part of the struggle for a Ukrainian bourgeois national republic because it represented only the bourgeoisie, not the nation.[53]

M. Frenkin (1968) pointed out that the Rada exploited Bolshevik mistakes in the national question and had considerable success in Ukrainizing the tsarist army. He explained the Bolsheviks were prepared to Ukrainize, but only if referendums carried out among the soldiers indicated their agreement. Frenkin also described how the Bolsheviks circumvented the efforts of the Rada and "attracted the masses" to their side.[54]

Conclusion

POLISH INTERPRETATIONS OF UKRAINIAN HISTORY

In 1947, W. Konopczynski observed that historiography would not be "scientific" if it did not pose research questions, or look for truth in the struggle with illusions, or progress methodologically. He continued:

> Neither is the evolution of historiography dependent on changes in the prevailing view of the past; optimism or pessimism concerning one's ancestors, the sins or merits of kings, estates, the entire nation, or the triumph of some idea regarded today or in the past as holy—all of this will always actively concern the historian, but progress in historiography is not dependent on the dominance of certain tendencies, or political preconceptions or philosophical observation. It lies in deepening [inquiry] into problems, sharpening critical thought and extracting facts from sources and secondary materials....
>
> Of course, let each generation write its own history, but not from nothing because history would stop being a science when father, son, and grandson no longer shared one truth.[1]

Konopczynski did not examine the possibility that people could share illusions as well as truth and implied that unless interpretive change flowed from research it could not be "progress."

Interwar Polish historiography about Ukraine included some pioneering studies. The few historians who wrote on Casimir's campaigns against Galicia concluded that his annexation had been legitimate even without a specific succession agreement with George II, thanks to the Piast inheritance system—which obviated the need for such a document. Historians studying Ukrainian lands in the Unions of 1386 and 1569 explained that they had not become a third entity in the Polish-Lithuanian state because their nobles had not asked for separate status. Historians also unearthed new details concerning the political place of Rus lands in Jagiello's plans, as well as the reactions of Rus magnates in 1569 to the threat of dispossession if they didn't agree to incorporation.

Historians writing about Ukrainian church history pointed out that the Brest Union had been primarily the work of Rome, and, with the exception of Lewicki, they claimed it served Polish interests. Monographs demonstrated that a basically loyal Orthodox Church had been tolerated as well as supported by a state that enacted no anti-Orthodox legislation until the second half of the seventeenth century. Historians emphasized the decline of the church prior to the Union and noted that Orthodox prelates had differed over whether or not to accept and exploit cossack support in their struggle with the Uniates. They also pointed out that Ukrainian and Russian Orthodoxy differed in ritual as well as in organization. Chodynicki's magisterial study provided Polish readers with details of the struggle for Orthodox rights in the *Sejm* as well as a discussion of the church's role in cossack attempts to ally with Poland's Protestant enemies.

Articles about the cossacks illustrated the political and social dilemma this social group presented the Crown. Most concluded that as of 1630, if not earlier, they represented not only a social force but also a national and religious power. Rawita-Gawronska reiterated the prewar view of early-seventeenth-century cossacks as primitive bandits, but recognized that Khmelnytsky, near the end of his life, as well as Vyhovsky and Mazepa, had been motivated by "national" political ideals and had sought to create a separate Rus state. Historians published original studies on campaigns in which Poles, Catholics, Orthodox, and cossacks had fought together, as well as a number of detailed studies on the Hadiach treaty that concluded that both sides shared the blame for its failure. There was no monograph devoted exclusively to the Haidamak revolt. One article mentioned that it could have been influenced by Enlightenment ideas. Except for Wolinski, who admitted that Poles had been to blame, those who mentioned the revolt in a broader monograph retained the prewar interpretation of it as one in a series of explosions of primitive bloodlust provoked by the Russians.

Four noteworthy studies by interwar Polish historians on the nineteenth-century Ukrainian national movement summarized its evolution and ideas, and showed that it had been part of the general European phenomenon. Whereas popularizers claimed that in Eastern Galicia Austrians had "thought up" a Ukrainian nation to weaken the Poles, academic historians realized the Austrians had used but not created the Ukrainian movement and that Poles as well as Ukrainians were to blame for the national conflict in Galicia. Most of the articles published in interwar Poland about Ukrainian events between 1917-1921 focused on military history. The few historians who looked at the political history of those years regarded the Central Rada as the culmination of the national movement—a failed attempt at statehood. ZUNR, if mentioned, was regarded as an Austrian tool.

The 30 surveys reviewed in this book shared an image of Polish-ruled Ukrainian lands as legally acquired integral parts of Poland and Ukrainians as basically loyal subjects. Authors differed in their explanations of why this population took up arms against Poland. The 15 surveys that echoed the prewar conservative-romantic view, or the "Cracow School" interpretation, tended to blame foreign intrigues and/or the bloody-mindedness of Ukrainian leaders for the violence. The remainder, which included Wasilewski's survey history of Ukraine, resembled the prewar positivist view. These explained that in some instances Polish intransigence or shortsightedness justified the actions of Ukrainian leaders and that there was a national as well as social and religious dimension to Polish-Ukrainian relations. *Wiedza o Polsce* (1931-1932) saw pre-nineteenth-century Ukrainian affairs in the positivist framework and the nineteenth-century Ukrainian national movement from the neoromantic perspective.

The surveys explained that Western Ukraine had been annexed via legal succession. Positivist historians added that economic interests had played a role in Casimir's politics. They discussed the Unions as political events with mixed consequences for Poland, while the neoromantics saw them as manifestations of the "Jagiellonian idea"—a term used to refer to a conscious plan that Jagiello supposedly had to form a vast Polish-dominated East European monarchy. The term encompassed the notion that Poland had a mission to civilize its eastern neighbors. Whereas Śliwinski and Arnold attributed the Brest Union to intolerance and condemned it and its consequences, most of the other reviewed authors who were critical of it criticized only the means used to implement it. Most of the authors of both interpretive persuasions stressed that the religious conflict was basically an Orthodox-Uniate rather than an Orthodox-Roman Catholic affair and claimed that rebel leaders alleged religious persecution to justify their violence. Most authors also regarded cossack revolts as social in nature, but treated them as understandable responses to persecution and explained the political dilemma this group of servitors had presented the Crown. Only one survey history explicitly characterized the cossack revolts as national. Interestingly, neoromantic popular histories and textbooks either did not mention Ukrainian uprisings or dismissed them as products of intrigues and fanaticism, but neoromantic academic surveys explained them in terms of social conflict. Only two historians mentioned persecution of Orthodoxy as a cause of the Haidamak revolts. The rest saw them as mindless rebellion provoked by Russia.

While neoromantics tended to disparage Khmelnytsky by attributing his political plans to foreign intrigues and drink, positivists noted that he had intended to create his own duchy, if not a state. Historians of both persuasions, however, agreed about the importance of the Hadiach accord and praised the wisdom of the cossack leaders who signed it. The 1654 treaty with Russia was seen as a political agreement with bitter consequences for Ukraine, and those who dealt with the Hetmanate drew attention to the diminution and final abolition of its autonomy. All the reviewed histories depicted the Ukrainian national movement in Galicia and ZUNR as products of Austrian intrigues.

With the exception of articles about ZUNR, the small body of interwar Polish academic historiography on Ukraine tended to focus on questions related to the legitimacy of the Polish presence in Ukraine and moments of Polish-Ukrainian cooperation. They did not dwell on differences and conflicts and avoided giving them national overtones. However, only conclusions relating to Casimir's campaign and the Hadiach treaty found their way into interwar histories of Poland, whose narratives otherwise reiterated facts known before the war. The reason was chronological. Whereas most of the survey histories were written in the 1920s, most of the good studies on the Ukrainian churches and the cossacks, and all of those on the national movement, appeared in the 1930s. It might also be argued that studies published in the 1920s on cossack issues dealt with subjects too remote and specialized for inclusion in survey histories of Poland. This does not imply that had these articles appeared sooner, interpretations inevitably would have been different. Halecki's early articles on the Lublin Union did not result in the elimination of the "Jagiellonian idea" from neoromantic interpretations of Polish history. Ukrainian historians who challenged Polish interpretations, it should be added, were simply ignored by almost all authors of Polish survey histories. Conversely, Polish studies demonstrating the liberal nature of Polish policy toward the Orthodox could not have seriously challenged or displaced the prevailing neoromantic and positivist interpretations. While adherents of the former, for whom Catholicism by definition was "good," were in any case loathe to admit that persecution existed, partisans of the latter view were not disposed to attach particular significance to persecution since they did not think religion in itself could cause major socio-political movements.

Except for some articles written between 1949 and 1953, such as those that sought to illustrate how seventeenth-century Polish peasants had "united" with the Ukrainian "liberation struggle," most postwar Polish historiography about Ukraine reflected high academic standards. Studies dealing with Ukrainian subjects were few, but among them at the center of historians' interests, as before the war, were the cossacks. Church history was displaced as the second most popular research subject by the Ukrainian national movement and the events of 1917-1921.

Tomkiewicz convincingly demonstrated that the cossacks had always been overwhelmingly Ukrainian, while Seredyka provided a detailed survey of Ukrainian-Russian relations between 1648 and 1649, illustrating their relationship to the Polish succession. Majewski's valuable examination of the Hadiach treaty explained cossack motivations in terms of family and status interests, while studies on Casimir IV and Galicia claimed that the king had planned his campaign well and that at least during his lifetime the newly annexed region had been an autonomous third part of the kingdom. Kuczynski argued that there was no "Jagiellonian idea" before the nineteenth century and that the Union of 1386 was a purely political consequence of a given set of circumstances. No articles dealt specifically with Ukraine in 1569 or the Union of Brest. In his excellent study on the Haidamaks, Serczyk identified rising grain prices and bad harvests as crucial preconditions of the revolt, along with religious persecution, and he explained that Haidamak leaders had no control over the excesses of their followers. Polish historians provided a detailed administrative history of the Ukrainian church in pre-partition Polish lands, a valuable quantitative study of Polish colonization in fourteenth- and fifteenth-century Galicia, as well as studies of the frequency and impact of Tartar raids in the province 100 years later. Horn's study of emigration patterns suggested that peasants fled to towns rather than to central Ukraine.

Studies written between 1949 and 1953 on the national movement sought to illustrate the profound historical significance of "revolutionary solidarity" between individual nineteenth-century Polish and Ukrainian radicals. More serious work began only in the 1960s when Polish historians studied the national movement in tsarist as well as Habsburg Ukraine and presented it as part of the broader European phenomenon of nationalism that evolved from cultural interests into political demands. Kozik demonstrated that the movement in Galicia was not merely an Austrian intrigue, although Vienna did use it. Historians dealing with the events of 1917-1921 provided balanced accounts of the Central Rada, its relations with the Bolsheviks, and the reasons for the failure of the former and the victory of the latter. By the 1970s, specialist monographs depicted the Rada and ZUNR as the culmination of the national movement that had legitimately demanded a Ukrainian nation-state. Articles on ZUNR were more detailed than those on the Rada and drew attention to Western economic interests in the region. While Zaks blamed the allies for the Polish occupation because they had allowed Poland to keep Western Ukraine, Deruga assigned greater significance to the Polish political interests that had wanted to control the region. Historians studying Pilsudski's Ukrainian policy drew attention to Polish opposition to it and also questioned the wisdom of his plan to federate with Petliura's Ukraine.

The sections of the major multivolume history of Poland dealing with Galicia from 1918 to 1920 incorporated previous research on Western interests in the area, but most of the important articles on the subjects reviewed here appeared after the publication of this survey. Research published before the publication of the two Polish surveys of Ukrainian history and the single-volume surveys of Polish history did not appreciably influence their interpretation of Ukrainian history. From the available pool of monographs, historians tended to incorporate information supporting the required schema, which was based on Party guidelines issued between 1944 and 1953.

Ukrainian history was a sensitive topic since it involved the past of a territory under Soviet control, and the official interpretation was an amalgam derived from prewar Polish positivist historiography and radical socialist writings, both critical of Polish presence in the east, and extrapolations from Soviet formulas such as "National Liberation War of the Ukrainian people," "anti-feudal" revolts, bolshevik hegemony over the "revolutionary movement," and "international solidarity" of the "laboring classes" or "revolutionaries." The result was a more dispassionate and balanced view than the Soviet-Russian, and from a Ukrainian perspective the Polish interpretation was even sympathetic. But this must not detract attention from the political roots of the official Polish view.

Survey histories published between 1949 and 1953 portrayed Poland as the aggressor in the east and ignored accepted knowledge that questioned this image. Casimir's annexation of Galicia, for example, was labeled a "conquest" or "seizure," the Union of 1569 was presented as political blackmail, and the Union of Brest as a Jesuit plot. Russia was described as Ukraine's "natural ally" in 1654, and Arnold even used the term "reunion" to refer to the Pereiaslav treaty. Instead of balanced description, accounts of the Haidamaks and the Ukrainian national movement in Galicia depicted Polish gentry as the cause of all ills and unequivocally condemned all Polish activity.

After 1956, accounts in survey histories became less dogmatic and authors muted condemnation of "Polish imperialism," but their interpretation still followed the imposed guidelines. The official interpretation of Ukrainian history may be criticized for reading later borders, differences, and ideas too simply into the past, for minimizing if not ignoring Polish-Ukrainian interaction, and for viewing Ukraine as a territory where Poles were occupiers who only oppressed and persecuted. Postwar Polish historians never examined or clearly explained how the history of the Polish state should be separated from the history of the nation, although from the 1960s survey histories tended to devote less attention to Ukrainian issues and more to the subject of Poles in Ukraine and Ukraine's impact on Poland. Yet, postwar historians no longer justified past Polish control over eastern territories, and in their writings Ukraine figured as a territory with a distinct national history. The few histories of Poland that did deal with Ukrainian issues at length, provided dispassionate factual accounts of the pre-1920 period and avoided generalization.

The three postwar Polish histories of Ukraine used Soviet categories and formulas, particularly in their accounts of Ukraine during the Revolution, but each left little doubt in readers' minds that at least until the twentieth century, Ukraine's past was distinct from that of its two main neighbors. Published after the publication of much of the reviewed monographs, these surveys tended to omit the research that blatantly challenged or contradicted official Soviet views. Thus, Serczyk and Podhorodecki incorporated research on the Haidamaks and ZUNR, but not Seredyka's or Deruga's work on Russian-Ukrainian relations, or Majewski's findings on the Hadiach treaty. Likewise, Serczyk's account of the Ukrainian revolution in his *Historia* differed markedly from his balanced 1967 article on the subject.

The Soviet influence on Polish treatment of Ukraine's past was most obvious in accounts of late-nineteenth- and early-twentieth-century events, and may be contrasted with the post-1956 official interpretation of Poland's past. Polish historians after 1963, if not 1956, when they restored professional ethics to their craft, could write with the implicit assumption that social liberation was possible only in an independent Poland. This legitimized social revolution in terms of national liberation as well as class struggle, and permitted incorporation into the image of Poland's past information and problems that otherwise would have been ignored. Explanation of why peasants didn't support native elites who fought to regain statehood required a different kind of presentation and incorporated different facts than narratives that assumed the aim of social struggle was "abolition" of feudalism or capitalism. The authors of Polish histories of Ukraine did not apply such a typology to early-twentieth-century events in Ukraine. In accordance with the official Soviet view, imposed through censorship if necessary, when dealing with this subject they did not equate social liberation with national political independence and thus did not depict either ZUNR or the Central Rada as institutions representing national liberation.

Only Jasienica's very popular survey departed significantly from the official schema. In particular, his depiction of Ukraine between 1340 and the eighteenth century as an integral part of Old Poland contravened the official view. His was the only post-1945 survey history of Poland that attempted to illustrate the profound impact each society had on the other, and to provide detailed accounts of issues glossed over or ignored in other surveys. Jasienica reminded readers that in the seventeenth century, cossack uprisings reflected not only internal problems, but had been linked to the European diplomatic game. He argued the only solution for both nations had lain in the formation of a tripartite union that in 1569 had not been attempted because the Ukrainian elite did not propose it and that failed in 1659 due to political circumstances.

Among those who examined the impact of Marxism on the post-war Polish interpretation of the country's past there was no agreement. Dissident Catholic historian B. Cywinski, who perhaps represented popular opinion, complained there was too much Marxism in Polish historiography.[2] Conversely, a Western scholar concluded that it had proved impossible to impose an interpretation of the national past alien to the Polish sense of their national identity, and a method at odds with objective scholarship. In short, the regime failed to reshape the traditional interpretation despite its power, institutions, and funds.[3] It might be added that Poles tended to reject "communist" historiography simply because it was official, which meant, in turn, they tended to dismiss the favorable, if circumscribed, image of Ukraine found in official histories.

Historians also disagreed about the postwar treatment of Ukrainian history. In 1953, Oswald Górka noted that because of border changes and Poland becoming an almost homogeneous nation-state, it had become possible to look objectively at cossacks, Ukraine, and Bohdan Khmelnytsky, not only as part of Poland's past but as the history of a brother nation.[4] In 1978, Serczyk wrote that the source of old conflicts between Poles and Ukrainians had disappeared and more than ever before Polish historians could look calmly and without bias at the main problems of Ukrainian history. There are no more troublesome questions of borders or religion or national antagonisms, he wrote, that can't be reduced to social questions, "and now class differences do not separate us."[5] Cywinski claimed that the guidelines were too restrictive and expressive of Russian interests. He listed disapproval of all eastern policy, stress on national differences between Poles and Ukrainians, the idea that Poland was an occupier in its eastern lands whereas Russia had a mission in the west, the argument that Polish colonization east of the Bug River was without lasting cultural consequences, and the critical attitude to the Union of Brest and sympathy for the Orthodox in Poland, as "falsifications" that reflected official propaganda in Polish history books used in schools.[6] What is known of the proceedings of the Polish-Soviet Commissions on Historical Textbooks gives yet a third perspective. Soviet Russians reviewing 1970s-era Polish histories of Poland complained that the books were too nationalistic. They disliked Polish use of the term "Muscovite," the failure to call 1648 a national revolt or Khmelnytsky a Ukrainian, the use of terms like "triumph of Polish arms" and "lands once part of Poland," and the failure to differentiate the Russia of the tsars and of Lenin. Clearly, the presumption that history was primarily a national story remained strong on both sides.[7]

The post-1945 official Polish interpretation of Ukraine's past would not qualify as "progress," in Konopczynski's opinion. Nevertheless, this interpretation did represent a major reorientation in Polish historiography. The "official elite" version of history was imposed by Moscow. It was defective because it never clearly specified on what basis minorities were to be included or excluded from narratives and because it downplayed the discontinuity, diversity and plurality on lands once ruled by Piasts, Jagiellonians, Riurykoviches, Romanovs, Habsburgs, and Hohenzollerns. Yet the official view cannot be dismissed as reprehensible, and it did have native Polish roots. Between 1982 and 1991, there was increased discussion of Ukrainian issues in the academic and popular press, but no scholarly survey of national history appeared with an interpretation markedly different from earlier ones.[8]

THE SOVIET-RUSSIAN INTERPRETATION OF UKRAINE'S PAST

Historiography in the USSR was more strictly controlled than in Poland, and after 1934 was debased to a greater degree by use as a tool of political integration. As late as 1931, Piontkovsky still condemned as nationalist and "russificatory" the tsarist conception of the evolution of the Russian state that explained it as a combined product of Russian, Belarussian, and Ukrainian cores. Such accounts, he insisted, denied the distinctiveness of each nation.[9] By 1939, what Piontkovsky had condemned was part of an official Russocentric interpretation that read "friendship of nations" beyond 1917 into medieval times, ignored or skirted the issue of Russian domination in the tsarist empire, and minimized national diversity, differences, and conflicts within it. The history of the USSR excluded so much from non-Russian historical memories that its imposition was tantamount to "intellectual colonization."[10]

As an account of the past of a multinational state, the official "history of the USSR" was not unique. Historians who wrote it, like their counterparts elsewhere who wrote histories of other multinational polities, had to connect different entities and create a credible narrative continuity. The Soviet regime was not unique in sponsoring interpretations of history that justified the existing order, and although post-1934 official Soviet accounts of the past were tendentious and inadequate, some Soviet historians did write accurate and truthful studies on some subjects. What was damnable in the Soviet situation was the use of force against and/or intimidation of recalcitrant scholars. Historians after 1934 risked their lives, and after 1956 their jobs, if they did not follow Party directives. To survive professionally, historians had to partake in the debasement of historiography. This involved treating non-Russian territories as integral parts of the larger Russian whole and minimizing, if not ignoring, diversity, plurality, and Russian–non-Russian conflicts in the past.

The "history of the USSR" was fundamentally a history of Russia extended over all the territories ruled from Moscow and Petersburg. It reflected Stalin's wish to institutionally merge the RSFSR into the USSR and paint a Russian face on the country. The "history of the USSR" differed somewhat from the tsarist image of "Russian history," but both neglected diversity and specificities and impeded the evolution of Russian national self-consciousness by identifying Russia and its past with an empire rather than with a specific native territory.[11] The attempt to integrate and unify the Soviet polity had as its counterpart an historiography that bowdlerized non-Russian pasts because it omitted so much from them. Official histories of the USSR and the Republics obscured rather than explained relations between the "core" and the "periphery," between the general and the specific.

Consequently, as "national history" was slowly dissociated from chauvinism in the West, historiography in the USSR continued to legitimize Russian domination of a multinational Eurasian state. Only a few years before the disintegration of the USSR, in 1988, did the Party begin to lessen its grip on historical scholarship and give historians more leeway to discuss this particular issue. Until then, the official statist "history of the USSR" made ritual references to the diversity and plurality of its subject matter, but the narrative focused on the country as seen from the center and used paradigms and categories derived from Russian history to study non-Russian pasts.

The Russocentrism of official USSR historiography after 1934 becomes particularly evident if it is compared with "British history," which rarely, if at all, confused the term "English" with "British."[12] In contrast to the Russian practice of trying to include non-Russians in the empire and the USSR into "Russian history," English historians did not attempt to incorporate Celts, Scots, or Irish within "English history." Neither did the British government ever use the concept "British history" as an ideological tool to integrate the United Kingdom.

After 1934 USSR historians had to write within a rigid administrative structure, using "Marxist-Leninist" method and terminology and *a priori* politically determined guidelines, of which the most important were issued in 1934, 1937, 1947, and 1953. Fundamental concepts found in these various resolutions included an assumed Eastern Slavic "brotherhood" derived from a medieval proto-Russian nation that was supposed to have been the basis of a "common historical process." It was assumed that a "desire" for "reunion" with Russians was a major historical force in Ukraine's past, that "oppression" led to uprisings, and that vicious "class struggle" represented a mass aspiration for social liberation from feudalism and then capitalism. Axioms relevant to the nineteenth and early twentieth centuries included the idea that the proletariat represented "progress" and could not be nationalistic, that nationalism was tantamount to "counterrevolution," that the Bolsheviks represented the proletariat, and that the Bolshevik seizure of power in 1917 was a "socialist revolution" whose course was basically the same throughout the tsarist empire. More generally, the past was fitted into a pattern of unilinear evolution marked by stages, and it was assumed that at any given moment a "progressive" option existed. Study was limited effectively to subjects related to "evolution," and research focused on those aspects of the past that "propelled" or "retarded" the "process." Trends were extrapolated from evidence that corresponded to the assumed model, while evidence that did not correspond was rationalized away or ignored.

The regime did provide non-Russians in the USSR with "national histories," but in the face of guidelines and central control over ideology and scholarship after 1934 that intensified after 1947, these accounts cannot be regarded as "national history" in the accepted meaning of the term. The official interpretation of a given region's past incorporated only such elements from the native "national historiography" as complemented its Russocentrism. Non-Russian "national history" found expression only in shifts of emphasis and nuances in treatment of particular issues that stressed what was particular or different in Republic pasts. Central Committee support for "reformists" was limited and rare, and they never overcame the resistance to interpretative change of those who dominated the institutions and made their careers imposing and promulgating the official view. Simple inertia reinforced the administrative structure of academia to ensure historiography identified and emphasized "unity," pro-Russian sentiment, and "All–Russian" phenomena in the Republics, at the expense of the particular and the local.

The internal logic of the final product was imposing. Since Eastern Slavs had been a united proto-Russian nation, and the Russians were the "leading nation" in the USSR, Ukrainian-Russian "reunion" in 1654 was "progressive." Since re-establishment of lost national commonality was beneficial and desirable, it followed that any differences between Ukraine and Russia were minimal and could be justifiably ignored or de-emphasized as historically insignificant. What was significant in Ukraine's past was whatever may have had favorable association with Russia or was similar to an event in Russia. From such a perspective, issues particular to Ukraine such as colonialism, the cossack social structure and federalist-populist political tradition, or the role of nationalism in the 1917 "Ukrainian revolution" became anomalies or obstacles that divided "fraternal nations" or weakened the "revolutionary struggle" of "fraternal peoples."

The official view resembled the pre-1917 tsarist interpretation, yet it was also similar to pro-Russian, "loyalist," or "Russophile" views of Ukrainian history written by Ukrainians in the eighteenth or nineteenth century. But this did not make the official Soviet interpretation less "Russian" or more legitimate from the twentieth-century Ukrainian perspective. In the final analysis, the post-1934 official Soviet interpretation of Ukraine's past was a "Russian" interpretation.

After 1934 the line between Russian and non-Russian history was vague but it did exist, and its location on the field of distinctiveness versus uniformity shifted with political circumstances. Between 1939 and 1947, and in the mid-1950s and mid-1960s, "reformist" historians had some leeway in interpreting guidelines and could stress what was distinctive or different in the Ukrainian as opposed to the Russian past. But the majority of survey histories of the USSR and the Republics obfuscated and ignored diversity. They emphasized Russian-Ukrainian "unity" and "All-Russian" phenomenon in the non-Russian provinces of the tsarist empire at the expense of indigenous events and organizations.

A "liberal" political climate in the mid-1960s fostered theoretical discussions on paradigms or typologies that in deductive systems of thought, such as Marxism-Leninism, play an important role in scholarship. The alternative typologies that emerged during these debates were reflected in the interpretative shifts and increased information found in "reformist" survey histories of Ukraine and the USSR.

The 1967 history of the Ukrainian SSR, for instance, contained less passages about Russian munificence and assistance to Ukrainians throughout time than did the 1955 edition. Its account of the nineteenth-century national movement in particular marked an improvement from the earlier edition. The text categorized this phenomenon as "progressive" and part of the "revolutionary struggle" rather than a hostile current apart from it. Perhaps it was not fortuitous that the two-volume 1967 survey had the smallest press run (50,000 copies in Ukrainian and Russian) of the three official multivolume histories of the Ukrainian SSR. Nevertheless, the narrative was still centered on the 1947 and 1953 guidelines and did not cover issues such as the reformist initiatives of elites, the cossacks in international politics, or benefits of Polish rule. The 1967 survey did not examine Polish or Russian administration in Ukraine and compare degrees of autonomy, it did not deal adequately with the Uniate church or motivations of individuals, nor did it even provide a credible account of Russian-Ukrainian relations.

Official historiography, with its monotonous style, compared development in Ukraine only with events in Russia and was not geared to stimulate readers to compare Ukraine with Ireland, India, Belgium, or Brittany. Readers going through these texts would be unlikely to ask themselves, for instance, whether Brittany and Belgium developed as they did because the former, like Ukraine, remained part of a larger state, France, after 1789, while the latter separated in 1830. Although Marx referred to a "civilizing function" of ruling classes, Soviet accounts of medieval and early-modern history did not impress this on readers. The historical role of elites was generally downplayed and juxtaposed to that of the "masses," but a civilizing function was allotted to the Russian ruling class. Ukrainian elites, except for some who could be shown to have been pro-Russian, were depicted as nothing but "exploiters," a "reactionary" group that neither defended Ukraine nor developed its forces of production.

There were few Russian monograph studies dealing with the issues covered in this book. Studies by Semevsky, the young Picheta, Zaionchkovsky, Osipov, Lyzlov, and Volkov were informative, well written, and even pioneering. New information unearthed by these men could find its way into survey histories only if it illustrated *a priori* axioms and the broader scheme. USSR historiography was controlled and deductivist, and interpretation in survey history changed only with the consent of political authority.

Russian historians who worked on Ukrainian subject matter as well as authors of survey histories of the USSR, of course, could have agreed with official points of view. Nevertheless, interpretation in the final analysis was the prerogative of Party officials, not scholars. For this reason, the interpretation of Ukraine's past found in survey histories cannot actually be attributed to the authors listed on title pages. Available evidence shows that Stalin, V. Bystriansky, P. Drozdov, V. Manilov, M. Rubach, T. Skubytsky , S. Kovaliov, M. Lykholat, P. Pospelov, S. Chervonenko, and A. Rumiantsev were the real compilers of the post-1934 Soviet account of Ukrainian history.

APPENDIX: PERESTROIKA AND INTERPRETATION

Russian historiography traditionally associated the Russian nation with the tsarist state and gave only fleeting attention to non-Russians as part of Russian regional history. Ukrainians and Belarussians figured as "lost tribes," separated from Russians after the "Kievan period of Russian history," then as victims of foreign oppression, and finally as peoples "reunited" with Russia. Eclipsed during the 1920s, a variant of this interpretation was revived after 1934 as the "history of the USSR" that presented the past of the nations of the USSR not as a sum of its parts but as a single "historical process," characterized by a struggle of commoners of all nationalities against a comprador multinational ruling class. To this was added, in 1954, the claim that the three Eastern Slavic nations evolved from a proto–"old Russian nation" whose unity was shattered in the thirteenth century by the Mongol invasion. Thereafter, a "desire for reunion" determined Ukrainian and Belarus history until their respective "reunifications" with the Russians.[1]

The official Soviet interpretation, unlike its tsarist precursor, recognized cultural-linguistic differences between Russians and Ukrainians and allotted the latter a "national history," but like the tsarist view, neglected the institutional and socio-economic differences between the two nations. Despite formal obeisances to non-Russians, the "history of the USSR," like the tsarist history of Russia, confused Russian nationhood with the tsarist state and promoted an image of Russia as a unit rather than a highly diverse entity. The official interpretation minimized or ignored differences and conflicts between Russians and non-Russians, stressed similarities and the beneficial results of centrally initiated "objective" modernization policies, and presented the national histories of non-Russians as Russian regional history. Such a reading of Russian statist centralism and national homogeneity into the Eastern Slavic past associated Kievan Rus and Russia with the multinational Russian-dominated Soviet state, relegated distinctions between Eastern Slavs to the realm of culture and language, and implicitly justified assimilation of Ukrainians into the Russian nation. Since Eastern Slavs were the same in the past, according to official reasoning, it was inevitable that they would become one nation again. The USSR was even called the "new Rus" in the national anthem. Such logic, reinforced by the Marxist belief that centralization and integration must lead to national homogeneity, and that policies fostering cultural uniformity were desirable and necessary,[2] fixed Ukraine tightly into Russia's national self-image.

The image is captured in Ilia Glazunov's painting "One Hundred Centuries."[3] Among hundreds of historical persons and symbols arrayed in front of the Kremlin, this canvas depicts three Ukrainian symbols: the Kievan St. Sophia church, Bohdan Khmelnytsky, and the battle of Poltava. It also portrays the early Kievan princes—regarded as "Ukrainian" in Ukrainian historiography. Since the only other non-Russian figures are a pagan god and a Mongol, and there is nothing representing Finno-Ugric tribes or Belarus, Ukraine fits into the composition not as a subject people, or "younger brother," but as an organic part of the Russian whole. This image, unmindful of distinctions between Eastern Slavs, emerged during Gorbachev's trips to Ukraine, when he referred to Kiev as a "Russian city"and remarked that whatever happened in the USSR "we Slavs must stick together." Similarly, Solzhenitsyn's call for Russians to strip their revived national consciousness of its imperial dimension did not include Ukraine and Belarus among the undesired accruements.[4] The regime's success in disseminating this image may be gauged from popular confusion between the Russian part and the Eastern Slavic whole found in letters to editors during *glasnost,* complaining about the Ukrainian revival. One reader complained: "And is it necessary to divide the Russian land? All Ukraine was part of Kievan Rus. Kiev—was the capital of Russia [Rossiia] for four hundred years. Ukraine—this is the quintessential [*iskonno*] Russian land."[5] In a poll asking Russians their national identity, 43 percent of the respondents said they were "Russian," while 42 percent said they were "soviet."[6]

Under Gorbachev, Russians began rediscovering their pre-1917 national culture. This revival included debate over Russian identity, and slowly Russians began to delineate the tsarist and Soviet states from the Russian nation.[7] With the political separation of Russia from the USSR, the mental separation of "Russia" from "Soviet" will become easier. It remains to be seen if Russian historians abet the latter tendency and begin drawing clear boundaries between the histories of the three Eastern Slavic nations.

Among the first critics of the official treatment of Russian and non-Russian relations was A. Iakovlev who spoke of the tendency to "embellish" Russian as well as non-Russian history.[8] Later, CC officials, at a session of the All-Union Ideological Commission, stated that the "history of the USSR" cannot continue to stress Russian history and "should indeed be a history of the peoples of the USSR."[9] Some Russian intellectuals also questioned the official treatment of Russian and non-Russian relations. Gavriel Popov drew attention to the dilemma posed by the fact that one nation's glory is often another's shame, and observed that understanding Russian relations with non-Russians would be complicated because the centralized system had used a circumscribed version of Russian history to oppress non-Russians and make them forget their pasts.[10] Sergei Baruzdin condemned two fundamental tenets of the official view of non-Russian history during the 1989 All-Union Writers Congress. He dismissed the idea of Russian "elder brothers" as Stalinist, and called for rejection of the post-Stalin innovation that all non-Russians had "voluntarily joined" Russia.[11]

Very few Russian historians took issue with the treatment of non-Russians in official historiography.[12] One reformist historian called for a major overhaul of the conception of Russian-Turkmen relations.[13] Another pointed out that the Belarussians had their own Western orientated state after the fall of Kievan Rus and questioned whether Polish control over Belarus was as bad, and Russian control as good, as habitually depicted. Pointing out that "reunification" with Russia cannot be regarded as Belarussia's only possible historical alternative, he called for revision of the prevailing interpretation.[14] There were no similarly critical articles on Ukrainian-Russian relations. Reformists admitted that not all non-Russians joined the Russian state voluntarily and that all forms of incorporation had to be studied, but some continued to regard the Ukrainian-Russian seventeenth-century "reunification" as simply a "form" of annexation like conquest and "joining." A. Novoseltsov, then head of the All-Union Academy Institute of USSR History, observed that ruling classes had come to agreements with tsars that included national autonomy and that the tsars were interested in subjugating incorporated regions, yet he claimed Ukraine's "reunion" was distinct from conquest or "joining."[15] As of 1991, only one Russian historian had called for the rejection of this politically imposed term.[16]

The failure of Russian historians to begin a critical reassessment of Russia's colonial past, and to ask if the servitude of their own nationality was the price of empire, converged with the views of senior academic administrators who promoted the official Russocentric interpretation of Russian–non-Russian relations. S. L. Tikhvinsky, then Deputy Chair of the Institute of Social Sciences of the All-Union Academy, Secretary of the Institute of History, an editor of *Voprosy istorii,* and member of the Praesidium of the USSR Academy of Sciences, for instance, listed among shortcomings of 1970s Republic historiography the "revival of nationalistic treatments of the past of certain nationalities" and "idealization" of Republic national histories. He accused historians in the Republics of not dealing adequately with past Russian "fraternal aid." Tikhvinsky criticized all Republics except the Russian SFSR and did not indict the "history of the USSR" for being Russocentric.[17] He even called for more centralization: "The time has come to decisively break with the fallacious tendency [*porochnaia tendentsiia*] of dividing scholarship into Ukrainian or Azeri, central or peripheral. There is one Soviet historical scholarship firmly based on Marxist-Leninist socialist internationalism."[18] The president of the All-Union Academy asserted that pre-eighteenth-century fatherland history was in "good condition."[19] Gorbachev, meanwhile, in December 1989, quoting Dostoevsky about the bighearted Russian striving for universal union, claimed that the "friendship" of Soviet nationalities was a desirable legacy of the tsarist period, when they all had been "united" around Russia. He drew attention to the "great role" of the Russians, their internationalism and humanitarianism, and how they had taken non-Russians "under their wings."[20]

Although the official version of the past was formulated and imposed by Moscow, the task of ensuring the conformity of historians in Ukraine belonged to the Ukrainian Party. The Kiev apparat performed this task well in the last two decades of the Soviet regime. As yet there is little evidence about Ukrainian Party politics during the late 1980s, but it seems likely that the new leadership in 1990, as part of its strategy to undercut the organized non-party opposition and legitimize continued communist rule, decided to exploit Ukrainian nationalism. This tactical shift included sanctioned change in historiography.

Ukrainian reformist writers and academics began to dispense with the stultifying language and concepts of DHM and to openly criticize the historical establishment and the prevailing image of Eastern Slavic relations later than did their Russian colleagues. But the Ukrainians, much more so than the Russians, focused on the shortcomings of the official version of Ukrainian-Russian relations. As elsewhere in the USSR, Ukrainian writers were more outspoken than "reformist" historians, who limited their criticism to declamatory renunciations of the interpretation of particular issues and concentrated on publishing popular descriptive essays on previously ignored subjects. "Reformists" published sympathetic articles about Mazepa, portraying him as a hero instead of a traitor, and questioned the nature and results of 360 years of Russian rule.[21] They observed that Mazepa had been a statesman who envisaged a Ukraine founded on "humanity and democracy" and had heralded the ideals of the French Revolution. One author explained that the hetman did not betray Peter I, but that the tsar and his predecessors betrayed Ukraine by limiting its autonomy.[22] In a critical look at Ukrainian-Russian relations, a writer reviewed the long-ignored subject of the diminution of cossack autonomy between 1654 and 1687 without mentioning the obligatory formula of "friendship" that equated non-Russian political autonomy under tsarist overlordship exclusively with "desires" of local elites to exploit their vassals.[23] Articles appeared pointing to tsarist economic exploitation of Cossack Ukraine, its colonial status vis-à-vis Russia, and the statist aspects of Ukraine's past and questioning the belief that Russia had exclusive right to the legacy of Kievan-Rus.[24] In a departure from Stalinist-Marxist canons, some began to study ruling elites and mentality in Ukraine, while others reminded readers of the neglected issue of "Western" and "nativist" tendencies in early-modern Ukraine.[25] Reformist historians stopped categorizing nineteenth-century Ukrainian intellectuals and activists who were not socialist-radicals as "right-wing" and unworthy of attention. They stopped referring to "decisive" influences of Russian "revolutionary democracy" on the Ukrainian national movement, and one historian pointed out that Russian radicals' attitudes toward the Ukrainian national movement were at best patronizing and condescending.[26] By the end of 1990, even the official *Ukrainskyi istorychnyi zhurnal* began publishing "reformist" opinions.[27] Noteworthy was a critique of the official view of 1917 in Ukraine that listed inconsistencies and gaps and argued that non-Bolshevik parties had the initiative in the first months of the revolution. The author noted that the Ukrainian national-liberation movement, like all others, was "progressive" and must be treated accordingly.[28]

But except for M. Braichevsky's analysis and critique of the official account of early-modern Ukrainian-Russian relations, written in the early 1960s and published in Ukraine in the spring of 1990,[29] reformist Ukrainian as well as Russian historiography on the eve of the disintegration of the USSR had not critically analyzed the official historiography of Ukraine and Russia. A few declarative condemnations of the old view were not matched by debate around alternative interpretive models, nor scholarly refutation of the old view, its conceptual categories and methodology. This failure represented a lacuna in thought and can hinder interpretive revision and the construction of better accounts of the past. Consequently, neo-nationalist-populist, neo-Slavophile and/or neostatist accounts of national history, derived from turn-of-the-century historiography remain, by default, prime candidates as alternative interpretations in the near future.

In the late 1980s, Ukrainian reformists focused their energies either on reiterating or reprinting officially condemned populist-nationalist and statist interpretations. These depicted Ukrainians as a "Western" nation that for centuries struggled for statehood against Polish and Russian oppression. This restricted image of the past had political utility for reformers inasmuch as it helped reconstitute the stunted Ukrainian national consciousness. But such utilitarian concern also risked distracting Ukrainian, as well as Russian scholars, from the need to scrutinize turn-of-the-century nationalist interpretations as thoroughly as Stalinist views.

Right up to its demise in 1991, the Party monopolized jobs and resources, but in the 1980s reformist historians had begun to group around alternative organizations such as "Memorial" and the Shevchenko Learned Society—reestablished in late 1989—and they predominated in the Institute of Social Studies in Lviv. Simultaneously, *glasnost* had eased restrictions on dissemination of information and allowed reformists to address the public directly. Reformists, more interested in currying favor with the public than the apparat, stopped using the language and categories of DHM. They began writing factual articles devoted to ignored subjects, reprinted nineteenth-century articles, sometimes condemned the old view, and occasionally made interpretive generalizations. "Conservatives" still dominated the Academy Institute of History, the academic press, and most university departments.[30] Some of them published work on previously ignored topics, and most shared with reformists a conviction that the key to proper or "true" history lay in unhindered access to and use of primary sources. Their essays and books, as a rule, were reworded versions of the "old" interpretation and contained no revisionist generalizations and declarative condemnations of the old.[31] "Conservatives" had even formulated a short modified alternative official interpretive schema of Ukrainian history that categorized Ukrainian history as "tragic" and noted that the country had been subject to the same "forces" as Europe. The authors did not stress Eastern Slavic ethnic affinity or highlight Russian influences and "assistance," and they devoted particular attention to Ukrainian statehood as well as the destructive impact of tsarist centralism on Cossack Ukraine. Yet the outline invoked an "old Rus legacy," claiming it had been part of the "liberation movement's" ideology in the seventeenth century, and still called the consequences of the "reunion" of 1654 "progressive." The survey characterized the ensuing conflict between cossacks and tsars over Ukrainian autonomy as "merely" a conflict between ruling classes.[32]

After five years of *glasnost* and criticism of the prevailing view of Russian–non-Russian relations by ministers, reformist historians, and outspoken writers, the historical establishment equivocated but still used DHM and had not formally revoked that part of the official interpretation that highlighted historical similarities and stressed the commonality of the Russian, Ukrainian, and Belarussian "historical process." The reluctance of conservatives to jettison the old official view and their domination of academic institutions may be attributed to inertia and continuing Party control over scholarship. Although in the late 1980s the apparat in Ukraine had considerable autonomy in ideological matters, only in 1990 did it permit establishment historians to make major interpretive revisions and formulate a new official version of Ukrainian history. This project was incomplete in 1991, but had official historiography developed, it might have become similar to the quasi-Marxist Polish Annales school of the 1970s.[33] Simultaneously, the Party excluded reformists from influential positions in academic institutions, and still controlled printing equipment and paper. The dissemination of reformist views was also limited by the high prices of the independent publications for which many of them wrote. Moreover, reformist historiography about Ukraine was usually in Ukrainian but Ukrainian language books in 1989-1990 were only 19 percent of total books published in Ukraine. This represented 2 books per person per year, while in Russia 12 Russian books appeared per person per year.[34]

The Party in Ukraine up to 1991 was still in control and it could and did dismiss from their jobs historians who left its ranks or who became too critical.[35] The Ukrainian apparat permitted some reformists into some academic institutions and stopped enforcing the old guidelines, but ensured its men held the key executive positions and the ministries. The Ukrainian CC did sanction an extensive program of document publication and republication of nineteenth-century historical classics, as well as the study of previously ignored subjects.[36] Yet the fact that anonymous academic plans were still compiled in the wake of Party resolutions spelled out in *Kommunist Ukrainy* that made no mention of the decisive role of reformists and popular pressure in "restructuring" historiography showed clearly that the administrative structure of scholarship and its control mechanisms were intact. More significantly, as of 1991 no one had criticized Tikhvinsky or the established periodization. The crucial resolutions of 1947-1951 were officially retracted and annulled, but not those of 1934, 1937, and 1953—which, at most, were merely mentioned in introductions and then ignored.[37]

In the face of strong public interest in history and a Party unsure of itself, some conservatives played to both sides. In one instance, a historian admitted at conferences that Ukraine's incorporation into the tsarist empire was not as simple as hitherto imagined and was not merely a result of "reunion" in 1654, but in his publications he used the phrases, concepts, and ideas of the old interpretation.[38] In another case, authors examined the long-ignored issue of early-modern Ukrainian statehood, but they retained the Marxist conflict theory of the state and, in accord with the old Russocentric interpretation, did not mention a treaty signed with Poland in 1649 that marked the formal recognition of cossack proto-statehood.[39]

Thus, just before the USSR was dissolved, historiography was slightly liberalized and pre-Stalinist, and non-Soviet interpretations had begun to reappear. In Ukraine some non-Soviet nationalist-populist and statist interpretations were slated for republication in mass editions. But Party control was strong, and only one alternative independent academic institution existed in Ukraine (the Shevchenko Learned Society in Lviv). Establishment academics were compiling a new "official interpretation" of Ukrainian history, which they already had published in textbook and popular form. Although reformist historians, enjoying public confidence, had begun reprinting non-Soviet surveys, they had not begun working on an alternative scholarly synthesis incorporating non-national methodologies and concepts. A modern account of past relations between Eastern Slavs that could bolster the national and civic consciousness of all sides without fomenting integral-nationalism was lacking.

The disintegration of Party control was a necessary but insufficient condition for improved scholarship and historical writing that would generate interpretations fostering equality and tolerance and not feelings of superiority and enmity. Among the remaining obstacles also were the enhanced prestige of pre-Soviet interpretations, regarded as "good" or "true" simply because they had been repressed. In Ukraine, there was popular conviction that Russian rule was disastrous, while in Russia, Ukraine constituted an inalienable part of the national self-image. There was also the legacy of ideological Manicheanism. Raised and trained in a system that reduced everything in society to politics, Ukrainians and Russians were prone to idealize and politicize previously condemned views. Insofar as such a mentality treats historical writing in purely normative terms and continues to influence historians, it will impede the evolution of non-ideological, dispassionate academic historiography. This could mean that in spite of the best efforts of a minority, represented by Danilov and Afanasiev in Russia, or Dashkevych and Isaevych in Ukraine, historiography might simply change uniforms. From being a tool of "bad" communism it could become nothing more than a tool of "good" Ukrainian or Russian historical nationalism.[40]

Western historians reading reformist Ukrainian historiography will be struck by its limited subject matter and dated philosophical assumptions. In part, this is the understandable result of 60 years of isolation from the international scholarly community. "Reformist" writing, additionally, was the product of intellectuals who saw themselves as representatives of an oppressed nation struggling against central authority. From their perspective, the non-national interpretive focus of modern sociological, psychological, and comparative historiography was undesirable insofar as it undermined the pressing task of reviving a horribly stilted national consciousness. A similar dilemma was faced by nineteenth-century Polish historians, who, although familiar with the latest developments in methodology, eschewed them as novelties unsuitable for what they thought was more important. Polish intellectuals then, like most reformist Ukrainians a century later, saw themselves as representatives of a nation without a state, historical writing as a tool to build national consciousness, and modern methods as mere experimentation that would detract from efforts to bolster and develop patriotism.[41] In short, concern for social utility determined that the dominant interpretation of Polish history at the beginning of the twentieth century was neoromantic, and that neopositivism, "integral history," and Marxism remained confined to a small circle of historians with little influence on society. Perhaps the popular nationalism produced by such historiography had its merits at the beginning of the century. But whether this force was desirable in Europe at the end of century, and whether century-old interpretive schema are the best way to reanimate Ukrainian national pride and self-worth are open to question.

The issue of social utility and methodology affects reformist Russian historiography similarly. Russians outside the ruling elite are in soul-searching upheaval and agony. They have learned that their government systematically lied to them, misused their nationalism, and provided little in return for sacrifices. In reaction, extremists as well as moderates, exhibited symptoms of an inferiority complex and injured pride characteristic of colonized rather than colonizers.[42] In reaction to non-Russian images of Russians, rather than the regime, as the oppressor, some Russians exhibited exaggerated nationalist self-assertion and used "Russophobia" as a term to discredit and dismiss criticism of Russia and Russians.[43] Among Stalinist, neo-Leninist, right-wing, and probably even most liberal Russians, accusations of colonialism by non-Russians added insult to injury, since Russians shared a preconception of their nation as a disinterested, spurned benefactor that rarely if ever besmirched itself with colonial repression. Part of this image is the interpretation of history that identifies East Slavs as basically the same peoples, Russians as modernizers, and Ukraine as a region whose association with Russia was desirable and historically justified. Given these circumstances, reformist critique or rejection of Stalinist and/or pre-1917 versions of Russian-Ukrainian relations, or the Eastern Slav affinity myth, could just as likely provoke a chauvinist backlash as mollify Russian nationalism. At the risk of oversimplification, it might be claimed that reformist Ukrainian historians risked abetting integral-nationalism by *not* adopting new interpretive schema, whereas their Russian colleagues faced a similar risk if they did adopt new schema.

In the nineteenth century, Jakob Burckhardt was a much better historian than Heinrich von Treitschke. The former, however, had less impact on contemporaries than the latter who won fame as the popularizer and apologist for Bismarck's "blood and iron" policies. In Russia and Ukraine at the beginning of the 1990s, historians faced the temptation to become latter-day Treitschkes. Some reformists, aware of the dilemma posed by utility and methodology, knew they would better serve their countrymen as modern Burckhardts. These were the most amenable to the proposition that knowing modern methodologies was a necessary precondition for new syntheses of national history.

ABBREVIATIONS TO NOTES

BU -	*Bolshevyk Ukrainy*
IM -	*Istorik Marksist*
ISSSR -	*Istoriia SSSR*
IZ -	*Istoricheskie zapiski*
IZh -	*Istoricheskii zhurnal*
KH -	*Kwartalnik Historyczny*
LR -	*Letopis revoliutsii*
PH -	*Przegląd Historyczny*
PHum -	*Przegląd Humanistyczny*
PM -	*Prapor Marksyzma*
PMLP -	*Pid Marksystsko-Leninskim Praporem*
PP -	*Przegląd Powszechny*
SR -	*Slavic Review*
SST -	*Studies in Soviet Thought and Society*
Studia zDZSRRiES -	*Studia z Dziejów ZSRR i Europy Środkowiej*
UIZh -	*Ukrainskyi istorychnyi zhurnal*
VI -	*Voprosy Istorii*
ZDSPR -	*Studia z Dziejów Stosunków Polsko-Radzieckich*

NOTES

Notes to Introduction

1. H. Butterfield, *The Whig Interpretation of History* (London, 1973), p. 12.
2. P. Burke, ed., *A New Kind of History: From The Writings of Lucien Febvre* (London, 1973), p. 258.
3. M. I. Finley, *The Use and Abuse of History* (London, 1974), pp. 11-33, 193-214; J. H. Plumb, *The Death of the Past* (Toronto, 1969).
4. For Barthes, Derrida, Kristeva, and Foucoult, meaning, thought and language, even in liberal-pluralist societies, are defined by power, not by their relation to empirical evidence or reality. Such extremist relativism makes scholarship indistinguishable from science-fiction or utterances at a monkey's tea party and reduces analysis to tautological propositions. Rules of evidence are not a rhetorical device. The underlying assumptions of this book derive from Dilthey, Collingwood, and Kuhn, who argue that interpretations can be better or worse.
5. From the 1930s, listings of scholars in the USSR were incomplete. For the 1920s see *Nauka i nauchnye rabotniki SSSR*, parts 5-6 (Leningrad, 1926-1928).

Notes to Chapter 1

1. M. Papierzyńska-Turek, *Sprawa ukraińska w Drugiej Rzeczypospolitej 1922-1926* (Warsaw, 1979); S. Mauersberg, *Szkolnictwo powszechne dla mniejszości narodowych w Polsce w latach 1918-1939* (Warsaw, 1968), pp. 9-26, 59-103, 191-211; A. Chojnowski, *Koncepje polityki narodowościowej rządów polskich w latach 1921-1939* (Warsaw and Krakow, 1979); S. Mikulicz, *Prometeizm w polityce II Rzeczypospolitej* (Warsaw, 1971).
2. K. Sochaniewicz, "Stan, organizacja i postulaty badań nad historją ziem południo Ruskich," *Pamiętnik IV powszechnego zjazdu Historyków Polskich* (Lviv, 1925), p. 9.
3. O. Górka, *Dziejowa rzeczywistość a racja stanu Polski na południowym wschodzie* (Warsaw, 1933). On Sienkiewicz's image of Ukraine, see T. Jodełka, ed., *Trylogia Henryka Sienkiewicza: Studia, szkice, polemiki* (Warsaw, 1962); W. Czapliński, *Glosa do Trylogii* (Wroclaw, 1974).
4. E. Maleczyńska and A. Gilewicz, *Materiały i wskazówki do nauczania historii ziemi czerwieńskiej* (Lviv, 1933).
5. K. Lewicki, "Dzieje kozaczyzny: Przegląd literatury za lata 1918-1935," *Ziemia Czerwieńska* 2, no. 1 (1936): 134-48; "Przegląd najnowszy literatury do dziejów prawosławia (unia) w Polsce," *Ziemia Czerwieńska* 3, no. 2 (1937), pp. 211-31.

6. J. Maternicki, *Idee i postawy: Historia i historycy polscy 1914-1918* (Warsaw, 1975), pp. 313, 371-97.
7. M. Papierzyńska-Turek, *Między tradycją a rzeczywistościa: Panstwo wobec prawosławia* (Warsaw, 1989), pp. 92-101.
8. G. Lovmiansky and L. Zhitkovich, "Istoriia SSSR v istoriografii narodnoi Polshi," *ISSSR*, no. 1 (1960): 207-23; H. Łowmianski, "Dzieje narodów ZSRR . . . (do konca XVII w.) w historiografii Polski Ludowej," *ZDSPR* 5 (1969): 3-18; M. Tanty, "Historia ZSRR . . . XIX-XX wieku w historiografii Polski Ludowej," *ZDSPR* 5 (1969): 19-34.
9. P. Kalenychenko, "Suchasna polska istoriohrafiia pro Ukrainu," *Pytannia novoi ta novitnoi istorii*, no. 13 (1971): 126-38, "Polska marksystychna istoriohrafiia pro Ukrainu periodu feodalizmu," *Seredni viky na Ukraini* 1 (1971): 214-26.
10. S. Zabrovarny, "Istoriia Ukrainy v doslidzhenniakh istorykiv PNR," *Nasha kultura*, no. 3 (1975), pp. 10-12; no. 4, pp. 12-14; no. 5, pp. 10-13; no. 6, pp. 10-13; no. 7, pp. 12-14; no. 8, pp. 13-15; no. 9, pp. 11-13; no. 10, pp. 12-13.
11. S. Zabrowarny, "Ukraiński ruch narodowy w Galicji XIX i początku XX wieku w pracach historyków polskich," *Studia z filologii rosyjskiej i słowianskiej* 14 (1987): 85-106. A prewar survey noted the first academic work on the Ukrainian question in Galicia appeared in 1934. See M. Tyrowicz, "Galicja, 1772-1914," *Ziemia Czerwieńska* 1 (1935): 131.
12. P. R. Magocsi, *Galicia: A Historical Survey and Bibliographic Guide* (Toronto, 1983), pp. 29, 225-26.
13. W. Serczyk, "Ukraina w historiografii polskiej: Potrzeby i nadzieje," *Studia z filologii rosyjskiej i słowianskiej* 14 (1987): 37-48. T. Biernacek, "Gwoli historycznej ścisłości (O mniejszości ukraińskiej w II Rzeczypospolitej)," *Slavia Orientalis*, no. 1-2 (1990): 144-52. This involved, for example, referring to Polish-Ukrainian events in 1918 as "the Polish struggle for Lviv" instead of "the Polish-Ukrainian War."
14. Cited in J. Borys, *The Sovietization of Ukraine 1917-1923* (Edmonton, 1980), pp. 137, 295; 52-72, 160-170. Zinoviev cited in W. R. Batsell, *Soviet Rule in Russia* (New York, 1929), p. 117.
15. B. Krawchenko, *Social Change and National Consciousness in Soviet Ukraine* (London, 1985); R. Sullivant, *Soviet Politics and the Ukraine* (New York, 1962).
16. S. A. Piontkovsky, "Velikoderzhavnye tendentsii v istoriografii Rossii," *IM*, no. 17 (1930): 25-26; Piontkovsky, *Burzhuaznaia istoricheskaia nauka v Rossii* (Moscow, 1931), pp. 94, 99.
17. B. Krupnytsky, *Ukrainska istorychna nauka pid sovietamy (1920-1953)* (Munich, 1957), p. 93; O. Ohloblyn, *Dumky pro suchasnu sovietsku istoriohrafiiu* (New York, 1963), p. 5.
18. A. Avtorkhanov, *Polozhenie istoricheskoi nauki v SSSR* (Munich, 1951); P. K. Urban, *Smena tendentsii v sovetskoi istoriografii* (Munich, 1959); K. Shteppa, *Russian Historians and the Soviet State* (New Brunswick, NJ, 1962); L. Tillet, *The Great Friendship* (Chapel Hill, NC, 1969).
19. G. Enteen, "Two Books on Soviet Historiography," *World Politics* 20, no. 2 (January 1968): 348-49.

20. For example, L. A. Openkin, "Mekhanizm tormozheniia v sfere obshchestvennykh nauk," *ISSSR*, no. 6 (1989): 3-15.
21. G. Barraclough, *Main Trends in History* (London, 1979), pp. 149-53; J. Sheenan, "What Is German History? Reflections on the Role of the Nation in German History and Historiography," *Journal of Modern History* (March-December 1981): 1-23.
22. E. H. Dance, *History the Betrayer* (London, 1960), pp. 126-45; D. Thomson, "Must History Stay Nationalist?" *Encounter* (June 1968): 22-28; M. H. Berman, *The Treatment of the Soviet Union and Communism in Selected World History Textbooks, 1920-1970* (Ann Arbor, MI, 1976), pp. 16-33.
23. R. Szporluk, "The Soviet West—Or Far Eastern Europe?" *East European Politics and Societies*, no. 3 (1991): 471-73. See also E. Gellner, *Nations and Nationalism* (Ithaca, NY, 1983).
24. J. Armstrong, "The Autonomy of Ethnic Identity, Historic Cleavages and Nationality Relations in the USSR," in *Thinking Theoretically About Soviet Nationalities*, ed. A. Motyl (New York, 1992), pp. 26-32.
25. E. Allworth, "Flexible Defenses of a Nationality," in *Nationality Group Survival in Multi-Ethnic States*, ed. E. Allworth (New York, 1977), p. 19.
26. B. Cywiński, *Zatruta humanistyka* (Warsaw, 1980), an unofficial publication; J. Leftwich-Curry, ed., *The Black Book of Polish Censorship* (New York, 1984), pp. 318-69.
27. A. D. Smith, *The Ethnic Revival* (Cambridge, 1981).
28. R. Szporluk, "The Ukraine and Russia," in *The Last Empire*, ed. R. Conquest (Stanford, 1988), pp. 151-82.
29. W. Connor, *The National Question in Marxist-Leninist Theory and Strategy* (Princeton, 1984); D. Boersner, *The Bolsheviks and the National and Colonial Question* (New York, 1981); R. Szporluk, *Communism and Nationalism* (New York, 1988), pp. 193-204; G. Gleason, *Federalism and Nationalism* (Boulder, CO, 1990), chaps. 2-3.
30. C. Herod, *The Nation in the History of Marxist Thought* (The Hague, 1976).
31. A. Low, *Lenin on the Question of Nationality* (New York, 1958); R. Szporluk, *Communism and Nationalism*, pp. 205-240.
32. H. Carrere d'Encausse, "Determinants and Parameters of Soviet Nationality Policy," in *Soviet Nationality Policies and Practices*, ed. J. Azrael (New York, 1978), p. 48.
33. R. Szporluk, "History and Russian Ethnocentrism," in *Ethnic Russia in the USSR: The Dilemma of Dominance*, ed. E. Allworth (New York, 1980), pp. 41-54.
34. A. M. Sakharov, "O znachenii otechestvennoi istorii," *ISSSR*, no. 4 (1965): 5.
35. *Trudy Pervoi vsesoiuznoi konferentsii istorikov marksistov* (Moscow, 1930), I: 448-467. Exchanges outside the chambers were sharper, according to O. Hermaize, "Isha Vsesoiuzna konferentsiia istorykiv-marksystiv u Moskvi," *Visti Vseukrainskoi akademii nauk*, no. 1 (1929): 16-17.
36. M. Redin, "Za bilshovytskyi povorot u vykladanni istorii," *BU*, no. 11 (1931): 88-89.
37. "Zamechaniia po povodu konspekta uchebnika po 'Istorii SSSR,' " *Krasnyi arkhiv* 75 (1936): 6. The term "history of the USSR" first appeared in "O prepodavanii grazhdanskoi istorii v shkolakh SSSR," *Krasnyi arkhiv* 75 (1936): 4.

38. F. Barghoorn, *Soviet Russian Nationalism* (New York, 1956); A. Motyl, *Will the Non-Russians Rebel?* (Ithaca, NY, 1987), pp. 3-51.
39. L. Yaresh, "The Formation of the Great Russian State," in *Rewriting Russian History*, ed. C. Black (New York, 1962), pp. 200-2.
40. This statement was not published until 1941. R. H. McNeal, ed., *I. V. Stalin. Sochineniia* (Stanford, 1967), I [XIV]: pp. 2-10.
41. G. Aleksandrov, "O nekotorykh zadachakh obshchestvennykh nauk v sovremennykh usloviakh," *Bolshevik*, no. 14 (July 1945): 17.
42. B. N. Ponomarev, ed., *Istoriia SSSR* (Moscow, 1966), I: xxviii.
43. *Izvestiia*, December 21, 1988. V. I. Lebedev et al., *Istoriia SSSR s drevneishikh vremen do kontsa XVIII v.* (1939); B. D. Datsiuk et al., *Istoriia SSSR* (1963); P. I. Kabanov and V. V. Mavrodin, *Istoriia SSSR* (1966); Iu. Kondufor and V. N. Kotov, *Istoriia SSSR* (1980).
44. V. D. Koroliuk et al., *Istoriia Polshi* (Moscow, 1956), I: 123, 189.
45. S. Velychenko, *National History as Cultural Process: The Interpretation of Ukraine's Past in Polish, Ukrainian and Russian Historiography* (Edmonton, 1992); D. Saunders, *The Ukrainian Impact on Russian Culture* (Edmonton, 1985), pp. 239-253.
46. A. Besancon, "Nationalism and Bolshevism in the USSR," in *The Last Empire*, ed. R. Conquest, pp. 1-13.
47. This conclusion is shared by Ia. Dashkevych, a respected Ukrainian historian whom I interviewed in November 1988.

Notes to Chapter 2

1. I am grateful to Sergei Kirzhaev of the Central Academic Library in Kiev for this information. On control over culture in general between 1919-1922, see C. Read, *Culture and Power in Revolutionary Russia* (New York, 1990), pp. 159-230.
2. M. Fainsod, *How Russia is Ruled* (Cambridge, MA, 1963), p. 169; L. R. Graham, *The Soviet Academy of Sciences and the Communist Party, 1927-1932* (Princeton, NJ, 1967).
3. V. Marchenko, *Planirovanie nauchnoi raboty v SSSR* (Munich, 1953), pp. 9, 12, 18; A. Avtorkhanov, *Memuary* (Frankfurt-am-Main, 1983), pp. 377-78. W. Vucinich, *Empire of Knowledge* (Berkeley, CA, 1984), pp. 72-314.
4. Vucinich, *Empire of Knowledge*, pp. 302-04; N. Heer, *Politics and History in the Soviet Union* (Cambridge, MA, 1973), p. 42; L. Tillet, *The Great Friendship*, (Chapel Hill, NC, 1969), p. 276; H. Rogger, "Politics Ideology and History in the USSR: The Search for Coexistence," *Soviet Studies* 16 (January 1965): 253-75.
5. L. Tillet, *The Great Friendship*, p. 251.
6. V. Golovskoy, "Is There Censorship in the Soviet Union? Methodological Problems of Studying Soviet Censorship," Kennan Institute for Advanced Russian Studies, Occasional Paper, no. 201 (Washington, 1985), pp. 21-22.
7. I. Krypiakevych, *Bohdan Khmelnytskyi*, 2d ed., ed. Ia. Isaevych (Lviv, 1990), p. 7.
8. Ibid.

9. R. Gul, "Tsenzura i pisatel v SSSR," *Sovremennyia zapiski*, no. 67 (1938): 442-45; I. Gorokhoff, *Publishing in the U.S.S.R.* (Bloomington, IN, 1959), pp. 73-83; L. Vladimirov, "Glavlit: How the Soviet Censor Works," *Index on Censorship*, Autumn 1972, pp. 31-43.

10. *Zvedenyi pokazhchyk zastarilykh vydan, shcho ne pidliahaiut vykorystanniu v bibliotekakh hromadskoho korystuvannia ta knyhotorvelnii sittsi* (Kharkiv, 1954). There were at least 19 indexes published between 1934 and 1961. See S. Bilokin, "Na polytsiakh spetsfondiv u rizni roky," *Slovo i chas*, no. 1 (1990): 71-73. In 1989 all such lists were annulled. In *Zhovten*, no. 7 (1989): 81, a reader noted that in 1950 truckloads of works removed from the Chernivtsi University Library were burned at the local hydro station. A 1925 CC resolution instructed officials to remove undesirable books from village libraries. See *Izdatelskoe delo v SSSR (1923-1931)* (Moscow, 1978), p. 59. The prewar Ukrainian GLAVLIT archive was lost during the war.

11. J. Maternicki, *Historiografiia polska XX wieka* (Warsaw, 1982), pp. 19-38.

12. J. Dutkiewicz and K. Śreniowska, *Zarys historii historiografii polskiej Część III* (Lodz, 1959).

13. E. Valkenier, "The Soviet Impact on Polish Historiography, 1946-1950," *Journal of Central European Affairs* 11, no. 4 (January 1952): 372-96; "Sovietization and Liberalization in Polish Post-War Historiography," *Journal of Central European Affairs* 10, no. 2 (July 1959): 149-73; P. Hubner, *Nauka polska po II wojnie światowej: Idee i instytucje* (Warsaw, 1987), pp. 37, 91. For an exchange concerning who reluctantly followed, exuberantly led, or quietly sabotaged the Stalinization of Polish historiography, see P. Hubner, "Przebudowa nauk historycznych w Polsce (1947-1953)" and M. Małowist, "Kilka uwag do artykułu Piotra Hubnera," *PH*, no. 3 (1987): 451-492.

14. B. Fijałkowska, *Polityka i twórcy (1948-1959)* (Warsaw, 1985), pp. 415, 424, 524-25.

15. E. Valkenier, "The Rise and Decline of Official Marxist Historiography in Poland 1945-1983," *SR*, no. 4 (1985): 663-80. On Party control of the Academy, see J. Jedlicki, "Pałac," *Res Publica*, no. 5 (1987): 105-6; M. Głowinski, "Pałac i Rudera," *Res Publica*, no. 1 (1988): 81-83. "Jeszcze jeden głos zbiorowy w sprawie sytuacji w PAN," *Res Publica*, no. 2 (1988): 119-21.

16. W. Serczyk, "Eastern Europe in the 16th-18th Centuries," *Acta Poloniae Historica* 32 (1975): 94.

17. E. A. Mierzwa, "V Narada Komisji ekspertów doskonalenia treści podręczników historii," *Wiadomości historyczne*, no. 1 (1988): 85.

18. The 1981 Code appears in translation in G. Schopflin, ed., *Censorship and Political Communication in Eastern Europe* (London, 1983), pp. 124-35. See also *Dziennik ustaw Rzeczypospolity Polskiej*, no. 19 (May 1952), art. 14.

19. Cited in S. Fitzpatrick, *Education and Social Mobility in the Soviet Union 1921-1934* (New York, 1979), p. 69.

20. A. W. Gouldner, *The Two Marxisms* (New York, 1980); P. M. Vaillancourt, *When Marxists Do Research* (New York, 1986); Z. A. Jordan, *The Evolution of Dialectical Materialism* (New York, 1967).

21. The qualification about the decisive influence of "the base" in "the final analysis" resolves nothing without specification of time limit. See J. Scanlan, "A Critique of the Engels-Soviet Version of Marxian Economic Determinism," *SST* 13 (1973): 11-19.
22. E. Hobsbawn ed., *Pre-capitalist Economic Formations* (New York, 1965), pp. 9-66.
23. Z. A. Jordan, *Evolution*, pp. 297-361.
24. L. Kolakowski, *Main Currents of Marxism* (New York, 1981), II: 210-11; A. Besancon, *The Rise of the Gulag: Intellectual Origins of Leninism* (New York, 1981), pp. 210-11.
25. Z. A. Jordan, *Philosophy and Ideology* (Dordrecht, 1963), pp. 443-45.
26. E. Zhukov, *Methodology of History* (Moscow, 1983), p. 178.
27. Summarized in H. Stuart Hughes, *Consciousness and Society* (Brighton, 1979), pp. 33-113.
28. P. Mattick, *Anti-Bolshevik Marxism* (London, 1978), pp. 170, 176-80. Mattick argues that Marxism is not affected by the new physics, which does not bother with objective reality except if it is recognized by man.
29. K. Korsch, "The Present State of the Problem of Marxism and Philosophy," reprinted in *Marxism and Philosophy* (London, 1970), pp. 111, 117.
30. A. Besancon, *Rise of the Gulag*, p. 194.
31. Z. A. Jordan, *Evolution*, pp. 364-69.
32. L. Kolakowski, *Main Currents*, III: 4.
33. A. Donoso, "Stalinism in Marxist Philosophy," *SST* 19 (1979): 113-41; Z. A. Jordan, *Philosophy*, pp. 478-79.
34. See T. Blakeley, *Soviet Scholasticism* (Dordrecht, 1961); J. Scanlan, *Marxism in the USSR* (Ithaca, NY, 1985); J. Keep, ed., *Contemporary History in the Soviet Mirror* (New York, 1967); C. Black, ed., *Rewriting Russian History* (New York, 1962).
35. Z. A. Jordan, *Philosophy*, pp. 57-58; A. Walicki, *Stanisław Brzozowski and the Polish Beginnings of 'Western Marxism'* (Oxford, 1980).
36. J. Lewandowski, "Głosy historiograficzne," *Zeszyty historyczne*, no. 27 (1974): 199.
37. B. Fijałkowska, *Polityka i twórcy*, p. 516.
38. J. Topolski, ed., *Dzieje Polski* (Warsaw, 1986), pp. 9-10.
39. S. Petroff, *The Red Eminence* (Clifton, NJ, 1988), pp. 55-57.
40. It would be useful to examine the relationship between Party organization and Shelest's "liberalization." S. Fortescue, "Research Institute Party Organizations and the Right of Control," *Soviet Studies*, no. 2 (1983): 175-95.
41. See N. Heer, *Politics and History*.
42. B. Cywiński, *Zatruta humanistyka*, pp. 5-6; A. Dorpalen, *German History in Marxist Perspective* (Detroit, 1985), pp. 24-62.
43. C. Calhoun, *The Question of Class Struggle* (Chicago, 1982), p. 219.
44. During a lecture on ideas and politics in early modern Ukraine that I presented in 1988 at the Institute of History of the Academy of Sciences, some of those present did not understand the subject because they had been schooled in a methodology and used a vocabulary that attached little if any significance to how people explain their own behavior. My paper and some of the comments were published as

Politychni ta sotsialni idei na Ukraini u 1550-1648 rr. / dyskusiia z kanadskym istorykom/ (Kiev, 1989).
45. F. Thom, *Langue de Bois* (Paris, 1987); P. Fidelius, *Jazyk a moc* (Munich, 1983); J. W. Young, *Totalitarian Language* (Charlottesville, VA, 1991).
46. P. Vaillaincourt, *When Marxists do Research*; "Zadachi sovetskoi istoricheskoi nauki na sovremennom etape ee razvitiia," *VI*, no. 5 (1973): 16.
47. "Osnovnye zadachi izucheniia istorii SSSR feodalnogo perioda," *VI*, no. 11 (1949): 5.
48. "Osnovni postanovy do metodolohii i tekhniky naukovoi publikatsii dokumentiv dlia potreb naukovo-istorychnoho doslidzhennia," *Radianskyi arkhiv*, no. 4-5 (1931): 53.
49. B. Popov, "K voprosu o nashykh publikatsiiakh istoricheskikh dokumentov," *Arkhivnoe delo*, no. 3 (1935): 48.
50. *Pravila izdaniia istoricheskikh dokumentov* (Moscow, 1956), p. 3.
51. *Pravila izdaniia istoricheskikh dokumentov v SSSR* (Moscow, 1969), pp. 14, 16.
52. Cited in A. Besancon, *Rise of the Gulag*, pp. 192, 302.
53. "Zamechaniia po povodu konspekta uchebnika po 'Istorii SSSR,' " *Krasnyi arkhiv* 75 (1936): 6.
54. N. Heer, *Politics and History*, pp. 52-3, 208.

Notes to Chapter 3

1. J. V. Stalin, *Problems of Leninism* (Moscow, 1947), pp. 378-89; J. Barber, *Soviet Historians in Crisis* (London, 1981), p. 131.
2. S. Semko, P. Iarovy, M. Sobol, and S. Korolivsky, "Za bilshovytskyi povorot u vykladanni istorii," *BU*, nos. 1-2 (1932): 104.
3. A. Avtorkhanov, *Memuary* (Frankfurt-am-Main, 1983), pp. 375-79.
4. J. Barber, *Soviet Historians*, pp. 6-11; S. Fitzpatrick, "The 'Soft' Line on Culture and Its Enemies: Soviet Cultural Policy, 1922-27," *SR*, no. 2 (1974): 286-87; A. E. Levin, "Anatomy of a Public Campaign: 'Academician Luzin's Case' in Soviet Political History," *SR*, no. 1 (1990): 97-100.
5. E. H. Carr, *Socialism in One Country* (London, 1970), II: 219-32, 241; A. Avtorkhanov, *Stalin and the Soviet Communist Party* (Munich, 1959), pp. 102-07; T. H. Rigby, "Early Provincial Cliques and the Rise of Stalin," *Soviet Studies*, no. 1 (1981): 3-28.
6. S. Fitzpatrick, "Cultural Revolution as Class War," in *Cultural Revolution in Russia*, ed. S. Fitzpatrick (Bloomington, 1984), pp. 18-39; G. M. Enteen, "The Stalinist Conception of Communist Party History," *SST* 29 (1989): 261; Interview with Ia. Dashkevych, November 1988.
7. Interview no. 7, November 1988.
8. Fond X in the manuscript division of the Central Academic Library in Kiev was opened to scholars in 1989 and contains the records of the All-Ukrainian Academy of Sciences' Historical-Archaeographical Commission for 1929-1934. Mss. 7109 and 7608 provide examples of unsigned bureau reports on draft essays and seminar presentations. Mss. 7012-59 provide a breakdown of subjects related to the study

of revolutionary movements and lists of assigned personnel. See S. Kirzhaev, "Dokumenty pro diialnist Arkheohrafichnoi komisii Vseukrainskoi akademii nauk," *Arkhivy Ukrainy*, no. 6 (1989): 5-12.
9. M. N. Pokrovsky, "Leninizm ta istoriia Rosii," *LR*, no. 1 (1929): xvi.
10. N. Tokin, "Bolshevistskoe ponimanie partiinosti istoricheskoi nauki," *Borba klassov*, nos. 9-10 (1932): 38-69.
11. K. Radek, "Nedostatki istoricheskogo fronta i oshibki shkoly Pokrovskogo," *Istoriia v shkole*, no. 3 (1935): 19. Radek condemned Pokrovsky for having written, among other things, the first sentence of the previous quote.
12. O. Kasymenko, "Znachennia prats I. V. Stalina u stvorenni marksystko-leninskoi istorii Ukrainy," *Visnyk Akademii nauk URSR*, no. 12 (1949): 44.
13. "Lenin as Historian," *The Modern Encyclopaedia of Russian and Soviet History*, ed. Joseph L. Wieczynski (Gulf Breeze, FL, 1988), 49: 210-22.
14. V. Zatonsky, *Komunist*, July 13, 1926.
15. H. Kostiuk, *Zustrichi i proshchannia: Spohady khyha persha* (Edmonton, 1987), pp. 197-98. I was not able to locate a published version of this speech. This idea was not incorporated into the celebrations of the tenth anniversary of the Revolution. See *Visti Vseukrainskoho Tsentralnoho Vykonavchoho Komitetu*, November-December 1927, passim.
16. J. V. Stalin, *Sochineniia* (Moscow, 1954), 8: 152
17. K. Shteppa, *Russian Historians and the Soviet State*, p. 141; G. M. Enteen, "Marxist Historians during the Cultural Revolution," in *Cultural Revolution in Russia*, ed. S. Fitzpatrick, p. 167. See also comments by A. Ciliga, who taught at the Communist University in 1929-30, in his *Russian Enigma* (London, 1979), pp. 74-82.
18. P. Harin, "Iak ne treba pysaty istorii," *LR*, no. 6 (1928): 323, 328.
19. P. Gorin, in *Trudy Pervoi vsesoiuznoi konferentsii istorikov marksistov* (Moscow, 1930), I: 449-51; J. Mace, *Communism and the Dilemmas of National Liberation* (Cambridge, MA, 1983), pp. 97-98; P. Gorin, *M. N. Pokrovsky* (Moscow, 1933), p. 44.
20. Promotion to head the institute in 1929 suggests cooperation with the authorities, though Rubach was supposedly profoundly shocked when he realized his polemics contributed to the deaths of Iavorsky and other historians. Interview no. 4, November 1988.
21. M. Rubach, "Reviziia bilshovytskoi skhemy rukhomykh syl i kharakteru revoliutsii 1905-1917 rr.," *BU*, nos. 17-18 (1929): 20-41. Similar in tone was an earlier article by a V. Manilov, who wrote soon after Zatonsky's above-mentioned comments and ponderously explained why the Ukrainian Central Rada did not play the "progressive role" Iavorsky claimed it had. See his "Iz istorii vzaimootnoshenii Tsentralnoi Rady s Vremennym pravitelstvom," *LR*, no. 3 (1927): 7-25; no. 4, pp. 7-31; no. 5, pp. 67-99; 1928 no. 1, pp. 65-85.
22. Review of Iavorsky's *Istoriia* in *IM*, no. 12 (1929): 284-85. Similar criticism was leveled earlier by Gorin in *Pravda*, February 10, 1929.
23. "Dyskusiia z pryvodu skhemy istorii Ukrainy M. Iavorskoho," *LR*, no. 2 (1930): 180-237; no. 3-4, pp. 176-238; no. 5, pp. 287-324; "Rezoliutsiia zahalnykh zboriv Ukrainskoho t-va 'Istoryk-marksyst,'" *PM*, no. 1 (1930): 226.

24. "Kliasova borotba na istorychnomu fronti Ukrainy," *Na dopomohu partnavchanniu*, no. 2 (1930): 30; M. Volin, "Kliasova borotba ta istorychnyi front," *Na dopomohu partnavchanniu*, no. 3 (1930): 9-14; no. 6-7, pp. 9-16.
25. Z. Hurevych's review of M. Svidzinsky's *Kurs istorii Ukrainy* in *LR*, no. 1-2 (1930): 278-89; "Rezoliutsiia Tov-va istor. mark-tiv z pryvodu kontseptsii istorii Ukrainy t. V. Sukhino-Khomenka," *LR*, no. 5 (1930): 430-31.
26. T. Skubitsky, "Klassovaia borba v ukrainskoi istoricheskoi literature," *IM*, no. 17 (1930): 31-38.
27. T. Skubytsky, "Proty fashystskoi teorii 'samostiinosti' i 'sobornosti' Ukrainy," *BU*, no. 1 (1934): 49-72.
28. T. Skubytsky, "Proty platformy kontrrevoliutsiinoho bloku ulamkiv natsionalistiv i trotskistiv u pidruchnyku istorii Ukrainy," *PMLP*, no. 3 (1935): 104-122.
29. "Meanwhile, we propose that district residents concentrate on all who show interest in the above-mentioned book. . . . You are to inform our secret agents of this and order them to intensify their surveillance of such individuals." S. Dukelsky, *ChK na Ukraine* (1923; repr. Benson, VT, 1989), p. 29.
30. M. Rubach, "Federalisticheskie teorii istorii Rossii," in *Russkaia istoricheskaia literatura v klassovom osveshchennii*, ed. M. N. Pokrovsky (Moscow, 1930), II: 91-97, 103, 108. Rubach submitted his article in 1926. It was part of a larger unpublished study.
31. *Trudy Pervoi vsesoiuznoi konferentsii*, I: 131. The relations between these men have yet to be studied.
32. F. Iastrebov, "Tomu deviatoho persha polovyna," *PM*, no. 1 (1930): 133-49; "Natsional-fashystska kontseptsiia selianskoi viiny 1648 r na Ukraini," *Zapysky Istorychno-arkheohrafichnoho instytutu*, no. 1 (1934): 55-120; I. Kravchenko, "Fashystski kontseptsii Hrushevskoho i ioho shkoly v ukrainskii istoriohrafii," *Zapysky Istorychno-arkheohrafichnoho instytutu*, no. 1 (1934): 9-54; M. Rubach "Burzhuazno-kurkulska natsionalistychna ideolohiia pid mashkaroiu demokratii 'trudovoho narodu,' " *Chervonyi shliakh*, no. 6 (1932): 118-35; no. 7-8, pp. 118-26; no. 11-12, pp. 127-36.
33. N. Horenshtein, "Proty natsionalizmu u vyvchenni istorii ekonomichnoi dumky na Ukraini," *BU*, nos. 5-6 (1934): 99-113.
34. I. I. Smirnov, "Natsionalisticheskaia kontrrevoliutsiia na Ukraine pod maskoi istoricheskoi nauki," *Problemy istorii dokapitalisticheskikh obshchestv*, no. 5 (1934): 55-75.
35. "Zamechaniia po povodu konspekta uchebnika po 'Istorii SSSR,' " *Krasnyi arkhiv* 75 (1936): 6. Although cited by historians in 1934, the decree was not published until 1936. On Stalin's historical reading, see D. Volkogonov, *Stalin: Triumph and Tragedy*, trans. H. Shukman (London, 1991), p. 227.
36. "Pro pidhotovku kursu istorii Ukrainy," and A. Abramov, "Pered pochatkom velykoi roboty," *PMLP*, no. 2 (1935): 123, 158-60. On the commission were Voielynsky, Trehubenko, Abramov, Hurystrymba, Killer, Hrebenkina, Skubitsky, Huslysty, Chebotarev, Frid, Rakhmaninov, Premisler, Sosipenka, Lukanenko, M. Popov, and Dzenits.
37. P. Drozdov, "Reshenie partii i pravitelstva ob uchebnikakh po istorii i zadachi sovetskikh istorikov," *IM*, no. 1 (1936): 12.

38. *Izvestiia*, January 21, 1936, and February 2, 1936. *Pravda*, February 10, 1936.
39. "Braterskyi pryvit velykomu rosiiskomu narodovi," *Visti Vseukrainskoho Tsentralnoho Vykonavchoho Komitetu*, January 15, 1937.
40. *Pravda*, March 28, 1937.
41. "Postanovlenie zhiuri . . . po konkursu na luchshii uchebnik . . . ," *Pravda*, August 22, 1937.
42. D. Skuratovsky, "Do metodyky vykladannia istorii narodiv SRSR u serednii shkoli," *Komunistychna osvita*, no. 10 (1938): 60-64.
43. M. Petrovsky, "Istoriia Ukrainy v kursi istorii narodiv SRSR," *Komunistychna osvita*, no. 4 (1940): 39-47.
44. "Pisma Anny Mikhailovny Pankratovoi," *VI*, no. 11 (1988): 55, 67-70, 76-78.
45. M. Morozov, "Ob 'Istorii Kazakhskoi SSSR,' " *Bolshevik*, no. 6 (1945): 73-80. Published before Stalin's "Toast to the Great Russian Nation." The first favorable review appeared in *IZh*, nos. 11-12 (1944): 85-90.
46. *Pravda*, May 25, 1945.
47. S. Kovaliov, "Vypravyty pomylky u vysvitlinni deiakykh pytan istorii Ukrainy," *Literaturna hazeta*, July 25, 1946; repr. from *Kultura i zhizn*, no. 3 (1946); S. Petroff, *The Red Eminence*, (Clifton, NJ, 1988), pp. 55-58.
48. V. Horbatiuk, "M. Hrushevskyi ta ioho tak zvana shkola," *Naukovi zapysky Lvivskoho derzhavnoho universyteta. seriia istorychna*, no. 1 (1946): 3-39.
49. "Pro zhurnal 'Vitchyzna,' " *Vitchyzna*, no. 9 (1946): 35. An earlier Ukrainian CC resolution associated Shevchenko with Russian "revolutionary democrats": "T. H. Shevchenko 1914-1934: Tezy do 120-richchia z dnia narodzhennia," *Chervonyi shliakh*, no. 2-3 (1934): 6, 12. Historians began to write that there were sharp differences between Shevchenko and most other members of the brotherhood after a 1939 All-Union CC resolution explained that the poet was not anti-Russian and that his ideas echoed those of the Russian radicals. "Velikii syn ukrainskogo naroda," *Pravda*, March 6, 1939; F. Iastrebov, "T. H. Shevchenko i revoliutsiinyi rukh 30-kh-50kh rokiv XIX stolittia," in *Pamiati T. H. Shevchenko*, ed. S. Belousov (Kiev, 1939), p. 66; V. Horbatiuk, "T. H. Shevchenko i Kyrylomefodiivske tovarystvo," *Trudy istorychnoho fakulteta Odeskoho derzhavnoho universiteta* 1 (1939): 45-58.
50. "Do kintsia likviduvaty burzhuazno-natsionalistychni perekruchennia istorii Ukrainy," *BU*, no. 8 (1947): 1-10; "Prohrama dalshoho pidnesennia istorychnoi nauky," *Visnyk Akademii nauk URSR*, no. 7 (1947): 1-10.
51. K. Litvin, "Ob istorii ukrainskogo naroda," *Bolshevik*, no. 7 (1947): 41-56.
52. I. Mints, "Lenin i razvitie sovetskoi istoricheskoi nauki" *VI*, no. 1 (1949): 15.
53. "Za patrioticheskuiu sovetskuiu nauku," *Vestnik Akademii nauk SSSR*, no. 4 (1949): 10. More detailed condemnation of Mints for "belittling" Russians may be found in "V Akademii obshchestvennykh nauk pri TsK VKP(b)" and in M. Stishov, "Na istoricheskom fakultete MGU," *VI*, no. 3 (1949): 151-58. On the political background, see W. Hahn, *Postwar Soviet Politics* (Ithaca, NY, 1982), pp. 67-136.
54. D. Myshko, "Vichna druzhba rosiiskoho i ukrainskoho narodiv," *Visnyk Akademii nauk URSR*, no. 10 (1949): 68 -75; O. Kasymenko, "Znachennia prats I. V. Stalina," *Visnyk Akademii nauk URSR*, no. 12 (1949): 35-47; Kasymenko,

"Rozrobka i vysvitlennia osnovnykh etapiv istorii Ukrainy," *Naukovi zapysky Instytutu istorii Ukrainy* 3 (1950): 63-77; F. Shevchenko, "Istorychne znachennia vikovoi druzhby ukrainskoho i rosiiskoho narodiv," ibid., pp. 78-95.

55. *Pravda*, January 12, 1954; English text in J. Basarab, *Pereiaslav 1654: A Historiographical Study* (Edmonton, 1982), pp. 270-88. See also S. Velychenko, "The Origins of the Official Soviet Interpretation of Eastern Slavic History," *Forschungen zur Osteuropaischen Geschichte* 46 (1990): 221-53.

56. Interview with M. Lykholat, Kiev, October 1988. The drafts of earlier versions of the thesis and protocols of discussions are in CC archives in Moscow and Kiev.

57. In the postwar period republican academics formally had an important say over what they could research. Informally they could stretch the limits of the permissible significantly by bribing supervisory commissions to interpret projects, plans, and guidelines loosely. Interview no. 9, February 1990.

58. "Strogo sobliudat leninskoi printsip partiinosti v istoricheskoi nauke," *Kommunist*, no. 4 (1957): 17-29; "Za leninskuiu partiinost v istoricheskoi nauke," *VI*, no. 3 (1957): 3-19.

59. "Nerushimoe edinstvo partii i naroda," *VI*, no. 12 (1958): 5-6. The formulation makes explicit an identification in Stalin's 1934 "Zamechanie" that implicitly equated the "history of the USSR" with the "history of Rus" and all nations later part of the USSR.

60. O. Kasymenko, "Zavdannia rozvytku istorychnoi nauky Ukrainy," *Kommunist Ukrainy*, no. 8 (1958): 23-34.

61. F. Malanchuk, "Dvi kontseptsii mynuloho i suchasnoho Ukrainy," *Zhovten*, no. 1 (1972): 101-09; no. 3, pp. 97-107; no. 4, pp. 96-108; no. 5, pp. 110-21.

62. "Zadachi sovetskoi istoricheskoi nauki na sovremennom etape ee razvitiia," *ISSSR*, no. 5 (1973): 16.

63. On the initiative of Suslov and the All-Union ideological secretary Demichev, the secretary of the Kiev Party Committee, A. Sheveliev, organized a collective of authors to write this review. "O sereznykh nedostatkakh i oshibkakh odnoi knigi," *Kommunist Ukrainy*, no. 4 (1973): 77-82. After its appearance, unsold stocks of the book were burned. Interview no. 3, November 1988. Interview with Shelest in *Kyiv*, no. 10 (1989): 93-4.

64. I. F. Kuras, "Aktualnye zadachi istoricheskoi nauky," *Kommunist Ukrainy*, no. 1 (1975): 73-78. Interview no. 3, November 1988.

65. N. N. Lysenko, "Metodicheskie puti sviazi prepodavaniia istorii soiuznoi respubliki s obshchim kursom otechestvennoi istorii," in N. P. Kuzina et al., *Iz opyta obucheniia istorii soiuznykh respublik* (Moscow, 1979), p. 4; M. Lysenko, "Vyvchennia temy 'Ukrainski zemli v XIV-XV st.,' v elementarnomu kursi istorii SRSR i URSR v VII klasi vosmyrichnoi shkoly," *UIZh*, no. 5 (1961): 101-5; V. Hordiienko, "Vykhovannia uchniv molodshykh klasiv u dushi druzhby narodiv SRSR," *Metodyka vykladannia istorii ta suspilnykh nauk v shkoli*, no. 3 (1970): 40-48; N. Arkhipovna, "Z dosvidu roboty nad poniatiam 'vitchyzna' v kursi istorii SRSR u VII klasi," *Metodyka vykladannia istorii ta suspilnykh nauk v shkoli*, no. 4 (1973): 29-37. Arkhipovna noted students in Sevastopol identified their city and the USSR as "fatherland." There was no "Ukraine" interposed between the two.

66. B. Jakubowska, *Przeobrażenia szkolnej edukacji historycznej w Polsce w latach 1944-1956* (Warsaw, 1987), pp. 23-32.
67. Ibid., p. 78. Kuroczko's brother was active in Ukrainian cultural work before and after the war.
68. *Program historii dla klas III-IV i VI-VII szkol polskich dla dzieci polskich w ZSRR* (Moscow, 1944), pp. 118-22. Zh. Kormanova, "Minelo 30 s leshnem let," in *Slaviane v epokhe feodalizmu*, ed. L. V. Cherepnin (Moscow, 1978), p. 103.
69. J. Maternicki, "Zmiany w kształtowaniu obrazu przeszłości w szkole średniej w okresie trzydziestolecia PRL," *PHum*, no. 6 (1975): 82.
70. B. Jakubowska, *Przeobrażenia*, pp. 102-26.
71. Ibid., pp. 165-77, 195-217.
72. E. Valkenier, "The Soviet Impact on Polish Historiography 1946-1950," *Journal of Central European Affairs* 11, no. 4 (January 1952): 380.
73. IM, no. 6 (1938): 201; K. Shteppa, *Russian Historians*, pp. 198-201; P. K. Urban, *Smena tendentsii v sovetskoi istoriografii*, pp. 10, 59; A. I. Goriainov, "Sovetskaia slavistika 1920-1930-kh godov," *Issledovaniia po istoriografii slavianovedeniia i balkanistiki* (Moscow, 1981), pp. 5-21.
74. V. A. Smirnov et al., "Osnovnye problemy istorii Polshi," *Kratkie soobshcheniia Instituta slavianovedeniia*, nos. 4-5 (1951): 21, 34.
75. Ibid., pp. 123-76. The only direct attack on the treatment of Ukrainian history in prewar historiography was by J. Tazbir, "Fałsz historyczny i zdrada narodu w pracach O. Haleckiego," *KH*, no. 3 (1953): 181-84.
76. Reputedly Party Secretary Boleslaw Bierut decided not to publish the Soviet history in Poland. See J. Rupnik, *The Other Europe* (London, 1988), p. 194.
77. W. B. and J. Micigolski, "List do redakcji," *Nowe drogi*, no. 7 (1952): 139-43.
78. B. Baranowski, "Narodowo wyzwolencza walka ludu ukraińskiego w XVII wieku," *Nowe drogi*, no. 1 (1954): 28-44; M. Jakóbiec, "Wzmacniajmy więzy kulturalne między Polską Ludową a Ukrainą Radziecką" *Nowe drogi*, no. 10 (1954): 81-94.
79. *Sesja naukowa w trzechsetną rocznicę zjednoczenia Ukrainy s Rosją, 1654-1954* (Warsaw, 1956), p. 5.
80. M. Ferro, *Comment on raconte l'historie aux enfants* (Paris, 1981), p. 213. I have not been able to locate this instruction, but three historians I interviewed in Poland did refer to "unwritten rules" to this effect. Among those involved were, presumably, Edward Ochab, Roman Werfel, and Zenon Kliszko. Minutes of Politburo meetings were rarely taken after 1948, and of those many were later destroyed. See P. J. Simmons, "Report from Eastern Europe," *Cold War International History Project Bulletin*, no. 1 (1992): 11.
81. *Pamiętnik VII powszechnego zjazdu historyków polskich* (Warsaw, 1948).
82. *I Kongres Nauki Polskiej. Sekcja nauk społecznych i humanistycznych*, series I (Warsaw, 1951); J. Sieradzki et al., *Pierwsza konferencja metodologiczna historyków polskich* (Warsaw, 1953); Z. Kormanowa, "Referat Podsekcji historii," *KH*, nos. 1-2 (1951): 260. E. Valkenier, "Sovietization and Liberalization in Polish Postwar Historiography," *Journal of Central European Affairs* 10, no. 2 (July 1959): 149-73.

83. *VIII Powszechny zjazd historyków polskich* (Warsaw, 1958); *II Kongres Nauki Polskiej. Sekcja XVII. Materiały Kongresowe* (Warsaw, 1973), p. 6.
84. Z. Wójcik, "U źrodeł polsko-ukraińskiej terażniejszości," *Znak*, no. 360-61 (1984): 1455, 1466; J. P. Himka, "Kościoł greckokatolicki a procesy narodotwórcze wśród Ukrainców w Galicji," *Znak*, no. 365 (1985): 49; J. Grabiszewski, "Ukraińcy w moich wspomnieniach," *Znak*, no. 365 (1985): 73; J. Radziejowski, "Ukraincy i polacy-kszałtowanie się wzajemnego obrazu i stereotypu," *Znak*, no. 360-61 (1984): 1480. These and other articles were to be published as a special issue of *Znak* devoted to Ukrainian-Polish relations, but permission was denied. Most of the articles subsequently appeared separately, while the uncensored proofs were circulated as a single volume by the underground. The issue appeared as originally planned in 1988 (*Znak* no. 395).
85. G. Schopflin, ed., *Censorship and Political Communication in Eastern Europe*, pp. 124-34.

Notes to Chapter 4

1. J. Dutkiewicz, K. Śreniowska, *Zarys historii historiografii polskiej. Część III*, pp. 103-263; A. Wierzbicki, *Naród—panstwo w polskiej myśli historycznej dwudziestolecia międzywojennego* (Warsaw, 1978), pp. 3-97; J. Maternicki, *Historiografiia polska XX wieku. Częśc I Lata 1900-1918* (Warsaw and Wroclaw, 1982).
2. S. Zakrzewski et al., *Historya polityczna Polski* (Warsaw, 1920-23), I: 327-8, 341.
3. Ibid., p. 459.
4. Ibid., II: 113-19.
5. Ibid., pp. 518-26.
6. Ibid., pp. 167-73, 213, 276-77.
7. Ibid, p. 317.
8. Ibid., pp. 341-42, 354.
9. Ibid., p. 432.
10. Ibid., pp. 541-551.
11. A. Szelągowski, *Obrazy z dziejów Polski* (Warsaw, 1920).
12. A. Szelągowski, *Dzieje Polski w zarysie* (Warsaw, 1921), p. 36; 1923 ed., p. 33.
13. Ibid., 1923 ed., p. 176.
14. Ibid., 1923 ed., p. 158; 1921 ed., p. 169.
15. *Polska: Jej dzieje i kultura,* 3 vols. (Warsaw and Krakow, 1927-32), I: 175-8.
16. Ibid., p. 193.
17. Ibid., p. 363.
18. Ibid., pp. 388-91.
19. Ibid., II: 35, 36, 47, 68.
20. Ibid., pp. 75-7.
21. Ibid., pp. 78-91.
22. Ibid., pp. 102-07.

23. Ibid., pp. 182, 241.
24. Ibid., III: 285, 687.
25. W. Sobieski, *Historja Polski* (Krakow, 1931), pp. 77-80.
26. Ibid., pp. 92, 130.
27. Ibid., pp. 138, 156.
28. Ibid., pp. 200-01.
29. Ibid., pp. 213-16.
30. *Wiedza O Polsce* (Warsaw, 1931-32), I: 147, 150, 155, 158, 181, 318.
31. Ibid., I, part 2, pp. 343, 349, 385, 374.
32. Ibid., pp. 390-400.
33. Ibid., pp. 411-12.
34. Ibid., p. 445.
35. Ibid., pp. 349, 582.
36. Ibid., pp. 605, 612, 616-17.
37. In order of publication: A. Wanczura, *Dzieje ojczyste dla wyższych klas szkol powszechnych* (Lviv, Warsaw and Krakow, 1920-21); J. Kisielewska, *Dzieje Polski Litwy i Rusi* (Warsaw, 1921); H. Pohoska and M. Wysznacka, *Z naszej przeszłości* (Warsaw, 1934); J. Friedberg, ed., *Zarys historii Polski*, 13th ed. (Warsaw, 1928).
38. J. Friedberg, ed., *Zarys*, p. 339; A. Lewicki, *Zarys historii Polski* (Warsaw, 1897), p. 320; *Dzieje narodu polskiego w zarysie* (Warsaw, 1899), p. 340. Two other versions of Lewicki's text contained little on Ukraine and were positivist rather than neoromantic in tone. H. Goldryng, *Skrócony podręcznik historji Polski*, 3rd ed. (Lodz, 1928); M. Bodzanowski, *Skrót historji Polski* (Warsaw, 1928).
39. J. Kisielewska, *Dzieje*, pp. 33-34.
40. Pohoska and Wysznacka, *Z naszej*, p. 156.
41. Wanczura, *Dzieje*, p. 101.
42. Friedberg, ed., *Zarys*, II: 149.
43. Ibid. 150.
44. Ibid., pp. 217-20, 228, 231-32, 244.
45. S. Arnold, Cz. Leśniewski, and H. Pohoska, *Polska w rozwoju dziejowym*, 2 vols. (Warsaw, 1929-1934); W. Jarosz, *Dzieje Polski* (Warsaw, 1921); Jarosz, *Opowiadania z dziejów Polski* (Lviv, 1933); Jarosz, *Opowiadania z przeszłości i teraźniejszości Polski*, 3 parts (Lviv, 1937-39); W. Martynowiczowna, *Historia* (Lviv, 1937).
46. Jarosz, *Opowiadania przeszłości*, kurs c, pp. 92, 98, 105, 119-20.
47. Jarosz, *Opowiadania z dziejów*, pp. 215-16.
48. S. K. Grobliński, *Historja Polski* (Lodz, 1915); L. Rydel, *Mała historya Polski* (Krakow, 1917); K. Zimowski, *Mała historya Polski* (Krakow, 1915) and *Większa historya Polski do roku 1919* (Krakow, 1921); R. Dobrzanski, *Skrót historii Polski* (Lviv, 1938).
49. Dobrzański, *Skrót*, pp. 133-34.
50. F. Markhlevsky, *Iz istorii Polshi* (Moscow, 1925), p. 11.

51. F. Markhlevsky, *Ocherki istorii Polshi* in his *Sochinennia* (Moscow, 1931), VI: xii, 64, 236, 260-61.
52. Z. Bukowiecka, *Książka Zosi: Opowiadania babuni o ojczyźnie*, 2 vols. (Warsaw, 1917-19); Bukowiecka, *Krótka historya Polski* (Warsaw, 1917); A. Chołoniewski, *Duch dziejów Polski* (Krakow, 1918); W. Dzwonkowski and H. Mościcki, *Odrodzenie Polski* (Warsaw, 1918); L. Rydel, *Dzieje Polski dla wszystkich* (Krakow, 1919); A. Śliwiński, *Polska niepodległa* (Warsaw, 1919); W. Smoleński, *Narod polski w walce o byt* (Warsaw, 1919); J. Kisielewska, *Historia Polski* (Warsaw, 1918); K. Czertwan, *Historia Polski* (Warsaw, 1942).
53. On the controversy surrounding the book, see A. Wierzbicki, *Naród—panstwo w polskiej myśli historycznej*, pp. 17-34.
54. Chołoniewski, *Duch dziejów Polski*, pp. 74-75.
55. Bukowiecka, *Książka Zosi*, p. 91.
56. Bukowiecka, *Krótka historya*, pp. 70, 74.
57. Smoleński, *Naród polski w walce o byt*, pp. 7-8, 38.
58. Rydel, *Dzieje Polski dla wszystkich*, p. 41.
59. Czertwan, pp. 30-32. This book was published by the Polish underground and the cover bore the title *Historia powszechna* (Wilno, 1934).
60. Kisielewska, *Historia Polski*, pp. 221, 224.

Notes to Chapter 5

1. J. Tomaszewski, "Kresy wschodnie w polskiej myśli politycznej XIX i XX w.," in *Między Polską etniczną a historyczną*, ed. W. Wrzesiński (Warsaw, 1988), pp. 97-105; J. Maternicki, *Idee i postawy: Historia i historycy polscy 1914-1918*, (Warsaw, 1975), pp. 398-97; K. Grunberg, *Polskie koncepcje federalistyczne, 1864-1918* (Warsaw, 1971).
2. *I Kongres Nauki Polski. Seria I zeszyt 3. Referat Podsekcji historii* (Warsaw, 1951), pp. 11, 13, 27; Z. Kormanowa, "Referat Podsekcji historii Sekcji nauk społecznych i humanistycznych: I Kongres Nauki Polskiej," *KH* 58 (1950-1951): 259, 268. The attitude is linked exclusively with the interwar "bourgeois state's" glorification of the Union.
3. Z. Kormanowa, "Programy nauczania i zagadnienie podręcznika," *Nowa szkoła*, no. 2-3 (1947-48): 78-79.
4. B. Szmidt, "O marksistowską koncepcję historji Polski," *Z pola walki*, no. 16 (1934): 214-24. See also J. Maternicki, *Kultura historyczna dawna i współczesna* (Warsaw, 1979), p. 259.
5. M. Dzhervis and U. Shuster, "Polsha," in *Bolshaia sovetskaia entsiklopediia* (Moscow, 1940), 46: 259-356.
6. A. F. Grabski, *Orientacje polskiej myśli historycznej* (Warsaw, 1972), pp. 41-52; Maternicki, *Kultura*, pp. 263-70. A. Bochenski, *Dzieje głupoty polskiej* (Warsaw, 1947), p. 105. Bochenski mentioned Ukraine once in 330 pages and basically agreed with Chołoniewski.
7. In order of appearance: *Skrót historii Polski na tle dziejów powszechnych* (Inowroclaw and Szczecin, 1946-47); W. Hoszowska and T. Szczechura, *Było to*

dawno ... *Opowiadania z dziejów ojczystych dla IV klasy szkoły powszechnej* (Warsaw, 1947); M. Dłuska, *Z naszych dziejów* (Warsaw, 1947); S. Arnold et al., *Historia Polski* (Warsaw, 1949); S. Missalowa, J. Schoenbrenner, *Historia Polski* (Warsaw, 1952); S. Arnold et al., *Historia Polski od połowy XV wieku do roku 1795* (Warsaw, 1953); S. Arnold et al., *Historia Polski do połowy XV wieku* (Warsaw, 1960).

8. Hoszowska, *Było to dawno*, p. 8.
9. Dłuska, *Z naszych dziejów*, pp. 65, 150, 176.
10. Arnold et al., *Historia Polski*, pp. 36-39.
11. Missalowa and Schoenbrenner, *Historia*, pp. 91-93.
12. Arnold et al., *Historia Polski*; Arnold, *Historia* ... *do roku 1795*, p. 89.
13. Missalowa and Schoenbrenner, *Historia*, p. 255.
14. E. Valkenier, "The Rise and Decline of Official Marxist Historiography in Poland 1945-1983," *SR*, no. 4 (1985): 663-80.
15. T. Manteuffl, ed., *Historia Polski*, 3 vols. (Warsaw, 1958-1972), I: 9-10, 273, 453, 536, 548, 620. For a detailed comparison of the final second edition with the first Stalinist version, see S. Kosciałkowski, "Spostrzeżenia nad ostateczną redakcją 'Historii Polski' wydanej przez P.A.N w Warszawie," *Teki Historyczne* 10 (1959): 3-74.
16. T. Manteuffl ed., *Historia Polski*, vol. I, part 2, pp. 252-4, 426, 439, 446, 612.
17. Ibid., pp. 515, 524-5, 548, 612.
18. Ibid., pp. 614, 665, 727.
19. Ibid., pp. 675-81, 727.
20. Ibid., vol. 2, pp. 57, 65.
21. Ibid., vol. 2, part 3, pp. 285-6, 383; vol. 3 part 1, pp. 295-6, 302, 345, 662-64, 667-69.
22. Ibid., vol. 4, pp. 120, 129, 263-67, 276, 279, 304.
23. Ibid., pp. 316, 337, 403, 415.
24. In order of publication, H. Samsonowicz, K. Groniowski, and J. Skowronek, *Historia Polski*, 2 vols. (Warsaw, 1967-1971); J. Topolski, ed., *Dzieje Polski* (Warsaw, 1975); J. Wyrozumski, J. Gierowski, and J. Buszko, *Dzieje Polski*, 4 vols. (Warsaw, 1978); J. Tazbir, ed., *Zarys historii Polski* (Warsaw, 1979); J. Topolski, *Zarys dziejów Polski* (Warsaw, 1982).
25. Wyrozumski, Gierowski, and Buszko, *Dzieje Polski*, vol. 2, part 1, pp. 148-49.
26. Topolski, ed., *Dzieje Polski*, pp. 100-01; Tazbir, ed., *Zarys historii Polski*, p. 299.
27. Wyrozumski, Gierowski, and Buszko, *Dzieje Polski*, vol. 2, part. 2, p. 356; vol. 3, p. 115.
28. Topolski, ed., *Dzieje Polski*, pp. 626-27, 645, 650.
29. H. Michnik and L. Mosler, *Historia Polski do roku 1795* (Warsaw, 1958); W. Hoszowska, *Opowiadania z dziejów Polski* (Warsaw, 1958); M. Dubas et al., *Historia Polski* (Warsaw, 1958); A. Gieysztor et al., *Millenium* (Warsaw, 1961); R. Pietrzykowski, *Krotki zarys dziejów Polski*, 2nd ed., 2 vols. (Warsaw, 1965-66); S. Arnold, *Zarys historii Polski* (Warsaw, 1962); M. Bogucka, *Dzieje Polski do 1795 r.* (Warsaw, 1964); M. Siuchiński and S. Kobyliński, *Ilustrowana kronika*

Polaków (Warsaw, 1967); A. Klubowna and J. Stępieniowa, *W naszej ojczyźnie* (Warsaw, 1971); J. Centkowski and A. Syta, *Opowiadania z dziejów Polski* (Warsaw, 1978).
30. Centkowski and Syta, *Opowiadania*, pp. 32, 60, 153.
31. Michnik and Mosler, *Historia Polski*, p. 231; Klubowna and Stępieniowa, *W naszej ojczyźnie*, p. 214.
32. Klubowna and Stępieniowa, *W naszej ojczyźnie*, p. 277; Bogucka, *Dzieje Polski*, p. 267; Dubas et al., *Historia Polski*, p. 169.
33. Klubowna and Stępieniowa, *W naszej ojczyźnie*, p. 322.
34. P. Jasienica, *Polska Piastów* (Warsaw, 1960), pp. 327, 330.
35. P. Jasienica, *Polska Jagiellonów* (Warsaw, 1963), pp. 60-67, 419.
36. P. Jasienica, *Rzeczpospolita obojga narodów*, 3 vols (Warsaw, 1967-1972), I: 219-23, 192, 310, 354. 370; II: 202-04.
37. Ibid., I: 228-30, 332, 445.
38. Ibid., II: 119-22, 158.
39. Ibid., p. 193.
40. Ibid., p. 216.
41. Ibid., III: 94, 97, 100.
42. Ibid., pp. 338, 350.

Notes to Chapter 6

1. A. Weryha-Darowski, *Kresy ruskie Rzeczypospolitej* (Warsaw, 1919), p. 7.
2. S. Zakrzewski and S. Pawlowski, *W obronie Galicji wschodniej* (Lviv, 1919), p. 12.
3. B. Gebert, *Z dziejów ziemie Czerwińskiej* (Lviv, 1921), p. 12. See also S. Łempicki, *Rola kultury polskiej na ziemiach południowo-wschodnich* (Lviv, 1938).
4. L. Wasilewski, *Ukraińska sprawa narodowa w jej rozwoju historycznym* (Warsaw and Krakow, 1925), pp. 33-34. On Wasilewski, see my *National History as Cultural Process: The Interpretation of Ukraine's Past in Polish, Ukrainian and Russian Historiography*.
5. Wasilewski, *Ukraińska*, pp. 87-90.
6. Ibid., pp. 186-89.
7. L. Kubala, "Ugoda Hadziacka," in *Wojny duńskie* (Lviv, 1922), pp. 120-21.
8. "Zerwanie ugody Hadziackiej," in ibid., pp. 251-56, and in *Przegląd narodowy*, May-June 1920, pp. 525-48.
9. A. Prochaska, "Wyhowski, tworca unii hadziackiej i jego rodzina," *Przegląd naukowy literacki* 46 (1920).
10. F. Rawita-Gawroński, *Kozaczyzna ukrainna w Rzeczypospolitej Polskiej: Do konca XVIII-go wieku* (Warsaw, 1923), pp. 91, 96, 107.
11. Ibid., pp. 110-20.
12. Ibid., pp. 158-59, 189, 224-26.
13. Z. Stroński, "Swawola ukrainna u schyłku XVI w.," *KH* 34 (1924): 311-30.

14. I. E. Chrąszcz, "Stosunki kozacko-tatarskie ... w I połowie 1649 roku," *Prace historyczne wydane ku uczczeniu 50-lecia akademickiego koła historyków Uniwersytetu Jana Kazimierza we Lwowie* (Lviv, 1929), pp. 295-312.
15. I. E. Chrąszcz, "Poddanie się Chmielnickiego Turcji w roku 1650," *Sprawozdanie Dyrekcji Panstwowego Gimnazium w Jaworowie za rok szkolny 1928/29*, pp. 1-17.
16. W. Tomkiewicz, "Powstanie kozackie w r. 1630," *PP* 187 (July-August 1930): 104-28.
17. W. Tomkiewicz, "Unia Hadziacka," *Sprawy Narodowościowe* 11, nos. 1-2 (1937): 1-31.
18. W. Tomkiewicz, *Kozaczyzna ukrainna* (Lviv, 1939), pp. 58, 84.
19. K. Tyszkowski, "Kozaczyzna w wojnach moskiewskich Zygmunta III (1605-1618)," *Przegląd historyczno-wojskowy*, no. 1 (1935): 37-86. Pioneering as well was his "Stosunki ks. Konstantego Wasyla Ostrogskiego z Michałem hospodarem Multanskim," in *Księga pamiętnicza ku czci Oswalda Balzera* (Lviv, 1925), vol. 2., pp. 641-49. He argues that Michael allied with the Orthodox in the Commonwealth against Chancellor Zamoyski in an attempt to counter Polish policies against him in Moldavia and Wallachia.
20. K. Lewicki, "Geneza idei Unji brzeskiej," *Prace historyczne wydane ku uczczeniu 50-lecia akademickiego koła historyków Uniwersytetu Jana Kazimierza we Lwowie*, p. 229.
21. K. Lewicki, "Sprawa unji Kosciola Wchódniego z Rzymskiem w polityce dawniej Rzeczypospolitej," *Sprawy Narodowosciowe* 7, no. 5 (1933): 491-58, 650-71.
22. K. Lewicki, *Książe Konstanty Ostrogski a Unia brzeska 1596 r.* (Lviv, 1933), pp. 44-5.
23. W. Tomkiewicz, "Cerkiew dyzunicka w dawnej Rzeczypospolitej Polskiej," *PP* 201 (November 1933): 160-71; (February 1934): 202, 216, 206.
24. K. Chodynicki, *Kościoł prawosławny a Rzeczpospolita Polska* (Warsaw, 1934), pp. 2-3, 119-20, 138, 173-74. S. Ptaszycki, in *Stosunek dawnych władz polskich do Cerkwi ruskiej* (Lviv, 1930), argued that the state had never persecuted the Orthodox, who had always been better off under Polish than under tsarist rule.
25. Ptaszycki, *Stosunek dawnych*, p. 336.
26. Ibid., pp. 512-44.
27. J. Woliński, *Polska i kościoł prawosławny* (Lviv, 1936), pp. 106-13.
28. O. Halecki, "Litwa Rus i Żmudz jako części składowe Wielkiego Księstwa Litewskiego," *Rozprawy Akademii Umiejętności*, seria II, 34 (1916): 214-54.
29. O. Halecki, "Wcielenie i wznowienie państwa Litewskiego przez Polskę (1386-1401)" *PH* 1 (1917-18): 1-146.
30. H. Łowmianski, "Wcielenie Litwy do Polski w 1386," *Ateneum Wileńskie*, no. 12 (1937): 36-145; repr. in *Lituano-Slavica Posnaniensia* 2 (1987): 37-124.
31. H. Paszkiewicz, *O genezie i wartości Krewa* (Warsaw, 1938).
32. O. Halecki, *Przyłączenia Podlasia Wołynia i Kijowszczyzny do Korony w roku 1569* (Krakow, 1915), pp. 105-10, 162-63.
33. Ibid., pp. 178-79, 192.
34. O. Halecki, *Unia Lubelska* (Krakow, 1916), pp. 29-30

35. O. Halecki, *Dzieje Unii Jagiellonskiej*, 2 vols. (Krakow, 1919-1920), I: 264-65, II: 298, 341.
36. H. Łowmianski, "Uwagi w sprawie podłoża społecznego i gospodarczego Unji Jagiellońskiej," in his *Studia nad dziejami Wielkiego Księstwa Litewskiego* (Poznan, 1988), pp. 401-03.
37. Ibid., pp. 447-49.
38. S. Kot, "Gniewy o unię," *Studia historyczne ku czci Stanisława Kutrzeby* (Krakow, 1938), II: 363-65.
39. F. Podleski, *Zagadnienie 'ukraińaskie' na tle stosunków austrjackich* (Lviv and Warsaw, 1935); T. Głuziński, *Sprawa ukraińska* (Warsaw, 1937).
40. L. Wasilewski, "Sprawa podziału Galicji na tle stosunków austriacko ukrainskich," *Przegląd wspołczesny*, July-September 1925, pp. 459-64.
41. J. Gołąbek, *Bractwo sw. Cyryla i Metodego w Kijowie* (Warsaw, 1935).
42. M. Handelsman, *Ukraińska polityka ks. Adama Czartoryskiego przed wojną krymską* (Warsaw, 1937), pp. 14, 23, 66, 79, 91-92.
43. J. Skrzypek, "Ukraińcy w Austrii podczas wielkiej wojny i geneza zamachu na Lwów," *Niepodległośc* 19, no. 1 (1939): p. 28.
44. Ibid., pp. 70-71; no. 2, p. 220.
45. Ibid., no. 2, pp. 216-19.
46. H. Jabłoński, "Ministerium spraw polskich Ukraińskej Republiki Ludowej 1917-18," *Niepodległośc* 20, no.1 (1939): 65-88; no. 2, pp. 260-68.
47. J. Ursyn-Zamarajew, *Pierwsze walki i niepodległośc Ukrainy* (Kiev and Krakow, 1920).
48. E. Paszkowski, *Zawierucha ukraińska* (Warsaw, 1919), pp. 27, 42, 51, 56, 60.
49. Ibid., p. 55.
50. S. Zakrzewski, "Wpływ sprawy ruskiej na państwo polskie w XIV w.," *PH* 23 (1921-1923): 104. L. Ehrlich, *Starostwa w Halickiem w stosunku do starostwa Łwowskiego w wiekach średnich (1390-1501)* (Lviv, 1914) provides a detailed administrative history of the province.
51. S. Zakrzewski, "Dwa przyczynki interpretacyjne polsko-ruskie z lat 1338 i 1340," *Sprawozdanie Towarzystwa Naukowego w Lwowie* 7 (1927): 95-103.
52. H. Paszkiewicz, *Polityka ruska Kazimierza Wielkiego* (Warsaw, 1925), pp. 48-49, 58-9, 85, 108-09.
53. Ibid., pp. 190, 267-68.
54. Ibid., pp. 254-56.
55. A. Gilewicz, "Przygotowania do rewolucji chłopskiej w Polsce w latach 1767-1769," *Roczniki dziejów społecznych i gospodarczych* I (1931): 1-36.
56. M. Karas and A. Podraza, eds., *Ukraina: Terażniejszość i przeszłość* (Krakow, 1970), pp. 264-65.
57. Ibid., pp. 258, 271-73.
58. Ibid., pp. 289-91.
59. Ibid., pp. 303-10.
60. W. Serczyk, *Historia Ukrainy* (Warsaw and Krakow, 1979), p. 100.
61. Ibid., pp. 150-53, 161; L. Podhorodecki, *Zarys dziejów Ukrainy*, 2 vols. (Warsaw, 1976), I: 298-300.

62. Serczyk, *Historia Ukrainy*, pp. 200-1; Podhorodecki, *Zarys dziejów*, II: 27.
63. Serczyk, *Historia Ukrainy*, pp. 241-43; Podhorodecki, *Zarys dziejów*, II: 151-53.
64. Serczyk, *Historia Ukrainy*, pp. 290, 310; Podhorodecki, *Zarys dziejów*, II: 151-53.
65. Censors told the author to remove his remarks concerning the state-building activities of the Rada. Interview with W. Serczyk, September 1990.
66. Serczyk, *Historia*, pp. 339, 346.
67. B. Baranowski, "Geneza sojuszu kozacko-tatarskiego," *PH* 37 (1948): 276-87.
68. W. Tomkiewicz, "O składzie społecznym i etnicznym Kozaczyzny," *PH* 37 (1948): 252-53.
69. S. Arnold, "Polska szlachecka wobec walki narodowo-wyzwolenczej ludu ukraińskiego w wieku XVII," *Sesja naukowa w trzechsetną rocznicę zjednoczenia Ukrainy z Rosją, 1654-1954*, pp. 9, 15.
70. Z. Libiszowska, "Stosunek polskich mas ludowych do walki narodowo-wyzwolenczej na Ukrainie w latach 1648-1654," *Sesja*, p. 25.
71. O. Górka, "Bohdan Chmielnicki," *Sesja*, pp. 92, 101.
72. M. Wawrykowa, "Z dziejów walki narodu ukraińskiego z ekspansją Polski," *Sesja*, pp. 111-29.
73. J. Seredyka, "Stosunki ukraińsko-rosyjskie w 1648 r.," *Zeszyty naukowe Uniwersitetu Wrocławskiego. Historia* 3, seria A, no. 23 (1960): 174-80. The text did not explicitly state that Khmelnytsky's offer to support the candidacy of the tsar to the Polish throne was merely a ploy and only mentioned this in a footnote. Yet the Russian language summary (p. 189) stressed the point as if it were a key issue in the article. This implied Seredyka's article conformed more closely to the official Soviet view than it in fact did.
74. J. Seredyka, "Stosunki ukraińsko-rosyjskie w I połowie 1649 r.," *Zeszyty naukowe Wyższej Szkoły Pedagogicznej w Opolu. Historia*, no. 2 (1961): 172, 182-84.
75. J. Perdenia, "Z zagadnień społeczno-ekonomicznych na Prawobrzeżniej Ukrainie," *Rocznik naukowo-dydaktyczny WSP w Krakowie (Historia)*, no. 14 (1962): 83-99.
76. J. Perdenia, *Stanowisko Rzeczypospolitej szlacheckiej wobec sprawy Ukrainy na przełomie XVII-XVIII w.* (Wroclaw and Warsaw, 1963).
77. Z. Wójcik, *Dzikie pola w ogniu* (Warsaw, 1961), pp. 81, 108, 129.
78. Ibid., pp. 214, 217-20.
79. R. Majewski, "Struktura społeczna a orientacja polityczna na Ukrainie Prawobrzeżnej (1659-1662)" *Rocznik Przemyski* 11 (1967): 105-38.
80. W. Serczyk, "Rzeczpospolita i kozaczczyzna," *Studia historyczne* 1977, no. 1, pp. 3-22.
81. H. Jabłoński, "Druga Rzeczpospolita a Galicja Wschódnia," *Wiedza i życie*, no. 10 (1948): 903-11.
82. H. Jabłoński, *Polska autonomia narodowa na Ukrainie* (Warsaw, 1948), pp. 29, 59, 67, 36-37; repr. in H. Jabłoński, *Z rozważań o II Rzeczypospolitej* (Warsaw, 1987), pp. 244-356.
83. L. Grosfeld, "Prawidłowośc i specyfika polskiego imperializmu," and E. Struminowa, "Ukraina zachodnia . . . jako teren ekspansji polskiego im-

perializmu," in *Pierwsza konferencja metodologiczna historyków polskich*, ed. L. Sieradzki, II: 283, 302, 481-88.
84. Z. Młynarski, "Polsko-ukraińskie braterstwo od 1905 do czasów najnowszych," *Sesja*, p. 224.
85. H. Jabłoński, "Zarys dziejów Ukrainy Radzieckiej," *Sesja*, p. 287.
86. Ibid., p. 296.
87. W. Serczyk, "Rewolucja 1917 roku na Ukrainie," *Zeszyty naukowe Uniwersytetu Jagiellońskiego. Prace Historyczne*, no. 20 (1967): 130, 141.
88. J. Kozik, "Ukraina wobec procesu federalizacji," in *Z dziejów państwa radzieckiego*, ed. W. Serczyk (Krakow, 1972), pp. 56-82.
89. J. Radziejowski, "Ruch narodowy i rewolucyjny na Ukrainie," *Studia z DZSRRiES* 9 (1973): 79-82.
90. K. Lewandowski, "Międzynarodowe uwarunkowania powstania państwowości ukraińskiej w 1917 roku," *Studia zDZSRRiES* 16 (1980): 73-101.
91. H. Jabłoński, "Z dziejów genezy sojuszu Piłsudski-Petlura," *Zeszyty naukowe Wojskowej Akademii Politycznej*, no. 5 (1961): 40-58; repr. in *Z rozważań o II Rzeczypospolitej*, pp. 360-81.
92. J. Kukułka, "Sprawa Galicji Wschodniej w stosunkach polsko-francuskich przed podpisaniem Traktatu Wersalskiego," *Studia z najnowszych dziejów powszechnych*, no. 5 (1963): 170-73.
93. Z. Zaks, "Les aspects internationaux de la question de la Galicie orientale 1918-1923," *Fasciculi historici*, no. 6 (1973): 83-93. This is a synopsis of her doctoral thesis. Her published articles based on the thesis are "Walka dyplomatyczna o naftę wschodniogalicyjską 1918-1923," *ZDSPR* 4 (1969): 37-60; "Galicja Wschodnia w polskiej polityce zagranicznej (1921-23)," *ZDSPR* 8 (1971): 3-36; "Problem Galicji Wschodniej . . . (1920)," *Studia z DZSRRiES* 8 (1971): 79-109.
94. Z. Zaks, "Galicja wschodnia w polityce Zachodnio-Ukraińskiej Republiki Ludowej i Ukraińskiej Republiki Ludowej w drugiej połowie 1919 r.," in *Narod i państwo*, ed. T. Cieslak (Warsaw, 1969), pp. 387-405.
95. Z. Zaks, "Radziecka Rosja i Ukraina wobec sprawy państwowej przynależności Galicji Wschodniej 1920-1923," *ZDSPR* 6 (1970): 19-96.
96. A. Deruga, "Początek rokowań między Pilsudskim a Petlurą," *SZDSPR* 6 (1970): 55, 58. Deruga examined Polish-Ukrainian relations in detail in his *Polityka wschodnia Polski wobec ziem Litwy, Białorusi i Ukrainy (1918-1919)* (Warsaw, 1969). He argued that the ZUNR represented a "national liberation movement" and that Polish expansion was motivated by big landowners' desires to regain their huge losses.
97. S. Kieniewicz, "Stosunki polsko-ukraińskie w latach 1820-1870," *Sesja*, pp. 133-34, 140, 155; L. Bazylow, "Braterstwo polsko-ukraińskie (1864-1904)," *Sesja*, p. 164.
98. E. Hornowa, "Prześladowanie ukraińskiej kultury przez rząd carski," *Zeszyty naukowe WSP w Opolu, seria A Filologia Rosyjska* 9 (1972): 115-22.
99. J. Kozik, *Ukraiński ruch narodowy w Galicji w latach 1830-1840* (Krakow, 1973), pp. 61, 206.
100. Ibid., pp. 273, 40-41, 53.
101. J. Kozik, *Między reakcją a rewolucją* (Krakow, 1975).

102. R. Radzik, "Instytucjonalny rozwoj ruskiego ruchu narodowego w Galicji wschodniej w latach 1848-1863," *KH*, no. 4 (1981): 963-64.
103. Z. Guldon, "W kwestii udziału Ukrainy w handlu zbożowym z Gdanskiem w II połowie XVI i I połowie XVII w.," *Zapiski historyczne*, no. 3 (1965): 67-74.
104. M. Horn, "Chronologia i zasięg najazdów tatarskich na ziemie Rzeczypospolitej Polskiej w latach 1600-1647," *Studia i materiały do historii wojskowości* 8, part 1 (1962): 3-71; and his *Skutki ekonomiczne najazdów tatarskich z lat 1605-1633 na Ruś Czerwoną* (Wroclaw, 1964).
105. M. Horn, *Walka klasowa i konflikty społeczne w miastach Rusi Czerwonej w latach 1600-1647 na tle stosunków gospodarczych* (Wroclaw and Warsaw, 1972); E. Hornowa, *Stosunki ekonomiczno-społeczne w miastach ziemi Halickiej w latach 1590-1648* (Opole, 1963).
106. A. Janeczek, "Polska ekspansja osadnicza w ziemi lwowskiej w XIV-XVI w.," *PH* 69 (1978): 597-620.
107. W. Serczyk, *Koliszczyzna* (Krakow, 1968), pp. 80-81.
108. J. Sieradzki, "Regnum Russia," *KH*, nos. 1-2 (1958): 505-06.
109. S. Kuczyński, *Studia z dziejów Europy Wschodniej X-XVII w.*, (Warsaw, 1965), pp. 186-88; "Program pierwszych Jagiellonów a tzw. idea jagiellonska," *Pamiętnik VIII zjazdu historyków polskich w Krakowie* (Warsaw, 1958,) vol. I, part 2, pp. 321-31.
110. J. Bardach, "Krewo i Lublin: Z problemow unii polsko-litewskiej," *Studia z ustroju i prawa Wielkiego Księstwa Litewskiego XIV-XVII wieku* (Warsaw, 1970), pp. 51-52, 55, 60, 62.
111. L. Bienkowski, "Organizacja Kościoła Wschódniego w Polsce," in *Kościoł w Polsce. Wieki XVI-XVII*, ed. J. Kłoczowski (Krakow, 1969), II: 867, 894.

Notes to Chapter 7

1. N. Cherepnin, *Russkaia istoriia* (Petrograd, 1911); 2nd ed., 1917; D. A. Zharinov and N. M. Nikolsky, *Byloe vokrug nas. Kniga dlia chteniia po Russkoi istorii* (Moscow, 1912); 2nd ed., 1919-1922; E. Zviagintsev, *Kratkii kurs russkoi istorii* (Moscow, 1913); 2nd ed., 1918; K. O. Veikhelt, M. N. Kovalensky, V. A. Petrushevsky, V. A. Ulianov, *Knige po Russkoi istorii dlia nachalnykh shkol i pervykh klassov srednikh uchebnikh zavedenii*, 5th ed. (Moscow, 1919).
2. N. A. Rozhkov, *Russkaia istoriia v sravnitelno-istoricheskom osveshchenii*, 10 vols. (Moscow, 1919-1924).
3. M. N. Pokrovsky, *Russkaia istoriia v samom szhatkom ocherke* (Moscow, 1920); repr. in his *Izbrannye proizvedeniia* (Moscow, 1967), vol. 3.
4. N. N. Vanag, *Kratkii ocherk istorii narodov SSSR* (Moscow, 1932), pp. 33, 35.
5. Ibid., pp. 45, 66-68.
6. Ibid., pp. 196-99, 211-13.
7. S. A. Piontkovsky, *Programa kursu istorii Rosii i SSSR dlia istorychno-ekonomichnykh viddiliv pedushchiv* (Kharkiv, 1933).
8. V. Bystriansky, "Kriticheskie zamechaniia ob uchebnikakh po istorii SSSR," *Pravda*, February 4, 1936; and *Istoriia v shkole*, no. 2 (1936): 17-25. The article

does not mention non-Russians nor does it refer to a negative historical role of the Muscovite state.
9. S. Dubrovsky, *Elementarnyi kurs istorii SSSR* (Moscow, 1936), p. 63.
10. I. I. Mints, M. Nechkina, and E. Genkina, *Elementarnyi kurs istorii SSSR* (Moscow, 1936), pp. 6-7.
11. Ibid., pp. 95, 115.
12. A. V. Shestakov, "Osnovnye problemy uchebnika 'Kratkii kurs istorii SSSR,'" *IM*, no. 3 (1937): 85-98.
13. A. V. Shestakov, ed., *Kratkii kurs istorii SSSR* (Moscow, 1937), p. 167.
14. B. D. Grekov, S. V. Bakhrushin, and V. I. Lebedev, *Istoriia SSSR: Tom I (s drevneishikh vremen do kontsa XVIII v.)* (Moscow, 1939-40), p. 74; 2nd ed., Ukrainian trans., Kiev, 1950, p. 114.
15. Ibid. 1st ed., I: 509, 528-29; 2nd ed., pp. 439, 458.
16. Ibid. 1st ed., pp. 482-83; 2nd ed., p. 553.
17. Ibid. 1st ed., p. 556; 2nd ed. p. 487.
18. Ibid. 1st ed., pp. 636, 638, 645, 674-75; 2nd ed., pp. 558-59, 567, 594-96.
19. M. V. Nechkina, ed., *Istoriia SSR: Tom II (Rossiia v XIX veke)* (Moscow, 1940), pp. 228, 235-36; 2nd ed., Moscow, 1949, p. 184. The bibliography of the second edition of volume 2 did not include articles on Ukraine published between 1917 and the 1930s.
20. Ibid. 1st ed., pp. 619, 623, 682; 2nd ed., pp. 703-05.
21. S. S. Dmitriev and M. N. Tikhomirov, *Istoriia SSSR* (Moscow, 1948), p. 82, 185, 188.
22. Ibid., pp. 379-80.
23. A. M. Pankratova and A. V. Fokht, "Ob uchebnikakh istorii SSSR dlia srednikh shkol," *IZh*, no. 11 (1940): 122.
24. A. M. Pankratova, ed., *Istoriia SSSR*, 3 vols. (Moscow, 1940), pp. 37, 91. The volumes were for grades 8, 9, and 10, respectively.
25. Ibid., 1940 ed., pp. 86-89; 1950 ed., pp. 197-99, 203; The term "reunification" appeared first in the 1948 edition; I: 196.
26. Ibid. 1955 ed., p. 202.
27. Ibid. 1940 ed., I: 204, II: 4; 1950 ed., p. 218, II: 5.
28. Ibid. 1950 ed., II: 76.
29. Ibid., 1940 ed., II: 179, 237-39; 1950 ed., II: 218, 283-85; 1950 ed., III: 55; 1955 ed., II: 283.
30. Ibid. 1940 ed., II: 239.
31. B. D. Grekov, ed., *Ocherki istorii SSSR: Period feodalizma IX–XV v.* (Moscow, 1953), part I, pp. 5, 22, 328; part II, pp. 520, 559.
32. N. M. Druzhinin, ed., *Ocherki istorii SSSR: Period feodalizma (konets XV v.–nachalo XVII v.)* (Moscow, 1955), pp. 702-14; N. M. Druzhinin, ed., *Ocherki istorii SSSR. Period feodalizma XVII v.*, pp. 694, 712-14, 668-69, 730.
33. Druzhinin, ed., *Ocherki . . . (konets XV v.–nachalo XVII v.)*, pp. 703, 719, 723-24.
34. Druzhinin, ed., *Ocherki . . . XVII v.*, pp. 693-94; Druzhinin, ed., *Ocherki . . . (konets XV v.–nachalo XVII v.)*, p. 7.

35. N. M. Druzhinin, ed., *Ocherki istorii SSSR: Period feodalizma (Rossiia v pervoi chetverti XVIII v.)* (Moscow, 1954), pp. 5-6, 18-19, 40; N. M. Druzhinin, ed., *Ocherki istorii SSSR: Period feodalizma (Rossiia v vtoroi chetverti XVIII v.)* (Moscow, 1957), pp. 16, 527-29, 537-37, 545-57; N. M. Druzhinin, ed., *Ocherki istorii SSSR. Period feodalizma (Rossiia vo vtoroi polovine XVIII v.)* (Moscow, 1956), pp. 582-600.

36. L. V. Cherepnin et al., *Istoriia SSSR: Tom 1 (s drevneishikh vremen do 1861 g.)* (Moscow, 1956), pp. 170, 254, 279, 374, 377; 2nd ed., (Moscow, 1964), pp. 386-87, 233, 199.

37. Ibid. 1st ed., pp. 380, 386-87.

38. Ibid. 1st ed., pp. 374, 382; 2nd ed., pp. 386, 392.

39. Ibid. 1st ed., pp. 820-21, 375, 379; 2nd ed., pp. 390.

40. A. L. Sidorova et al., *Istoriia SSR: Tom II (1816-1917, period kapitalizma)* (Moscow, 1959), pp. 115-21, 133, 200, 231, 248.

41. Ibid., pp. 276, 278, 559, 705; 2nd ed., Moscow, 1964, pp. 253-56, 535, 627.

42. B. N. Ponomarev, ed., *Istoriia SSSR s drevneishikh vremen do nashikh dnei*, 11 vols. (Moscow, 1966-67), I: xxviii, 587; II: 410-11, 435-36, 443-47, 459, 461-62.

43. Ibid., III: 67-74, 239, 496, 604, 616-18.

44. Ibid., IV: 9, 358, 360.

45. Ibid., IV: 361, 365-67.

46. Ibid., IV: 401.

47. Ibid., IV: 402, 376, 378.

48. Ibid., IV: 417-19, 449-50, V: 379, 381-86, VI: 309.

49. Ibid., VI: 11, 337-38, 456-57, 664.

50. Ibid., VI: 74-75, 183, 350, 670.

51. Ibid., VII: 190-98, 476, 530.

52. I. I. Smirnov, ed., *Kratkaia istoriia SSSR v dvukh chastiakh* (Moscow, 1963-64); A. M. Sakharov, I. D. Kovalchenko et al., *Posobie po istorii SSSR* (Moscow, 1965); V. Diadychenko, *Narysy z istorii SRSR* (Kiev, 1971).

53. A. M. Pankratova, ed., *Istoriia SSSR* (Moscow, 1958); B. D. Datsiuk et al., *Istoriia SSSR: uchebnoe posobie*, 2nd ed. (Moscow, 1963); F. I. Kabanov and V. V. Mavrodin, *Istoriia SSSR*, 2nd ed. (Moscow, 1966); V. T. Pashuto et al., *Illiustrilovannaia istoriia SSSR* (Moscow, 1974); V. V. Malkov, *Posobie po istorii SSSR* (Moscow, 1974); Iu. Kondufor and V. N. Kotov, *Istoriia SSSR* (Kiev, 1980); N. E. Artemov, ed., *Istoriia SSSR*, 2 vols. (Moscow, 1982).

54. Artemov, ed., *Istoriia SSSR*, I: 63, II: 62; Kondufor and Kotov, *Istoriia SSSR*, pp. 23, 105, 223.

55. Pankratova, ed., *Istoriia SSSR*, I: 51, III: 37-38, 160.

56. Pashuto et al., *Illiustrilovannaia istoriia*, pp. 59, 60, 132.

57. Malkov, *Posobie po istorii SSSR*, pp. 33-34, 209, 218.

Notes to Chapter 8

1. A. Santsevich and N. Komarenko, *Razvitie istoricheskoi nauki v Akademii nauk Ukrainskoi SSR* (Kiev, 1982), pp. 59-60.
2. Interview with S. Kulchytsky, Institute of History, Academy of Sciences of the Ukraine, February 1990.
3. *Bolshaia sovetskaia entsiklopediia* (Moscow, 1947), 55: 858-948. Picheta died in the summer of 1947 thus avoiding official condemnation.
4. "Postranichnaia razrabotka retsenzii k kursu istorii Ukrainy. Tom I Epokha feodalizma" (Kiev, 1949), pp. 122-31, 160-61, 172-74, 181-83. Discussions and protocols related to the postwar histories of Ukraine are in the Archive of the Institute of History of the Academy of the Sciences of Ukraine.
5. "Retsenzii na glavy i chasti kratkogo kursu istorii Ukrainy," (Kiev, 1948), pp. 6-10, 14, 45, 222.
6. There is no extended discussion of the matter in the reviews. A. M. Pankratova, *Postanovy TsK VKP(b) z ideolohichnykh pytan i zavdannia istorychnoi nauky* (Kiev, 1950) refers to a "history of the Ukrainian SSR" (p. 39). This is the first published reference I could find to this term.
7. There are detailed reviews of the non-sequiturs and absurdities in the 1953 *Istoriia* by V. Dubrovsky, "Nainoviisha sovietska kontseptsiia istorii Ukrainy," and D. Solovei, "Natsionalna polityka partii i uriadu SSSR v Ukraini u svitli deiakykh nainovishykh faktiv," *Ukrainskyi zbirnyk*, no. 6 (1956), pp. 71-108, 137-57. See also Iu. Lavrynenko, "Istoriia bez istorii," *Ukrainska literaturna gazeta*, no. 1 (1955). These include references to later Soviet criticism of the book for ignoring the particularity of Ukraine's past.
8. O. K. Kasymenko et al., *Istoriia Ukrainskoi RSR* (Kiev, 1953), I: 86, 91-92, 115, 137; A. K. Kasimenko et al., *Istoriia Ukrainy: Kratkii kurs* (Kiev, 1948), 42, 70; O. K. Kasymenko et al., *Istoriia Ukrainskoi RSR* (Kiev, 1955), I: 273, 123; S. Velychenko, "The Origins of the Official Soviet Interpretation of Eastern Slavic History," *Forschungen zur Osteuropaischen Geschichte* 46 (1990): 235.
9. *Istoriia* (1953), I: 173; *Istoriia* (1955), I: 187.
10. *Istoriia* (1953), I: 183, 215-17; *Istoriia* (1955), I: 198-200.
11. *Istoriia* (1953), I: 349, 338, 351; *Istoriia* (1955), I: 257, 332-23, 383; *Istoriia* (1948), pp. 191-92.
12. *Istoriia* (1948), pp. 214, 301, 303; *Istoriia* (1953), I: 396, 505, 508, 655; *Istoriia* (1955), I: 431, 547, 708.
13. *Istoriia* (1953), I: 214, 224, 242; *Istoriia* (1948), pp. 111, 116, 126; *Istoriia* (1955), p. 261.
14. *Istoriia* (1953), I: 288, 333-34, 351; *Istoriia* (1955), I: 363-64, 384.
15. *Istoriia* (1948), pp. 241-45, 256, 260, 411; *Istoriia* (1953), I: 428, 438, 445, 490, 675; *Istoriia* (1955), I: 483.
16. *Istoriia* (1948), pp. 289-90, 304, 323; *Istoriia* (1953), I: 490, 508, 536-37; *Istoriia* (1955), I: 761-65.
17. *Istoriia* (1948), p. 413; *Istoriia* (1953), I: 683.
18. *Istoriia* (1948), pp. 461, 476, 495, 499, 503-04, 513; *Istoriia* (1953), I: 779; *Istoriia* (1958), II: 16, 34, 66-67, 71, 78, 82, 87, 91, 156.

19. *Istoriia* (1958), II: 201-08.
20. *Istoriia* (1955), I: 244, 224; *Istoriia* (1953), I: 224, 205.
21. These studies will be examined in a future volume. For a survey, see I. Myhul, "Politics and History in the Soviet Ukraine: A Study of Soviet Ukrainian Historiography, 1956-1970," Ph.D. diss., Columbia University, 1973.
22. "Stenohrama zasidzhennia Vchennoi rady. Obhovorennia maketa i tomu istorii Ukrainy" (Kiev, 1965), p. 12-1.
23. Ibid, pp. 14-3, 28-1, 25-1, 16-1, 13-1, 29-1.
24. Ibid.
25. K. K. Dubyna et al., *Istoriia Ukrainskoi RSR u dvokh tomakh* (Kiev, 1967), I: 104, 106, 151-53, 159; A. H. Shevelev, ed., *Istoriia Ukrainskoi RSR u vosmy tomakh desiaty knyhakh* (Kiev, 1977), vol. I, part 1, p. 350; vol I., part 2, pp. 69, 73, 75, 22-24, 96-97, 199, 233, 272.
26. *Istoriia* (1967), I: 166, 332-34; *Istoriia* (1977), vol. I, part 2, p. 228; II: 445-49, 454.
27. *Istoriia* (1967), I: 122, 131, 175-80, 258; *Istoriia* (1977), vol. I, part 2, pp. 112, 161, 178-79, 181, 192; II: 128, 370, 396, 21-23, 62-65.
28. *Istoriia* (1977), II: 583; A. N. Chistozvonov, "Nekotorye aspekty problemy genezisa absolutizma," *VI*, no. 5 (1968): 46-62.
29. *Istoriia* (1955), I: 312, 380; *Istoriia* (1967), I: 260, 290, 319; *Istoriia* (1977), II: 71, 221, 223, 228, 240.
30. *Istoriia* (1967), I: 365, 454-56, 573-74, 604; *Istoriia* (1977), III: 325, 331, 348, 351, 354; IV: 6.
31. *Istoriia* (1967), I: 162, 166, 222, 239; *Istoriia* (1977), I, part 2, pp. 246; II: 35, 82.
32. *Istoriia* (1967), I: 248-49, 252, 259-60, 290-91, 320; *Istoriia* (1977), II: 84-85, 93, 133, 225, 322, 333, 399-402, 581.
33. *Istoriia* (1967), I: 398, 402, 408, 456, 572; *Istoriia* (1977), III: 125, 175, 181-82, 194, 272-73, 397, 441; IV: 18.
34. *Istoriia* (1977), III: 444-48.
35. *Istoriia* (1966), I: 486-87, 535; *Istoriia* (1977) III: 471, 476-79; IV: 69-71.
36. *Istoriia* (1977), IV: 282-84, 302-04, 319-24; *Istoriia* (1967), I: 632, 642, 662-68.
37. *Istoriia* (1967), I: 662, 663, 672; *Istoriia* (1955), II: 761, 762; *Istoriia* (1977), IV: 321-322.
38. *Istoriia* (1967), I: 733-35; II: 8-9, 24-25, 39, 54-57.
39. *Istoriia* (1977), IV: 383-418; *Istoriia* (1979), V: 31 34, 95, 97, 151, 175, 203-05.
40. *Istoriia* (1967), II: 145, 151; *Istoriia* (1977), V: 513-20.
41. V. Diadychenko and V. Spytsky, *Istoriia Ukrainskoi RSR: Metodychni vkazivky do vyvchennia kursu*, 2nd ed. (Kiev, 1962); P. Lavrov et al., *Istoriia Ukrainskoi RSR: Prohramma do kursu* (Kiev, 1963); I. Hurzhyi, ed., *Knyha dlia chytannia z istorii Ukrainskoi RSR* (Kiev, 1970); I. Rybalka and V. Dovhopol, *Prohrama kursu 'Istoriia Ukrainskoi RSR'* (Kiev, 1981).
42. O. K. Kasymenko, *Istoriia Ukrainskoi RSR: Populiarnyi narys* (Kiev, 1960); I. Rybalka, *Istoriia Ukrainskoi RSR* (Kiev, 1978); Iu. Kondufor, ed., *Istoriia Ukrainskoi RSR. Korotkyi narys* (Kiev, 1981).

43. K. K. Dubyna, ed., *Istoriia Ukrainskoi RSR* (Kiev, 1965); K. K. Dubyna et al., *Istoriia Ukrainskoi RSR (naukovo-populiarnyi narys)* (Kiev, 1967); V. Diadychenko, F. Los, and V. Spytsky, *Istoriia Ukrainskoi RSR* (Kiev, 1961).
44. Kasymenko, *Istoriia (1960)*, pp. 145, 35; Dubyna et al., *Istoriia* (1967), p. 35.
45. Kasymenko, *Istoriia (1960)*, pp. 93, 99; Dubyna, ed., *Istoriia* (1965), pp. 84, 103; Dubyna et al., *Istoriia* (1967), pp. 81, 92.
46. Kasymenko, *Istoriia (1960)*, pp. 165, 182, 136; Dubyna, ed., *Istoriia (1965)*, pp. 136, 138, 156-57, 189, 200; Dubyna et al., *Istoriia* (1967), pp. 116, 142, 174.
47. Kasymenko, *Istoriia* (1960), pp. 213; Dubyna, ed., *Istoriia* (1965), p. 236; Dubyna et al., *Istoriia* (1967), p. 193.
48. Kasymenko, *Istoriia (1960)*, pp. 222, 230, 239; Dubyna, ed., *Istoriia* (1965), pp. 247-50, 261, 287; Dubyna et al., *Istoriia* (1967), pp. 199, 210, 210-21, 231.
49. Diadychenko, Los, and Spytsky, *Istoriia* (1973), p. 76; 1974 ed., p. 74.
50. Ibid. 1973 ed., p. 39; 1974 ed., p. 38.
51. Ibid. 1968 ed., pp. 66, 75-77; 1973 ed., pp. 76; 1972 ed., pp. 65.
52. Ibid. 1964 ed., pp. 18, 21, 108, 120, 123; 1968 ed., pp. 27, 31, 66; part 2, pp. 12, 28.

Notes to Chapter 9

1. A number of these debates are reviewed in C. E. Black, ed., *Rewriting Russian History* (New York, 1962) and in S. Baron and N. Heer, eds., *Windows on the Russian Past* (Columbus, OH, 1977).
2. "Doklad E. N. Burdzhalova . . . (na vstreche s chitateliami 19-20 iunia 1956 g. v Leningradskom otdelenii Instituta istorii AN SSSR)," *VI*, no. 9 (1989): 92-93.
3. E. Kingston-Mann, *Lenin and the Problem of Marxist Peasant Revolution* (New York, 1985), pp. 44-45, 103; T. Cox, *Peasants, Class and Capitalism* (Oxford, 1986), pp. 46, 61.
4. N. Morokhovets, *Istoriia Rossii v period promyshlennogo kapitalizma* (Moscow, 1929); T. Shanin, *Russia as a 'Developing Society,'* 2 vols. (London, 1985-1986), I: 159-64, II: 152-53, 280-83; M. Lewin, *The Making of the Soviet System* (New York, 1985), pp. 292-93.
5. P. K. Urban, *Smena tendentsii v sovetskoi istoriografii*, pp. 48-53. For reference to censored proceedings, see P. G. Galuzo, *Agrarnye otnosheniia na iuge Kazakhstana* (Alma Ata, 1965), p. 27.
6. His "O nachale 'niskhodiashchei' stadii feodalnoi formatsii," *VI*, no. 9 (1959): 123-37; "Sotsialno-ekonomichni prychyny posylennia kripatstva v krainakh skhidnoi Evropy v XV-XVII st.," in *Tezy dopovidei XVII naukovoi sesii Kyivskoho instytutu narodnoho hospodarstva* (Kiev, 1965), pp. 126-28 (unavailable at time of writing).
7. G. Zaidel, Z. Lozinsky, A. Prigozhin, and S. Tomsinsky, eds., *Spornye voprosy metodologii istorii* (Kharkiv, 1930); A. G. Prigozhin, *Karl Marks i problemy sotsio-ekonomicheskikh formatsii* (Leningrad, 1933); and his *Karl Marks i problemy istorii dokapitalisticheskikh formatsii* (Moscow, 1934). A Soviet review of this debate is L. V. Danilova, "Stanovlenie marksytskogo napravleniia v sovetskoi istoriografii epokhi feodalizma," *IZ*, no. 76 (1965): 62-119. See also J. Barber,

Soviet Historians in Crisis, 1928-1932 (London, 1981), pp. 46-67; and L. Yaresh, "The Problem of Periodization," in Rewriting, ed. C. Black, pp. 49-55.

8. L. Yaresh, "The Problem of Periodization"; S. Baron, "The Transition from Feudalism to Capitalism in Russia: A Major Soviet Historical Controversy," *American Historical Review* 77 (June 1972): 715-29; A. Gerschenkron, "Soviet Marxism and Absolutism," *SR*, no. 4 (1971): 853-69.

9. L. V. Cherepnin, "Nekotorye voprosy istorii dokapitalisticheskikh formatsii v Rossii," *Kommunist*, no. 1 (1975): 71-2.

10. V. I. Shunkov, et al., *Perekhod ot feodalizma k kapitalismu v Rossii* (Moscow, 1969), pp. 14-15, 266, 405; S. D. Skazkin, ed., *Teoreticheskie i istoriograficheskie problemy genesisa kapitalizma* (Moscow, 1969), pp. 200-1. For the Western Marxist perspective, see R. Hilton, ed., *The Transition from Feudalism to Capitalism* (London, 1973).

11. S. Piontkovsky, "Istoriografiia krestianskikh voin v Rossii," *IM*, no. 6 (1933): 80-119; L. Yaresh, "The 'Peasant Wars' in Soviet Historiography," *SR*, no. 3 (1957): 241-59; V. V. Mavrodin, "Sovetskaia istoricheskaia literatura o krestianskikh voinakh v Rossii XVII-XVIII vekov," *VI*, no. 5 (1961): 25-37. For a discussion of Engels see J. Bak, ed., *The German Peasant War of 1525* (London, 1976), pp. 89-131.

12. S. G. Tomsinsky, "K metodologii istorii krestianskikh dvizhenii v dokapitalisticheskuiu epokhu," *Pod znamenem marksyzma*, no. 6 (1930): 134-50; and his *Ocherki istorii feodalnokrepostnoi Rossii* (Moscow, 1934); "Soveshchanie po istorii krestianskikh voin v Rossii," *VI*, no. 2 (1956): 69-79; E. I. Indova, A. A. Preobrazhensky, and Iu. A. Tikhonov, "Klassovaia borba krestianstva i stanovlenie burzhuaznykh otnoshenii v Rossii," *VI*, no. 12 (1964): 27-53; A. M. Sakharov, "O dialektike istoricheskogo razvitiia Russkogo krestianstva," *VI*, no. 1 (1970): 17-41. See also L. V. Cherepnin, ed., *Krestianskie voiny v Rossii XVII-XVIII vekov* (Moscow, 1974), pp. 5-25, for a review of post-Stalin literature.

13. E. I. Antonov, "Obsuzhdenie stati E. I. Indovoi . . . ," *VI*, no. 1 (1965): 164-69.

14. V. V. Mavrodin, "Po povodu kharaktera i istoricheskogo znacheniia krestianskikh voin v Rossii," in *Krestianskie voiny*, ed., L. V. Cherepin, pp. 44-45. Mavrodin did not mention Peter I.

15. E. M. Zhukov et al., *Vsesoiuznoe soveshchanie o merakh uluchsheniia podgotovki nauchno-pedagogicheskikh kadrov po istoricheskim naukam* (Moscow, 1964), pp. 162-65, 311, 348. On the significance of this conference, see K. Marko, "History and Historians," *Survey*, no. 56 (July 1965): 72-82.

16. *Istoriia i sotsiologiia* (Moscow, 1964), pp. 127, 129, 137, 177, 311; A. L. Sidorov, ed., *Ob osobennostiakh imperializma v Rossii* (Moscow, 1963), p. 10.

17. P. G. Galuzo, "K leninskim otsenkam predposilok obedineniia natsionalnykh dvizhenii v Rossii i revoliutsionnoi borby rabochago klassa za sotsializm," and M. Rubach, "Ukrainskoe natsionalnoe dvizhenie, ego kharakter i dvizhushchie sily (1910-febral 1917)," in *Natsionalnyi vopros nakanune i v period provedeniia Velikoi Oktiabrskoi Revoliutsii* (Moscow, 1964), pp. 8-9, 22-35. See also the conference report in *ISSSR*, no. 5 (1964): 215-19; and P. Vorobei, "Sovetskaia istoriografiia natsionalnogo voprosa na Ukraine," in *Nekotorye problemy otechestvennoi istoriografii i istochnikovedeniia* (Dnipropetrovsk, 1972), pp. 35-37.

18. *Vsesoiuznoe soveshchanie*, p. 29. No one asked why this idea was not relegated to the list of "mistakes" of the Stalin period.
19. Most glaring for our purposes is Lenin's failure to explain why blocs of capital should form on the basis of nation-states. A. Brewer, *Marxist Theories of Imperialism: A Critical Survey* (London, 1980), p. 116; A. Mack, "Theories of Imperialism," *Journal of Conflict Resolution*, no. 3 (1974): 518-19; and B. Warren, *Imperialism: Pioneer of Capitalism* (London, 1985), pp. 50-80.
20. In the pre-Stalin years there seems to have been only one discussion of the relationship between the Marxist theory of imperialism and tsarist colonialism: E. Drabkina, *Natsionalnyi i kolonialnyi vopros v tsarskoi Rossii* (Moscow, 1930). Drabkina argued that because "feudal military" imperialism was based on supranational ties of landowning elites, "all national" (that is, supra-class) liberation fronts were impossible, "bourgeois revolutions" could not bring "real" national liberation, and national autonomy would splinter the working class. See also J. Barber, *Soviet Historians*, pp. 68-69. One of Pokrovsky's articles on pre-1861 tsarist imperialism has been translated and published in R. Szporluk, ed., *Russia in World History* (Ann Arbor, MI, 1970), pp. 117-30.
21. D. Boersner, *The Bolsheviks and the National and Colonial Question* (New York, 1981); R. Lowenthal, "On National Democracy: Its Function in Communist Policy," *Survey*, no. 47 (April 1963): 119-26.
22. A. L. Sidorov, ed., *Ob osobennostiakh imperializma v Rossii*; M. Agursky, "The Bolshevik Revolution as a Revolution of National Liberation," *The Journal of Communist Studies*, no. 2 (1987): 178-84.
23. A. F. Galuzo, *Agrarnye otnosheniia*, pp. 5-32.
24. During the Stalin terror, individuals would destroy their own copies of books that were "criticized" or condemned. Interview nos. 3 and 4, November 1988.
25. J. Kren, "Czech Historiography at a Turning Point," *East European Politics and Societies*, no. 2 (1992): 162-63.
26. V. Picheta, "Verkhovnyi tainyi sovet i Malorossiiskya dela," *Ukrainskaia zhizn*, no. 3 (1916): 32-53; Picheta, "Kniaz A. I. Shakhovskoi i vopros ob upravlenii Malorossi," *Ukrainskaia zhizn*, nos. 10-11 (1916): 43-47; Picheta, "Ukraina i moskovskoe samoderzhavie," *Ukrainskaia zhizn*, nos. 3-6 (1917): 65-83.
27. I. Rozenfeld, *Prisoedinenie Malorossii k Rossii, 1654-1793 gg*. (Petrograd, 1915).
28. V. I. Semevsky, *Kirillo-mefodievskoe obshchestvo* (Petrograd, 1918).
29. A. Iarynovich, *Galichina v eia proshlom i nastoiashchem* (Moscow, 1915), pp. 7-10, 39; P. R. Magosci, *Galicia*, p. 30; N. M. Pashaeva, "Galitsiia pod vlastiu Avstrii v russkoi i sovetskoi istoricheskoi literature: Bibliografiia," in V. D. Koroliuk, ed., *Mezhdunarodnye sviazi stran Tsentralnoi, Vostochnoi i Iugo-vostochnoi Evropy i slaviano-germanskie otnosheniia* (Moscow, 1968), pp. 295-394. See also *Knizhnaia letopis*, 1914-17 (reprint ed., 1964 vols. 20-29).
30. Magosci, *Galicia*; Pashaeva, "Galitsiia"; M. Korduba, *La Litterature historique sovietique-ukrainienne*, 2nd ed. (Munich, 1972). A valuable bibliography of Soviet works published between 1921 and 1972 may be found in issues of *Arkhivy Ukrainy* for 1958-1972.
31. V. Picheta, "Osnovnye momenty v istoricheskikh sudbakh narodov zapadnoi Ukrainy i Belorusii," *IM*, nos. 5-6 (1939): 67-98. Similar was his *Osnovnye*

momenty istoricheskogo razvitiia zapadnoi Ukrainy i zapadnoi Belorussii (Moscow, 1940). B. Grekov, "Sudba naseleniia galitskikh kniazheskikh votchin pod vlastiu Polshi," *IZh*, no. 12 (1944): 37-43 is the only Russian article dealing with a problem related to the social and legal impact of early Polish rule in Galicia.

32. V. Picheta, "Polsha na putiakh k kolonizatsii Ukrainy i Belorussii," *IZ* 7 (1940): 60-90.
33. *Metodicheskie ukazaniia i bibliografiia po izucheniiu spetskursa 'Osvoboditelnaia voina ukrainskogo naroda 1648-1654'* (Dnipropetrovsk, 1980); A. V. Santsevych, *Ukrainska radianska istoriohrafiia* (Kiev, 1984); I. S. Khmel et al., *Istoriografiia istorii Ukrainskoi SSR* (Kiev, 1986); *The Lvov Church Council. Documents and Materials 1946-1981* (Moscow, 1983), pp. 207-22.
34. There is no single comprehensive bibliography of this subject. See I. Handros, N. Horbachova, and E. Landa, "Zhovten ta hromadianska viina na Ukraiini," *LR*, nos. 3-4 (1932): 319-54; nos. 5-6, pp. 216-41; Iu. M. Hamretsky et al., *Istoriografiia Velikoi Oktiabrskoi sotsialisticheskoi revoliutsii na Ukraine* (Kiev, 1987), pp. 5-57, 214-21; O. S. Pidhainy and O. I. Pidhainy, *The Ukrainian Republic in the Great East-European Revolution: A Bibliography*, vols. 5-6 (Toronto, 1971, 1975); J. Lawrynenko, *Ukrainian Communism and Soviet Russian Policy Toward the Ukraine: An Annotated Bibliography* (New York, 1953).
35. N. Rubinshtein, "Klassovaia borba na Ukraine v XVII v.," *Borba klassov*, no. 4 (1936): 36-46.
36. V. Mavrodin, "Borba ukrainskogo naroda ... i prisoedinenie Ukrainy k Rossii," *Propaganda i agitatsiia*, no. 7 (1948): 20-29.
37. K. Osipov, *Bogdan Khmelnitskyi* (Moscow, 1939).
38. V. Picheta, "Bogdan Khmelnitskyi—diplomat i strateg," *Izvestiia Akademii nauk SSSR, Seriia istorii i filosofii*, no. 2 (1944): 49-59.
39. Osipov, *Bogdan Khmelnitskyi* (Moscow, 1939), p. 8; 2nd ed., 1948, p. 12.
40. Ibid. 1939 ed., pp. 336-39; 1948 ed., pp. 346-54.
41. Ibid. 1939 ed., pp. 350-60; 1948 ed., pp. 393-404.
42. S. F. Kalashnikova, "Sotsialno-ekonomicheskoe i politicheskoe polozheniia Ukrainy nakanune osvoboditelnoi voiny," *Uchenye zapiski Moskovskago gosudarstvennogo pedagogicheskago instituta, Kafedra istorii SSSR* 60, no. 2 (1949): 43-99.
43. G. M. Lyzlov, "Polsko-russkie otnosheniia," *Kratkie soobshcheniia Instituta slavianovedeniia*, no. 24 (1958): 73.
44. G. Georgievsky, "Mazepa i Menshikov," *IZh*, no. 12 (1940): 72-83.
45. V. K. Putilov, "Deiatel gadiachskogo soglasheniia s Polshei P. I. Teteria," *Uchenye zapiski Leningradskogo gosudarstvennogo universiteta*, no. 73 (1940): 175-79.
46. M. Ia. Volkov, "Iz istorii borby za ukrainskii rynok vo vtoroi chetverti XVIII veka," *Vestnik Moskovskogo universiteta, seria IX, Istoriia*, no. 1 (1961): 56.
47. A. Dmitriev, *Gaidamachshchina* and *Koliivshchina* (Moscow, 1934).
48. Ia. Golovchiner, "Krestianskoe vostanie 1768 goda na Ukraine," *IZh*, no. 1 (1939): 70-79.
49. P. A. Zaionchkovsky, "Kirillo-mefodievskoe obshchestvo," *Trudy Istoriko-arkhivnogo instituta*, no. 3 (1947): 175, 179, 19, 193, 199, 203. See *Pravda*

Ukrainy, October 5, 1946, for an attack on Ukrainian historians who were writing in the same vein as Zaionchkovsky.
50. P. A. Zaionchkovsky, *Kirillo-mefodievskoe obshchestvo* (Moscow, 1959), pp. 55, 65, 78, 90, 101.
51. R. Eideman and N. Kahurin, *Hromadianska viina na Ukraini* (Kharkiv, 1930), pp. 7-9 68-70.
52. P. Gorin, "O roli proletariata," *Bolshevik,* no. 1 (1930): 45-48.
53. E. Gorodetsky, "Legende o 'neitralitete,'" *IM,* no. 4 (1937): 100-23; Gorodetsky, "Tsentralna Rada-oplot vserossiiskoe kontrevoliutsii," *IM,* nos. 8-9 (1935): 111-32. Gorodetsky's view soon replaced those in the 1936 *Istoriia grazhdanskoi voiny v SSSR,* which depicted relations between the Rada and Provisional Government as basically hostile. M. Gorky et al., *The History of the Civil War in the USSR* (Moscow, 1937), I: 119.
54. M. S. Frenkin, "Nekotorye voprosy deiatelnosti Tsentralnoi rady i ee voiskovykh organov v . . . Velikoi Oktiabrskoi sotsialisticheskoi revoliutsii," *Trudy Moskovskogo gosudarstvennogo istoriko–arkhivnogo instituta,* no. 26 (1968): 28-57.

Notes to Conclusion

1. W. Konopczyński, "Dzieje nauki historycznej w Polsce," *PP* 228 (1949): 27, 158.
2. B. Cywiński, *Zatruta humanistyka* (Warsaw, 1980).
3. E. Valkenier, "The Rise and Decline of Official Marxist Historiography in Poland 1945-1983," *SR,* no. 4 (1985): 663.
4. O. Górka, "Bohdan Chmielnicki—jego historycy postac i dzieło," *Sesja,* p. 66.
5. W. Serczyk, *Hajdamacy* (Krakow, 1972), p. 7
6. B. Cywiński. Summarized in M. Piłka, "Deformacje w wykładzie historii w podręcznikach dla szkół średnich," *Zeszyty historyczne,* no. 61 (1982): 3-31.
7. "Recenzja z Moskwy o polskich podręcznikach historii," *Zeszyty Historyczne,* no. 57 (1981): 73-91.
8. T. Chynczewska-Hennel's *Świadomość narodowa szlachty ukraińskiej i Kozaczyzny od połowy XVI do połowy XVII wieku* (Warsaw, 1985) sparked a sharp exchange of opinions. See *PH,* no. 2 (1986): 331-51; 1987, no. 3, pp. 533-56. The debate included reference to Polish work on early-modern Ukraine published between 1982 and 1987. Also see the special issue of *Znak,* no. 395 (1988) and *Slavia Orientalis,* nos. 3-4 (1989), and nos. 1-2 (1990).
9. S. A. Piontkovsky, *Burzhuaznaia istoricheskaia nauka v Rossii* (Moscow, 1931), pp. 19, 94. An example of what Piontkovsky was criticizing is provided by B. D. Grekov's *Feodalnye otnosheniia v kievskom gosudarstve* (Moscow, 1936), pp. 16-17; and Grekov, *Kievskaia Rus* (Moscow, 1939), p. 9. In the first book Grekov compared Kievan Rus to Charlemagne's empire, because three nations traced their roots from each polity. In the second he added that the "Russian nation," which he now used as a synonym for Eastern Slavs, had played the "leading role" in the political successes of the Kievan state.

10. R. Szporluk, "The Ukraine and Russia," in *The Last Empire*, ed. R. Conquest (Stanford, 1988), pp. 151-82.
11. R. Szporluk, "Dilemmas of Russian Nationalism," *Problems of Communism* (July-August 1989): 16-33.
12. J. G. Pocock, "British History: A Plea for a New Subject," *Journal of Modern History*, no. 4 (1975): 601-28; Pocock, "The Limits and Divisions of British History: In Search of the Unknown Subject," *American Historical Review*, no. 2 (1982): 311-36.

Notes to Appendix

1. K. Gerner, "An alternative to Moscow: Ancient Rus, Modern Ukraine and Byelorussia, in *Nationalism in the USSR*, ed. A. Bon and R. van Voren (Amsterdam, 1989), pp. 68-86.
2. W. Connor, *The National Question in Marxist-Leninist Theory and Strategy* (Princeton, 1984); R. Solchanyk, "Molding 'The Soviet People': The Role of Ukraine and Belorussia," *Journal of Ukrainian Studies* (Summer 1983): 3-19.
3. The picture was published as the centerfold in *Ukraina*, no. 3 (1989). On Glazunov, see V. Krasnov, "Russian National Feeling: An Informal Poll," in *The Last Empire*, ed. R. Conquest, pp. 109-32; V. Osipov, "Lgushchee isskustvo ili lgushchaia kritika"; and L. Sarin, "Beres za kist, spasai Rossiiu," *Strana i mir*, no. 4 (1988): 74-83. For reformist Ukrainian criticism of the Russian conception of Ukraine as a quaint part of Russia, see R. Szporluk, "Dilemmas of Russian Nationalism," *Problems of Communism* (July-August 1989): 30.
4. A. Solzhenitsyn, "Kak nam obustroit Rossiiu," *Literaturna gazeta*, September 18, 1990. For a Ukrainian reply, see R. Ivanchenko, "Iakshcho v nas vidibraty istoriiu," *Literaturna Ukraina*, October 11, 1990, p. 6.
5. *Komosomol Donbassa*, July 2, 1990. *Uchitelskaia gazeta*, September 25, 1989, called Riuryk the first ruler of "Rossiia" instead of "Rus," while a letter to the editor in *Molod Ukrainy*, October 15, 1989, referred to Russification of Ukrainians as a reestablishment of earlier unity.
6. R. Solchanyk, "Ukraine and Russia: Before and After the Coup," *Report on the USSR*, September 27, 1991, p. 17.
7. R. Szporluk, "The Eurasia House: Problems of Identity in Russia and Eastern Europe," *Crosscurrents*, no. 9 (1990): 3-15; "Russkaia kultura na perekhrestke mnenii," *Druzhba narodov*, no. 6 (1990): 163-93; no. 7, pp. 201-28. R. Moroz, "Rosiiska inteligentsiia i natsionalne pytannia na tli glasnosti i perebudovy," *Suchasnist*, nos. 7-8 (1990): 171-85, argues that most of the literary elite are indifferent to non-Russian concerns.
8. A. N. Iakovlev, "Dostizhenie kachestvenno novogo sostoianiia sovetskogo obshchestva i obshchestvennye nauki," *Vestnik Akademii nauk SSSR*, no. 6 (1987): 68.
9. "Ideologicheskie problemy mezhnatsionalnykh otnoshenii," *Izvestiia TsK KPSS*, no. 6 (1989): 82, 87.
10. G. Kh. Popov and N. Adzhubei, "Pamiat i 'pamiat,' " *Znamia*, no. 1 (1988): 192-93.
11. *Literaturna gazeta*, no. 10 (1988). In a letter to the editor, a Russian sympathetic to Ukraine wrote, "Why among us Russians living in Ukraine, as well as other republics, is there such boorishness in our attitude to the native population? This

manifests itself . . . in feelings of superiority that too often leads to dislike of Russian speakers." *Dzvin*, no. 7 (1990): 155.

12. M. Von Hagen, "Soviet Historiography and the Nationality Question," *Nationalities Papers* (Spring 1990): 55.
13. M. A. Annanepesov, "Prisoedinenie Turkmenistana k Rossii: Pravda istorii," *VI*, no. 11 (1989): 70-86.
14. S. M. Dumin, "Ob izuchenii istorii Velikogo Kniazhestva Litovskogo," *Sovetskoe slavianovedenie*, no. 6 (1988): 97-101; K. Mihalisko, "Historian Outlines Revisionist View of Belorussia's Past," *Radio Liberty Research*, no. 415 (1988).
15. "Natsionalnyi vopros i mezhnatsionalnye otnosheniia v SSSR: Istoriia i sovremennost," *VI*, no. 5 (1989): 41, 55-56; V. Sarbei, "Vsesoiuznyi 'kruhlyi stil,'" *UIZh*, no. 3 (1990): 154.
16. Sarbei, "Vsesoiuznyi 'kruhlyi stil,' " p. 152. The respected historian Dmitrii Likhachev still used Russian, Rus'ian, and Eastern Slavs as synonyms. Sentences such as "The Russian land, or more correctly, the land of Rus', i.e., the whole land area of the future Ukraine, Belorussia and Great Russia . . ." and "Rus' remained united even after its split" make relations between the Eastern Slavs as intelligible as the mystery of the Holy Trinity. N. N. Petro, ed., *Reflections on Russia: Dmitrii S. Likhachev* (Boulder, CO, 1991), pp. 161, 73.
17. S. L. Tikhvinsky, "Ianvarskyi (1987 g.) Plenum TsKKPSS i istoricheskaia nauka," *VI*, no. 6 (1987): 3-13.
18. S. L. Tikhvinsky, "Zadachi koordinatsii v oblasti istoricheskoi nauki," *ISSSR*, no. 1 (1988): 119.
19. G. I. Marchuk, "O zadachakh Akademii nauk SSSR vytekaiushchikh iz reshenii XIX Vsesoiuznoi partiinoi konferentsii," *Vestnik Akademii nauk SSSR*, no. 2 (1989): 11.
20. *Izvestiia*, December 24, 1989.
21. Iu Barabash, "Ivan Mazepa—Shche odna literaturna versiia," *Kyiv*, no. 12 (1989): 145.
22. V. Marochkin, "Hirka chasha Ivana Mazepy," *Ukraina*, no. 23 (June 1989): 14-16; and his "Ivan Mazepa: Pravda i vyhadky," *Ukraina*, no. 6 (February 1990): 11-12. An accompanying esay by M. Braichevsky refers to Peter I's policies as "imperialist colonialism."
23. Iu. Khorunzhy, "Ni z kotrym hosudarem . . . ," *Ukraina*, no. 16 (May 1989): 20-22; Khorunzhy, "Aki v robotu ehipetsku," *Ukraina*, no. 25 (September 1990): 22.
24. M. Braichevsky, *Literaturna Ukraina*, October 12, 1989; I. Lysenko, "Istoriia Ukrainy—nove vysvitlennia," *Ukraina*, no. 41 (October 1989): 5.
25. Ia. Dzyra, "Zhadaimo pravednykh hetmaniv," *Ukraina*, no. 1 (January 1990): 23; Ia. Dashkevych, "Hetmanska Ukraina," *Pamiatnyky Ukrainy*, no. 2 (1990): 11; P. Sas, "Ukrainsko-polskyi myslytel doby vidrodzhennia . . . ," *UIZh*, no. 1 (1991): 87-98; I. Paslavsky, "Pysav mandrovanets iakoho zvut Vyshenskym," *Dzvin*, no. 1 (1991): 152-59.
26. P. Fedchenko, "Shevchenko, Kulish i Kostomarov u Kyryllo-Mefodiivskomu tovarystvi," *Radianske literaturoznavstvo*, no. 7 (1989): 29-36; Fedchenko, "Apostol pravdy i nauky," *Slovo i chas*, no. 7 (1990): 36-41; O. Romaniv and Ia. Hrytsak, "NTSh, Etap diialnosti," *Visnyk Akademii nauk URSR*, no. 3 (1990):

69-78; Ia. Dzyra, "Henii i komentatory ioho tvorchosti," *Literaturna Ukraina,* April 5, 1990, p. 7; O. V. Lysenko, *Prosvity naddniprianskoi Ukrainy u dozhovtnevyi period* (Kiev, 1990); M. Kuhutiuk, "Radykalna partiia v Skhidnii Halychyni," *UIZh,* no. 10 (1990): 55-62.

27. "Ukrainske kozatstvo . . . (Materialy 'kruhloho stolu')," and I. Hoshuliak, "Politychni aspekty istorii hromadianskoi viiny na Ukraini," *UIZh,* no. 12 (1990): 12-29,36-46.
28. Ia. Hamretsky, "Do vyvchennia natsionalno-vyzvolnoho rukhu na Ukraini v 1917 r.," *UIZh,* no. 12 (1990): 60-72.
29. M. Braichevsky, "Pryiednannia chy vozziednannia," *Narodna hazeta,* nos. 1-6 (1990). This essay was first published in the West.
30. V. Shevchuk was the first to openly criticize the Institute of History of the Ukrainian Academy of Sciences. See his "Bez korenia krona mertva," *Kultura i zhyttia,* February 7, 1988, p. 6; see also R. Ivanchuk, "Dukhovne zdorovia i nihilistychnyi virus," *Kyiv,* no. 4 (1988): 119-21. Iu. Kondufor, the head of the institute, replied in "Zhaiane nadoluzhuvaty," *Kultura i zhyttia,* March 13, 1988, pp. 2-3; and "Zavdannia dalshoho rozvytku istorychnykh doslidzhen v Ukrainsky RSR u svitli rishen XXVII zizdu KPRS," *UIZh,* no. 4 (1988): 5-19. See also "Pidvyshchuvaty rol suspilnykh nauk u zdiisneni reformy politychnoi systemy," *UIZh,* no.5 (1989): 150, and "Pidvyshchuvaty efektyvnist istorychnykh doslidzhen," *Visnyk Akademii nauk URSR,* no. 9 (1989): 13. By 1991, Kondufor had changed his tone remarkably; see his "Istoriia i sohodnia," *Visnyk Akademii nauk URSR,* no. 2 (1991): 9-19.
31. For example, O. Motsia, "Davnoruska narodnist," *UIZh,* no. 7 (1990): 3-13; V. Sarbei, *Ocherki po metodologii i istoriografii istorii Ukrainy* (Kiev, 1989); Sarbei et al., *Istoriia Ukrainskoi SSR* (Kiev, 1989). By mid-1991, many of these historians had begun to distance themselves from the official views they propounded earlier. For example, see Motsia's comments in "U poshukakh istorychnoi pravdy ('kruhlyi stil')," *UIZh,* no. 10 (1991): 3-5; V. Sarbei, "Do pohliadiv M. P. Drahomanova na natsionalne pytannia," *UIZh,* no. 9 (1991): 60-70.
32. Iu. Kondufor, S. Kulchytsky, V. Sarbei, V. Smolyi, and I. Khmil, "Ukraina: Dialektyka istorychnoho rozvytku," *Kommunist Ukrainy,* no. 9 (1989): 13-20; no. 11, pp. 42-51. Similar was V. H. Sarbei et al., *Istoriia Ukrainy v zapytanniakh ta vidpovidiakh* (Kiev, 1989).
33. See also Iu. Kondufor et al., *Ukrainska narodnist* (Kiev, 1990). This survey uses DHM categories and repeats the Eastern Slavic affinity myth. But the text is less polemical, less vulgar, and less simplistic; the euphemism, metaphor, and jargon are minimal; and it even includes an interesting discussion about pre-nineteenth-century culture, ideology, and mentality. A critique of DHM methodology appeared the same year and argued the case for "Western Marxism," Iu. Kanyhin, "Vid istmatu do intelektualizmu," *Visnyk Akademii nauk URSR,* no. 11 (1989): 19-29.
34. V. Sydorenko and V. Tytarenko, "Pokhmuri hrymasy rynku," *Literaturna Ukraina,* January 31, 1991, p. 3.
35. D. Tabachnik was fired from the Institute of History after he had published an interview with the former First Secretary of the Ukrainian Party, P. Shelest. During

the summer of 1990 reformist Ukrainian scholars mentioned in conversation that they would lose their jobs if they quit the Party and that friends who had been "too active" in RUKH were dismissed from their positions for trivial pretexts.

36. See "Istorychna nauka: Novi rubezhi," *Radianska Ukraina*, December 15, 1989; "Respulikanska prohrama rozvytku istorychnykh doslidzhen... istorii Ukrainskoi RSR," *UIZh*, no. 11 (1990): 3-9; no. 12, pp. 3-11.
37. "Pryntsypova politychna otsinka," *Literaturna Ukraina*, June 21, 1990. The first direct criticism of the 1934 and 1936 decrees and Stalin's use of nationalism appeared in 1990: V. B. Kobrin, "Pod pressom ideologii," *Vestnik Akademii nauk SSSR*, no. 12 (1990): 31-33, 36.
38. "Vsesoiuznyi 'kruhlyi stil,' " *UIZh*, no. 3 (1990): 153; V. Sarbei, "M. M. Arkas i ioho 'Istoriia Ukrainy-Rusi,' " *UIZh*, no. 7 (1990): 100-14; and his comments in the introduction to the 1990 reprint edition of Arkas's history. V. Zamlinsky, *Bogdan Khmelnitskyi* (Moscow, 1989) does not deal with differences among Ukrainian leaders over the Russian alliance, Khmelnytsky's internal policies, or cossack autonomy. The book was favorably reviewed by V. Kotliar, "Slovo pro Bohdana," *Kommunist Ukrainy*, no. 2 (1990): 90-93. The first anthologies by "conservative" historians focus on legal, political, and mentality history instead of socio-economic subjects and Ukrainian-Russian "friendship." See O. I. Hurzhyi et al., *Problemy ukrainskoi istorychnoi medievistyky* (Kiev, 1990); V. Smolyi, ed., *Feodalizm na Ukraini* (Kiev, 1990).
39. V. Smolyi and O Hurzhyi, "Stanovlennia Ukrainskoi feodalnoi derzhavnosti," *UIZh*, no. 10 (1990): 10-20. The article did not cite articles by reformists.
40. P. Tolochko formally expressed concern over this issue at the summer 1991 General Meeting of the Ukrainian academy. "Vystupy uchasnykiv sesii," *Visnyk Akademii nauk URSR*, no. 8 (1991): 5-6.
41. For a discussion of this dilemma and its resolution in Polish historiography, see J. Maternicki, "Polska refleksia teoretyczna i metodologiczna w dziedzinie historii w okresie neoromantyzmu i modernizmu," *PHum*, no. 7 (1979): 33-56; "O nowy kształt historii," *Dzieje najnowsze*, no. 1 (1980): 119-72.
42. A. Sinyavsky, "Russian Nationalism," *Radio Liberty Research Bulletin*, December 19, 1988, pp. 25-35; V. Krasnov, "Pamyat: A Force for Change?" *Nationalities Papers*, 19 no. 2 (1991): 167-82.
43. Liberals dismissed the notion. See A. Shmelev, "Po zakonam parodii," *Znamia*, no. 6 (1990): 213-25. The USSR academy accorded the term respectability by allotting an article to it and an interview with its inventor, I. Shafarevich. See B. A. Lapshov, "Ob istokakh imperskogo myshlenniia, zoologicheskogo antikommunizma i politicheskoi russofobii," *Vestnik Akademii nauk SSSR*, no. 11 (1990): 83-87; I. Shafarevich, "Ostaius dissidentom," *Vestnik Akademii nauk SSSR*, no. 11 (1990):88-99.

INDEX

Afanasiev, Iu. 220
Agrarian Program of Social Democracy, The 181, 183
Akademia Umijtnoci (Krakow) 31, 69-70
Aleksandrov, G. 24
Alexander II 129
Algasov, A. 135
Anti-Dühring 34
anti-Semitism 57-8, 141
Arnold, S. 81-2, 90, 123, 201
Artemov, N 152-3
Association of Marxist Historians (AHM) 31, 63
Austria (Habsburg Empire) 11, 13, 64-5, 72, 75, 77-8, 80, 82, 86, 92, 94-5, 101-3, 113-5, 120-2, 129-30, 159, 161, 163, 167, 173, 175, 192, 200-2
Austro-Marxism 19, 115, 126

Bahaly, D. 50
Bakhrushin, S.V. 50, 157
Balzer, O. 131
Bar Confederation 77-8, 99, 105, 118, 131
Bardach, J. 132
Baranowski, B. 64-5, 122-3
Baruzdin, Sergei 215
Barycz, Henryk 88
Bauer, Otto 115, 126
Bazilevich, K.M. 59
Bazilov, M.V. 50
Belarus 16, 61, 111, 140, 143, 147, 153, 192, 207, 213-5
Belinsky, V. 152-3
"Bernstein revisionism" 56
Berr, Henri 36, 39
Bezborodko, O. 195
Biernacek, T. 13
Bobinski, Stanisaw 82-3
Bobrzynski, M. 96
Bochenski, A. 88

Bogdanov, M. 37
Bogoliubsky, Andrei 5-6, 119, 137-9, 145, 147-8, 152-3, 158, 165
Boiko, I. 59
Boleslaw I (the Brave) 83-4
Bolshaia sovetskaia entsiklopediia 155-6
Bolsheviks and Bolshevism 5, 6, 13-14, 22, 27, 49-50, 52, 92, 95, 103, 118-9, 122, 126-8, 145, 152, 162, 172, 174-6, 178, 181, 197, 209
Books of the Polish Nation and its Pilgrimage 192
Braichevsky, M. 217
Bratstva 107
Brest-Litovsk Treaty 21, 119, 128
Bruckner, Alexsander 73-4
Bujak, F. 39
Bukharin, N. 51, 55
Bukowiecka, S. 83-4
Burdzhalov, E. 180
Bystriansky, V. 137, 212
Byzantine Studies 63

Capital 19, 184
Carpathian Ukraine 15
Casares resolution 16-17
Casimir IV (the Great) 70, 72, 73, 75-8, 81, 89, 91, 93, 95-7, 101-2, 104, 110, 113, 116-7, 119, 124, 131, 139, 145, 148, 166, 192, 199, 201-4
Catherine II 105, 121, 131
Catholic church 70, 76, 91, 96-7, 103-5, 107-10, 116, 131, 141, 149, 200-2
Censorship Code (Polish, 1981) 66
Centkowski, J. 95
Central Asia 137, 147, 151, 189-90
Central Committee (CC) 29, 48, 50, 137, 148, 153, 155, 157, 214; Ideological Department of 29, 34
Central Committee (Poland) 32

Central Committee (Ukraine) 57; Culture and Learning Department 59
Central Executive Committee 27
Central Rada 6, 52, 78, 86, 95, 102-3, 115, 118-9, 122, 126-8, 138, 144, 148, 152-3, 156, 161-2, 172, 174, 176-8, 194, 196-7, 201, 203, 206, 209
Charles XII 120, 124
chauvinism 16-18, 21, 89
Checkaniuk, A. 164-5
Cherepnin, L.V. 59
Chervonenko, S. 212
Chief Administration for Literary and Press Affairs (GLAVLIT) 30
China 60
Chodynicki, Kazimierz 109-10, 200
Chołoniewski, A. 83
Chrząszcz, I. 105
"Civil Board of the Eastern Lands" 78
collectivization 14, 127
colonialism 20-2
Comintern, the 51
Commission on the History of the October Revolution and the History of the Communist Party (ISTPART) 29, 51
Communist Party of the Soviet Union (CPSU) 1, 2, 6, 14, 18-19, 21-2, 50, 58; resolutions 1, 32; Culture and Learning Department of 59
Communist Party of Western Ukraine 51
Congress of Polish Learning, First (1950) 65, 87
Congress of Polish Learning, Second (1973) 65
Constituent Assembly (Russia, 1917) 14
Contribution to the Critique of Political Economy 34
Contribution to the Question of the Development of the Monist View of History 34
cossacks 6, 25, 52-4, 58, 60, 64, 70, 72-7, 79-81, 83, 89-91, 94, 96-8, 103-7, 109, 112, 117, 119-20, 122-5, 131, 136, 140, 141, 156, 160-1, 164, 191, 194-5, 200, 202, 206, 211, 219
Council of Ambassadors 11
Counter-Reformation 70, 94
Crimea 15, 125, 153
Cyril-Methodius Brotherhood 6, 57, 102, 114, 118, 121, 136, 142, 144, 151, 172, 176, 192-3, 196

Cywinski, B. 206
Czartoryski, Adam 114
Czechoslovakia 19, 65
Czertwan, K. 85-6

Danilov, A. 220
Dashkevych, Ia. 220
Datsiuk, B. 153
Decembrist movement 118
Department of Orthodox Affairs (Poland) 109
Deruga, A. 129, 204-5
Development of Capitalism in Russia, The 49, 181, 187-9
Diadychenko, V. 152, 177
dialectical historical materialism (DHM) 27, 33-6, 40-2, 139, 146, 172, 179-82, 190-1, 218
Dłuska, M. 89
Dmitriev, A. 142
Dmytro of Horai 97
Dobrzanski, R. 82
Donetsk Republic 152
Drahomanov, Mykhailo 162, 164
Drozdov, P. 54-5, 155, 212
Dubas, M. 95
Dubrovsky, S.M. 137-8
Dudykevych, B. 157
Dubyna, K. 176-7
Dzieje narodu Polskiego w zarysie 78
Dzieje Polski w zarysie 72
Dziennik Kijowski 115
Dzwonkowski, Wodzimierz 76

Eidemanis, R. (Eideman) 196-7
Encyclopedya Polska 69
Engels, Friederich 19, 23, 33-5, 41, 48, 180, 184
England 90, 190
Erde, D. (Rakhstein) 196

February Revolution 144, 151-2
Febvre, Lucien 2
Feldmann, W. 13
Finley, Moses 2
First Methodological Conference (1951) 126
First Universal 175
Foundations of Leninism 37
France 16, 25, 83, 90, 92, 114, 121, 127, 145, 160, 177, 211, 216

Franko, Ivo 66
Frenkin, M. 197
Friedburg, J. 78-9

Galicia (Habs prov 1795-1918)(*see also* Western Ukraine*) 7, 11, 13, 25, 58, 66, 75, 77, 83, 88, 90, 92, 114-5, 118, 122, 161-2, 167, 173
Galicia, Eastern (bef 1795, after 1918, Halychyna, W.Uk.) 7, 11, 13, 72, 79-80, 84, 92, 95, 102, 113, 122, 128-9, 144
Galicia, Polish occupation of (1340s) 6, 57, 70, 73, 76, 89, 91, 96, 101-2, 113, 117, 139, 143, 145, 147, 166, 192, 199, 204
Galician Radical Party 92
Galician Revolutionary Committee 93
Galician Soviet Republic 93, 176
Galuzo, P.G. 186, 189
Gdansk (Danzig) 101
Gellner, E. 17
Genkina, E. 137
George II of Galicia 70, 73, 78, 116, 166, 199
Georgievksy, G. 194-5
German Ideology, The 184
Germany 16, 53, 63, 65, 75, 82, 85-6, 95, 103, 114-5, 119, 122, 126, 128, 131, 140, 144, 153, 162-3
Gierowski, J. 94-5
Gilewicz, A. 116-7
glasnost 16, 214
Glazunov, Ilia 214
Głuzinski, T. 113-4
Gołąbek, J. 114-5
Golovchiner, I. 195
Gorbachev, Mikhail 4, 16, 214, 216
Gorin, P. 50-2, 157, 197
Górka, O. 12-13, 31, 123, 206
Gorky, Maxim 158
Gorodetsky, I. 197
Great Soviet Encyclopaedia 42
Greece 2, 74, 76
Grekov, B. 50, 157
Grodecki, Roman 73
Guldon, Z. 130

Habsburg Empire (*see Austria*)
Hadiach Treaty (1659) 6, 64, 71-2, 75-7, 80, 82, 92, 94, 97, 99, 103-6, 114, 118, 120, 125, 141, 144, 147, 149, 193, 194-5, 200, 202-3, 205
Haidamak revolts 6, 71-2, 75, 77-8, 80, 82, 84, 86, 92, 94-5, 99, 105, 107, 109-10, 113, 116-8, 120, 131, 141, 149, 158, 166, 193, 195, 200, 202-3, 205
Halecki, Oskar 73, 111-13, 202
Handelsman, Marceli 31, 114-5
Higher Party School (Kiev) 164
Historia Polski (1958-1972) 91-2
"historiography of citizens" 2
History of the CPSU (B) 37
"history of the USSR" 3, 20-5, 47, 61, 137, 182, 186, 208
History of Ukraine (1948) 155
Hitler, Adolf 39, 63
Hitler-Stalin Pact 12
Holland 109
Holubutsky, V. 59, 182
Horenshtein, N. 54
Horn, Mauricy 130-1, 203
Hornowa, E. 129
Hoszowska, W. 89
hromady 6, 118, 144, 149, 161, 172-3
Hrushevsky, M. 51-4, 57, 135, 157, 173
Hungary 73
Huslysty, K. 59

Iakovlev, A.I. 56, 214
Iarynovich, A. (A. Nikolsky) 192
Iavorsky, Matvei 51-3
Iefymenko, A. 135
Imperialism: The Highest Stage of Capitalism 187-90
India 189-90
"Index of Information Not to Be Published in the Open Press" 31
Institute of Red Professors 47, 136
International Committee on Intellectual Co-operation 16
International Peace Bureau 16
Ireland 19, 190
Isaevych, Ia. 220
Istoriia grazhdanskoi voiny v SSSR (1935) 47
Istoriia Kazakhskoi SSR (1943) 55-6
Istoryk Marksyst 52
Istoriia Polshi 64
Istoriia SSSR (1939-40) 190

Istoriia Ukrainskoi RSR (1967) 191
Istoriia Ukrainy: Kratkii kurs 135, 156-7
Ivan III 140
Ivan IV 132
Ivanenko, G. 62
Izvestiia 55

Jabłonowski, A. 96, 124
Jabłonski, Henryk !15, 126, 128
Jadwiga 73
Jagiello 72-3, 84, 111, 113, 200-1, 207
"Jagiellonian idea" 73, 75, 77-9, 88, 97, 131, 201-3
Jagiellonian University 32, 117
Janaczek, A. 131
Jarosz, W. 81-2
Jasienica, Pawe (Lech Beynar) 96-9, 125, 206
Jesuits 72, 77, 79, 89, 107-8, 143, 145, 156, 163, 166
Jews 5, 13, 103-4, 141, 162
Joseph II 102

Kabanov, F. 153
Kaganovich, L. 54, 155
Kalashnikova, S. 194
Kalmucks 123
Kasymenko, O. 58-60, 176-7
Kazakhstan 55-6, 189
Keep, John 180
Kharkiv Soviet government 103
Khmelnytsky uprising (1648) 52, 54, 58, 64-5, 71-2, 74, 76-7, 79, 81-2, 84-5, 89-92, 94, 98, 102, 104, 106, 108, 110, 117, 120, 122-5, 135-8, 140-1, 143, 146-7, 149, 152, 156, 158, 160, 168, 185, 191-2, 193-4, 200, 206-7, 214
Kieniewicz, Stefan 90
Kiev, sack of (1169) 6, 119, 135, 137-9, 145, 147, 149, 158, 165
Kievan Rus 21, 56-7, 139, 142, 158
Kievan Ukrainian Government-in-Exile 61
Kisielewska, J. 78-80, 85-6
Kliuchevsky, V. 135
Kołankowski, Ludwig 76
Kommunist Ukrainy 219
Kondufor, Iu. 152, 176
Konopczynski, W. 70-1, 199, 207
Konspekt lektsii po istorii Rossii (Algasov) 135

Kormanowa, Z. 62-4, 88
Korniechuk, A. 59
Korsch, K. 37
Kostomarov, N. 144
Kot, S. 113
Kovaliov, S. 56-7, 156, 212
Kozik, J. 127, 129-30, 203
Krakow, University of 31, 88, 96, 201
Kromer's chronicle 112
Krupnytsky, B. 15
Krzywicki, Ludwig 38
Kubala, Ludwig 103-4, 106, 125
Kuczynski, S. 203
Kukułka, J. 128
Kula, W. 39
Kulikovo, Battle of 158
Kuroczko, E. 62-3
Kwartalnik instytutu Polsko-Radzieckiego 66

League for the Liberation of Ukraine 48
League of Nations 16-17
Lenin, V.I. 11, 14, 19-21, 33, 35-8, 44, 47-50, 54, 103, 121-2, 127, 142, 150, 153, 158, 162-3, 173-5, 177-8, 180-1, 184-8, 196-7, 207, 221
Lewandowski, K. 128
Lelewel, J. 131
Lewicki, K. 13, 78, 107-8, 200
"liberalization" 26
Libiszowska, Z. 123
Lithuania 17, 33, 70, 73, 77-8, 82, 84, 94, 96, 111-13, 116-7, 119, 132, 143, 192
LITKONTROL 30
Los, F. 177
Łowmianski, Henryk 111, 113
Lunacharsky, A. 44
"Luxemburgism" 88
Luxemburg, Rosa 38
Lviv, University of (Lwów) 31, 39, 71
Lykholat, Andryi 59, 212
Lytvyn, K. 57, 59
Lyzlov, G. 194, 211

Magdeburg Laws 41, 110
Magocsi, P.R. 13
Maiarov, M. (Biberman) 196
Main Board for the Protection of State and Military Secrets in the Press 30-1

Index

Main Office for Control of Press Publications and Public Performances (GUKPPiW) 33
Majewski, R. 125, 203, 205
Malkov, V. 153
Małowist, M. 131
Manilov, V. 212
Marchlewski, Feliks 82-3, 88
Martynowiczowna, W. 81
Marxism (and Marx) 18-21, 33, 35-8, 41, 48, 53, 139, 142, 150, 168, 180-1, 184, 189, 206, 211, 221
Marxism and Linguistics 38
Marxism and the National Question 23
Marxist-Leninism 1, 3, 27, 33, 43, 50, 60, 161, 209 see also under DHM
Masons 114
Materialism and Empirio Criticism 37
Maternicki, J. 13
Mavrodin, V.V. 153, 185, 193
Mayakovsky, V. 44
Mazepa I, Hetman 71-2, 75, 77, 80, 92, 94, 96, 98-9, 102, 105, 107, 117-18, 120, 124, 138-9, 141, 144, 146, 149, 157, 160, 168-9, 193, 195, 200, 216
"Memorial" 218
Menshikov, Prince 71, 194
Michiewicz, Adam 114
Michnik, H. 95
Minin uprising 55
Ministry of Education (Poland) 31
Ministry of the Interior (USSR) 30
Ministry of the Interior (Poland) 31
Mints, I.I. 47-8, 57-8, 137, 157, 186
Missałowa, S. 90
Molotov, V. 54
Mongols 25, 119, 147, 160, 213-4
Moscow historical conference (1928) 50-4
Muscovy 143

National Democrats (Poland) 12, 69, 88, 92
"national history" 16-21
National History as Cultural Process 5-6
nationalism 16-17, 19-20, 39
Nazarenko, I. 59
Nechkina, M. 137
Nemirych, Iuryi 71, 195
neo-Kantians 36

neoromanticism 69, 73, 75, 78, 83, 89, 96
New Knowledge 37
New Physics 37
non-Russian history within USSR 5, 15-16
Novoseltsov, A. 215
Nowe Drogi 64

Ocherki iz istorii Polshi 82
Ohloblyn, O. 15
"Old Ruthenian" 25
On the Origin of Species 34
Orwell, George 42
Orthodox Church 6, 12-13, 70-4, 76-7, 79-81, 83-6, 91, 94, 97-8, 105-10, 116-8, 125, 131-2, 140, 145, 166, 168, 195, 200-2, 207
Osipov, K. (O. Kuperman) 193-4, 211
Ostrozhsky, Prince Kostiantyn 79, 81, 107-9

pan-Slavism 59
Pankratova, A.M. 55, 59, 144, 153
Pannakoek, A. 37
paper allocation 30
Pareto, W. 36
Party Bureaus (*biuro tsykł*) 28, 48
Pashuto, V. 153
Paszkiewicz, H. 111, 116
Patriarch of Jerusalem 108
Paszkowski, E. 115-6
Peasant War in Germany, The (Engels) 184
Perdenia, J. 124
Peter the Great 120, 124, 138-9, 141, 147, 152, 161, 168-9, 194-5, 216
Petliura, S. 81-2, 93, 128-9, 204
Petrovsky, M. 139
Piast state 71, 116, 132, 199, 207
Piatakov, G. 14
Picheta, V.I. 50, 59, 139, 156, 191-3
Pilsudski, Jozef 11-12, 69, 81-3, 90, 92-3, 103, 128-9, 204
Piontkovsky, S. 15, 205
Planck, Max 36-7
Plekhanov, G. 34-5, 38
Podhorodecki, L. 119-22, 205
Podlassia 112
Podleski, F. 113-4
Podolynsky, M. 54
Pokrovsky, Mikhail 21-2, 33, 49, 51, 138, 193

Poland, Partition of 11-12. 6
Polish Communist Party (PZPR) 62-3, 66, 90
Polish Germans 12
Polish Historians Conference (IV) 12
Polish Historians Conference (VII) 65
Polish Historians Conference (VIII) 65
Polish Historical Association (PHT) 32, 90
Polish liberals 12
Polish-Lithuanian Commonwealth 6, 77, 91, 97-8, 104, 107-8, 112, 125, 147, 200
Polish Marxism 38-9
"Polish Military Organization in the Borderlands" 81
Polish occupation of Russia (1610-12) 25
Polish Revolt (1863) 103
Polish Socialist Party (PPS) 12
Polish Soviet Committee on Issues related to Polish Children in the USSR 62
Polish-Soviet Commission on History Textbooks 17-18, 207
Polish-Soviet Commission for the Improvement of the Contents of History and Geographical Textbooks 33
Polish Workers Party 38
Polonocentrism 3
Polska jej Dzieje i Kultura 73-4
Poltava, Battle of 169, 214
Ponomarev, Boris 24, 148, 150-1, 186
Popov, Gavriel 214-5
Popov, N. 50
positivism 69, 73, 76, 81-2
Pospilov, P.M. 59
Postyshev, P. 50
Pozharsky uprising 55
Poznan, University of 31, 39
"pragmatic schema" 25-6
Pravda 59
Priselkov, M. 135
Prochaska, A. 104
Program historii dla klass III-IV i VI-VII szkol Polskich dla dzieci polskich w ZSRR 62
proletariat, history of 5
Proletarskeia revoliutsiia 47
Propaganda and Agitation Department (AGITPROP) 28, 31, 39, 56, 58
Propaganda Secretariat (Poland) 33
Provisional Government 52, 174, 177-8, 185, 197

Prussia 11, 80, 84, 96
Pugachev uprising 55
Putilov, V. 195

Questions of Leninism 37

Radek, Karl 49
Radziejowski, J. 127-8
Radzik, R. 130
Radziwill, M. 113
Ranke, Leopold von 16
Rawita-Gawronski, F. 71, 104, 200
Red Army 14, 103, 138, 144, 197; Political Directorate of 39
Redin, M. 22
"reformism" 26, 29, 60
Renner, K. 115
Republic Institutes of Marxism-Leninism 28
Republican Commissariats of Education (SOVNARKOM) 28
Republican Central Committees (CC) 28
Revolutions of 1848 19, 75, 77, 82, 90, 102, 113-4, 118, 121, 130, 161
Riga Treaty of 1921 11, 93
Rozenfeld, I. 192
Rozhkov, Nikolai 135
Rozumovsky, Hetman 120-1, 195
Rubach (Rubanovych), Mykhailo 51, 53, 157, 186, 212
Rubinshtein, Nikolai 139, 193
Rumiantsev, A. 59, 212
Rus' 6, 70, 73, 75, 78, 81, 83, 91, 96-8, 101, 104-5, 109, 111, 116, 123, 131-2, 142
Russian Patriarchate 74
Russkaia istoriia (Pokrovsky) 135-6
Russkaia istoriia (Priselkov) 135
Russkaia istoriia (Sivkov) 135
Russocentrism 3, 21, 25
Rutkowski, J. 39
Rybalka, I. 176
Rydel, L. 84-5

Sakharov, A. 152
Samsonowicz, H. 93-5
Sangushko, R. 112
Sashkevych, Markian 102
Secret Diplomatic History 143
secret police 30, 53

Sejm 75, 103-4, 109, 111-12
Semevsky, V.I. 192, 211
Senate, Polish 70-1, 76, 79-80, 109-10
Serczyk, W. 13, 119-22, 125, 127, 131, 203, 205
Seredyka, J. 124, 194, 203, 205
Seventh Congress of Polish Historians (1948) 63
Shcherbakov, A. 39
Shelest, Petro 40, 60
Shestakov, A. 47, 138-9, 141-3
Shevchenko, F. 57, 59, 66, 80, 102, 152, 158, 172, 176, 196
Shevchenko Learned Society 218, 220
Short Course history of the CPSU 50
Shumsky, O. 51
Shuvalov, P.I. 195
Sidorov, A.L. 59
Sienkiewicz, Henryk 13
Sigismund III 85, 107, 117
Sivkov, K. 135
Skarga, Piotr 79, 81, 85
Skoropadsky, Hetman 103
Skrzypek, J. 114-5
Skubytsky, Trokhym 51-3, 157, 212
Slabchenko, M. 139
Slavic Academic Commission for the Study of the History of the Slavs 63
Śliwinski, A. 85-6, 201
Smirnov, I. 54, 152
Smolenski, W. 84
Sobieski, King Jan 107
Sobieski, Wacaw 73, 75-6
Sochaniewicz, K. 12
Socialist Academy 27
Society of Marxist Historians 22, 50
Society of Militant Dialectical Materialists 28
Solzhenitsyn, A. 214
Sorel, G. 36
"special collections" (SPETSFOND) 31
Spytsky, V. 177
Stadion, F. 75, 95
Stalin, Josef 1, 3, 14-16, 20, 23, 28, 33-4, 37, 44, 47-51, 54-6, 126, 137-8, 141-2, 144, 147, 155, 157-8, 160, 162-4, 180-2, 186, 188, 190, 197, 208, 212, 221
State Committee on Publications 30
State Committee for Public Education 25

State Planning Commission (GOSPLAN) 28; Cultural and Scientific branch of 28
Stronnictwa i programmy polityczne w Galicyi 13
Stronski, Z. 105
Suslov, Mikhail 39, 56, 59-60
Sweden 92, 94, 99, 106, 109, 117, 120, 125, 195
Syta, A. 95
Szelągowski, Adam 71-2
Szmidt, B. 88
Szporluk, Roman 17

Tatars 25, 74, 76-8, 85, 89, 96, 112, 116-7, 122-3, 125, 130, 153, 160, 203
Tazbir, J. 93-4
Teteria, Pavlo 195
Teutonic Knights 96, 111, 113
"Thesis on the Reunification of Ukraine with Russia" (1953) 58-60, 144-6, 158, 164, 194
Tikhomirov, M.N. 59, 142
Tikhvinsky, S.L. 215, 219
Time of Troubles, the 91
Tomkiewicz, Wadyslaw 105-8, 120, 123, 125, 203
Tomsinsky, S.G. 184
Topolski, J. 39, 93-5
Torchyn Manifesto (1767) 95, 116-7, 131, 166
Towarzystwo Milosnikow Historii (Warsaw) 31
Towarzystwo Naukowe (Lviv) 31
Towarzystwo Przyjacioł Nauk (Poznan) 31
Toynbee, Arnold 16
Transylvania 74, 105, 109, 120
Trapeznikov, S. 39
Treaty of Nystadt (1721) 161
Treaty of Pereiaslav (1654) 6, 58, 60, 65, 71, 82, 90-1, 98, 104, 106, 108, 117, 123, 125, 136, 137-8, 149, 152, 158, 164, 168, 194, 204, 210
Treitschke, Heinrich von 222
Trotsky, Leon 14, 48
Turkey (Ottoman Empire) 70, 72, 74, 76-7, 79, 82, 89, 105-6, 117, 121, 124, 131-2, 143
Turkmenia 215

Tymieniecki, Kazimierz 76
Tyszkowski, Kazimierz 107

Ukraine and Russian Revolution 5, 50, 174-5, 193
Ukraine in 1812 5, 25
Ukraine, People's Republic of 6, 11, 115
Ukrainian Academy 49, 54, 58
Ukrainian church 13, 62, 107-8
Ukrainian Marxism 51, 53
Ukrainian national movements 6, 13, 25-6, 57, 101-2, 114, 118, 121, 195-6
Ukrainian National Democrats 92
Ukrainian National Republic 12
Ukrainian Party history organization (ISTPART) 196
Ukrainian Social Democrats (SDs) 126-7
Ukrainian Socialist Revolutionaries (SRs) 126-7
Ukrainian SSR 3, 4, 15, 103, 127, 155-79
Ukrainian Writers Union 59
Ukrainian-Polish Compromise (1914) 78
Ukrainization 50
Ukraino nashe Radianske (1970) 60
Ukrainskyi istorychnyi zhurnal 217
UNESCO 17
Uniate Church 12, 70-1, 74, 79, 102-4, 108, 110, 113-4, 130-2, 156, 166, 192, 201, 211
Union of Krevo (1386) 6, 64, 70, 72-3, 77-8, 81, 111-12, 142, 145, 148, 159, 192, 199, 201, 203
Union of Lublin (1569) 6, 64, 70, 72-3, 75-6, 77-9, 82, 84-5, 89, 91, 93, 95-6, 111-12, 117, 119, 132, 138, 145, 147, 148, 159, 166, 192, 199, 201-2, 204
Union of Brest (Church Union) (1596) 6, 58, 64, 70, 72, 76, 79, 81-5, 89, 91, 94, 107-10, 117, 119-20, 125, 132, 138, 143, 145, 147, 148, 156, 193, 200-1, 203-4, 207
United States 127
Ursyzn-Zamarajew, J. 11

Vanag, N.M. 136-7
Vatican, the 58, 107, 145, 163
Vilnius (Wilno), University of 31
Volkov, M. 195, 211

Volyn 11, 12, 111-12, 116-7
Voprosy istorii 58, 60, 215
Vyhovsky, Ivan 71-2, 75-6, 96, 98, 102, 104, 106, 125, 141, 144, 146, 149, 160, 168, 195, 200

Wanczura, A. 78-9
Warsaw, University of 31
Wasilewski, Leon 101-3, 114, 201
Wawrykowa, M. 123-4
Western Ukraine (*see also Galicia, Eastern*) 6, 11, 12-13, 15, 55, 58-9, 70, 81, 88, 90, 93, 101-2, 107, 116, 142, 156-9, 162, 169
Western Ukrainian People's Republic (ZUNR) 6, 11, 81-2, 86, 95, 122, 126-9, 145, 163, 175-6, 186, 193, 201-4
What the Friends of the People Are 35
"whig history" 24
White Russian Army 176
Wiadomoci Historyczne 66
Wiedza o Polsce (1932) 76, 201
Wierzbicki, J. 112
Wladyslaw IV 72
Wójcik, Z. 125
Wolinsky, Janusz 109-10, 200
World War I 16, 18, 72, 82
World War II 5, 28, 39, 49, 88, 184
Wrangel, General 129, 176
Wyczanski, A. 39
Wysznacka, M. 78-9, 81

"Young Europe" 114
Yugoslavia 60

Z Pola Walki 88
Zabrovarny, S. 13
Zaionchkovsky, P. 195-6, 211
Zakrszewski, Stanisaw (Kazimierz Brzo) 69-70, 101, 116
Zaks, Sophia 128-9, 204
Zaporozhian Sich 167, 177
Zarys historii Polski 78
Zatonsky, V. 50
Zboriv Treaty (1649) 76
Ziber, M. 5
Zinoviev, G. 14, 48

GPSR Compliance

The European Union's (EU) General Product Safety Regulation (GPSR) is a set of rules that requires consumer products to be safe and our obligations to ensure this.

If you have any concerns about our products, you can contact us on

ProductSafety@springernature.com

In case Publisher is established outside the EU, the EU authorized representative is:

Springer Nature Customer Service Center GmbH
Europaplatz 3
69115 Heidelberg, Germany

www.ingramcontent.com/pod-product-compliance
Lightning Source LLC
LaVergne TN
LVHW041624060526
838200LV00040B/1429